Hollywood Heyday

75 Candid Interviews
with Golden Age Legends

DAVID FANTLE *and*
TOM JOHNSON

McFarland & Company, Inc., Publishers
Jefferson, North Carolina

ISBN (print) 978-1-4766-6805-5 ∞
ISBN (ebook) 978-1-4766-3283-4

LIBRARY OF CONGRESS CATALOGUING DATA ARE AVAILABLE

BRITISH LIBRARY CATALOGUING DATA ARE AVAILABLE

Cover design by Dan Augustine;
cover photographs © David Fantle and Tom Johnson

Printed in the United States of America

*McFarland & Company, Inc., Publishers
Box 611, Jefferson, North Carolina 28640
www.mcfarlandpub.com*

For Fred and Gene

"It's totally impossible to break into showbiz, but someone does it every day."

—Fred de Cordova, producer of *The Tonight Show* starring Johnny Carson, Interview at NBC, summer of 1981

Table of Contents

Foreword by Robert Wagner   1

Preface: Origin Story   3

Vaudeville Was Not a Place! *Will Ahern* and *Eddie Parks*   7

It Ain't Easy Being Green *Eddie Albert*   11

Alphabet Soup *Steve Allen*   15

Read All About Him *Ed Asner*   19

That Nimble Tread *Fred Astaire*   24

Having (Less Than) a Ball with Lucy *Lucille Ball*   27

What's the Buzz? *Rona Barrett*   31

The Biggest in the Business *Milton Berle*   34

Dog Day Afternoon *Jacqueline Bisset*   38

Blanc's Slate *Mel Blanc*   41

The Importance of Being Ernest *Ernest Borgnine*   44

Comedy in Three Acts *George Burns*   49

Measuring Up *James Cagney*   55

What Makes Sammy Run? *Sammy Cahn*   59

The-Great-Minneapolis-Kidnap-Caper *Frank Capra*   63

Stardust and Residuals *Hoagy Carmichael*   72

The Gamine *Leslie Caron*   75

Jacked! *Jack Carter*   79

"Beautiful Dynamite" *Cyd Charisse*   82

"Mannix": The Last Interview *Mike Connors*   86

Festering *Jackie Coogan*   90

Fred and Ed (and Johnny) *Fred de Cordova* and *Ed McMahon*   93

Angie *Angie Dickinson*   98

Testy(monial) Sparring with *Stanley Donen*   102

You Must Remember This *Julius Epstein*   107

Common and Preferred *Peter Falk*   110

With a Song in Her Heart *Kathryn Grayson*   113

Man Tan *George Hamilton*   117

This One's for the Birds *Tippi Hedren*   123

Holy Moses!—Heston on High *Charlton Heston*   126

All the Best Lines *Al Hirschfeld*   131

On the Road with "Old Ski Nose" *Bob Hope*   135

"To the Greats Without a Microphone" *George Jessel*   141

"How Do You Like Them Apples?" *Shirley Jones* and *Rod Steiger*   144

The Real McCoy *DeForest Kelley*   151

Passing Time with *Gene Kelly*   154

The Last of the Great Anchormen *Ted Knight*   158

Clock Watching with *Martin Landau*   161

The Art of Perfect Timing *Burton Lane*   164

Janet and Tony and the Art of Crowd Control *Janet Leigh* and
     Tony Curtis   166

Mum's the Word *Mervyn LeRoy*   173

Jerry-Rigged *Jerry Lewis*   176

"Great Songs, Drudge Assignments, It Never Mattered"
     Jay Livingston and *Ray Evans*   180

Nice and Easy Does It Every Time *Karl Malden*   184

The "Toy King" *Louis Marx*   187

Frankly Speaking *Billy May*   190

Baked Alaska *Virginia Mayo*   194

Tops in Taps *Ann Miller*   196

MGM's Amazing Technicolor Dreamcoat *Vincente Minnelli*   200

TV's Funniest Shrink *Bob Newhart*   203

The Great American Flyers *The Nicholas Brothers*   206

Fred Astaire's Silent Partner *Hermes Pan*   209

Of Mockingbirds and Maniacs *Gregory Peck*   212

Maledictions in a Minor Chord *André Previn*   216

Unsinkable *Debbie Reynolds*   221

The Merchant of Venom, Defanged *Don Rickles*   225

Behind the Tinsel *Mickey Rooney*   228

The Also-Ran *Benny Rubin*   231

A Delicate Balance *Eva Marie Saint*   234

The Pen Is Mightier Than the Clarinet *Artie Shaw*   238

By George! *George Sidney*   242

The Untouchable *Robert Stack*   247

A Long Meander with RJ *Robert Wagner*   252

Benchwarmer *Eli Wallach*   259

A Friend of Dorothy *Charles Walters*   262

Lullabies and Nightmares *Harry Warren*   267

A Short Take on The Three Stooges: *Jules White*   273

In the Swim with Neptune's Daughter *Esther Williams*   275

His Favorite Things *Robert Wise*   279

Afterword: A View from the Terrace   285

Index   287

Foreword
by Robert Wagner

What audacity!

And I say that with admiration. These two guys from Minnesota have accomplished something that might be unique, given the fact they were just out of high school when they started interviewing immortal stars of the Golden Age of Hollywood; men and women that lit up our screens for decades with great performances.

The guys are too modest to crow about their achievements. So let me, by proxy, do it for them.

Dave and Tom weren't just a couple of nervy 18-year-olds when they made that first trip to see Fred Astaire and Gene Kelly back in 1978. They had resolve and determination and weren't content, like most people would be, to just see old movies and write fan letters. Don't get me wrong; that's perfectly fine (I get heartfelt fan mail each week), but they took it one giant leap further—they sought out and visited the stars on their home turf and got it all down on tape and in their notebooks.

Millions of people from throughout the world worshipped (and with good reason), the likes of Astaire, Kelly, James Cagney, Lucille Ball and Gregory Peck—but no one else, to my knowledge did what these guys did—hopped a plane from Minnesota to Hollywood—and captured an intimate and personal side of them that few have captured in print before.

These are candid interviews with many stars that rarely, if ever, really opened up. Somehow Dave and Tom got them all to open up and the result is always informative, enlightening and often very funny.

Some of the people profiled in these pages have been in my heart for years as I was fortunate to work with quite a few of them and call them my dear friends. To this day I'm thankful that I was a part of that Golden Age and I'm so happy that Dave and Tom have chronicled so well that period in our show business history.

When I received the first draft of their book, I couldn't put it down, and I'm sure you'll find yourself in the same happy predicament; immersed. But apart from the scintillating stories and wonderful photos they took, at its root, "Hollywood Heyday" is really a memoir about Dave and Tom—not just what they did, but how they did it. And it's been 40 years in the making.

I highly recommend that you take this journey with them and bask in the stories about these irreplaceable stars. I loved this book and I know you will too!

Robert Wagner is an American television and movie star who was a fundamental part of Hollywood's heyday, well-known for his roles in TV series ranging from the classic It Takes a Thief *to the popular favorite* Hart to Hart. *He's still busy with recurring roles in a variety of popular series such as* NCIS *and* Futurama.

Preface:
Origin Story

Time flies when you live a life that is celebrity adjacent.

It doesn't seem that long ago when we began chronicling Hollywood chiefly through the recollections of the artists who starred, directed, wrote, choreographed or composed musical scores for that era's movies and television shows. But it was long ago, a lifetime ago; 40 years (and counting) now.

Looking back, our predilection for old movies and vintage TV shouldn't have come as much of a surprise; all the signifiers were there, as telling as genetic markers. We loved history and felt mostly out of step with the contemporary stars lionized by our peers in the mid– to late–1970s. In our view, Peter Frampton or KISS was small potatoes compared to Ella Fitzgerald.

But it was one seminal event—a movie collage of cinematic moments culled from Golden Age films—that became the catalyst leading to the stories contained in these pages.

The year was 1974 and *That's Entertainment!*, the compilation film of Metro-Goldwyn-Mayer Studio's most wondrous musical moments had just opened wide in theaters across the country. A new generation of movie fans that hadn't been born during MGM's heyday could now watch Gene Kelly joyously dancin' and singin' in the rain, Judy Garland belting out "Get Happy," or Fred Astaire and Eleanor Powell whirling around each other like syncopated pinwheels to Cole Porter's sublime "Begin the Beguine."

To millions of moviegoers, *That's Entertainment!* was a revelation; to us—a couple of St. Paul, Minnesota teenagers—it was galvanizing. Like many kids growing up in the Twin Cities of Minneapolis and St. Paul, we dutifully watched the *Mel Jass Matinee Movie* on local television in the early afternoons and for years had been treated to campy double-bills like *I Was a Teenage Werewolf* and *The Brain That Wouldn't Die*. Entertaining as such B-grade fare could be, it could not remotely be classified as art. Artless was more like it.

So, when *That's Entertainment!* opened, our interest was piqued far beyond seeing a few choice snippets from those Arthur Freed Unit productions. We wanted to see the musicals—in their entirety—which gave birth to the clips. We wanted the main course, not just the appetizer. However, in an era before DVD's, streaming video or even video-cassettes, viewing what you wanted when you wanted was, to say the least, problematic.

Undaunted, we formed a film society that shuttled musicals (of our own choosing, of course) to nursing homes in the Minneapolis–St. Paul area. By renting 16-millimeter prints of the movies and then splitting the expense among the venues, we kept costs affordable for the nursing homes that signed on. We dubbed our organization "Films on Wheels," which seemed appropriate since most of our elderly audience were on wheels, too.

Later on, at the University of Minnesota, we expanded our hucksterish notion into a new film group ("The Song and Dance Cinema Society") with all proceeds, after expenses, donated to the Ronald McDonald House for children with cancer.

Although eventually sated by seeing practically every musical ever made, our interest took a new turn; we wanted to meet some of the leading lights of the films we so admired. By sheer luck, during the last years of the 1970s, many stars from Hollywood's Golden Age were still in the picture—if not exactly making pictures. What's more, an interview query with a stamped, self-addressed envelope for their reply was often all it took to get an affirmative response in those simpler days.

Just liberated from high school, in the summer of 1978, Fred Astaire and Gene Kelly (after talking it over between them, we always suspected) agreed to sit down and talk with us.

As vendors at Metropolitan Stadium in Bloomington, Minnesota, selling Schweigert hot dogs and Frosty Malts to hungry Minnesota Twins and Vikings fans, we figured we had put away enough money for a quick trip to Los Angeles to meet Astaire and Kelly and then get back in time to work the next Twins home stand. What we hadn't factored in was the cost of taxicabs and buses (we weren't old enough to rent a car in L.A.). Fortunately, we were able to book rooms at a budgetel called the Beverly Terrace Motor Hotel which had weekly rates that abstracted out to about $27 a night.

The visits with Astaire and Kelly, though brief, were transcendent. Their musical exploits had already attained an almost mythical status for us. In our star-struck minds, the dancers weren't tethered to *terra firma* (we weren't in a position to see them engaged in such prosaic pursuits as walking the dog or trimming the hydrangeas, something they both did).

So, in a way, it was an eye-opener to interrupt Astaire in his accountant's office while he was busily engaged not in some terpsichorean matter of the greatest creative urgency, but in the laborious chore of balancing his personal checkbook!

Did we experience even a momentary letdown at having our illusions shattered so completely? Hardly. Our appreciation for the hundreds of artists we've interviewed since has only deepened knowing that they were flesh and blood—some, like Astaire and Kelly, leavened with a touch of genius.

The next logical step in our fledgling journey toward becoming celebrity chroniclers was writing up notes from our interviews with Astaire and Kelly for the arts section of the *Minnesota Daily*, the student newspaper of the University of Minnesota where we enrolled that fall. From there, perseverance became habit and some habits are hard to break as we find that we're still interviewing movie and television stars 40 years later.

What we couldn't have known back in the summer of '78 was that our brief visit with the universally-revered Astaire was a "golden ticket" that opened the door to many interviews that most likely would never have happened otherwise. It gave us an agency we certainly didn't possess on our own. Thanks to Fred, for us, what came after was like Dorothy opening up her drab, sepia-toned farmhouse door and stepping into the glorious Technicolor of *Oz*.

The advantage of having met Astaire can't be overstated; he was an exemplar that cut across every tier of show business. For instance, in the mid–'80s we interviewed Stephen Sondheim in his townhouse in the Turtle Bay section of Manhattan. Sondheim was a man of such formidable genius that we quaked with nervousness just conversing with him about his Broadway career. He told us flatly that he wasn't a fan of Hollywood musicals and that the only one he liked was *The Wizard of Oz*. But when we dropped that we had met Astaire, Sondheim's eyes widened. "What was he like?" he asked sounding more like a bedazzled adolescent who just heard a tale out of school than the most respected composer/lyricist of the last 50 years. Not to be one-upped, he confided that Katharine Hepburn was his next-door neighbor and that sometimes he saw her taking out her trash.

One bittersweet consequence of interviewing celebrities decades ago who, at that time, were often up in years, is that most of them are gone now. But that's what makes this reportage about Golden Age Hollywood stars a kind of throwback reverie that we hope evokes some nostalgic moments of when movies were much-anticipated events with heavy velvet curtains that parted to a silver screen; an era when you could count the number of television channels on one hand.

As you read *Hollywood Heyday,* you might notice that some stories seem to intersect with each other. There's a reason for this; Hollywood, back in the studio system era, was a congenial company town knit together. Back then, actors were neighbors who knew, worked and socialized with each other. As Ann Miller told us about an impromptu reunion she had with several of her leading lady contemporaries years after their glory years at MGM had ended, when they got together and started dishing, everyone weighed in with overlapping anecdotes about this director or that leading man until their luncheon became a free-for-all, an irresistible gumbo of gossip that she said couldn't be printed in any reputable newspaper. Sometimes *Heyday* has that same kind of overlap.

"Don't quit your day jobs," Gene Kelly said, laughing, when, early on, we once confided to him that we'd like to try and carve out a living interviewing stage and screen stars. Gene's gentle admonishment proved prescient. Although we've never exited the 9-to-5 grind, we've had tremendous fun meeting the great, near great (and some merely grating) the last several decades.

Consider this cross-hatch of selected stories to be our roseate corollary to Kelly's bit of cautionary advice; a jubilant time capsule of dimming, bygone days that can see a bit of light once again if only for the time it takes to turn a page.

David Fantle, Milwaukee, Wisconsin
Tom Johnson, Sherman Oaks, California

Vaudeville Was Not a Place!

Will Ahern and *Eddie Parks*

Step, ball-change, flap, step.

The hard-driven finger plunks of stride piano played in counterpoint to the steel tones of Capezios in a tap dance, drifted down the steps of Will Ahern's Rainbow Rehearsal Studio in Hollywood, California as we bounded up. The delightful sounds, however, didn't mesh well with the waft of garlic from Palermo's Pizzeria right next door.

"Entertainers come to my studio to train in hopes of making it big in show business," Ahern quipped. "They might as well start with the quality of the air around here; they'll face audiences just as bad!"

Ahern's studio was located on Yucca Street, a block north of the fabled intersection of Hollywood and Vine and a stone's throw from the Capitol Records Tower which, back in 1980, seemed to loom over everything with architecture that looked like records stacked on a turntable.

When we visited, Ahern was a small, cuddly, silver-haired man with an elfin twinkle in his eye and a smile as twee as one of Santa Claus' helpers. He had a rhythm in his speech and urgency in his manner. It was his habit to entertain "at the drop of a hat" and to dazzle with his treasured lore of playing the Orpheum Vaudeville Circuit. We were pushovers.

Showbiz started for Ahern in 1909 in Waterbury, Connecticut, where Buffalo Bill's Wild West Show was performing for four days. He was a water-boy, slept in hay in a railroad flatcar, and got kicked in the pants by a mule with rubber horseshoes—all for a dollar a day. "I remember Annie Oakley used to shoot skeet with a shotgun," Ahern said. "She would always spray the crowd with spent buckshot."

Ahern (who was born in Waterbury in 1896) was so mesmerized that he ran away with the show and learned how to twirl a rope. He made his vaudeville debut in 1913 at the Lyric Theater in Bridgeport, Connecticut.

"When I got older I did a sort of Will Rogers act in vaudeville. I would tie knots in my lariat, and with each knot I would repeat: 'I'm not a cowboy, I am a cowboy' … I've been roping for 71 years."

It was a long career that included more than a few milestones. "I performed for President Woodrow Wilson at the Versailles Peace Conference after World War I (after serving a stint in the Navy). I made films with Mary Pickford in 1913. And I played the Palace Theater (vaudeville's Holy Grail) in New York City," Ahern said.

But admittedly, Ahern's greatest achievement came when he "lassoed" his wife Gladys into tying the matrimonial knot. They met in Chicago in 1919, formed an act and had been married for more than 50 years when we met.

"On the Orpheum Circuit we were billed as 'Will & Gladys Ahern in a Spinning Romance.' My wife did a toe dance inside my rope while I twirled it, then we both danced in it. That was back in 1921."

In their fast-paced 12-minute act, the Aherns pulled out all the stops in song, dance and comedy shtick to entertain.

"I sang 'Rancho Grande' with a sombrero hat on my head," Ahern said. "Gladys would come onstage, take my hat off and exclaim: 'I, Chiquita, will do the bolero/yes, I'm going to do that/and dance with my beau's sombrero/I will have the need of a hat.' I would grab it back from her; she would grab it from me and so on. I would then say: 'Who are you?' My wife would reply: 'I am Dona Jose Maria Lopez Dias Estado. That is my given name' I would tell her, 'You should give it back!'"

Bahrump-bump!

Nothing in show biz is as topical to its given time (or ages as rapidly) as humor, and Will and Gladys' antediluvian repartee groans quite a bit after being vacuum-sealed in a comedy pickle jar for nearly 100 years. But it was a more naïve, gentler era when popular entertainment was synonymous with family entertainment; and vaudeville was as all-American and "G-rated" as nine innings of baseball.

Will Ahern

To many people today, the word vaudeville itself might be easily mistaken for a single stop-light town in North Dakota or maybe images of a loud-mouthed performer with more nerve than talent. In reality, vaudeville as a force died in the 1930s, replaced by the easier access of movies and radio. It remained vivid only in the crystal-clear memories of a handful of men like Ahern, a fast-vanishing breed in the 1980s.

Vaudeville was perhaps the best leisure-time deal of the late 19th and early 20th century. For around 15 cents, the fluctuating cost of a balcony seat, one could while away three hours with seven acts of some of the greatest traveling entertainment in the country. From the Kita Banzai Jap Acrobatic Family to Ethel Barrymore in a one-act dramatic "playlet," vaudeville had something for everyone.

In the course of his own coast-to-coast travels on the Orpheum Circuit, Ahern acquired invaluable theatrical seasoning that performer's in the 1980s, much less now, couldn't get anywhere else. From Wahpeton, North Dakota, to New York City, he played to every kind of audience and pandered to most mentalities.

"After a few years on the boards I began to pick up inside information that makes or breaks a really great vaudeville act," Ahern said. "When performing in the southern states, audiences had a different lingo; a sort of drawl. Vaudevillians, to be understood, had to be slower and more distinct in intonation. In West Virginia, Ohio and Pennsylvania, you would hit the steel mill and coal mine towns. The crowds were 80 percent foreign, so I eliminated most the dialogue and did my act in pantomime (this despite the fact that Will and Gladys spoke German, French, Italian and Spanish). New York, Chicago and Philadelphia were cosmopolitan. You couldn't fool audiences there so you had to snap up the pace of your act."

Orpheum performers played one week in each theater and then moved on. Cities and audiences changed with the frequency of every troupe train out of town and the posting of each new vaudeville bill. But some prejudices remained.

"At the St. Paul Orpheum I shared the bill with four colored boys in a dance act called 'The Dixie Four,'" Ahern said. "One of the four came backstage after the show, he was very upset. He said that the restaurant around the corner (Carling's Uptown Café) refused to serve them. I got them sandwiches—to go. The town of Wahpeton, North Dakota had different concerns, against tobacco. Wahpeton is just across the border from Minnesota and they had an absolute rule against smoking of any kind within the city limits. I remember vaudevillians had to buy their cigarettes and cigars in Minnesota and smoke them there."

As a married man, Ahern lived a fairly monastic life. Many vaudevillians were habitual cardsharps and pool hustlers when they weren't "knocking 'em in the aisles." In his spare time, Ahern counseled his fellow performers in Ben Franklin's doctrine of thrift: A penny saved is money not hustled.

"As long as you didn't gamble, you were all right," Ahern said. "During the train junket from St. Paul to Winnipeg, I would go back to the men's room and find different acts shooting craps and rolling dice. In a single night a guy would often lose his entire previous week's pay. I used to tell them that they should go to the box-office after the first performance, draw out $150, and send it straight home. That way they would show some profit."

Ahern told us in his "dotage" that he still saw some profit (he received a residual check of less than $2 the month before we spoke) for his last performance on film—*Hello, Dolly!*—in 1969 when he was 73. In the movie, Ahern, with flossy muttonchops, plays a groundskeeper leisurely cleaning up a park. He and Barbra Streisand meet whereupon Ahern daintily waltz's "Dolly" around the green in an impossibly precious moment to the tune "Dancing." At the end, Ahern, winded, doffs his bowler hat to her and resumes spearing errant trash with his garbage spike.

At that moment a gentleman doddered in from the other room and smack-dab into our conversation. He announced to us that he would be playing the part of an old vaudevillian who taps dances from Los Angeles to New York City wearing Bermuda shorts in Marty Feldman's upcoming film *In God We Tru$t*.

"I'm an old friend of Will's. The name's Eddie Parks of Coogan & Parks Orpheum vaudeville renown," he said rather immodestly. "I first played the Orpheum Circuit around 1909. I was just a 16-year-old kid." Dapper in a suit and tie, Parks was in his mid–80s then and had cheeks so bulbous it looked like he was storing nuts for a harsh winter.

Eddie Parks

Parks' partner, Jack Coogan, was the father of Jackie Coogan, co-star with Charlie Chaplin in *The Kid* and later "Uncle Fester" on TV's *The Addams Family*.

"Jack Coogan and I would do comedy, buck, soft-shoe and eccentric dancing," Parks said. "During our soft-shoe number, we did dialogue. It was called 'patter between the steps.' It went like this:

> PARKS: "Do you remember Jones the playwright?"
> COOGAN: I certainly do."
> PARKS: "Tell me, which one of his productions did you like best?"
> COOGAN: "His oldest daughter, Lizzie."

Headline acts like "Coogan & Parks" usually drew salary figures requisite with the depth of their talent. But often they had to sell themselves with as much élan to the booking offices as they did to paying audiences. In fact, offstage, Coogan and Parks had a pretty successful bait and-switch scheme with Parks playing the *flaneur*.

"We drew big salaries because Coogan would go into Orpheum booking offices and say: 'My partner has rich parents so he doesn't need money. He can pick and choose his jobs.' Then I would stroll in and the bookers would fall all over themselves to offer us big money."

Parks was married in 1911 and like Ahern he built a new act with his wife as partner. Although they promised to love, honor, cherish and obey, those vows apparently stopped short of the stage door.

"We did a song and conversation. She would sing, 'I will admit I'm fond of animals and such, but when it comes to insects...' Then she would look over at me with disdain and walk offstage. I would then turn to her and reply, 'Just for that, when you die and are cremated, I hope they find klinkers in your ashes.'"

The battle of the sexes jousting continued.

"I'd then say that gorgeous little gal was in a beauty contest in Atlantic City. Last year she was MISrepresented and this year she's MISunderstood. My wife would walk on again as I talked to the audience. She would trip and look at her shoe. Here's the patter:

ME: "What's the matter?"
HER: "I've got a loose heel."
ME: "What?"
HER: "A loose heel."
ME: "Now listen, Lucille!"

A popular stereotype of old vaudevillians used to be that of a grinning goof whose sunny disposition was totally at variance with the hard realities of life outside the close-knit camaraderie of show business; but Ahern and Parks had sincere upbeat personas.

"I've always like small towns like St. Paul," Parks told us. "When I was a young man I acquired the capacity to enjoy the simple pleasures that every small town offered. Many people in our business became what I call 'show-wise.' They can't go from here to across the street without a bored smirk. They've lost all the wonder and fascination of life."

From looking after the welfare of his vaudeville colleagues to feeding flocks of nesting birds outside his home, Ahern also remained an unquenchable optimist.

"I take care of about 400 blue jays, blackbirds and sparrows every day. I spend $30 a week on birdseed," Ahern said. "I have four stray dogs and I don't gamble, smoke, drink or run around—except to and from the studio."

Ahern's Rainbow Rehearsal Studio, in spite of a few generations of dust and that transient Neapolitan odor from next door, was another example of his benevolence. He hadn't raised his rates in 30 years.

"I'm not interested in making money," he said. "I keep low rates to help the singers, dancers, acrobats and comedians who need a place to perfect their routines. You know, when my studio was over a Greyhound Bus Station, the Broadway character actor—and vaudevillian—Jack Barton used to tell people that if their act wasn't working out during rehearsal at Ahern's, they could catch a bus out of town. Fortunately, Rainbow is a good luck rehearsal hall for Carol Channing and Bob Hope. When I retired from performing, I didn't divorce myself from show business. I just found another outlet; I love it too much."

Vaudeville wasn't a place. But, looking back maybe it was, for a few brief years at least, at the Rainbow Studios—just one flight up.

It Ain't Easy Being Green

Eddie Albert

He's best remembered as the eternally optimistic "Mr. Douglas" on the campy '60s sitcom *Green Acres*, who, with his society doyenne wife played by Eva Gabor, abandoned his citified existence and thriving legal practice on Park Avenue for a hardscrabble farmer's life somewhere near Hooterville, USA.

In reality, Eddie Albert, 86 when we met him in 1994, lived in the posh West Los Angeles community of Pacific Palisades. However, he truly did have a green thumb, managing to make his front lawn yield more of a bumper crop than his television farm ever did. "My yard is nothing but vegetables," he told us. "I eat what I grow, and I grow just about everything—you name it!"

Indeed, in a spot where most Angelenos plant orange trees and yucca plants, Albert had row upon furrowed row of carrots, beans, lettuce and herbs coming up in an array that would have made organic restaurateur Alice Waters of *Chez Panisse* drool enough to fill the nearby sprinkling cans. But we learned Albert's commitment to the environment reached far beyond subsistence farming to enhance his own dinner table. For years, he had been a vocal activist speaking out in support of such causes as preserving family farms in the Midwest and particularly conserving the nation's dwindling topsoil. Soil conservation not acting was Albert's true taproot.

"I was a citizen long before I was an actor," he said, responding to our question of whether his status as a performer has hurt his credibility as an expert in environmental matters. "Most people don't realize that the whole world hinges on a little thing called topsoil. When Europeans first settled this continent, we had 18 inches of it, on average. Now we're down to about five or six inches. When it goes, we're finished as a nation."

Down and dirty pronouncements notwithstanding, Albert believed we have "a couple of generations" to reverse this trend. "Agriculture is what built America … Omaha, Minneapolis … Chicago," he said. "What has happened is that we are very close to doing the same thing that happened 3,000 years ago in the Middle East which is now nothing more than sand, scorpions and spiders. The Sahara was once covered with trees. The Cedars of Lebanon was once a great forest. It's all dead. In California, for example, we have 20,000 new desert acres every year and the same is true for the other five or six southwestern states."

The conversation moved from Albert's sitting area in front of a large fireplace to a bench in his tree-shaded backyard. Crowned with a healthy shock of snow-white hair, Albert was dressed in a white T-shirt and a blue down-filled vest, continuing (visually at least) the environmental guru theme to which he adhered. Capping off this "clean look," Albert was shod in a pair of boots constructed from some indeterminate synthetic fabric that made him look like he was ready to play a round of lunar golf with an Apollo astronaut.

Edward Albert Heimberger began his show business career as a "song-and-dance-patter-man" on a radio broadcast out of Minneapolis, Minnesota. Announcers kept referring to him as Hamburger instead of Heimberger (food analogies resonate throughout his life and career), so he dropped his last name altogether. "I was pretty bewildered back then, without a clear-cut profession. It was the Depression and after 1929 only an idiot would study business in school; it wasn't very chic," Albert said. "Show business felt the effects of the Depression later than almost anything else. I guess that's why I gravitated toward it."

After landing some minor radio work and small theater parts in New York, Albert was cast by the legendary stage director George Abbott in the Broadway play, *Brother Rat*, followed in short order by another Abbott production, *Room Service*.

"Most people are familiar with the Marx Brothers movie version of that show," Albert said. "They brought their own kind of frenetic energy to the thing, which wasn't the way it was originally intended. The brothers were marvelous, but the show never really worked as a movie."

Eddie's green acres

Albert made his film debut in the Warner Bros. production of *Brother Rat*. His co-star in the movie had an activist bent that he translated into a long run in the White House—Ronald Reagan.

"Ronnie wasn't a very good comedian, but as a straightman he was fine," Albert remembered. "Even in those days—1938—he liked politics. And when he was asked to speak, he was better than anyone else. He like the idea of the politics and he dug into it. The showmanship was more important than the substance and he was very good at that."

And then Albert said something eerily prophetic: "It's all image and media hype now and, unfortunately, it will probably be that way for some time; some years."

With World War II looming, Albert took time out of his contract work at Warner Bros. to trek to Mexico and turn up facts about Nazi activities south of the border. For cover, he joined the Escalante Brothers Circus as part of a "trapeze act." In between shows he gathered information about German U-boats in Mexican waters that he promptly turned over to Army intelligence. When the Japanese bombed Pearl Harbor, Albert enlisted in the Navy.

"I was with the first wave of Marines at Tarawa," he said. "I piloted a Higgins Boat, and when I neared the beach there were about 600 dead Marines floating in the water. The tide was too low and all the boats got hung up on a reef hundreds of yards from the beach. We had to unload the guys and they had to make it to shore on their own. The machine guns were drilling them. It was hell. To this day, I often think of those brave Marines. The only survivors were those too wounded to kill themselves. I stayed on the beach and reported to Shoup (General David M. Shoup, commander of the 2nd Marine Division) when a message was sent back: 'The ending is in doubt.' I was very proud to be with the Marines."

Albert choked up and needed a few seconds to compose himself when he talked of that bloody battle more than 50 years before. What he didn't mention was winning a Bronze Star with a Combat "V" for rescuing 47 Leathernecks stranded offshore, but then very few veterans of The Greatest Generation ever seem to recollect their heroics.

The bucolic pastures of Hooterville are literally a world away from the war-torn coral atolls of the Central Pacific, a place Albert said he was reluctant to revisit even in memory. Ironically, *Green Acres,* which aired between 1965 and 1971, paralleled another turbulent period in our history. Perhaps the absurdity of the show was an effective metaphor for what was taking place thousands of miles away in Vietnam. Quite naturally, memories of working with Mr. Kimball, Mr. Haney, Sam Drucker, Eb, and even the prescient pig, Arnold Ziffel, evoked fonder memories.

"It was the most fun I ever had," Albert said. "It was superior writing, really quite subtle in its own way. And working with Eva Gabor was great." Albert was also justifiably proud of his film work, which included two Best Supporting Actor Academy Award nominations for *Roman Holiday* and *The Heartbreak Kid* and costarring roles with the likes of Errol Flynn and Humphrey Bogart.

A widower since 1985, Albert was married for almost 50 years to singer, actress and dancer Margo. They had two children, Maria and Edward Jr., who followed in his father's acting footsteps appearing in such movies as *Butterflies Are Free*, *The Greek Tycoon*, *Midway* and *Guarding Tess.*

"Both of my parents believe strongly in giving something back to the community, or society as a whole," Edward Jr. told us when we talked to him about his dad. In a case of the apple not falling very far from the tree, Edward's home was a 10-acre working ranch in Malibu. But instead of growing vegetables like his father, Edward and his wife tended to a menagerie of horses, goats, sheep and assorted dogs and cats.

"My dad's always been an advocate for the underdog," Edward said. "In fact, I don't think he realizes the magnitude of the work he's done. Even at his age, he hasn't slowed down."

Ultimately, however, reminiscing about the past was a zero-sum gain for Albert. He was too busy thinking about his next road trip, a junket to Washington, D.C., where he said he'd talk to some senators about the topsoil threat. Then it was on to Europe to spread the "manure" there. After all, Albert said, "If manure can make crops grow, maybe the verbal version will plant a few ideas with people."

Just like at home, Albert was happy to keep spreading it around.

Alphabet Soup

Steve Allen

Conjuring up the singular Steve Allen isn't easy. It may be impossible, a contradiction in terms. Characterizing his talent is like encountering a railroad roundhouse with dozens of tracks stretching out infinitely in every direction from the terminus. Creator and first host of *The Tonight Show* ... acknowledged master of ad-lib comedy ... author of 43 books ... playwright ... jazz pianist ... composer. They all describe the artist Noel Coward (a polymath himself) once called, "The most talented man in America."

Before we met him for the first time in 1980, his publicist, in a well-meaning effort to help us synthesize Allen's versatility, gave us a handout entitled "Steve Allen: A to Z." It was a piece of paper with the 26 letters of the alphabet running down the left side of the page, each with a corresponding talent (e.g., "A"—Author, "C"—Composer, etc.) all the way to "Z" which might have had "Zither player" notated after it. It was an odd exercise in taxonomy being given an alphabetical list with Allen's accomplishments, however it did prove two things; the man had a formidable utility and a surpassing ego to match.

But it was his gift for musical composition that Allen himself ranked above all others, with ad-lib comedy a distant second. "Somebody once compared me to the great old Hollywood songwriter Harry Warren," Allen said. "Harry wrote a lot of good tunes but never made it into the front rank of his peers like Berlin, Gershwin and Porter."

The comparison is apt if a bit self-serving. Of the more than 5,200 songs Allen composed before he died in 2000, 1,000 had been published with a handful achieving bonafide hit status including, "This Could Be the Start of Something," "Picnic," "Impossible," "Gravy Waltz," and the Bing Crosby–Andrews Sisters hit, "South Rampart Street Parade."

When we met, Allen was 73 and worked out of a nondescript office building in Van Nuys, California (not exactly the garden spot of the San Fernando Valley)—his nerve center where we talked music ("M"—Musician on the list). Amid a phalanx of file cabinets containing *Tonight Show* stills, radio and television scripts, kinescopes, etc., hung a framed one-sheet poster of *The Benny Goodman Story*, the 1955 biopic that starred Allen in his feature film debut as the "King of Swing."

That day Allen was a bit late getting started and caromed into his office with a large leather valise slung over his shoulder so jammed with books, scripts and files that it looked like it might emit its own gravitational field. Dressed casually, Allen wore his trademark horn-rimmed glasses low on his nose and despite the flurry of his entrance, which created a momentary tizzy among his small staff, his other trademark (a toupee so flat you could practically land a fighter jet on it) remained unruffled.

"The great kick of doing the Goodman movie was getting to hang out with Lionel Hampton, Gene Krupa, Teddy Wilson, Harry James and all the guys," Allen remembered. "I didn't get to know Benny, nobody did, not even the men who played with him. His emphasis was on the music—other people didn't exist for him."

For the role, Allen was coached in correct fingering techniques by veteran clarinetist Saul Yaged. "Saul is still the world's number one Benny Goodman fan—perhaps to his own detriment," Allen said. "He knew all of Goodman's solos, his tone, everything. He was to Goodman what Oscar Levant was to George Gershwin. But at least Oscar composed his own melodies, whereas what Saul did for a living was *be* Benny." In telling us about Yaged, Allen spelled out each letter of his name for us, something he did repeatedly with almost every name he mentioned. As journalists ("J" on our own minuscule list if we had one), we appreciated Allen's assist for accuracy in our reporting.

According to Allen, the decision of who would play the lead in the movie came down to a choice between himself and Tony Curtis. "Leonard Feather once told me that Benny cast the deciding vote himself," Allen said. "Benny thought Tony looked too much like a 'pretty boy' and that I resembled him more. Secondly, Benny said that as a jazz musician, I would have the right attitude. Tony would have to fake it."

Allen contemplating

Allen's jazz pedigree was an outgrowth of the popular music he grew up listening to on the radio in Chicago in the early 1930s. "I was a big Eddie Duchin fan in those days. He was as influential as Sinatra and Presley to kids my age, 12 or 14," Allen said. "Duchin created a certain style to a medium-tempo ballad. Every American teenager who had access to a piano learned them very fast, including myself."

While attending Hyde Park High School on Chicago's South Side (Mel Tormé was a classmate), Allen said he discovered jazz. "Chicago has always been a good music town. I had heard jazz before, but to me, it was just one of 19 different aspects of the popular music that I loved," Allen said. "Many classic jazz performances are built around popular tunes by Berlin, Gershwin, Johnny Mercer, etc. Take Coleman Hawkins' rendition of 'Body and Soul.' He didn't write the song, but thank God he recorded it."

For the record, Allen's show business debut wasn't cutting up in comedy clubs, but playing jazz piano as a teenager in trios and with a small band on the South Side. "My first gig paid 50 cents," he said. "It sounds comical now, but in those days, 50 cents could buy a meal in a restaurant. I remember I played for two hours in a saloon near the corner of 63rd Street and Cottage Grove, just down the street from my high school. Later I gigged a couple of times with Mel Tormé who was a drummer then."

Allen always played by ear and to this day can't read music. "I wish I had taken the time to learn," he said, "but after a while it seemed like it would have delayed the progress I was making in the clubs." Any regrets were tempered by the knowledge that his idol, Erroll Garner, never learned to read music either. "To this day, I think Erroll can swing a room or a record better than any other pianist. Great as some of the others are, there is just some little extra mystery ingredient that knocks me out," Allen said. "And then there is the other totally separate Garner brain that plays ballads in the lacy, romantic, emotional style that may or may not be jazz depending on how you define it."

Years later, Allen realized a dream by booking Garner as a guest on *The Tonight Show*. "It was like being a kid in a candy store," he said gleefully. "I would say, offhandedly, let's get Lester Young and we would get him. One night I was on stage before we went on the air and suddenly I saw Lester walk in. Nobody paid attention to him; they were all doing 40 different things. But I recognized his porkpie hat and tenor case. I had never met him and didn't know how much TV he watched. I said, 'Mr. Young, welcome to our show.' At that point he realized he was talking to the host. He looked real close at me; we were standing practically nose-to-nose, and replied 'Many eyes.' It was a hip reference akin to 'I only have eyes for you' or 'I have eyes to quit this job.' Lester had his own special language and it influenced many jazz musicians."

Allen themed many of those early *Tonight Show*s around jazz. One memorable episode featured Hoagy Carmichael who had offered kind words of encouragement to Allen as early as 1948. "He was one of the first people to record a number of mine," Allen said. "It was a tune called, 'An Old Piano Plays the Blues.'"

Allen's favorite show had Richard Rodgers in the spotlight performing his songs for 90 minutes. "We had Andy Williams, Steve Lawrence and Eydie Gorme and Pat Kirby all sitting unrehearsed around the piano with Dick," Allen said. "It came off like a sing-along in somebody's home, it was that intimate. In those days I think the only person we didn't get was Charlie Parker. But we got almost everyone else." A quarter century after the airings of most of those shows, Allen was rediscovering gold in the record vaults of his office. "Just a few days ago I came across three different piano performances by Bill Evans. We'll make a 30-minute video out of that lovely find."

In the show's early days, Allen staffed the *Tonight* orchestra with the best jazz side-men to be found in New York. In the tradition, subsequent hosts Jack Paar, Johnny Carson and Jay Leno all recruited excellent jazz musicians including such leaders as Doc Severinsen and Branford Marsalis.

By Allen's own estimate, he had written and recorded material for six jazz CDs. His latest, *Steve Allen Plays Jazz Tonight* (1993, Concord Jazz, Inc.), contains a baker's dozen of swinging tracks, including a few Allen compositions. "I've always been puzzled when I read that some rock group called the Four Garbage Cans are now into the seventh month of production on their new album," Allen said. "I don't put it down, but I don't understand it. I did my *Tonight* CD in one night."

Indeed, inspiration for a song could hit Allen anywhere; driving down the freeway, at home noodling with chords on the piano, or even during a deep sleep. Allen respected his peripatetic muse by keeping a handful of tape recorders within reach at all times. "My biggest hit, 'This Could be the Start of Something' hit me in a dream," Allen said. "I was writing the score of *The Bachelor*—the first television musical. Just before I awakened in the morning, I thought of the melody and the first seven or eight lines of the lyric. Thank God it was a morning dream, because you never remember your early night dreams."

Allen liked "96 percent" of the jazz he heard in 1980, much of it on radio station KLON in Los Angeles. "Just take the piano players," he said. "The good players of today stand up very well to the legends of 30 or 40 years ago. The young players tend to have more chops. In the old days there was only Art Tatum who had that facility. One CD I particularly like is *Kenny Barron Live at Maybeck Recital Hall* (Volume 10, Concord Jazz, Inc.)."

After musing long and hard about his abundant contribution to so many different areas of show business, Allen shrugged. "I haven't directly decided anything much in my life."

Perhaps expecting a pat answer from a man who spent a career refusing to be pigeon-holed—despite the attempt at A to Zed categorization—was just too easy.

... *On Comedy*

Thirteen years later, the quick wit and nonstop flow of quips and puns were decidedly absent during our second interview with Allen. Instead, a sense of smugness pervaded his office when we got around to discussing the how, what and why of being funny. That's not to say that Allen was uncooperative or unfriendly. We learned quickly that for him, talking about comedy was serious business.

"I get laughs in quite a few different ways," Allen said. "Most comedians don't, I suppose. I do some very broad, burlesque, vaudeville, slapstick sort of things in my night-club act. I do a character called 'Senator Phillip Buster' who wears a silly wig, mustache, baggy pants, and tells big, broad jokes. On the other hand, some of my material is more sophisticated or controlled. My brain works in some of the same ways as Groucho's did in that whatever someone says, I turn it around and make some dumb joke out of it."

We reminded Allen of the time Groucho had a contestant on his TV show *You Bet Your Life* from Pottstown, Pennsylvania. "I remember Pottstown very well," said Groucho. "I played there years ago. I was heavily panned in Pottstown." Allen laughed in his familiar abrupt fashion (kind of like a Buick backfiring short bursts out the exhaust pipe) and said, "Yes, that's an acceptable example of the type of play on words I would do."

In an unusual analogy, Allen compared sports to variation in comedic style. "There really can be no such thing as a decathlon champion of comedy," he explained. "You can make up such a category in your own head and elect your own man. It's like taking the best guy in high jumping and the fastest guy in the 100-meter dash and saying which is the best athlete. You can't. You're talking about two different ballgames. The same specialization is found in the field of comedy. The reasons we laughed at Groucho have nothing whatsoever to do with why we laugh at Steve Martin. They're just funny in two different ways."

We were surprised when Allen admitted he enjoyed the work of almost all other comedians. "The real mystery is why five percent of them don't amuse me," he said. "I really don't understand that because some of the ones that don't amuse me are quite successful. I probably am entertained by more comedians than any other comedian. That may strike you as odd. The fact that I'm at the head of the list doesn't mean a damn. The more important fact is that most comedians aren't amused by their peers. I never quite understood why. I don't know whether it's an unconscious jealousy, misunderstanding of different styles, or whatever it might be." The only brand of comedy Allen said he didn't enjoy was dirty humor. "I laugh not only at comedians, but people, dogs, wallpaper, whatever."

On July 27, 1953, Allen originated and hosted what became over the intervening decades a television institution—*The Tonight Show*. The original program was a talk show only on certain nights, Allen said. The show would occasionally present a live 30-minute drama, a political debate or it would book the Basie Band to jam for 40 minutes.

Allen said the material was 97 percent spontaneous and only 3 percent written. We mentioned that the Johnny Carson format was fairly uncontroversial. "Johnny wants no controversy at all," Allen conjectured. Nevertheless, he occasionally does some just as a way of getting people off his back who bring up the subject. He would prefer not to get into any of that."

On the subject of talk shows, Allen was withering. "It takes no talent to host a talk show. I don't mean that as a cute statement. Yet on the other hand, of the few hundred talented people in the business, very few can run a talk show. Marlon Brando would fall off the desk in three seconds, as would most movie stars. And yet there are some people with no talent whatsoever who are very successful at talk shows. I run into journalists who are better than any of these guys and they're not on the air. It has something to do with one's projection over the air."

According to Allen, intelligence (innate or otherwise) is also not a guarantor for late night hosting success. "It certainly makes it easier for those of us who are intelligent," he laughed, "but I won't give you any names of those in the other category."

Read All About Him

Ed Asner

"Mary, you got spunk…. I hate spunk!"—Lou Grant to Mary Richards on *The Mary Tyler Moore Show*

Spunk. Whether he likes it or not, the word characterizes Ed Asner, both personally and professionally. The "Lou Grant" character that Asner debuted in 1970 on *The Mary Tyler Moore Show* had a gruff exterior that was mostly bluff engineered to hide a gooey center of grudging sensitivity.

From the WJM newsroom in Minneapolis to the *Los Angeles Tribune* city desk as the titular star of his own spin-off series, even extending to his curmudgeonly voiceover as Carl Fredricksen in the 2009 animated hit, *Up*, the Lou Grant spunk has remained a commodity audiences can count on.

Over the years, in Studio City, California, we frequently experienced Asner's spunk firsthand.

A favorite dining spot near Tom's home was Spark Woodfire Grill, an Italianate hybrid restaurant on Ventura Boulevard, which featured on its menu a Margherita Pizza with crust as thin as construction paper. The Grill was also in Asner's restaurant rotation and he was frequently there dining with friends. We'd always stop to say "hi" since Asner is one of the most approachable pedigreed actors in Hollywood. That said, before we reached the table, he would usually exclaim in a low rumble (just theatrical enough to be overheard): "Uh-oh, here comes trouble!"

When we first encountered Asner in 1980, three years after Mary Richards had turned off the lights at WJM, he looked much the same as he did in that last episode with a ruddy complexion, stocky build and a ring of brown hair around his head like a laurel wreath on the head of a Caesar.

We chatted with him in his office at CBS soon after a Screen Actors Guild strike had closed down Hollywood entertainment production for nine weeks. In his office that day was Johnny Green famed MGM musical director and composer ("I Cover the Waterfront," "Body and Soul") who left just as we entered having cajoled Asner into agreeing to moderate a Musician's Guild of America fundraising event.

At that time, Asner, a lifelong hardcore liberal, was the last actor to cross the musicians' picket line after an agreement had been tentatively reached with the Guild. It reflected a political and professional bent that could be traced to his years as a journeyman laborer doing odd jobs throughout the Midwest.

"One of my first jobs was selling encyclopedias," he told us. "I threw-up from the training. It was scumbag time, the degrading hard sell. I tried to sell shoes and then went to work on an automobile assembly line in Kansas City. That didn't work out, so after nine or 10 months, I traveled to Chicago and worked as a taxicab driver. I finally wound up in a steel mill in Gary, Indiana. I really appreciate the blue-collar worker."

Asner's first professional acting experience came as a member of Paul Sills's Chicago Playwrights Repertory Theater, a company that fostered Elaine May, Mike Nichols and Barbara Harris among others.

"Before I got out of the army, I was stationed in France, and I got a letter from Paul Sills who I had known from the University of Chicago Theatre," Asner said. "Sills wrote that he was starting a little professional theater on the Near North Side and asked if I wanted a job. He said hopefully he could pay me $50–$60 a week. Suddenly my life fell into place. It was a 180-seat theater, which we slept in. The second floor had been an old chop suey joint and bookie front."

Spunk personified!

The Chicago Playwrights Theatre, Asner remembered, was not an immediate hit among the city's theater critics. The avant-garde stance and presentation of modern playwrights was not always appreciated or understood.

Asner was first cast in *La Ronde*, by Schnitzler, but the play incurred the displeasure of the Catholic Church and closed after only two performances. He was then cast as the lead in *Woyzeck* by Buchner. It was a hit and ran for two years. Asner quit the Chicago Playwrights Theatre when it became improvisational.

"I felt it was too much fun to improv," he said. "I wanted to seek renown as an actor, not an improvisationalist. I wanted to be tested. You can put that down to feelings of Jewish middle-class guilt."

As an out-of-work actor just relocated to New York City, Asner told us he devised a method for canvassing the city with his resume and headshots that was as effective as it was simple.

"I began looking for work by making the rounds, looking up anybody and everybody I could. One of the few times I ever did anything intelligent for myself, I came to New York expecting nothing. I set myself up a grid pattern of the city. I would drop off my picture and resume to any and all agencies knowing full well that most of them were dumped in the wastebasket before I reached the door."

For Asner, acting was always about finding "outlets" and occasionally suffering the slings and arrows of the New York critics. "I was in a production of *The Tempest* in New York, and Brooks Atkinson reviewed it," Asner said. "It was his next-to-last review before retiring and he likened my voice to that of a train conductor. I diverted myself from his criticism with the thought that I would not have time to get on stage in something else and make that S.O.B. eat his words concerning my talent."

For six years Asner acted in such plays as *The Three-Penny Opera*, *Ivanov* and *Henry V* for Joseph Papp's Shakespeare in the Park. But Asner's subsequent decision to move to Hollywood was not a natural outgrowth of his experience on the stage. "I could have stayed in New York forever, but I was discovered by the Burt Leonard people who did the television shows *Naked City* and *Route 66*," he said.

Asner's success led to his first TV series role as a character on *Slattery's People*. It was short lived. "They couldn't find a way to use me properly. In the first 10 shows they didn't use me in two of them."

Then came *The Mary Tyler Moore Show*. Asner said that he and just about every other actor in Hollywood tested for the part of Lou Grant. "I read for the two producers and then came back a week or two later and read with Mary. I think that Gavin MacLeod tested for my role. The producers didn't think he was right for it, but asked him if he would be interested in the role of Murray Slaughter. Happy ending."

The irony is that up to that point in his career Asner had assiduously avoided comedic roles. "I came in highly recommended with really very little basis to substantiate that recommendation," he said, "but they were impressed with the grunting reality of what they saw and they felt that they could pump me up into the blowhard character that Lou turned out to be."

Asner credited Ethel Winant, a vice president in charge of talent at CBS at the time, for a big promotional push of his untapped comedy potential. Winant also lobbied hard for Valerie Harper and Cloris Leachman to be cast in the show.

"And Grant Tinker (a co-founder of MTM Enterprises and Moore's husband at the time) had seen me do a character akin to Lou—a police chief in a 20th Century–Fox film I was involved in. (Asner played Sheriff Muntz in the made-for-TV movie, *The House on Greenapple Road* in 1970, the same year *The Mary Tyler Moore Show* debuted.) But the rest of the officialdom at CBS had grave doubts as to whether I could do the comedic aspect of Lou Grant so we had to prove them wrong."

To make the suits at CBS true believers that he could induce belly laughs, Asner drew on the example of his two older brothers. "They had certain areas of bombast," Asner said. "I was kind of shy and retiring. To put the 'oomph' into the comedic Lou Grant, I brought in their high points."

During the seven-season run of *The Mary Tyler Moore Show*, Asner remembered only a couple of occasions in which artistic disagreement among cast members flared into petty vendetta. "Most of the time we were secure enough with one another that no animosity was aroused. A couple of times, however, Ted Knight and I got into personal conflict, even though we were the best of friends. Once during a Friday night performance, I brought my hate with me onstage. I was deadly. I learned that it is a professional necessity to quell any anger before going onstage, or else everyone's performance will suffer. Being around Ted Knight certainly stimulated and provoked any comedic sensibilities I had. He is the funniest man I've ever known.

"And I'm delighted with *The Mary Tyler Moore Show* being a big part of my legacy," he added. "It's work I'm proud of. It never dates. It has legs."

Asner said he keeps in touch with McLeod, Betty White (Sue-Ann Nivens) and Valerie Harper who played Mary's best friend, Rhoda Morgenstern on the show. For the last several years Harper has battled lung cancer that has spread into membranes surrounding her brain. "Valerie's a fighter; she's a tough Guinea!" Asner said.

Lou Grant (the series) aired in 1977 on CBS, the same year that *The Mary Tyler Moore Show* ankled. It marked a rare instance of a beloved comic character in one hit series morphing quickly into a more dramatic persona in another.

"Well, they were writing an hour show and I began to look into myself and realize that what they had wanted me to do when we started out, to retain the flavor of *The Mary Tyler Moore Show* into an hour format, that wasn't going to work," Asner said. "I had to find this other guy that I ended up with which came out of my soul.

"Frankly, I was amazed and delighted that they found a way to turn this comedic character based on my two older brothers into my somber personality for the hour-long show. I'm thrilled that it worked."

Asner believed that there was an "everyman" aspect to his role of Lou Grant that allowed the character to grow, develop and most importantly, remain popular. "No amount of adversity can keep him down for long. As Chuckles the Clown on MTM used to say: 'A little song, a little dance, a little seltzer down your pants.'"

Still, the character had changed by the time the first season of *Lou Grant* aired in 1977. "We found that the old *Mary Tyler Moore*–era character wasn't working. Everyone was miserable," he said. "The Jamaican episode was the old comedic Lou Grant, but some of the scenes on the beach were somber and they augured in the new Lou Grant."

During the last two years, *Lou Grant* used its newspaper-related episodes to explore such complex social issues as race relations, spousal abuse and abortion. We asked Asner if he thought that a one-hour format was enough time to do justice to such weighty and complex issues.

"If you are dealing with a newspaper, and not an all-out comedy, then you have to deal with issues that a newspaper deals with. I'm amazed that we handled these problems as completely and succinctly as we did."

Indeed, professional journalists applauded *Lou Grant* for its realistic depiction of the workings of a newspaper city desk. "In the beginning I felt guilty about that," Asner said. "They applauded us so loudly, it really helped. But I challenged that we were that dramatically effective. In the third year I felt we began to merit their praise."

Although never high in the ratings, *Lou Grant* had a respectable audience share.

Nonetheless, in 1982, the network cancelled the show due to what many considered to be Asner's vocal stances on various political issues. "My own personal involvement in politics at the time concerning El Salvador certainly created the panic at CBS," said. "I try to run every time I hear someone say they got into journalism as a career because of *Lou Grant*. I hate to take that responsibility, especially seeing as how poorly journalists are treated these days.

"You can't take away the power of an investigative reporter," Asner continued. "I don't care how many internets or *Huffington Post*s you have; you still need a reporter with feet on the ground. It's called the dumbing down of America, and they're doing a good job about that."

Recently we spoke with Asner again. The intervening years had turned his florid complexion pale and his hair white. Still stocky, he looked a bit like one of those kid toy bop bags that bounces back up after you hit it—especially if the bag was in the shape of a large-sized white bowling pin. The metaphor is not entirely outlandish. At 86, Asner's still impassioned; still a firebrand for the underrepresented and the "have-nots." And no matter what, he bounces back up.

We talked a bit about the 2016 presidential race. As always, Asner didn't mince words.

"It's become an entertaining spectacle," he said. "Statesmanship and dignity seem to have flown out the window on the Republican side. I'm delighted that the Democrats haven't been dragged into a dogfight like the Republicans have. I'm just hoping the American people will exercise a good deal of restraint and not just try to satisfy their animal urgings.

"It's extremely upsetting that Trump has gotten this far," he continued in high dudgeon, a bit of that old ruddiness flushing his cheeks. "I don't like the man. I do think it's refreshing when he calls a spade a spade when it's necessary and I'd like to see that extended throughout the election campaign. But he's been saved by it because he doesn't have a day job to go back to. Still, we're soon to be a yahoo country because our elections are based on money. I think it's disgusting and calling yourself a democracy when money rules is the biggest bunch of crap I ever heard."

Reluctant to end the visit on such a downbeat note, we asked Asner if he'd like to follow up the success of *Up* with more voicework.

"I did voiceovers before *Up* and I'm continuing to do them after *Up*. I just did an episode of *SpongeBob SquarePants* the other day. Whenever I can do a voiceover, I leap at it. I enjoy the work and you don't have to shave."

At the risk of embarrassing him, we told Asner that we thought he was a kind of national treasure—like a dented old family jalopy with quite a bit of mileage on the odometer but also precious history. "We know you hate to hear that, but the hell with it, it's true," we admonished figuring we'd get in the first dig because the best defense is a good offense, right?

Asner mumbled something unintelligible, guttural, like he was horking up a mouthful of pasta that had just gone down the wrong pipe at Spark Woodfire Grill.

Like any decent reporter would, we asked for clarification: "We missed that, what you said. You'd like to kill us?"

"Kiss you, you idiots! Now get lost, you're trouble!"

Spunk … with a gooey center!

That Nimble Tread

Fred Astaire

For us, meeting Fred Astaire in late June 1978 was both a genesis and a culmination.

It was the culmination of idolatry that bordered on obsession—a single-minded adulation so engulfing that as teenagers, before we even met Fred, we started a cinema society just to rent and see films in the Astaire canon that rarely popped up in movie theater retrospectives or aired as afternoon matinees on TV. It was also the defining event that started us down our decades-long path of entertainment journalism; although, in retrospect, we couldn't possibly predict that "beginning" nearly 40 years ago. Fred was our lodestar.

After a dogged two-year campaign of "snail-mail" correspondence with Astaire (via his secretary Jaye Johnston), a brief window of availability for us to meet him in Los Angeles opened up in the crawlspace between graduation from high school and taking our first summer session at the University of Minnesota. Fred said that he'd be in town the whole month and that he'd be happy to see us if we could arrange transport out to L.A.

We got cracking.

At 18 years old, we weren't legal to rent a car in California, so we reserved rooms at the Beverly Terrace Motor Hotel on Doheny Drive at the eastern edge of Beverly Hills. Fortunately, back then, even the rarified purlieus of Beverly Hills contained a few budget hotels with weekly rates and life-saving kitchenettes. Even better, our visit was scheduled to take place at the Brighton Way offices of Fred's accountant and The Terrace was a short walk from there.

The man who had repeatedly been named as one of the world's best dressed men was, when we met him, wearing a blue sport coat, wide, red Christian Dior necktie, blue cotton pants, a red and blue designer belt and Gucci black leather shoes. (We also noticed that some part of Astaire's chic attire had the distinct redwood odor of being recently liberated from a cedar trunk.)

Fred greeted us with a "hi fellas, sit down" informality that mirrored his persona in films. It was just the kind of introduction that at once put us at ease and deflated any notions we might have harbored about exactly how to visit with a certifiable national treasure.

After all, Astaire is considered without serious exception to be the greatest dancer the movies have ever known. His 31 musical films spanning from 1933 to 1968 established a measuring rod of excellence by which all other musical comedy work is judged. Landmark movies such as the series of 10 films Astaire made with Ginger Rogers are enduring classics and have been acknowledged as a major influence in the work of dancer/choreographers such as Gene Kelly, George Balanchine and Bob Fosse. Simply put, he was as *sui generis* as anyone we ever had the good fortune to interview.

As Fred settled into a nearby chair, we noticed that his ankles swelled out of his shoes like a couple of globular ball bearings. The effect seemed odd until we comprehended that after the better part of a century stomping the hell out of rehearsal hall floorboards, any such ankles—bulbous or not—would be fortunate if they were still attached to legs, let alone be proportionately as slender as the rest of Astaire's lithe frame.

To break the ice, we asked Astaire if he had ever visited Minnesota during his vaudeville days. "About all that I remember positively is that my sister Adele and I performed in Minneapolis and St. Paul around 1909 (when Fred was nine years old) on the Orpheum Circuit," he said haltingly, almost apologetically. We certainly couldn't fault him for not recalling 71-year-old specifics about two towns he probably only glimpsed from a stage door.

Astaire's modesty and deference (which were unfailing and continuous) didn't register completely with us during our visit. It would take months; even years, before we fully realized and appreciated that aspect of his character. During our careers we've interviewed many stars from Hollywood's Golden Age and they often shared a trait of genuine humility about their talent or film legacy, some were even squeamish talking about it. But after being in the limelight and under public scrutiny for decades, most seemed to attain a placid, healthy perspective about their lives and careers.

That said, no one we've interviewed since Fred has ever surpassed his innate courtesy which, in practice, was as natural as a drawn breath.

Dapper Fred

We mentioned that we had recently shown his 1948 musical *Easter Parade*, co-starring Judy Garland, to a St. Paul nursing home audience, and that immediately after the screening an elderly resident innocently asked us if it was one of our home movies.

The statement flabbergasted Astaire. "You mean she thought that *you* guys filmed it yourselves?" he asked incredulously. Gimlet-eyed, Fred cracked a thin smile and gamely fought to retain a measure of self-control. But his composure finally shattered into convulsive laughter. Eventually he collected himself and said that after a 45-year career of fielding detailed questions on every aspect of his films, this was the first time anyone ever mistook his work for someone else's home movie.

With disco dancing the national rage at the time, we asked if he ever tripped the light fantastic in local Los Angeles nightclubs. Astaire replied that disco was just free-style fun and could not possibly be compared with exhaustively rehearsed choreography of musical films. As if to make that point emphatic, he improvised a couple of dance steps (still seated in his chair). Fred did a kind of scissors step crossing his feet back and forth while he thrust one arm out front. At the same time, he twisted his other arm around the back of his neck; his long, tapering fingers sprouting up behind his head like five giant eagle feathers on a Sioux war bonnet.

The agility of those legendary feet—even at the age of 78—and his marvelously expressive hands which seemed to have no end, demonstrated that Astaire had lost little of the precision that characterized numbers like his adagio with the wooden coat rack in *Royal Wedding* or his synchronized golf dance from *Carefree*.

"After seeing *Saturday Night Fever*, I voted for John Travolta as Best Actor at the 1978 Academy Award ceremony," Astaire said. Travolta's tense, sexually-charged dancing was, according to Astaire, an interesting extension of the delinquent character he portrayed.

We talked about the nostalgia craze for old movies that seemed to grip the nation a few years before and which had been partly fueled by *That's Entertainment!*, the artful 1974 compilation of some of the finest moments from MGM musicals. The movie heralded a re-reckoning of the work of Astaire, Gene Kelly, director Vincente Minnelli and many others. However with that popular rebirth, came innumerable requests for interviews and a rash of unauthorized biographies about the artists that gave those glorious movie musicals their special luster. It was a subject that didn't really interest Fred who liked to live in the present and would much rather discuss instead the "good new days."

"My 1959 autobiography *Steps in Time* is, and can only be, the definitive source on my career," Fred explained. He told us that because of the "rediscovery" of his films, he was continually hounded by interviewers and authors intent on asking questions for which he says he has long since forgotten the answers. Astaire said that one author in particular, British writer Michael Freedland, was quite insistent on getting—quite literally—some face time with Fred.

"He kept telephoning for days wanting a posed photograph of the two of us for the dust-jacket of a book he was writing about me. When I finally agreed to a short photo session, he arrived at my house with his wife and kids, but luckily without his overnight luggage." Freedland got his selfie (taken by the small pool in Fred's backyard) which subsequently adorned the back cover of his 1976 illustrated biography on Astaire.

As if in prescient acknowledgment of the distance we had traveled just to chat with him about his movies, Fred did tell us about how his famous gravity-defying number in *Royal Wedding* was filmed—the one where he danced (seemingly weightlessly) on the walls and ceilings of his London hotel suite to the Alan Jay Lerner–Burton Lane tune, "You're All the World to Me."

"The room was a square set built inside a barrel that could be rotated like a hamster treadmill," Astaire told us. "I, of course, never left the ground, but it looked like I did. The cameraman rotated with the room and was upside down and sideways and all kinds of ways. That was the trick."

Astaire's tireless perfectionism is the stuff of legend and has been recognized with a trunk full of awards from an honorary Oscar and Emmy Awards to Kennedy Center and American Film Institute honors. But Fred told us that he found his greatest pleasure in the victories of several racehorses he owned. As a discussion topic, Astaire's thoroughbreds won by a country mile over his classic movies.

"My filly Triplicate won the 1946 Hollywood Gold Cup," he said proudly and then added conspiratorially, "She beat Louis B. Mayer's mare when I was under contract to Mayer at MGM."

Our visit at an end, Astaire ushered us out of the office as unassumingly as he had greeted us. It reminded us of a certain air of nonchalance that we had seen in a 1933 film called *Flying Down to Rio* when Fred coaxed a lissome gal named Ginger onto a dance floor for the first time to "try out" a new dance called "The Carioca." In that instant, musicals became airborne in a way that they had never been before.

In 1978, walking back out onto sun-bleached Brighton Way, we were levitating a bit too!

Having (Less Than) a Ball with Lucy
Lucille Ball

Her career spanned more than a quarter century in an industry with a turnover rate as rapid as some Third World dictatorships. Her last name bounced from Ricardo to Carmichael to Carter with regularity. But she never really needed a last name because to the world she was simply known as "Lucy."

The acclaim she earned when her first series, *I Love Lucy*, premiered in October 1951 (in 2012, it was voted the greatest TV show of all time in a public poll conducted by ABC News and *People* magazine) was long overdue. Lucille Ball—first as a platinum blonde and later as the redhead we all came to know—arrived in Hollywood in 1933 as a "poster girl" in the Samuel Goldwyn film, *Roman Scandals*, which starred googly-eyed comic, Eddie Cantor.

So began a 17-year apprenticeship in movies, where she could be seen briefly in a few Astaire-Rogers musicals, on the receiving end of cream pies thrown by The Three Stooges and as the object of the collective desire of the Marx Brothers. Occasionally, Lucy would land meatier assignments such as the role of the crippled singer in Damon Runyon's *Big Street*, the title role in *Du Barry Was a Lady* and good parts in a few Bob Hope pictures.

But all that had happened long before we interviewed Lucy in 1980 at her home on Roxbury Drive in Beverly Hills where she lived with her second husband, comedian Gary Morton. Known as "The Street of Stars," Lucy had Jimmy Stewart, Rosemary Clooney and Ira Gershwin as close Roxbury Drive neighbors.

It was a bit discomfiting walking up to her front door—being careful to stay on the sidewalk and not leave a footprint on the manicured lawn—while hearing tourists in an open-air Starline tour bus sneer at our effrontery, exclaiming in loud tones: "Who in the hell do they think they are!" To the gawkers, the fact that we were on a mission dressed in suits and carrying our customary accoutrements (shitty camera and intermittently functioning Panasonic cassette tape-recorder) didn't seem to distinguish us from mere impetuous boobs with more nerve than class.

Luckily Lucy's public relations man, Howard McClay, was expecting us and we disappeared inside without a backward glance.

She was waiting for us in her living room. Sitting in an overstuffed chair and smoking a cigarette, Lucy looked fit but physically slight and wore a brown pants suit, tinted, oversize sunglasses and a green kerchief that was wound tightly around her head as if she expected to buck a strong headwind and not the gentle graze of her air-conditioner. Her trademark red hair practically pulsated with an orangish tint that would have startled Donald Trump.

We seated ourselves on the sofa next to her white toy poodle that looked to be as well coiffed as any Angeleno just released from a Vidal Sassoon rinse and set. As Morton hovered noticeably in the background, Lucy spoke candidly about her life and career, and unleashed some insights (insults) on the present state of television that would have given any self-respecting network executive reason to jump off a bridge.

Only once did she get into a momentary snit and that's when we asked her why, according to facts printed in a volume of *Current Biography*, she ran away from her upstate Jamestown, New York, home at a tender age to embark on a stage career on Broadway.

We surmised the question would be a cute lead-in to recollections about her childhood and budding show business ambitions. Instead, Lucy fixed us with a cold stare (at least that's what we figured; we couldn't see her exact expression behind the tint of her sunglasses). You'd have thought we just strangled her dog.

Lucy slowly rose from the couch and looked ready to kick our abashed asses out the door and over the fence into Jimmy Stewart's yard.

"If I'd have known you'd be asking these kinds of personal questions, I would not have agreed to this interview," she said in a quick, clipped way that left no margin for misinterpretation.

We had thought any facts about her life that we gleaned from *Current Biography*—a reference source universally accessible in libraries and as unimpeachable as a set of the *World Book Encyclopedia*—would hardly be objectionable. Perhaps we were naïve. In any case, we were wrong. For an instant we both felt like emitting one of Lucy's characteristic "Waaaaah's"; her forlorn wallow whenever she felt defeated or overwhelmed on TV.

Instead, mortified, we redirected—quickly. But in that moment, as flop-sweat beaded our brows, and we began to redact our prepared questions, we experienced firsthand the old axiom about comedians, that often they have no sense of humor about themselves.

Perhaps we "pushed a button" or caught Lucy in a moment of pique about something else; we'll never know. Offstage she could well have been the funniest person in the room, but the Lucy we interviewed that September day came across as a tough-as-nails, pensive businesswoman who didn't sugarcoat anything.

As a television pioneer who triumphed over huge odds, battled a paternalistic sexism throughout her career and was the first woman to build and run a bonafide Hollywood studio (Desilu Productions) maybe that was to be expected.

We took a cue from Lucy's poodle that had rolled deferentially over on her back. We too, in our way, genuflected to the alpha in the room and Lucy, placated, sat back down in her chair.

* * *

Fantle & Johnson: *Why did the article in* Current Biography *say: "much of the information about Lucy's early life is vague and contradictory?"*

Lucy: You'll find that out if you read some of the scurrilous unauthorized biographies that have been written about me. They take the first two pages and make you out a bum that ran away from home and had an unhappy childhood. You are 80 years old or there must have been some reason why you left. I went to dramatic school when I was 15 and there was nothing vague or contradictory about that, except in the three unauthorized book versions of my career. There is one good book by Bart Andrews (*Lucy & Ricky & Fred & Ethel*, Popular Library, 1977).

Have you ever had any formal musical training?

I never studied, musically, and God knows it looks like it. I attempted to take up what is called eccentric dancing but teachers told me I was ill-equipped for that. They wrote my mother a letter saying that she was wasting her money, which she was, because I couldn't do anything. I've gotten away with my dancing in many musical films only because I could rehearse for weeks. The little stuff I did on my television show was satirically done. I don't mean that each step was out and out satire, but it was easy enough for me to master. Same with my singing. I never could sing, although I've done a lot of singing. My mother also wasted her perfectly good money on piano lessons, which I can't play.

Were there any tell-tale signs of inherent comedic ability when you were young?

I certainly didn't notice any. All I knew was that I wanted to perform and I took every chance that I got at school … church … Kiwanis and Elks clubs. Wherever I was needed—sweeping up, selling tickets—I would pitch in.

Have you always been as physical and vivacious as you appear on the screen?

I've always loved physical comedy. I don't do one pratfall after another, inasmuch as people have made such a thing out of that. Our show was void of a lot of things that television is doing in triplicate these days. I counted once, and in all my 25 years on television, there have not been more than five or six shows where I threw pies or did deliberate pratfalls. I've used trampolines, stilts, animals and even jumped out of planes, but these flowed naturally out of the plot predicaments. People don't really hear me when I say this. I'm glad you have your tape recorder on.

What did you do to survive during those early struggling years in New York City?

I literally starved. I was young, very backward and awkward. Vaudeville was the only thing I knew so I tried to break in. Unfortunately for me, vaudeville was already dead and gone. The lack of food and work forced me into modeling. I finally became a showgirl and my first job in Hollywood was as a showgirl. I came out here to Los Angeles only expecting to stay for six weeks. I've never left.

You worked with the Marx Brothers in the film, Room Service. *Were they as crazy offstage as they were onstage?*

Yes, all except one, who was an extraordinary, sensitive, intelligent and adorable man. That was Harpo.

Would you prefer the old studio contract system to the way actors make their way in show business today?

In retrospect I'm sure everyone would. I certainly would. I never objected to any of the hype. I have always been very much in favor of the big umbrella, the poppa, the help and the build that a star would get from the public relations department. In addition, they took beautiful publicity photographs. Nowadays the kids are begging for the old departmental specialization. They have to do everything themselves, including writing, producing, directing, raising funds and selling their project.

Do you watch your television shows, and what do you look at when you view them?

I usually watch Vivian (Vivian Vance, who played Ethel on *I Love Lucy*, died in 1979). God bless her! I used to enjoy working with Vivian. We would almost play act and pull a little extra out of each scene. I would rather look at a compilation like the *25 Years of Lucy* special than just watch one particular show. There are, of course, a few exceptions such as the special I made with Dean Martin.

What was the production schedule like for I Love Lucy?

The first couple of years it was 'round the clock, seven days a week because we were innovating so many new things. We trained hundreds and hundreds of people. We invented three-headed monsters for shooting close-ups, medium-shots and long-shots at the same time. We also shot in sequence like a play. We didn't make our audience sit and wait for hours. They came in to watch and we got them out as quickly as possible.

How did you manage to get stars of the magnitude of William Holden and John Wayne to appear on your show?

There was a time when people weren't doing television. Desi had the idea of trying to get these stars for guest appearances once television became accepted a little more. When we got Duke Wayne and Bill Holden, we didn't have trouble getting any more stars.

How important were audience ratings in the early days of television?

They certainly were not as stupidly important as they are today. But there is no way of accurately gauging the effect because there was less competition back then. *I Love Lucy* never had any problems with the ratings.

How much, besides your acting, did you contribute to the show?

I just acted. I had great writers. Vivian, Bill, Desi and myself would naturalize the dialogue a bit, especially where Desi was concerned. Soon writers would write the scripts just the way we talked naturally. Throughout all the years, we did very little ad-libbing. That was not our forte.

Your shows are seen all over the world in syndication. Why do you think the show remains so fresh and popular?

I think it covers many generations of understanding. The little kids understand it, the next generation understands it, mom and pop understand it and remember it, as do grandma and grandpa. For sheer escapism, I don't think there has been a better executed show. People can watch our show and get away from all of the sex, violence, blood and guts and all of that. Even before our show was dubbed in other countries, people could identify with our domestic predicaments.

Do you watch much television?

I never watch soap operas but I do enjoy game shows. I never had a chance to watch game shows when I was doing a weekly series. The other shows I get to look at are the news, *60 Minutes*, *20/20* … 15/15, 8½—whatever they call them. I'm not saying I don't enjoy shows like *The Incredible Hulk* or *Real People*. It's just that I get more out of a show like *60 Minutes*.

How would you evaluate the present state of television?

Chaotic, downhill, leaving us.

Do you have any favorite current performers, comedic or otherwise?

Alan Alda in *M*A*S*H** and some other people in that show and *Taxi* are two of the finest programs on the air. I really don't watch many other shows.

Can you understand why Laverne and Shirley *is often compared to your show?*

Well, it is about two girls involved in different situations. Many others have done it besides us. But those slapstick premises were all copied from the *I Love Lucy* writers. There are only so many jokes that people can do, only so many situations that a comic can get in or out of. I like *Laverne and Shirley,* but I don't laugh at it.

Who can make you laugh?

In person I laugh at Dean Martin, my husband Gary Morton, Ann Sothern and I used to laugh at Betty Grable. Very few people can give me a real belly laugh.

In the early '70s you came back to the big screen in a musical version of Mame.

The film broke all box office records in New York City. If they hadn't stopped the public relations work, the film would have been a bigger hit. Warner Brothers Studios were going through some terrible happenings with that horrible picture, *The Exorcist*. They had seven deaths on that film! All the people at that studio were out on extremes working on that movie. They were like a bunch of paramedics running around the world trying to catch up with the violence that was plaguing their crew. The whole studio was spooked with *The Exorcist*. That in itself is a story that should be written. Not everyone knows this.

You recently made news when you were hired by NBC President Fred Silverman to act as creative consultant for that network.

There is a certain expertise in knowing how to do my type of half-hour comedy show. The network still feels the need of having more situation comedies. People are still packaging such shows, but the network is not doing a very good job of selecting any after they have been put together. That's why I took the job.

* * *

Our interview at an end, we left Lucy contentedly puffing away in her chair. She had chain-smoked during the interview and there seemed to be a palpable air of certitude about the wisdom she had just imparted that haloed around her like the hazy cloud of cigarette smoke.

Lucy's PR man, McClay, showed us to the front door and as we stepped outside, another tour bus slowed so people could take pictures, this time of a couple of nondescript guys fumbling for their sunglasses in the midday glare.

What's the Buzz?

Rona Barrett

We all know that television stories about celebrity minutiae have become as ubiquitous in our culture as the seemingly unending array of photos of Kim Kardashian's ample backside. The major networks and cable shows dutifully cover celebrity gossip, the more salacious of course, the better. And nowhere is that more in evidence than the "Gotcha" moments (in addition to a surprising number of legitimate scoops) engineered by TMZ.

But back in the 1960s, such "fluff journalism" (at least on TV) was nascent. And the face of it was Rona Barrett, a frosted blonde pixie with a Joey Heatherton hairdo and a "New Yawkish" speech cadence that had some viewers lunging for their remotes.

For her time, Barrett (now 80 and living in northern California) was the grand dame of gossip. She even had her own catchphrase sign-off ("That's Hollywood") which, combined with her sly, knowing stare, she ended her weekly gossip and interview segments on ABC. In a Warholian era where "everyone will be famous for 15 minutes," Barrett ruled a celebrity news caliphate that stretched from coast to coast. But instead of Walter Winchell's famed Table 50 at the Stork Club, Barrett's locus of power was a chair at KNBC in Los Angeles.

In fact, prefiguring the later arrival of Barbara Walters, Barrett was the first to develop in-depth probing TV specials about entertainment and political celebrities. At her height, she even and had a series of magazines covering the entertainment industry including *Rona Barrett's Hollywood*.

In 1991, Barrett retired to her ranch in Santa Ynez, California where she currently runs the Rona Barrett Foundation which caters to senior citizens in need. Back in 1982 when Barrett was reporting out of her suite of offices at NBC, we sat down with her and learned quickly that the word "gossip" is not part of her lexicon.

"I began to resent the word gossip as applied to me when I learned that it carried an innuendo of trivia and a stigma of nastiness, everything that I abhor. I work hard at my craft," she said.

Perseverance and an unflagging belief in her own capabilities, Barrett told us, were responsible for her success. By her own admission she "gnawed" her way into network television in Los Angeles. "I drove people crazy at KNBC," she said. "I kept applying for a job there. They never turned me down but they never said yes, either. Finally they said, 'For God's sake let's put her on the air and she can bomb and then we'll be finished with her.'"

As a child, Barrett was a victim of muscular dystrophy and wore leg braces. Her move from New York City was precipitated by the fact that whenever it snowed, she felt like a "caged animal." At the age of 13, armed with nothing more than sheer bravado, Barrett stormed singer Eddie Fisher's Los Angeles office and convinced him that she should be head of his national fan club.

"I saw through Eddie Fisher my own way to escape," she said. "At 13, I believed that famous people were perfect people and that if I could attach myself to a faultless human being, my life would be perfect. All the pain, suffering and indignation would fade away. It hasn't."

Barrett's entire pre-foundation career was spent reporting about celebrities. At the same time, she made a concerted attempt to legitimize herself and her profession to her peers and the American public at large. "People think that this job is so easy. They're all under the impression that you wake up in the morning and say to yourself: 'Well, today should I interview Rock Hudson or James Arness?'" Barrett said. "I've spent 20 years accumulating the knowledge and experience to be able to do my job thoroughly and efficiently, to put it all in perspective. You can't take somebody off the street and tell them to report on Hollywood."

In the 1980's, dignity and respect were the intransigents Barrett searched for as she nomadically bounced from network to network. That was the reason for her move to NBC and a short-lived co-anchor spot on *The Tomorrow Show* with Tom Snyder. Sublimating his own blimp-sized ego was never Snyder's hallmark, and Barrett left the show in a mutual rancor that made her the subject of—dare we say it—gossip! NBC also tried Barrett out on her own program after she left Snyder, but that too, bombed.

In an effort to dismiss any similarities between herself and such Hollywood columnists as Louella Parsons and Hedda Hopper, Barrett said that she tried to reflect the shifting attitude in the U.S. "Louella and Hedda were very moral people but their job was to expose the immorality of others. I don't do that. I expose immorality from a business standpoint," Barrett said. "I feel the public really isn't interested anymore in who is sleeping with

Rona, dishing

whom. It may sound pompous, but I think people are seeking something more spiritual. They want to find out how stars overcame obstacles enroute to their success, even if it's as silly as learning how to cook."

Celebrities interviewed by Barrett back then seemed to sense that same concern. They knew that her interviewing technique was to penetrate as deeply as possible into their emotional psyches (just as Walters would do years later) to try to discover what really made them tick. Often Barrett probed the common ground of misery that the celebrity might have experienced during their childhood—something Barrett could certainly empathize with.

"I've listened to Dudley Moore explain about how his sense of humor sprang from the compensation he continually made because of the clubfoot he was born with," she said. "His parents were outraged and humiliated at having produced a child who wasn't physically normal.

"Another interview I vividly remember is when Daniel J. Travanti of *Hill Street Blues* talked to me about his alcoholism. He said that if you ever want to do a chronic alcoholic a favor, you should fire them."

Triumphing over daunting disabilities; exorcising personal demons and finding a therapeutic peace via the stories of others who have faced down similar pain were Barrett's pocket aces time and again in her interviews. So what if they sometimes sounded suspiciously like the plot threads of a Tinseltown screenplay.

As Barrett might've said herself: "That's Hollywood!"

The Biggest in the Business

Milton Berle

Milton Berle was a venerated member of the Friars Club … a long-standing member … no doubt the biggest member; a man almost as storied for the outsized tripodal blessing God saw fit to give him as he was for his career as an early pioneer on TV, thus earning the sobriquet, "Mr. Television."

Berle was instrumental in founding the club (a spin-off of the New York Friars) in 1947 when he got together a group of actors including Bing Crosby, Eddie Cantor, Jimmy Durante and George Jessel. In 1961, the California club moved into a building on Santa Monica Boulevard in Beverly Hills which featured a white, windowless Space Age façade (appropos in the age of Sputnik) but which looked to us, from the outside at least, like a well-favored parking ramp. Through the decades, the Friars became ground zero for countless booze-fueled "roasts" where the "Man of the Hour" was ripped mercilessly by a dais of members who were more than up to the task.

In the mid 1990s we were waiting when Berle shambled into the Beverly Hills branch of the club with his longtime gagman Buddy Arnold in tow as the staff and fellow Friars greeted him with a reverence reserved only for comic Grand Poobahs. Berle clearly relished the kudos and his exalted position and usually, we were told, returned the salutations with what everyone expected—a quick one-liner, a gentle insult or an off-color joke (in this case, all three simultaneously).

"You know what a Lawrence Welk cigar is? A lot of shit with a band around it."

And then to us: "Got some questions? Ask me the fuckin' questions."

But before we could blurt one out, Berle told us what he said was a "new joke."

"A Japanese guy, a Polish guy and a Jew are sitting together," he said. "The Japanese guy says, 'See this smallest cellular phone in the world that I got? I can make millions if I sell it on QVC for $39.95. The Polish guy says, 'That's nothing.' He takes a tiny microcircuit out of his pocket. 'See that, it's a satellite. I get 5,000 stations on this.' All of a sudden, the Jew farts and says to the other two guys, 'You'll pardon me, I got a fax coming in.' That's one of the great fuckin' jokes."

No doubt about it, Berle was all-in from the get-go. And in that instant we realized why columnist Walter Winchell decades ago had anointed Berle "The Thief of Bad Gags."

Once upstairs in the main dining room (aptly named the Milton Berle Room), Berle promptly jibed about the temperature. "It's so damn cold in this room," he railed to no one in particular. "What are they doing, hanging meat in here?" Score one for the jowly old-timer. A few minutes into the interview, Berle had "warmed up" sufficiently to shed his fedora and ancient Hart Schaffner & Marx beige raincoat that he wore rain or shine (giving him a 1950's–era, worn-down-to-the-nub businessman look that seemed more at home in New York's garment district than in the palm-tree'd purlieus of Beverly Hills).

Back then, Berle, 86, held court in his private corner booth. With trusty cigar in hand that he deftly waved for emphasis like a conductor's baton accentuating verbal beats

Berle's overbite

and cues, he regaled us with anecdotes from his rich traveling trunk of show business memories. Berle, who held the title *abbot emeritus* at the Friars had been a fixture there since the age of 12 when entertainer Eddie Cantor brought his young and impertinent new find into the New York branch to "show off" to show business cronies Fred Allen, DeWolfe Hopper and Enrico Caruso.

"I'll never forget that day in 1920," Berle recalled. "I put on a long pantsuit and dark glasses. Cantor introduced me as a young entertainer who was going to be famous some day. Fred Allen smirked, 'That'll be the day!' So there I was, this kid clowning and trading lines with the big guys. And Caruso was at the table. He spoke broken English and ate like there was no tomorrow and smoked 25 cigars a day. I told him I thought he was wonderful and he said to me, 'Next week my performance I do it at Werba's Theater.' He died shortly after that, so I caught him at the end."

Cantor's prophecy for young Milton quickly came true. Berle was one of five children born to Moses and Sarah Berlinger in New York City. "Stage Mother" Sarah elected Milton to become a star and bring financial security to the family. With his trademark Bugs Bunny jowls, Berle played "the kid" in dozens of silent films starring the biggest names of the day— Charlie Chaplin, Douglas Fairbanks, Mary Pickford, Marie Dressler and Mabel Normand.

"I hadn't seen Chaplin in 50 years since *Tillie's Punctured Romance* where I played a young kid he had to slap," Berle said. "In 1966–67, I was staying at the Dorchester in London and I called his office to speak with him. His secretary said he was busy. He was shooting *The Countess of Hong Kong* with Brando and Sophia Loren. He got back to me and sent a Daimler-Benz to pick me up for lunch. I had to jog his memory. It had been

50 years but then he remembered. I said, 'I still feel that slap you gave me.' He said, 'Well, realism.' I said, 'Do you remember how much you paid me that day? I think it was $2.75.'"

When growing pains cut short his cute kid status in films, Berle began a slow but steady climb to vaudeville stardom, eventually headlining at New York's famed Palace Theater. It was a career nurtured every step of the way by his mother.

"My mother was with me all the time," he said. "She out-gypsied Gypsy Rose Lee's mother. She was my chief helper and my main stooge in the audience. She was with me at every show I did in vaudeville, even the lean days when I was playing five shows a day for a paltry sum. She was also my severest critic. But her instinct was right on the nose most of the time."

Berle said that his mother (like Mama Rose) was a frustrated actress who grew up in an era when a young lady going on stage risked being labeled a harlot by polite society. So, she poured all her energies into her "Little Miltie."

"My mother, Minnie Marx (the Marx Brothers' stage mother) and George Gershwin's mother were all good friends," Berle said. "She was pushy but terrific. Back in 1901, my mother enlisted in the New York Police Department as one of its first police women. She was a private detective and a store detective." Sarah Glantz Berle, née Berlinger also gained everlasting show business notoriety as a laugh-starter during her son's stage appearances and for pilfering other comedians material that Berle then used in his own act—sometimes when he was on the same bill with them but before they could use the jokes themselves.

"She had a real good high laugh and she would sit in different parts of the theater during different shows," Berle remembered. "She would go: 'HAAAA, HAHAH HA.' Then I'd ad-lib, 'Lady, which joke are you working on?' Then I would hear that laugh during the next show in another part of the theater and I would say, 'That woman moved!' Later I would bring her out on stage and she would come out wearing her fur coat—when I could afford to buy a mink coat—and I said, 'This coat was bought by other comedians.'"

The 1930s and '40s brought Berle continued success in vaudeville, radio and the legitimate stage. While other comics such as Bob Hope and Jack Benny ruled the radio waves, Berle admitted he had only limited success in that medium. "I never made it big on radio because I was too visual," he said. "You had to see me. It was because of this realization that I took the early plunge into television although a lot of people thought I was crazy."

In June 1948, Berle entered the newfangled world of television and Tuesday nights would never be the same again. He became, literally, an overnight sensation and his *Texaco Star Theater* soon was responsible for selling more televisions than the collective sales effort of Philco, Admiral and Zenith. TV proved the perfect medium for Berle's no-holds-barred style of physical comedy and sight gags. He admitted that the Texaco show was, in effect, a televised vaudeville show. "The Texaco Show started with a live audience," Berle said, "and no one would take that challenge. I had worked in vaudeville with live audiences and you only had one chance; you got what you saw and you saw what you got. And you couldn't do it over again."

Early in the run of the program, Berle was dubbed "Mr. Television." Another nick-name, "Uncle Miltie," came about by accident. "I received a lot of complaints from parents who wrote and told me their kids wouldn't go to sleep until our show was over," Berle said. "So I went on the air and told all the children watching to 'listen to their Uncle Miltie' and go to bed right after the show. Shortly after that spot I was in a parade in

Boston and a couple of workmen in hardhats yelled 'Hi, Uncle Miltie.' I had no idea when I first used it that the name would stick."

During his seven-year run on primetime (including two years under the sponsorship of Buick), Berle would go to any lengths for a laugh. A pie in the face, a pratfall—even dressing in drag—was all part of his repertoire. Ironically, milking laughs was the farthest thing on his mind when he first donned a bustier and girdle in the 1930s.

"It had nothing to do with show business. It had everything to do with making it with a girl I met," he said. "It was in the '30s and I was in my 20s and met this gorgeous girl from Texas who came to New York City to become a model. I took her out for a couple of weeks all the while trying to figure out where I can make love to her. You see, she was staying at an all-girl's hotel, the Barbizon, and I was still living in a suite of rooms at the Essex House with my mother!" Finally, Berle devised a way to circumvent both his mother and the hotel desk clerk (men weren't allowed past the lobby).

"I went to the Brook's Costume Company and picked out a dress, complete with towels for padding for a bust," he said. "I wore these high heels that just about killed me. I put on a blonde wig and make up and had a stole. I made it past the desk clerk and into the elevator where this one girl gave me a look like she just met the Elephant Man. It was well worth it until the next morning when I tried to leave. My feet were swollen from the shoes. So here I am in drag, barefoot and walking back to where I lived, about 10 blocks away."

About a decade later Berle again dressed in drag, this time for a larger audience. "Our show aired on Valentine's Day so we thought it would be funny if I'd come on stage in drag, rip off my clothes to reveal my suit underneath and go into my monologue. That's how it started. Later we did a June bride in drag, Cleopatra, and a lot of different things."

As we were getting up to leave, Berle told us he had one more "unprintable" joke for us about a guy who visits his doctor.

> GUY: Tell me doctor, I've got something growing, what is that?
> DOCTOR: I don't know how to tell you, but you have a penis growing out of your forehead. The longer it stays, it will continue to grow.
> GUY: Gee, cut it out!
> DOCTOR: I can't do that. It's attached to your brain and you'll die.
> GUY: Doctor, do you mean to tell me that I have to get up every morning, go to the John, look in the mirror and see this?
> DOCTOR: You won't see it; your balls will be covering your eyes.

Zowie! A literal dickhead joke from the guy who'd been a penis punch line for eons. We felt honored.

Berle did not live long enough to see his beloved Friars fall to the wrecking ball in 2011. He passed away in 2002 at the age of 93. That said, throughout the interview, Dave said an image of those Russian nesting dolls—Matryoshka's—kept reverberating through his head, the ones that decrease in size as they are placed inside each other, one after the other. The symbology was apt. For all his full-court press, Uncle Miltie's current world as an octogenarian had wizened to a small circumference where he regaled stragglers in a favorite corner of his personal booth in an eponymous room that existed in "his club."

Although his reign as "Mr. Television" had ended decades ago and his fame had scaled down considerably to where he was only sought out by minutiae-obsessed historians (and possibly Joe Franklin), it nonetheless struck us that Berle was content, assured that his legacy (raunchy gags notwithstanding) was secure. For the living Matryoshka that he had become, it seemed enough.

Dog Day Afternoon

Jacqueline Bisset

The fabled devotion of dogs to their human caretakers has earned them the title of "man's best friend" and the status (continually jockeying with cats) of America's most popular pet. Hollywood celebrities, like everyone else, are not immune to this imprinting. Quite the contrary, even more than we civilians, stars often need the incessant reassurance and unswerving love-without-qualification that dogs readily provide. Best yet, for the price of a dish of Alpo, dogs are bought cheap compared to the omnipresent retinue of paid flunkies and sycophants that some stars feel they must have.

Through the years we've seen proof of this a dozen times over: Lucille Ball and her poodle who had a disposition as skittish as her master; Gregory Peck and Howard, his German Shepherd, who was inseparable from a chew toy (an empty plastic Hawaiian Tropic suntan oil bottle) that added a snap, crackle and occasional pop underscoring to our whole interview; Director Stanley Donen's collies that shed so much white fur on our dark suits, we looked like a couple of Himalayan Yetis' at the end.

In one career first (and last) we even "interviewed" Eddie, the rambunctious little Parson Russell Terrier from the sitcom *Frasier*. The article was for a cigar magazine, and for the cover photo, Eddie's trainer got him to gently mouth a Havana cigar. The banner headline read, "Eddie Doesn't Smoke Dogs." On later visits to NBC's PR department, we saw that magazine cover dutifully tacked up to almost every cubicle wall we passed.

But no dog ever made quite the impression that Jacqueline Bisset's pooch did during our visit to her Benedict Canyon hacienda one cold and rainy Sunday afternoon. "I've always had pets all my life," she said. "I haven't had many because I travel too much. It's really an indulgence." More on that later.

Back in 1996, when we met Bisset for the first time, Hollywood didn't quite seem to know what to do with her, possibly because of the paucity of roles that called for the classic triumvirate of patrician beauty combined with talent and a kind of in-born grace— precisely the qualities Bisset (like Grace Kelly and Audrey Hepburn before her) had demonstrated in spades during her long career in films. Bisset, like Hepburn, was trained in ballet and it's what accounted for her elegant carriage in films like *Bullitt* with Steve McQueen to recent guest spots in TV series like *Rizzoli & Isles* and *Dancing on the Edge*.

"I've never liked to be part of any formula or cookie-cutter recipe when it comes to selecting projects," Bisset told us. "I like to find an interesting story, and, hopefully, it will become popular. I'm not against success, of course, but who's to say exactly what is a 'big' or 'small' film? If it fills the screen and packs some emotion, then it's big by my standards."

At 52, Bisset was striking with what had to be the squarest jawline and highest cheekbones this side of Mount Rushmore. Her auburn hair was tousled and her most prominent feature; her light, slightly translucent jade-green eyes seemed to shimmer in whatever ambient light was reflected whenever she moved her head. She was willowy and wore black leather pants, a cotton pullover top and no makeup—not that she needed even a smidge.

"I exercise regularly—a lot of fast walking usually," Bisset said. "I also believe that what you think shows on your face. I work especially hard to eliminate any negative stuff in my life. People who are dissatisfied create dissatisfaction in others. People who are bored breed boredom. I'm always on the lookout for generosity, not petty bickering, and, of course, love is paramount."

Enter the dog, a recently acquired mixed-breed puppy that as soon as we sat down, began to teeth on Bisset's shoe. As a doleful *Gaelic* ballad from Enya (perfect mood music for a dank afternoon) wafted into the living room from a CD player located somewhere in the house, Bisset told us she and her dog were in the "get to know each other" phase. "He's a bit of a challenge," she said.

Bisset wanted to talk about her most recent film, a Warner Bros. release called *Dangerous Beauty*. Set in Venice during the Renaissance, Bisset played a courtesan in the film who attempts to teach her daughter (Catherine McCormack) the tricks of the trade.

"It's sure to be a truly beautiful film," she gushed. "It has epic sweep to it. I'm just looking for a piece of language; an opportunity to recite some decent lines. This movie was written with a lot of depth and resonance."

At about this point the dog began to move up Bisset's leg from the shoe, gently lapping at her leather pants along the way like a painter swabbing a flagpole. During the interview, Bisset had sunk casually and comfortably in the chair with her back braced against one of the armrests, one leg dangling over the opposite arm and the other leg (the one getting all the undivided attention) touching the tile floor.

"Puppy, puppy, c'mon," she pleaded, but the dog was undeterred. Bisset pushed him away with enough force that he slid on his ass a few feet across the porcelain tile squares.

Dangerous Beauty marked nearly 50 feature film performances for the actress born Jacqueline Fraser-Bisset in Weybridge, Surrey, England. Her father was a Scottish doctor and her mother a lawyer of French and English descent. Growing up, Bisset never harbored dreams of becoming an actress—ballet was her passion.

"We didn't have a television and we never went to the cinema," she said without a trace of regret. "I was exposed to really good ballet from an early age. I, myself, wasn't very good technically, certainly not good enough to become a professional dancer, but I was totally obsessed nevertheless. To me, no one epitomized grace like Margot Fonteyn."

With her aspirations of becoming a prima ballerina out of reach, Bisset snagged some modeling assignments that dovetailed into her being cast as an extra in a few European films. In 1966 she landed her first speaking role in director Roman Polanski's *Cul-de-Sac*.

Polanski was just the first in a long line of notable directors who put Bisset through her paces. Others included Stanley Donen (*Two for the Road*), George Seaton (*Airport*), John Huston (*The Life and Times of Judge Roy Bean*), Peter Yates (*The Deep*), Francois Truffaut (*Day for Night*), Sidney Lumet (*Murder on the Orient Express*) and George Cukor (*Rich and Famous*).

"I had very mixed feelings about George Cukor," Bisset said. "He was very autocratic; very bossy. I had a certain amount of admiration for his legend and we got along quite well privately. On the set, he didn't really want to hear anything from me except as an actress. He liked what he called 'humdingers.' Women were 'humdingers.' He actually paid much more attention to men. I could tell. In *Rich and Famous* the speeches were pure sex—wonderful.

"I asked George if I could change a line," Bisset continued. "He said, 'Nope.' I'm actually pretty good at improvising if I know who I'm playing. I like to explore the subtext. The subtext in *Rich and Famous* was fantastic. The dialogue had a beat, a cadence to it. The pauses were as important as the words."

Truth be told, Bisset confided that most directors with whom she's worked haven't lived up to their advance billing.

"I can almost mention on one hand the directors who were helpful to me," she said without a hint of malice. "There were maybe eight of them. I can remember almost every bit of meaningful direction I ever received because it was so scant, but it really doesn't matter. I finally figured out that direction has nothing to do with what I'm supposed to do. Direction is all about filming the scene correctly, getting into the eyes; lensing the right angles—the whole visual thing. Historically, I haven't generally been photographed to my full advantage."

Although loath to admit her status as a sex symbol, Bisset didn't rail against it either.

"We all know that men like their women younger," she said. "It's not just Hollywood. This business has a lot to do with sex and sex appeal. People tend to think of sexuality as the main ingredient young people have to offer. I beg to differ. I think older people exude bundles of sexuality. It's just that older men and women tend not to run around like cats and dogs in heat."

Responding to that verbal cue as if it were a command, Bisset's dog was back at it, but this time he ignored her leg and made repeated lunges at her, um, cul-de-sac.

"My God," she said. "What is wrong with you?" All we could do was sit, fidget slightly, pretend to look at our notebooks and try not to turn crimson.

But the dog wasn't giving up and continued to tussle and not be put off. "Jesus! I've got to take care of this," Bisset said getting out of what had become a defensive position in her chair; her hands a blur of kung fu countermeasures to protect her chastity.

She grabbed the dog by the collar and hauled him out of the room.

"I never knew what the phrase, 'Every dog has his day' meant until now," Dave whispered.

"Shut your yap, she might hear us," Tom said.

Bisset soon returned and made an awkward rather sullen apology (she didn't need to) and then picked up where she left off. "Youthful beauty connotes freshness and people tend to enjoy that," she said. "But, unfortunately, something much deeper is lost in translation. There is nothing more fascinating than letting the human voice, whatever its age, express heartfelt emotions. That is real exploration and it never fails to turn me on when I watch it."

Nearly 20 years before, Bisset in all her youthful, radiant splendor, made a worldwide splash in *The Deep*, a movie co-starring Nick Nolte and Robert Shaw. The opening scuba-diving sequence featuring Bisset in the wettest of t-shirts, was something not seen on the screen since Sophia Loren, as a Greek sponge diver in a clingy schmatta, rose like the goddess Amphitrite out of the Aegean Sea in 1957 in *Boy on a Dolphin*, in the process causing thousands of theater-seat shifts in cinemas across the U.S.

We began to embrace as interview subject matter what we took to be the portentous theme of the afternoon—sex—and told her that in a recent commercial-airing of the movie, her nipples had been fuzzed out by the censors. "I had no idea they did that," Bisset said, truly puzzled. "I would think that such an effect would only draw more attention to my boobs. God knows, they depict a lot more sex and nudity on TV today than what was portrayed in that tame scene."

Meanwhile, in another part of the house, intermittent snarls eventually gave way to sustained high-pitched whimpering that became a kind of soundtrack for the rest of the interview which didn't last long.

"Guys, I'm afraid I really have to take care of this. I hope you'll excuse me," an exasperated Bisset said.

As we stepped out of her house into the rain which had begun to pelt, we thought of that sage old bit of actorly advice attributed to W.C. Fields: "Never work with children or animals."

Flash forward 20 years later, almost to the day, and we had Bisset on the speaker-phone plugging her latest movie, a resounding dud called *The Last Film Festival*.

Her voice had that same posh, slightly silky accent we remembered from '96, but because it was disembodied, she sounded even sexier this time.

In the film (who's release had been delayed six years due to the death of costar Dennis Hopper during shooting), Bisset plays a counterfeit Italian movie diva with an ersatz Neapolitan accent about as believable as Chico Marx's "Tootsie Frootsie ice cream" dialect from *A Day at the Races*.

Producer-turned-director Linda Yellen encouraged Bisset to invent her character and accent almost entirely out of whole cloth which is not always a good idea unless you have the track record of Robert Altman or *are* Robert Altman. Nevertheless, Bisset had fun with it.

"Linda said that the film would have a lot of improvisation, and I really hadn't done that before," Bisset said. "I hesitated, and she said she sort of wanted me to put my character together myself; find a name for her and probably make her an actress.

"Any film that you're doing that's not a big budget and doing it in a great rush is always a degree of stress," she continued. "I'm a reasonably good sport with these things and I was interested to work with Dennis (Hopper). We didn't get to know each other well. He's more of a Method Actor. I felt very free with him, but didn't get to know him. We shared a large classroom at the school we were using for the setting of the festival. I had one corner of the classroom and he had another corner. We had partitions to cover the corners so we had privacy but we were very much in our own corners. I'm not a Method Actor at all. I have my own methods. I embrace the amount of knowledge I have of somebody rather than going right down to the ground and starting again."

Talking about a stillborn misfire was all well and good, but interest in what was Hopper's last film soon waned, at least for us. Taking a nostalgic tack, we reminded Bisset that we had a memorable interview in her home two decades ago and asked if she still lived off Benedict Canyon. She did.

"That Rhodesian Ridgeback Beagle or whatever it was that you had at the time was kind of boisterous," Dave asked. "Do you still have canine companionship?"

"Um … no," Bisset replied. We couldn't know if she had connected the dots or even remembered.

Probably not.

Doggone!

Blanc's Slate

Mel Blanc

Given the flaked out reputation Southern California had acquired over the years, it was just another ordinary weekday afternoon back in 1980 when we found ourselves talking with Bugs Bunny, Tweety Bird, Porky Pig, Daffy Duck and Barney Rubble. No, it wasn't a meet-and-greet with the costumed desperados who troll Hollywood Boulevard trying to extort tourists into paying for pricey posed shots, but an interview with the man who was responsible for creating those immortal animated cartoon voices along with more than 400 others—Mel Blanc.

We chatted in the Beverly Hills offices of Blanc Communications overlooking the traffic snarl of Wilshire Boulevard. Blanc, 72, was not wearing the customary three-piece suit and rep tie that might have been more emblematic for the founder of an immensely successful advertising firm (the company handled the accounts of 9 Lives cat food, Pepsi-Cola, Oscar Mayer and PaineWebber and Company). Instead, he was dressed in a green open-collared shirt with his favorite and most famous character stitched onto his pocket—Bugs Bunny. Staying in character, he greeted us with, "Eh, what's up youse two?"

"I'm a voice specialist," he declared at the outset, "due to the fact that I've created so many different voices. I'm not a copyist or impersonator. I've tried to be an original."

Blanc was born in San Francisco in 1908. Even as a child growing up in Portland, Oregon, he realized that he had the unique ability to create different voices. "I was quite popular in school," Blanc said (whose non-affected speaking voice was a close approximation of Barney Rubble's). "I used to entertain the kids and teachers at assemblies. The kids would laugh and the teachers would laugh. In fact, the teachers showed their appreciation for my entertainment by consistently giving me lousy marks."

During the '20s and early '30s, Blanc went through what seemed like a mandatory struggling period. His musical talents, not his voices, landed him much of his early work in show business. An accomplished musician on the violin, bass and tuba, Blanc got a

Drawing a Blanc

job on the NBC Radio Orchestra in San Francisco and later worked as the pit orchestra conductor at the Portland Orpheum Vaudeville Theater.

At 22, Blanc said he was the youngest musical director the theater ever had. As a kid, Blanc said the Orpheum was like a magnet for him. "I used to go a couple times a week just to see Jack Benny, never thinking that I'd eventually work with him. He was the most marvelous man I ever met. He was loved by everybody."

Along with his wife, Estelle, Blanc moved to Los Angeles in the mid–'30s hoping to land a job in motion pictures or network radio as a voice specialist. After months of hounding the offices of Schlesinger Productions, the animation factory that later became Warner Brothers' *Looney Tunes* and *Merry Melodies*, he was given a chance to audition for director Frank Tashlin, an animator and cartoonist who later became a film director especially adept at packing movies with outrageous sight gags and furious pacing.

"He asked me if I could do a drunken bull. I thought about it for a minute and said, 'yes.' When he asked me how he would sound, I told him that he would sound like he was a little loaded and looking for the sour mash. Tashlin loved it and gave me my first job in cartoons."

The idea that in his career Blanc had managed to create over 400 distinctly different voices is mind-boggling and on par with his estimate of contributing voicework to more that 3,000 cartoons for MGM, Walter Lantz, Hanna-Barbera, Warner Brothers and other studios and producers. "They would show me a picture of the character that was going to be in the cartoon. And then a storyboard that showed me what the character was going to do throughout the picture. Porky Pig, for example, was a timid little guy. I had to give him a timid voice. When I lecture at colleges, I tell the kids that I wanted to immerse myself in the life of a pig so I could authentically create a pig's voice. I went to a pig farm and I wallowed around with the pig for a couple of weeks. I came back to the studio and they kicked me out and said, 'Go home and take a bath.'

"Then they showed me a picture of Bugs and told me that he was a real stinker. I knew he was a tough character. I had to get a tough voice. So I thought either Brooklyn or the Bronx. I compromised and put the two of them together. That's how I got the voice for Bugs ... doc."

Almost as famous as Blanc's characters are the catchphrases associated with many of them. Such phrases as "Eh, what's up, Doc?," "I tawt I taw a puddy tat," and "That's all folks" have become part of the American vernacular. "'Eh, what's up, Doc?' was popular around 1932–33," Blanc said. "They were going to have him say, 'Hey, what's cooking?' and I said, 'Instead of that corny saying, why don't you use a modern expression like Eh, what's up, Doc?' They thought it was a good idea, and the expression has become synonymous with Bugs. Strange, Warners had all the catchphrases ("That's all folks" and "Sufferin' succotash" were also coined by Blanc) and the characters copyrighted and trademarked. I gave them all of those damn things and now I have to ask permission to use them."

Blanc said the only voice he out and out copied and didn't originate was Elmer J. Fudd, the implacable "wabbit" hunter always on the trail of Bugs Bunny. "Elmer Fudd was created by a man named Arthur Q. Bryan and he died about 30 years ago," Blanc said. "Friz Freleng came to me and said, 'Mel, you could do that.' I said, 'I can do it, but try to find somebody else. He tried and couldn't find anybody. Finally he came to me and said, 'Mel, it's just a couple of lines. Won't you try it?' I tried it. Friz said, 'That's it!' I've been doing it ever since."

The most successful prime-time TV cartoon show of all time (until the advent of

The Simpsons) and a personal favorite is *The Flintstones*. Blanc supplied the voice of Fred's neighbor and best friend, Barney Rubble, as well as the Flintstone's pet dinosaur, Dino. Blanc said that the producers of the show, Hanna-Barbera, wanted him to pattern Barney after Art Carney's "Ed Norton" character on *The Honeymooners*. He refused and demonstrated with a "Hey, Fred!" the difference between Barney and Carney.

On Jan. 24, 1961, a year into the run of the cartoon, Blanc's voice was almost stilled permanently when he was involved in a horrific traffic accident that broke every bone in his body. He was in a coma for three weeks. "I was in the obituary column in Honolulu," he said. "But the old adage 'the show must go on' held true. After two months in the hospital, I was brought home and put in a full-body cast. We recorded eight months of *The Flintstones* from my bedroom. My son fixed up a beautiful recording studio right in the house."

The technology of making cartoons has changed radically over the years, but Blanc feels some of the artfulness has been sacrificed to speed and other economies. "What they're doing now I called limited animation. The old Warner Brothers' cartoons were full animation. Every frame was drawn separately, whereas in limited animation they draw the face, you see the eyes blink, the mouth moves a little, the background is on a turntable, and you see the same damn thing over and over again."

According to Blanc, years ago, a 6½-minute cartoon employed 125 people, took nine months to make, and cost about $50,000. Today it takes the same number of people, one-tenth of the time to make a cartoon that costs around $350,000.

"I have found that you can count on your fingers the number of people who can do more than two creative voices," Blanc said. "Most of them are impersonators or copyists. A lot of them will do a voice and say that they created it. I say, 'Bullshit!' It was created by 'Schnozz' Durante or one of those other guys."

Blanc's voice finally fell silent in 1989 at the age of 81. Inscribed on his tombstone are the words: "Man of 1,000 Voices" and "That's All Folks." While preparing this story in August 2017 for this book, another voice actor from cartoon's golden age passed away a few weeks shy of 100. She was June Foray and she did voice work on *The Flintstones* although not, like Blanc, in service to one of the main characters. Foray did, however, carve out her own special vocal niche as the cartoon voice of Rocket J. Squirrel, Natasha Fatale, Nell Fenwick, Witch Hazel and Cindy Lou Who, among others.

As contemporaries, Blanc and Foray's pint size belied their big talent as actors who were heard but not seen. By providing a rich legacy that stands as a benchmark in quality, they and others paved the way for newer generations of, in Blanc's words, "voice specialists." It's a tradition that continues to echo.

The Importance of Being Ernest

Ernest Borgnine

The guttural (often sardonic) laugh coming as it did from that blockhouse middle and invariably followed by the most famous gap-toothed grin since Lauren Hutton began appearing in Revlon ads was all part of the Ernest Borgnine brand that worked so well in hundreds of movies and episodic television shows.

Whether (as a literal and figurative "heavy") he was torturing Frank Sinatra in *From Here to Eternity*, playing the nebbishy title character "Marty" in an Oscar-winning performance, or pulling a fast one on Joe Flynn's clueless "Captain Binghamton" in the TV sitcom *McHale's Navy*, Borgie was a crowd-pleasing staple; as reliably rock-solid as the immutable granite faces on Mount Rushmore. But spend a little time with him (as we did in 1998) and evidence of Borgie's family roots in the Piedmont of northern Italy came cascading out like a deep pour from a generous sommelier. Borgie was instantly ingratiating—*compiacente*—like we were long-lost prodigals from his extended *famiglia*. All that was missing, really, was a plate of Agnolotti, a glass of Barolo and the three of us talking over each other.

Chi mangia bene, vive bene!

We met Borgie in Southeastern Wisconsin where he was filming a small independent family-oriented feature called *The Last Great Ride*. The location was a large home in the exurbs of Kenosha but we visited with him in his trailer where, costumed in suspenders that were as taut as rubber bands. Borgnine nodded when we mentioned we were situated only a few miles from the birthplace of two other show business heavyweights—Orson Welles and Don Ameche.

Long a believer in alternative modes of transportation, like a latter-day "Ralph Cramden," Borgnine could often be seen tooling around the country behind the wheel of his retro-fitted "Borgie bus." "I have a ball with it," he said. "I drive it and take it all

Borgie suspendered

over the country. Don Rickles can't get over it. Milton Berle said, 'God I wish I had his courage.'"

Erness Effron Borgnine was born on January 24, 1917, in Hamden, Connecticut, and grew up in New Haven. An only child, Borgie took to sports but showed no interest in acting. After high school he joined the Navy, where he stayed for 10 years (reaching the rank of chief gunner's mate) at the end of World War II. After toiling in various factory jobs, his mother suggested that young Ernie, with his "forceful" personality, could possibly channel that energy into acting. He enrolled in the Randall School of Dramatic Arts and later joined the Barter Theater in Virginia, where he plied his newfound profession for four years. His big break came in 1949, when he landed a role in the Broadway production of *Harvey*. In 1951, Borgnine moved to Hollywood and made his film debut in *China Corsair* (1951).

Borgie's reputation as a screen "heavy" was laid when he played "Sgt. 'Fatso' Judson" in *From Here to Eternity* in 1953. Two years later he broke out of the mold, portraying the sensitive New York butcher "Marty Piletti" in *Marty*. Borgie won the Best Actor Oscar, besting a field of thoroughbreds that included Spencer Tracy, Frank Sinatra, James Dean and James Cagney.

Other screen credits include: *The Catered Affair*, *The Dirty Dozen*, *The Wild Bunch*, *The Poseidon Adventure* and *Escape from New York*. On the small screen, in the early 1960s, Borgnine starred as "Lt. Cmdr. Quinton McHale" in *McHale's Navy*.

Off-screen, Borgie (who died in 2012 at the age of 95) was married four times, including an infamously short marriage to Ethel Merman, which lasted all of 32 days. When we met him, he had been married to his last wife, Tova, a successful cosmetics company owner, since 1972.

* * *

Fantle & Johnson: The Wild Bunch *was selected by the American Film Institute as one of the 100 best films of the century. There's a scene where William Holden and the men are getting laid in a brothel, and you're the lone gang member sitting outside whittling on a piece of wood that's an unmistakable phallic symbol. Some say that scene—purposely placed there by director Sam Peckinpah—signaled to audiences that your character was a closeted homosexual. Any truth to that?*

Borgie: Oh my God almighty! Ain't that something? I always tell people this. I'd already finished up in the brothel! How stupid could people be? No, it was just like this. The man was done and he was out there waiting for the rest of the guys to come out, period. That's it you know.

Do you think The Wild Bunch *was too violent?*

No, it's nothing compared to what we have today. And yet at the time it was considered very violent.

Playing a heavy as you did, you also had a lot of interesting death scenes. Are those roles fun?

Well, it's always paid me well. It all started with *From Here to Eternity*. Then I got into being a bad guy, killing Lee Marvin with a pitchfork (*Violent Saturday* 1955). One thing led to another. Finally when I did *Marty*, somebody asked, "Marty? To be played by Ernest Borgnine? He's a killer!"

Rod Steiger played the role of Marty *first on live television. Did you see his performance?*

No, not until much later. They asked me if I wanted to see it and I said, "What for?" I wanted to give my own performance. I won't comment on his, but he did win an Emmy for it, which, hey, people thought was good. I won an Oscar for mine.

Winning an Oscar makes you a member of a very small, select fraternity. How important was winning for you?

I'm very proud of my Oscar for the simple reason that I think I got it on my own, through my own merit, through my own work and I'm very proud of it. I only received $5,000 for the film, with a promise of $5,000 more if I signed a seven-year contract. I never got it.

Winning the Oscar has got to be worth more than $5,000?

Oh my lord. I'd have done it for nothing.

You didn't even pursue acting until after you got discharged from the Navy, correct?

My mother asked me one day after I came back from the service, "Ernie, have you ever thought of becoming an actor? You always like to make a darn fool of yourself in front of people. Why don't you give it a try?" And I said, "Mom, that's what I'm going to be." It opened up a whole new life for me and 10 years later, I'm very happy to say, I had an Academy Award.

You took a supporting role in the NBC sitcom, The Single Guy. *Why didn't that show last longer?*

The thing that makes me mad and angry right now is the fact that they don't want people over 50 years of age on television anymore. That's unfortunate because there are so many of us out in Hollywood that would love to be working. They canceled the show because of some political reasons at NBC. The ratings were still good. It was fun and it was a challenge but I originally didn't want to get into it.

So if you weren't working, what would you do?

I could be out in my bus. But then again, how many thousands of miles can you do? Right now, I'm in the midst of writing my book. Do you want to hear how I came up with the name for the book?

Sure.

I think some of the oldsters will get a kick out of this. I was walking along 10th Avenue in New York City contemplating my fate about becoming an actor. And I'm saying to myself, "Why did I become an actor? I could be doing anything else that would at least be keeping my home and family together. And here I am running from pillar to post trying to find a job and I can't find a job." In those days you could only work once a month on television because they were afraid if you were seen too much you'd be out of business. The only ones who were working steady were people like Charlton Heston and Jack Lemmon. And I said, "Wait a minute. I can act as well as Charlton Heston, if not better, right?" So I'm walking along and suddenly I smell the hot chestnuts. The vendor at the corner is selling hot chestnuts. I walked up and it reminded me of my mother when she used to cut the chestnuts and cook them. And the whole house would be permeated by the beautiful smell of the roasted chestnuts. So I walked closer to the vendor. Not to buy any because I couldn't afford them—just to catch a smell. And I saw a sign on the vendor's cart that became my philosophy of life and the title of my book. It said: "I don't want to set the world on fire; I just want to keep my nuts warm."

(Borgie's best-selling autobiography was published in 2009 under the more prosaic title: *Ernie*)

As a movie star, wasn't it a big career risk for you to take a role in McHale's Navy?

Yes it was. As a matter of fact when my agent called and asked me if I wanted to do this, I said, "No, no, I'm through with television now." As far as I'm concerned, I'm an actor now, you know a motion picture actor and I'll stay with movies. He said, "Well, if you change your mind, call me." OK, fine. So the next morning as the good Lord would have it, there came a knock at my door. A young man is selling chocolate bars for some private school out in the San Fernando Valley. He said, "Would you like … and I said, sure, sure, how much are they?" I started digging for the money. And he looked at me and said, "Mister, I've seen your face before, are you in show business?" He asked me my name, and I kiddingly said, "James Arness." He said, "No, he's on *Gunsmoke*." And I said I was just pulling his leg. "My name is really Richard Boone," I said. He said, "No, he's in *Have Gun Will Travel*." All this kid had to do was look around the door corner and see my Oscar. I thought I'd get him now, so I said, "My name is really Ernest Borgnine." Absolutely no recognition of any kind! He said, "But I know I've seen you." I said, "Thanks a million son, here's your money." I picked up the telephone, called my agent and said, "Is the part still open? I'll do it." He asked me what changed my mind and I responded, "None of your damn business." A year later I'm on the road up in Oregon looking for a place to park for the night. And I stuck my head into this cabin and this fellow looked at me and said, "McHale, what are you doing here?" I thought, "Boy, that kid was right!"

Tom Arnold starred in a remake of McHale's Navy *in which you had a small role.*

They paid me well for it and I can't say another word about it. In the TV series, I had chemistry with those guys that spewed forth a sense of comedy. I'm sorry to say in the film they made, there was just nothing there.

You spent 10 years in the Navy. Did you ever see anything there resembling your McHale's-*type hijinks?*

Oh you'd better believe it. I was stationed on board a yacht during the war. And on this yacht, believe it or not, I had my own stateroom and I was the gunner's mate onboard. We had the run of the Atlantic Ocean you might say. It was the greatest thing since cut bread. We'd go out and get boxes of food for ourselves, steaks and everything else during the war mind you. And we'd trade in another box full of stuff just to get whisky and beer and everything else. And then we'd go out and have a ball on the beach.

After McHale's *you had no trouble going back into feature films.*

Oh yeah. That's what made it so easy and people just couldn't get over it. They asked, "How come you can go back and forth from motion pictures to television and everything else. You are one of the few who can do it." I said, "There's nothing different between television and motion pictures." It's the easiest thing in the world you know. A lot of people are great on that small tube. You get them up there on the great big tube, and they can't do it.

Have you always been comfortable with your character actor status?

Absolutely! I don't want to be a star all the time. You know how many headaches these people have? Let's see, I've got to carry this picture on my shoulders. That's why they have best supporting actors. I'm one of the very few actors that ever won an Oscar for not being a leading man, really, but rather for portraying a character.

You don't seem to wear your political leanings on your sleeve like many others in your profession. Is that an accurate statement?

It's a pretty private thing for me, but I did shoot six commercials for a group of people who are pushing for a national sales tax, instead of the IRS. What the heck…. I'm 81 years old and I like to speak my mind. As a legacy, on the day I die, I'd like to have a newspaper publish all the things that I find wrong in the United States today. And my first would be to get rid of the politicians. We put politicians into Congress and the Senate for what? For representation. But who do they represent? They represent not only their party, but the people who give them the money, the lobbyists.

What keeps you going at this breakneck pace?

My mother told me when I was a young man, "You know Ernie, if you can make one person laugh in the span of 24 hours, you have accomplished a great deal." And that's what I try to do, make somebody laugh in the span of 24 hours. That's it. If you can do that, it keeps you young, keeps you happy, and hey, what more can you ask out of life?

Comedy in Three Acts

George Burns

Act I

Our first meeting with George Burns came in a roundabout way, to put it mildly.

One night in the summer of 1978 we were trying to walk off extra helpings of Yorkshire Pudding outside Lawry's The Prime Rib on La Cienega Boulevard in Beverly Hills. We'd just put in a call to the Beverly Hills Cab Company for a lift back to our hotel. After what seemed an interminable amount of time (taxis weren't and aren't exactly ubiquitous in L.A.), a paint-chipped cab pulled up. Our cabby introduced himself—immodestly perhaps—as "Seymour Barish: God's gift to West Coast public transportation."

He was a bewhiskered old coot (maybe in his late 60s) dressed in Converse "Jack Purcell" sneakers, a grimy knit stocking cap and blue jeans that were so streaked with motor oil they looked as if they had seen service as his dipstick wipe rag. We asked to be driven to our hotel in Beverly Hills. Barish flipped the meter, gunned the engine and we were off.

Seymour's cab had to be one of the dirtiest in Southern California. Besides the absence of one door handle, there has a gaping hole the size of a basketball in the passenger floor of his taxi through which we could view the passing of each white stripe of highway divider as he drove. We worriedly asked Seymour if the opening was to be used as a passenger foot brake. "No," he replied, "it's the emergency exit in case of fire, but no one gets outta here without payin' first."

We could understand the need for an emergency exit; the back seat was littered with every kind of combustible detritus imaginable, including empty Coca-Cola bottles, cigarette butts and candy wrappers all amid a generous padding of yellowing back issues of the *Los Angeles Times*.

One of the articles, we noticed, contained an article about Barish. It said that he had recovered more than $1 million in stolen government bonds. Seymour explained to us that when driving home from work one night, he stopped his cab because he saw an abandoned wooden box that he thought he would convert into a "dandy breakfast table for the kitchen nook." But after discovering the amount of money inside, he took it down to the police station where he was promptly arrested.

"It seemed L.A.'s finest thought I had stolen the money," Barish said incredulously. "But what really burned me was that after the whole mess blew over, I wasn't even offered a reward."

Seymour also mentioned with a sly twinkle in his bloodshot eye that he knew our hotel intimately having lived there briefly two years before. He said he had driven "clientele" of some of the young ladies to it. This was startling news to us, especially since we were paying $27 a night for our rooms and thought we deserved better than a brothel. When we voiced our outrage to Barish, he suggested we double up with a couple of the ladies.

"Problem solved," he said. Or just begun, we thought.

We wondered if Barish had driven any movie stars around town. (This was a question we methodically asked of all our L.A. cabbies.) He pulled out an autograph book—we had thought it was his dispatch book—that contained such names as Humphrey Bogart, Lauren Bacall, Groucho Marx and George Burns. After 35 years of driving the Beverly Hills beat, Seymour said it might be more appropriate to ask which film stars he hadn't driven.

We were particularly interested in Burns' signature. Barish said that he and Burns were the best of friends and that if we wanted to meet him, he could drive us to George's house right away. We thought Barish was putting us on—and dared him to prove he wasn't joking.

As we cruised down Maple Drive in Beverly Hills, we began to squirm, and when we turned up Burns' driveway, we realized Barish wasn't bluffing. We had an acute case of stage fright and decided we couldn't just knock on Burns' front door unaccompanied and unwelcome; Seymour would have to come with us.

The three of us then trouped up the sidewalk and rang the doorbell. It was then that Barish, with the sudden spring of a bullfrog leaping off a dock, disappeared into a flower bush just off the front landing

We suddenly saw less of Seymour.

A drowsy houseboy answered and tersely informed us that Mr. Burns usually slept in the evening. We shot a glance at our watches; it was 10 p.m. Taking pity on a couple of flummoxed rubes, the houseboy gave us the number to Burns' office.

Embarrassed, and with a haste prompted by the long leash of Burns' pissed-off Doberman, we returned to the car. Barish, acting as if everything was status quo and that we hadn't noticed his reenactment of "The Celebrated Jumping Frog of Calaveras County," asked if we wanted to go anywhere else.

"To the hotel," we huffed.

"The bordello it is," Seymour said, preternaturally cheerful, as usual.

Upon arriving, we saw the meter had been run up to around $60. We paid Seymour and watched as he gleefully drove off in the direction of Sunset Boulevard rhythmically tooting his horn. We both figured it was probably a set-up and that in due course he'd double back and pay off his co-conspirator, the houseboy.

Next day…

After putting in a call to Burns' office located not far from our hotel, a place called Hollywood Center Studios, we met with some initial resistance from Burns' longtime assistant and all-around Man Friday, Jack Langdon.

"You want to interview George? Well, he's pretty busy these days, and besides, he happens to be out of town right now," Langdon said dismissively.

"That's not what George's houseboy told us last night when we knocked on the door," Dave said, our implacability put to the test. "We could practically hear Mr. Burns snoring upstairs." (A tad impertinent perhaps, but what did we have to lose?)

"Damn, you caught me!" Langdon said after a pause that seemed to last minutes. "If you can get your butts over here pronto, I'll work you in … but you gotta move fast!"

To say we made tracks is an understatement. We appeared at Burns' office faster than Seymour had disappeared off Burns' landing the night before.

Act II

Burns was quartered in the old Hollywood Center Studios on Las Palmas Avenue. Built in 1919, Hollywood Center was one of the oldest production facilities in town and the site of such television shows as *I Love Lucy*, *The Addams Family*, *Get Smart* and *The Rockford Files*. In the early 1980s it briefly saw service as the site of Francis Ford Coppola's Zoetrope Studios.

It seemed appropriate that the old lot would be the venue for our visit with a man who quipped more about his age than anyone since Jack Benny! George met us at the door with a couple of cigars, 85-cent El Producto Queens. He was Kewpie doll tiny and at the age of 82 his face had begun to transmogrify into every caricaturist's dream—a countenance vaguely resembling that of an impish chimpanzee.

"What do you fellas wanna talk about?" he said. We thought of a subject befitting both the venerable setting and the man.

Anyone who ever spent any appreciable amount of time with George Burns (either in the audience during one of his personal appearances or in his expansive circle of friends) came to learn that the comedian was a walking repository of vaudeville lore.

One of the things he loved best was to reminisce about the time he spent touring the Orpheum Circuit with his wife and partner Gracie Allen. So, we fired a few questions at him about our own hometown Orpheum Theater in St. Paul, a show palace that played host to a glittering parade of stage entertainment after its cornerstone was laid back in 1917.

As a downtown vaudeville house, the St. Paul Orpheum's footlights illuminated some of the finest stage performers in America. Stars of the caliber of George Jessel, Jack Benny and, of course, Burns & Allen played the "two-a-day" in St. Paul to audiences that could afford the 75-cent admission.

Here's what George had to say about the heralded and the unsung; all of whom worked without a net or a microphone.

*   *   *

Fantle & Johnson: *When were you first hired by the Orpheum Circuit?*
    Burns: In 1925. I was 83 then.

Did you play the St. Paul Orpheum before you teamed with Gracie?
    No. Before I met Gracie, they wouldn't let me into St. Paul.

What did your act consist of when you teamed with Gracie?
    We did an act called "Burns & Allen in Lamb Chops." I said: "Gracie, would you like a kiss?" She said: "No." I said: "What would you like?" She said: "Lamb chops." And that joke made us both stars.

What are your recollections of the St. Paul Orpheum?
    Large, beautiful—and with indoor toilets.

What were your impressions of playing St. Paul?
    Gracie and I always did love playing St. Paul because there was *a* great restaurant there…. I forgot the name of the hotel we stayed at in St. Paul because I lost the towels I stole.

What did you do between shows to kill time in St. Paul?
    We went to Minneapolis.

How was the audience in St. Paul?
    That's why we went to Minneapolis.

What were some of the most unusual acts you shared the bill with in St. Paul?
    Power's Elephants, Fink's Mules, Madame Burkhardt and her Cockatoos and Dainty Marie.

What was your salary on the Orpheum Circuit?
    The team got $400 per week. That was good money in those days.

Were there any other unusual incidents or events that happened while playing St. Paul?
    I'd say that during our careers Burns & Allen played the Orpheum Theater about 15 times, and we were never cancelled. That was *very* unusual.

*   *   *

Act III

The unmistakable smell of cigar smoke hit us like a third-stage smog alert. The pungent odor is what greeted all visitors to George Burns' Hollywood office.

Seventeen years after our first visit that office was still spartan when we visited George several weeks shy of his 99th birthday in 1995—just a few mementos strewn around from his 80-plus-year show business career. What was conspicuous was the framed photo on the wall of Burns' late wife and performing partner, Gracie Allen.

A slight digression: Years before, we had made a promise concerning Gracie Allen

Burns between drags

that we felt honor-bound to keep no matter how much time might have elapsed. Edward Buzzell, a child star in vaudeville who became a director at MGM and Columbia and who had put the Marx Brothers through their zany paces in *At the Circus* and *Go West*, had asked if we could act as envoys for him if we ever ran into Burns again. Buzzell said he had written something he wanted us to give to George.

"I knew Burns & Allen when they were in vaudeville," Buzzell told us when we had visited him in his condominium. "I was just crazy about Gracie; had a big crush on her. I even directed them as a team in the film *Honolulu* in 1939."

Hollywood being a fraternal town—especially for artists of that earlier era—it didn't strike us as peculiar that we would be enlisted as passenger pigeons between two codgers who had been friendly half a century before. What we didn't know was that 14 years would pass before we got the chance to give Buzzell's message to George, and by then we would be surrogates of a ghost.

"I'm an old man now (Buzzell was 85 when we met him and would die four years later in 1985) and I don't care if you read this," he told us as he handed over an envelope with a hand-written note inside.

This time Burns didn't meet us at the door. He was seated in a director's chair inscribed with his name and clutching his second favorite partner, a cigar of course. In between puffs, he sipped tea from a mug appropriately inscribed with the word "God"— a tongue-in-cheek reference to his starring role in the two *Oh, God!* films.

The day before our visit, Los Angeles—as it often is—was rocked by small tremors from an earthquake. We asked George if he had felt anything.

"I look forward to them," he said without missing a beat. "They're my form of aerobics."

"Here boys, have a cigar," he offered. We reminded him that is was the same 85-cent El Producto Queen he gave us when we first visited with him.

"OK, good. Come back in another 17 years and I'll give you another one," he deadpanned. (Burns died the next year after reaching the century mark.)

At the time, the almost-centenarian still smoked at least half a dozen stogies a day—"more when I'm working," he said between drags.

Although the air in Burns' office was definitely stale, his outlook was amazingly fresh. In a rare serious moment, he explained his formula for staying young and offered a topical message for youth of any generation.

"Get out of bed, keep working and love what you're doing. The most important thing is to fall in love with what you are doing. If kids focused on one thing that they would eventually like to do and just did it, they wouldn't have to be turned on by drugs. Your future will turn you on. I get turned on by show business. I smoke cigars and drink martinis, but I don't use any stuff. I don't need it."

Burns' career spanned more than seven decades, from vaudeville and radio to movies and TV. The anchor for more than 40 of those years was Gracie Allen. She retired from the act in 1958 due to ill health and died in 1964. And he always was the first to credit Allen for the success of the team, but Burns said playing the role of the straight man was not as easy as it appeared.

"You think its easy being a straight man?" he asked. "I just walked on stage and asked Gracie: 'How's your brother?' She'd go off on a long comic routine and then I would say: 'Is that so?' I had seven or eight of those. To be a straight man you have to have good ears. When the audience laughs, you don't talk. The minute they stop laughing, you say: 'Is that so?'"

George Burns made performance art out of growing old with retirement never part of his vocabulary. "Listen boys," he said. "You can't help growing older, but you don't have to get old."

Oh, that envelope Buzzell wanted us to deliver to George? It contained this poem:

I would like to tell a tale of Burns & Allen
And the first time we met in New York town.
She was gentle, she was pretty, nothing like the city,
So I ushered her around.
I courted her with flowers and more flowers.
She responded and I almost went insane.
Right then I determined she be jeweled in mink and ermine,
Though I didn't have a penny to my name.

We were young and unafraid; we were smart and made the grade.
We were clever and never missed a beat.
We played the Music Hall and The Palace.
Gracie had the whole world at her feet.
The things I wrote, I wrote just for Gracie.
The fans all clamored for autographs,
Smoked my cigar, she got all the laughs.
We had love, we had life, we had humor.
We had music, we had singing, we had talk.
I do it all alone now but she's with me…
… with me since the first time in New York.

Measuring Up

James Cagney

He was 5 ft. nothing but he was larger than life. And he was no "tough guy."

James Cagney who died on Easter Sunday in 1986 at the age of 86 at his beloved farm in Stanford, New York, was the antithesis of tough. He was a doting husband and father with a penchant for poetry and a soft-spot for song-and-dance men, "hoofers," he called them. Cagney, more than almost anyone we ever met, was a gentleman of the old school where one's word was his bond and personal integrity was everything.

It was 1979, on St. Patrick's Day, when we visited Cagney at his rustic house just off Coldwater Canyon Drive in Beverly Hills. Cagney had granted just a handful of interviews since filming his last movie, *One, Two, Three* in 1961. Shortly after our visit, however, he was deluged by reporters with requests for interviews to coincide with his "unretirement" film, *Ragtime*.

We entered Cagney's very private life as a couple of college journalists. At the time, we were freelance writers who hustled our stories to any newspaper or magazine that would print and pay for them. In addition, we wrote a regular celebrity interview column for the University of Minnesota's student newspaper, *The Minnesota Daily*. Our specialty was old Hollywood. The previous summer we had cadged a couple of sit-downs with Fred Astaire and Gene Kelly.

"If Freddie saw you, so will I," Cagney wrote us in late 1978. We could almost hear his frenetic cackle leap from the letter. He informed us that he would be spending the winter months in his Southern California home and that's where we could reach him. He preferred to stay year-round at his upstate New York farm, but his wife of more than 60 years, Billie, liked the warmer weather, he explained. That's all we needed to hear; we planned a spring break trip to Los Angeles.

Immediately upon arrival at our hotel on the outskirts of Beverly Hills, we phoned Cagney's unlisted number which he had provided to us in the letter. A woman answered.

"Hello, we were told to call Mr. Cagney to arrange a short visit," Dave told her.

"Who told you and how did you get this number?" she asked, bristling.

"Mr. Cagney," Dave said.

"Well, he can't see you." With that, she hung up.

We had not journeyed 2,000 miles to get the heave-ho from some anonymous voice on the end of a telephone line. We called again. This time, Dave was more assertive.

"Listen," Dave said. "We're students from the University of Minnesota and we flew from Minneapolis to see Mr. Cagney at his invitation."

"Hold on a moment," the woman tersely replied. The few seconds she was away from the phone seemed like an hour and a half.

"OK, be here in a half-hour. No cameras and no tape recorders," she commanded. It was like we were trapped in some old '50s noirish melodrama directed by Sam Fuller and stocked with his hardboiled dialogue.

"We'll be there," Dave said trying as much as he could to channel Richard Widmark in *Pickup on South Street*, and hung up the phone. We quickly hailed a taxi for Coldwater Canyon—a boulevard that bisects the Santa Monica Mountains and links West Los Angeles with the sprawling San Fernando Valley to the north.

When we arrived at Cagney's house perched on a sloping shoulder of the canyon, a woman who appeared to be in her mid–50s answered the door. She introduced herself as Marge Zimmerman, Mr. Cagney's assistant. We could tell by the brusque voice that she was the telephone mystery woman. We didn't know it at the time but Zimmerman was soon to be embroiled in controversy chronicled in a feature story in *Life* magazine. According to many of Cagney's old show business friends, Zimmerman had taken complete control of all aspects of his life—professional and personal—in much the same way that Groucho Marx's "helper," Erin Fleming had done with that comedian's life a decade earlier. Some of Cagney's friends had claimed that Zimmerman was motivated purely by the profit she could make leeching off Cagney.

But Zimmerman (as Fleming had been) was not without her defenders. Many testified that she helped keep the ailing Cagney stay vital by pushing him back into film and

The artful Cagney—gifted to the authors, a James Cagney painting reproduced on a postcard

television roles. To this day, her motives and the exact role she played in the actor's life are unclear.

In fairness to her, Zimmerman was friendly and cooperative to us in person. She ushered us into the den where Cagney was waiting. "Cag, I'd like you to meet two young men from Minnesota," she announced.

"Minnesota," Cagney said with astonishment. "What brings you here?"

"We came to meet you," Tom said. Seated on a rocking chair, dressed in a terrycloth bathrobe and with a severe case of morning bed head (his red hair had turned white and stood almost straight up as if at attention), Cagney replied: "Hell, you must be a six-footer!" What immediately stuck us was the classic, instantly recognizable (and often parroted) Cagney voice. Age had not diminished that high-pitched, Irish-by-way-of-Yorkville, New York City pitch and the machine-gun cadence that came with it.

We scanned the room. Like the rest of the house, it used a lumberyard's worth of wood paneling and was decorated in what might best be described as Western Americana. We saw a Frederic Remington sculpture as well as a large oil painting of Cagney in his role as Admiral William "Bull" Halsey from the 1960 film, *The Gallant Hours*. It was painted, Cagney told us, by his good friend and instructor, Sergei Bongart.

To us, Cagney looked every bit his 80 years. He suffered from diabetes, intermittent ischemic strokes and a heart condition. Shortly after our visit, he entered a hospital for treatment of sciatica, a painful lower back disorder. But like the characters he portrayed on the screen, he still seemed larger than life.

"What can I do for you boys?," he asked.

"We'd like to talk to you a little about the musical films you made." His face lit up with a broad grin.

He told us that as a self-taught dancer, when he was young, he would "acquire" steps from stage performers as he sat in the audience watching vaudeville acts, and then immediately swap them with other aspiring hoofers on the streets of Manhattan.

There was nothing remotely deviant in this and it was considered an accepted, widespread practice, Cagney told us, provided one used the proper discretion and didn't cop an entire routine outright.

Tom mentioned that he had read an anecdote about how the great black tap dancer Bill "Bojangles" Robinson once gave a recital for a group of dance experts who all stared intently at his feet during the performance. "They should have been lookin' at my face, 'cause that's where I was sellin'," Bojangles said.

"Right, right!" Cagney laughed. "He knew!"

Cagney said that in the early days, choreographers charged large amounts to tailor a routine for a dancer, and it was just common sense for those less flush to pay a 15-cent admission to the local vaudeville house and get it secondhand at a more affordable price.

It was during those early years—in the 1920s—that Cagney formulated his distinctively stiff but rhythmic style of dancing and his raspy enunciation of song lyrics. The combination was potent enough to win him an Oscar as Best Actor for his portrayal of George M. Cohan in *Yankee Doodle Dandy* (1942), which he told us was his favorite screen role bar none.

Besides the flag-waving patriotism of the film (Cohan wrote "Over There" which became a galvanic rallying cry for soldiers going off to World War I) and coming as it did in the dark, early days of World War II, the movie was a revelation to many moviegoers showing a side of Cagney that didn't include smashing grapefruits into molls' faces or peppering coppers with a tommy-gun.

Seeing Cagney on the hoof was always an odd treat. His stocky torso was like a cinder block with arms and legs that flailed centrifugally about as when he ran up the proscenium wall or buck-and-winged his way down the White House staircase in *Yankee Doodle Dandy*. At times, watching Cagney dance, was like viewing the top half of a swathed mummy whose bottom half was hyper-animated, almost like a cartoon.

Cagney cited veteran hoofers Johnny Boyle and Harland Dixon as brilliant all-around dancers who had great influence on his personal style, but he acknowledged "Freddie" Astaire to be "the master of us all."

He said that he and Astaire had talked of making a musical together in the early 1950s, but due to previous commitments (Astaire was contracted to MGM at the time); their schedules never coincided long enough to make it a reality.

In 1961 Cagney retired as a movie actor and, when we met him, still felt no great urge to perform in front of the cameras. He did intimate to us that the only film offer he felt a tinge of regret in turning down was the role of Alfred Doolittle, Eliza's ne'er-do-well father in *My Fair Lady*, a character whose tremendous *joie de vivre* had impressed Cagney when he saw the original Broadway production.

Besides musicals, Cagney's other interest was raising Morgan horses on his farm. He told us that Morgans are utilitarian and good for both hard work and riding. Tom mentioned that his Irish great-grandparents raised horses on their farm in Greene County, Iowa.

"Well I'll be damned, my wife's from Iowa," Cagney said. His marital status was rare in Hollywood: he and his wife "Bill," as Cagney called her had been married for 58 years.

We had noticed Cagney's wife when we first came into the room. She was a tiny, unprepossessing woman wearing dark glasses who seemed to disappear into the chair in which she was sitting. Tom began to talk to "Bill" about Iowa and that the family farm grew mostly soybeans and corn but had once had quite a few hogs—"And not just the hired hands who crowded the kitchen table during lunch breaks," he said.

Cagney loved it! Not the conversation about his career, but the "farm talk" (which had moved on to an impassioned discussion about corn futures) between his beloved wife and a Midwestern teenager. It was evident that during Cagney's many years of stardom, it had been expected during public appearances and press junkets that "Bill" dutifully melt into the background. He was obviously delighted that a bit of that spotlight was now trained on her.

"Farmer's are the backbone of this country," he said joining in. "We drive across America each fall from New York to Los Angeles because I love to see this country and you can't see it from 28,000 ft. in an airplane."

"My grandmother always said that farmers are the biggest gamblers on earth dealing as they do with Mother Nature and what can happen at any time," Tom said.

"Vegas high-rollers are nothing compared to them," Cagney intoned. "Say, would you fellas like to have dinner with Bill and I tomorrow night?"

"Is that a rhetorical question?" we asked, caught flat-footed. Of course we accepted.

Because we had traveled to Cagney's house by taxi, we planned to make the two-mile walk down the canyon to Sunset Blvd., but Zimmerman wouldn't hear of it. Instead, she insisted on driving us back to our hotel in Cagney's 1961 Bentley. And here's a shameful confession, we got purposely lost so that Zimmerman could drive us around for a few extra blocks as we waved to pedestrians from the back seat acting all the while like half-assed Beverly Hills grandees.

Zimmerman told us to come to the Gingerman Restaurant the next night. Cagney, she said, loved to go there when the Beverly Hills Unlisted Jazz Band played, featuring actors George Segal (*The Owl and the Pussycat* with Barbra Streisand) and Conrad Janis (*Mork and Mindy*). We learned it was a weekly tradition for the Cagneys to dine there on those nights when they were in town.

Next night, when we arrived at the Gingerman on Bedford Drive, we found a line that extended around the block. After name-dropping to the hostess why we were there, we were promptly seated. A few minutes later, Zimmerman arrived.

"Order anything you want," she said, "and enjoy the tunes."

At the next table sat a trio of expensively dressed ultra-chic Beverly Hills trophy wives who we surmised were out of their element. They couldn't have been drawn to the band as they tried to keep time to the music by drumming their fingernails on the table at 2/4 beat to a "flat four" time signature.

After dinner, Zimmerman returned. It was time to meet the Cagney party. Sitting next to Cagney and his wife was the owner of the Gingerman, "Archie Bunker" himself—

Carroll O'Connor, who sized us up silently with a penetrating glance with would have stiffened even "Meathead." Cagney, wearing a Russian sailor's cap and blue blazer was having a grand time as he tapped his foot in time to the Dixieland stylings of the band. (What wasn't grand was the procession of tipsy well-wishers that crowded the table, including a soused character dressed in full-on yachting regalia who was a dead ringer for "Thurston Howell III" of *Gilligan's Island*.)

Due to Zimmerman's urging, public excursions had become commonplace for Cagney during the last couple of years. After we exchanged pleasantries, Cagney wordlessly reached over and gave us a couple of signed and dated postcards made from one of his own paintings, a still life of a vase of flowers, doubtless painted under the close tutelage of his instructor, Bongart. It was a touching gesture from a man famed—at least in the movies—for being a hard case; a tough guy.

We returned to our table to listen to the jazz, feeling 10 ft. tall.

What Makes Sammy Run?

Sammy Cahn

It wasn't a Steinway and didn't have white and black keys. In fact, the composing instrument of choice for four-time Oscar-winning lyricist Sammy Cahn (1914–1993) wasn't even a piano. He used a manual typewriter (which had given way to an IBM Selectric in his office when we visited) to create the quatrains and couplets to such American song standards as "High Hopes," "All the Way," "Three Coins in the Fountain," "I've Heard That Song Before," "Let It Snow," "Call Me Irresponsible," "Come Fly with Me," "(Chicago Is) My Kind of Town," "Love and Marriage" and dozens of others, mostly in collaboration with composers Jule Styne and Jimmy Van Heusen.

"I would rather be sitting and typing lyrics than anything in the world," he declared. As we came to find out, that statement was far from hyperbole; Cahn lived and breathed lyric writing, it consumed him. The interview in 1980 started out in the sunken living room of his home in Beverly Hills but quickly became a moveable feast with us literally following the peripatetic Cahn around his house from the typewriter in his office to the portable typewriter out by his pool.

Cahn began his musical education by writing parodies of popular songs while attending high school in his native New York City. "The greatest exercise for a beginning songwriter is to write parodies," he said. "Education is a tool, especially for a man who deals in words. I started to read voraciously when I was very young and, funny enough, I think I know all the most important words. I still hold my high school record for truancy, it's never been approached."

A 'born and bred New Yorker, Cahn (who dispensed with formality and received us naked from the waist up, his potbelly protruding over his belt like a second cousin of Buddha three weeks into the Scarsdale Diet) never lacked for patter. In fact, he was as loquacious as anyone we ever met who wasn't named Rod Steiger. "I would have given

The write stuff

my soul to be a performer," he confided. "If I would have been born 13 years earlier in 1900 instead of 1913, I would have been George Burns. So I took out my frustration in demonstrating my songs. I'm considered quite a lethal demonstrator. First of all, there's no such thing as a word sticking in my mouth when I sing it to you; it's singable because I couldn't be singing it otherwise."

Admittedly, Cahn's voice did have a thin, reedy "I'm Mario Lanza but only in the shower" quality of a true amateur. (Incidentally, Cahn wrote Lanza's biggest hit, "Be My Love" for the film *The Toast of New Orleans*.) The only difference was that he was brazen enough to sing in public, a circumstance he blamed on the fact that he was an unrepentant "ham." It was, however, kind of endearing to watch him dash back and forth from his desk to the piano to serenade us. To say that Cahn was enthusiastic about his work would be a gross understatement; his energy was kinetic and contagious.

Cahn—the Orphic bard of hipster lyricists—called his ability to write lyrics an unexplainable miracle. "I put the paper in and type. That's it. No margin for error, no paper strewn around the floor. It never fails. It's a miracle, and I'm pleased to be part of the miracle.

"I say this most modestly," he added. "I'm not calling myself a miracle. I'm calling *it* a miracle. The point is, I just sit and type, and there's no way in the world that it doesn't come out. It never fails. And I've learned after 50 years it will always come out. I don't write the songs as much as the songs write me."

When the tutelage of his parody days was behind him, Cahn began work at Columbia Pictures with songwriter Saul Chaplin. His most productive years came when he collaborated with Styne and Jimmy Van Heusen on such films as *Anchors Aweigh* (starring Frank Sinatra and Gene Kelly), *The Court Jester* (starring Danny Kaye), *The Tender Trap* (again with Sinatra to whom Cahn said he pledged his "everlasting allegiance"),

Peter Pan and *Thoroughly Modern Millie* (starring Julie Andrews, Mary Tyler Moore and Carol Channing).

One of Cahn's favorite stories was how he wrote the lyrics of "I've Heard That Song Before" which became a big hit for Sinatra. "I'd come out of a very low period in my life," he said. "I had just finished writing with Saul Chaplin and I was out of work, the most fallow period of my life. I got a call to write with a fellow named Jule Styne."

Styne played Cahn a melody and the lyricist immediately exclaimed: "I've heard that song before!" Styne shot back: "What are you, a tune detective?" "I didn't mean I had literally heard it," Cahn said, "I meant it as a title." Cahn then sang:

It seems to me I've heard that song before
It's from an old familiar score. I know it well, that melody

It's funny how a theme recalls a favorite dream
A dream that brought you so close to me

I know each word because I heard that song before

"I didn't write the song, it wrote me," he said. "Anyway, the song's a big hit and I'm out of my slump and I'm floating and I come to the Castle Argyle Apartments on Argyle Ave. in Los Angeles and there sit Paul Weston and Axel Stordahl making an arrangement of 'I've Heard That Song Before.' They say to me, 'There he is, he writes a song in 15 minutes and it takes us hours to make it sound good.'"

Cahn loved explaining the genesis of his songs almost as much as singing them to us. Following are a couple more stories with some of his quavering tenor thrown in for good measure.

"The Second Time Around"—"Very often I use certain sounds in lyrics. When I was writing 'The Second Time Around' with Jimmy Van Heusen. (Sammy sang):

Love's more comfortable the second time you fall
Like a friendly home the second time you call
Who can say what brought us to this miracle we've found?
There are those who'll bet love comes but once, and yet
I'm oh, so glad we met the second time around

Van Heusen didn't like the "et" sound and I understood what he meant. So I said to him, 'I like it and I'll tell you why.'" Cahn then sang a few bars of Lerner and Loewe's "I've Grown Accustomed to Her Face" from *My Fair Lady* in which he accented the "ack" sound. "Then Van Heusen understood what I was getting at," Cahn said.

"Call Me Irresponsible"—"It was originally written for Fred Astaire (for a musical film version of *Papa's Delicate Condition* that eventually starred Jackie Gleason when Astaire dropped out of the project to star in the film *Silk Stockings*). You can hear when you listen to that song that it was written for him. I said to Fred, 'You should have your name on every song that was written for you because you are a contributor by the sheer fact that you're going to do it.

"I'll never forget, the song was written at 11 p.m. in Jimmy Van Heusen's home in the Hollywood Hills," Cahn continued. "He and I had the *Papa's Delicate Condition* script and the word 'irresponsible' was replete through the script. So, Van Heusen was stretched out on the couch and I said to him, 'Hey, how do you like the title, 'Call Me Irresponsible'? It has a cadence and that cadence is the root to the whole song. Van Heusen thought about it, got off the couch, went to the piano and played it right away. But the genesis of it is that it has the most unsingable words. (Sammy sang):

So, call me unpredictable
Tell me I'm impractical

But those notes made it beautiful. Later, I find myself in a room at Paramount Studios singing 'Call Me Irresponsible' to Astaire—one of the great thrills of my life. (Sammy sang):

Call me irresponsible
Call me unreliable
Throw in undependable, too

Do my foolish alibis bore you?
Well, I'm not too clever, I
I just adore you

Fred said, 'Stop!' and Van Heusen almost fell off the piano bench. 'It's one of the best songs I've ever heard,' Fred said. I said, 'It's one of the best half-songs you've ever heard. Wait until you hear the finish of the song.' He was delighted and then said, 'Do you know why you got this job? You got this job because (Johnny) Mercer is out of town.' I said, 'I consider that a high, high compliment.' Fred said, 'No, now let me give you the compliment. The next time Mercer leaves town, I won't be worried.'"

"The Tender Trap"—"When we wrote 'The Tender Trap,' Van Heusen and I, Jack Benny always used to ask us how we wrote it. So I said to him, seriously, 'When I hear the word 'trap,' I hear the word, 'snap,' so the song's finished, it's finished.' He said, 'What do you mean, finished?' I said, 'It's finished.' (Sammy sang):

You see a pair of laughing eyes
You're acting kind of smart, until your heart
just goes wap!

You're caught in the tender trap

It was my original instinct. So, I'm typing, 'you're acting kind of smart, until your heart just goes wap! Those eyes, those sighs, they're part of the tender trap.' Again, the song is writing me. The man who almost saved my sanity, probably my career, was Matisse. When someone asked Matisse to explain what he did, he said, 'I don't explain it because it isn't intellectual; it's intuitive.'"

In his short story, "My Lost City," F. Scott Fitzgerald wrote, "I once thought that there were no second acts in American lives." Clearly, he never fomented the idea of Sammy Cahn.

At the time we visited him, Cahn was fully immersed in his "second time around" writing special lyrics for corporate events. "It's a source of great revenue for me," he told us. "People send me specific information and I reduce it to the

The portable Cahn

song. And I ask you to believe that they're written as impeccably as I know how to write. I'm not being casual about it."

He shared with us an example of how he conjured new lyrics to melodies that are part of the American song canon—a "special lyric" he wrote for one, Steven Gray, for an IBM banquet in Rochester, New York set to the music of "The Tender Trap."

It all began way back in May
A phone call from a Mr. Gray
He said my name is Steve and I had to believe the chap
So you can see it's me and the IBM trap
And I'm a ham
Yes, I am
I mean the purest and without shame
I'll inform you I was flown here tourist
Some special lyrics I have made
Please do applaud, don't be afraid
The applause is how I'm paid in the IBM trap

"The requests for these kinds of lyrics are endless, infinite," Cahn said. "The world has radar on my typewriter." Cahn added that as a superstitious talisman, he finished each song with three exclamation points. "Nobody ever asked me why and I don't know why, it's just an affectation," he said. "I've never had to walk around with ideas for songs. The music speaks to me. Any number of people will come through that door and go to the piano and play me something and the music speaks. That's why I'm very humble about that miracle."

But Cahn's self-effacement stopped when young hopefuls sought him out for advice "If I could ever help amateurs out, I would," he said. "I found out you can't. You can't help people because by helping them, you don't help and here's the line: If you help salmon upstream, you get lousy salmon."

Inspiration for a new song lyric was never more than a phone call away, he said. "People always ask me what comes first, the words or the music. It's the phone call. If the phone stops ringing, I will stop writing." For Cahn, the phone never stopped ringing. Nonplussed but nonetheless bemused that his career as a lyricist transformed into an altogether new hybrid, Sammy, no doubt, would've had the last, choicest words on the phenomenon, maybe summoning from his trunk a classic lazily and most memorably trilled with sangfroid to spare by Dean Martin; lyrics that articulated exactly what he wanted to say:

I've sunshine enough to spread,
It's just like the fella said
Tell me quick, ain't that a kick in the head?

The-Great-Minneapolis-Kidnap-Caper

Frank Capra

We weren't taking any chances.
Uppermost in our minds was the gloomy pall that descended when another great

director, William Wyler, died the day before we were scheduled to meet him. The only thing that could keep us from interviewing Frank Capra was if *we* dropped dead. And that wasn't gonna happen! Although, come to think of it, Minnesota was in the grip of a particularly nasty winter in January 1981 with engine blocks freezing in cars all over town and then crashing through their chassis to the icy roadways underneath. Better check the anti-freeze. Did we mention we weren't taking any chances?

Despite the inclement weather, the Minneapolis Film Festival was going full bore with its slate of screenings and seminars. Capra, who had flown in from his home in Palm Springs, California, was the honored guest and celebrity fulcrum around which many of the festivities spun. It was quite a casting coup for the festival organizers and they were milking it for all it was worth, guiding the diminutive director to and fro, albeit willingly, like a beagle on a leash.

Attempting to keep the lid clamped on our maverick tendencies, we tried negotiating through official channels with the frazzled talent wrangler to arrange some time with Capra and were strung along with vague, cheery promises that we'd get "a few minutes sometime … somewhere."

About midway through the festival, we realized that those minutes were not going to materialize unless we took a preposterous step. We decided to kidnap Capra.

After some checking, we found out that the director was billeted at the Sheraton-Ritz Hotel in Minneapolis. We drove downtown, inquired at the front desk and were told outright (without even a trace of suspicion) Capra's room number. In the morning crush of activity with guests checking in and checking out, we guessed that the staff was clueless about Capra's fame as one of Hollywood's great directors and, therefore, didn't have their proprietary antennae up—a real case of "Meet John Doe."

We promptly hiked it on up to his floor and knocked on the door. It was around 9 a.m. We didn't hear anything so we knocked again. We repeated this process a couple more times, along with some furtive salutations whispered into the tiny security peephole in the door (as if sound could penetrate the minuscule glass eyepiece), but we got no response—just dead silence.

We started to get worried; Capra after all, was in his 80s, and William Wyler's demise was still fresh in our memory banks. So we returned to the front desk and told a hotel manager our concern. He dispatched a worker with a set of keys to accompany us back to Capra's room. This time there was no knocking as the hotel guy inserted the key and opened the door. We scanned the room and there was no sign of Capra. At about that instant we heard the shower and saw steam coming from underneath the bathroom door. If we had moved as quick as the hotel guy—whose heightened sense no doubt told him to beat a hasty retreat down the hall or risk losing his job—we'd have been home free. But we didn't move fast enough.

Capra (who had heard us enter his room) flung open the door and let loose a stream of invective that would have made Redd Foxx blush. "I was in the fucking shower!" he screamed in a high-pitched voice that sounded like a party balloon, pinched at the nozzle, being deflated. His eyes were fixed and dilated now with more steam pouring out of his ears than from the superheated showerhead. He had a hotel towel hitched around his hips and would have used it as a weapon if his vitriolic rant wasn't already doing a thorough job. "God damn it, get the hell out!" he yelled literally in a lather, white flecks of saliva (or maybe soap) visible on his lips and chin.

We muttered some half-assed apology and then had the cheek to say we'd wait for him downstairs in the lobby. It was the longest, most mortifying half-hour of our lives.

In a film career that spanned four decades and garnered three Academy Awards, Capra provided the American movie-going public with a style of screen entertainment that was not only grand, but uniquely his. Capra's direct legacy to film was his vision of the triumph of homegrown virtue and morality against all odds.

This ideal found an effective showcase in the cinematic portraits he created for many of his leading men. The Mandrake Falls Vermonter who becomes heir to a large fortune but gives it away free as parceled farm acreage to the unemployed of the Great Depression; the U.S. Senator who refuses to be corrupted by his fellow politicians in Washington and stands up for his beliefs in front of Congress; the small-town savings and loan banker whose unbending faith in the inherent goodness of humanity enable him to face and defeat crisis after crisis—all are characters he created for such immortal films as *Mr. Deeds Goes to Town*, *Mr. Smith Goes to Washington* and *It's a Wonderful Life*.

Capra began his career in 1922 as a propman, film cutter and gagman for the Hal Roach Studios (Laurel and Hardy's alma mater), but later graduated to scriptwriting status while working for Mack Sennett. It was there that he played an instrumental part in forming the comedic style of silent screen star Harry Langdon, a pantomimist many pundits rank as just one notch below Chaplin and Keaton. It is in Langdon's persona of the oppressed underdog that one first discerns the seed that was to germinate full-blown into the character roles of Capra's greatest successes in the 1930s and '40s.

These characters—Mr. Deeds, Mr. Smith, George Bailey of *It's a Wonderful Life* and the rest—were often disparaged by the critics of the time for what was called their "unceasing morality and dedication to virtuous causes." Such characters, critics believed, only existed in folklore and legend. Nevertheless they symbolized the traditional American dream of an idealistic lone eagle that never compromises his beliefs or what he knows to be true. They mirrored closely those rugged individualists of our pioneer past. And in a world being torn apart by the deceit and aggression that was a prelude to World War II, it was a comfort to know that such people existed—even if it was only for a few minutes in a Frank Capra production.

In a few minutes, Capra (dressed more for a shotgun start on Palm Springs' golf links than for a sub-zero Minnesota winter's day) appeared in the lobby. He was minus any kind of wool or down-filled outer layer and was wearing an off-white blazer tailored from a synthetic fabric that probably "breathed" well enough in the desert but would be a miserable windbreak for the cold gusts we'd likely encounter outside (if we ever made it that far).

We could tell Capra was still upset, but, to his eternal credit, he decided to move past our breaking and entering episode.

"I do about six film festivals a year, and I think I'll have to cut down," he said. "I never get to see any of the cities I visit because I am programmed into doing interviews or seeing films from dawn to dusk. The only time I do get out its usually to some festival coordinator's house."

Jumping at this slight overture to make amends, we offered to squire Capra around on a select tour of the Twin Cities. He told us he wanted very much to see "Mark Twain's river—the Mississippi" and to attend Sunday church services.

We drove to the Cathedral of St. Paul with its copper-clad dome that looms on a hill overlooking downtown St. Paul and sidled into a pew (Capra skipped confession

Mr. Capra goes to Minneapolis

rightly figuring that we deserved his early-morning verbal torrent). After services, the recessional hymn was "My Country Tis of Thee." It was a tribute to the American hostages that had just been released from captivity in Iran. Capra sang all the verses from memory without once looking in the hymnal.

After church, we drove Capra around the Summit Hill area just up the incline from the cathedral. We cruised slowly past the governor's mansion, the old Commodore Hotel and F. Scott Fitzgerald's home where the Jazz Age author had completed his first successful novel, *This Side of Paradise.* We discussed the sad fact (in retrospect) that Fitzgerald—along with an army of other talented writers—seemed to have sold out to the sunshine and easy money that Hollywood offered in the late '30s and '40s. Ernest Hemingway was one of the few literary titans of that era who seemed to hold his ground.

"I'll tell you an interesting story about Hemingway that you won't believe," Capra piped up from the backseat. "I wouldn't have believed it myself, but the man who told it to me was Spencer Tracy.

"Spence was filming Hemingway's short story 'The Old Man and the Sea' down in the Caribbean when Hemingway invited him in for a drink in a little cantina. They were getting along well when suddenly, for no reason at all, Hemingway got up, turned around, and slammed his fist into the face of a waiter carrying a tray of food. The waiter went sliding across the floor as Hemingway sat down and continued the conversation as if nothing had happened. Spencer was in a state of shock and asked why he had done that. Hemingway said that he hit one of them every day just to show them who was boss. Spence said: 'Would you like to try that on me?' Hemingway told him that he didn't hit any of his friends, whereupon Spence said, 'I'm no friend,' and got up and left."

A shockingly sad example of "Papa" not being very fatherly—we were speechless. It's a good thing Capra wasn't. He continued: "I feel the true aim of any artist is to unify the world through his art, not divide it. I am like a lawyer or doctor. Through the medium of film and my particular work, I try to lobby for all of mankind."

Most of all, Capra wanted to see the Mississippi River. We knew a traverse through the St. Paul neighborhood of Highland Park (where we both grew up) that would take us over the river and afford a nice panoramic view of Fort Snelling. From the bluffs, Capra studied intently the swirls and eddies of the "Big Muddy" as it flowed south of the old, restored 1820s Army outpost and into a confluence with the nearby Minnesota River.

"This is the crux of Twain," Capra said delightedly. "He was a great writer and a great man."

Figuring we couldn't possibly top what Abraham Lincoln once called "The Father of Waters" with any other Twin Cities hotspot, we drove Capra back to the Sheraton-Ritz and deposited him curbside. "Hey guys, I'm hungry. Do you wanna eat?" he asked leaning in before shutting the car door. We reasoned that our unconscionable transgression of kidnapping Capra and obliterating his schedule couldn't possibly be mitigated by any halfhearted show of restraint at this late date, so we accepted his invitation. Besides, we were hungry too … for more anecdotes. So, we all sat down to lunch in the hotel's Cheshire Cheese Restaurant where we discussed Capra's directorial heyday during Hollywood's Golden Era.

* * *

Fantle & Johnson: *In your autobiography,* The Name Above the Title, *you wrote about many innovations that you devised to improve techniques in filmmaking. Is the teleprompter that we see on modern television cameras your invention?*

Capra: Well, it was the first time I ever heard of anybody doing it. I built a primitive model using wire between two spools, in which the cue-cards could be rotated. I then placed this on top of the movie camera. I did this for some of General George C. Marshall's speeches during World War II. Incidentally, I put a humorous switch on that idea in *It's a Wonderful Life*. During that scene where Jimmy Stewart and Donna Reed are living in that old dilapidated house without a cooking stove, they use a moving phonograph turntable and a thread spool to slowly roast a chicken over the fireplace.

An attractive aspect of your film work has always been the attention paid to the minutest details. In Lost Horizon, *during the scenes in the Himalayan Mountains, the frosty breath of Ronald Colman and the rest of the cast are clearly visible. This is a realistic effect we have seldom seen in movies of the 1930s and '40s that were filmed on back lots.*

The reason you could see the actor's breath was that we shot those winter scenes in an icehouse, with decorated backdrops painted to resemble snowy mountains. Previously I had tried putting little chicken-wire cages of dried ice in the performers' mouths. But as you might imagine the clarity of their dialogue suffered terribly, and I discarded the idea.

Did Harry Cohn, production boss at Columbia Studios, give you complete autonomy with regard to what films you could direct and which stars would appear in them?

Yes, he did. Harry Cohn was every kind of a so-and-so, but he was awfully smart. He trusted his talent. If he had confidence in someone, then that person would have complete control. But if anyone under contract ever gave in to him in an argument, then that person was fired. Cohn didn't know how to write or direct a film, so he didn't want his directors saying, "How do you want this Mr. Cohn?" He would say, "What the hell do I know about it!" He trusted people who had confidence in themselves, and who could stand up to his bullying.

What was the difference when you were under contract to Paramount?

They dictated absolutely what films I could and couldn't direct. Much of the time this was based on projected production costs. If I presented them with an idea that looked too expensive they would veto it immediately. The only reason I was able to direct the two Bing Crosby pictures, *Riding High* and *Here Comes the Groom,* was that I guaranteed Paramount that I could shoot them for less than $1 million, which was under their projected budget.

When you filmed the two Crosby movies, did you record the songs and dialogue live on the set, or did you use playback machines and record them in a soundproof booth somewhere else on the Paramount lot?

I recorded everything directly on the set. The music department at Paramount raised hell about this; they wanted to take the actors into a beautiful music stage, put them around a microphone, and after hours of rehearsal, record the songs onto a vocal track—a monumental dubbing job I thought unnecessary. I said, "This is ridiculous. Why don't we shoot the songs live on the set?" The music department replied, "The acoustics are bad; we can't." I countered with, "Well, I don't want anyone directing my actors." We were at an impasse.

Was this situation ever resolved?

Yes, we arrived at a compromise. In order to placate the music department and yet have full control over my actors, I rigged up a recording system of my own which we used for Jane Wyman's singing of "In the Cool, Cool, Cool of the Evening" from *Here Comes the Groom*. We shot this scene live on the set. But in order for Jane to hear the orchestra, which was on a separate soundstage at the other end of Paramount Studios, I used two tiny sound wires that we strung along the ground from the orchestra stage, across the lot, to our location. On the ends of the wires were two ear inserts that acted as a kind of miniature headphone set. Jane was then able to hear the orchestra music and sing the song live as we filmed. That song, "In the Cool, Cool, Cool of the Evening" won the Academy Award for Best Song that year (1951).

Riding High *and* Here Comes the Groom *were essentially movie comedies with music appended. Did you ever want to make a song-and-dance musical?*

My good friend Irving Berlin, one of our greatest songwriters, was always after me to do a musical picture with him. But I kept telling him I wouldn't know what to do with a musical comedy. He said, "What do you mean by that?" I said, "I don't know, all of a sudden some guy starts singing to a tune that materializes out of thin air, Irving, I'd probably break out laughing and never get the film done." Well, Berlin explained that the audience suspends their disbelief in such a case, and that's what makes musicals acceptable. I told him that I loved musicals in the theater and on the screen, but I would still probably break up if I ever directed one. Irving said, "If you ever get an idea for a musical film, call me up." Well, one day I did come up with an idea for a story in which the songs, I felt, would flow naturally from the plot. The story concerned a group of show people who ran a vacation inn just on the holidays.

This sounds familiar!

Yes, my idea became the musical *Holiday Inn* which was released in 1942 starring Fred Astaire and Bing Crosby. I was in the Army at the time making the *Why We Fight* series of films when I told Irving about it. He went wild with delight, exclaiming he could write a different song for each holiday. Since I was in the Army, I wasn't able to direct, but I gave the idea to Irving anyway and the musical was a big hit for Paramount.

We heard somewhere that when Harry Cohn bought the play You Can't Take It with You *for you to direct in 1938, you threw out music that had been written for it.*

Cohn couldn't believe it. He said: "Why the hell did you do it, a musical with no music?" I told him that I didn't like the music, and Cohn said the New York critics would eat me alive for tampering with *their* hit play. Well, when my film of *You Can't Take It with You* opened at Radio City Music Hall, I took Irving Berlin to the premiere. He thought it was a hell of a show. We walked home to the Waldorf Astoria, and when the elevator door opened, out came Moss Hart, who along with George S. Kaufman, was the author of the original Broadway version. Moss turned to me and said, "Frank, I liked it," and then walked out of the hotel. I died laughing but Irving was so embarrassed for me that he ran after Hart to get him to apologize.

You made State of the Union *with Katharine Hepburn and Spencer Tracy at MGM. What were your impressions of working there?*

It would have been impossible for me to be a director contracted at MGM. Twice I tried working there and twice they fired me before I started. The production bosses didn't like the idea of any director completely running the show, the old question of limited autonomy again. I made *State of the Union* (one of my best pictures) at MGM, because I wanted to work with Spencer Tracy. I had organized my own independent film company called Liberty Films and had come to an agreement with the studio executives that for the services of Tracy in my picture, MGM would have sole distribution rights when the project was completed. They owned a theater chain that stretched from coast to coast, so they stood to gain immensely as their own marketing agents. In addition, my company would rent MGM studio space and facilities, but I would retain complete autonomy on any matters pertaining to the production.

I soon realized that our mutual contract with regard to my undisputed autonomy wasn't—as is said—worth the paper it was written on. There were problems from the very start. I had a scene in the picture with five people in it and was just about to film when my MGM cameraman approached and said, "I can't shoot that." I asked him why not and he replied: "I can't carry that focus with a 2/4 lens; you'll have to move the actors a little out of line." Well, I wasn't about to re-block a scene I had been working on for the last half hour just to benefit my myopic cameraman. I said: "Change the lens to 4/9 and the focus will be perfect. I shouldn't have to tell you that." The cameraman was adamant against changing lenses, so after arguing fruitlessly, I fired him. I then put in a phone call to the production department telling them that I wanted to hire my own cameraman, and not one from MGM. They said the man I had fired was probably the best photographer on the lot. "That makes no difference, I want someone who I can work with," I said.

Later that day, an impeccably dressed white-haired old gentleman, obviously someone important, visited me on the set. He asked me what the trouble was, and I told him that my former cameraman had refused to change a 2/4 focal-length lens. He said, "I'm from the photography laboratory and we shoot all pictures here with 2/4 lenses; that way we can use the same developing process on all our movies." I couldn't believe my ears. "You mean you make no exceptions? This is ridiculous!" I said. The lab man told me that if I insisted, I could hire my own cameraman and use whatever lens I desired. I insisted.

As filming progressed on *State of the Union*, I began to see that every technical aspect of the picture was controlled by the department heads. The prop, set, makeup and sound men, to name just a few, all had bosses to account to. It was a machine studio; pictures were churned out with the regularity of a factory assembly line.

I guess that's why MGM films seem to have a style and sound that is interchangeable.

Yes, and they were all well done but not very individualistic. MGM pictures seem to exude a sheen like mass-made Grand Rapids furniture. Each picture looked like another; that was just their method of production. I believe one man, one film is the only way to make a movie. It is a director's responsibility to exercise complete authority on a film. The director is the only person with an overall conception of the film. It is he who will take the disjointed bits and pieces of film footage and relate them into a cohesive whole, the finished product.

Were there any actors or actresses you wanted to work with but couldn't because they were tenured to other studios at the time?

Yes, many. One actor I wanted to direct in a film was Jimmy Cagney. I wanted him for everything, but especially for the role of a small-time hood, "Dave the Dude," in *Lady for a Day* (1933). Unfortunately, he was contracted to Warner Bros. and our schedules never coincided long enough for us to make a picture together. Another star I would have loved to direct just once was Greta Garbo. But I got my share of fine actors, I have no complaints.

Do you think Hollywood is still producing fine films with a high level of craftsmanship?

Oh yes, today's filmmakers are creating some of the best movies. Film mechanics and techniques have advanced enormously since when I first started in this business, but I think the level of screenwriting has slackened recently. An inordinate amount of movies have sex and violence as their only attributes. None seem to have inspiring characters, people fighting for an idea. Instead, I find many films without a single sympathetic character. It's hard to sit through a picture when everyone in it is a jerk. This state of affairs has been brought about because the movie business is now dictated solely by cost and profit. A group of backers with sufficient financial resources decide to invest in a movie with only one motivation in mind: To make a quick buck. This stringent creative attitude allied with low budget outlays afflicts the quality of a film. Occasionally, however, when a director is given free artistic control, independent of business-oriented movie men, a fine picture will result.

What advice would you give to anyone aspiring to become a filmmaker nowadays?

Just submit material and don't get discouraged by rejection; any aspirant will have to face a great deal of it. Films are an art form, so if a person is born without a certain amount of creativity, he or she probably won't be well suited to the more imaginative aspects of moviemaking. Creativity, in most cases, cannot be learned. But skills can be. There are a thousand-and-one-jobs that go into making a film, from initial photography to final editing. Qualified and skillful people are always needed to fill these places. Film courses such as those offered by the American Film Institute, USC, and UCLA are good starting points for acquiring filmmaking skills.

* * *

Our day with Capra had wound down. We suggested that it might be a good idea if he checked at the front desk for any messages that came in that morning ... or afternoon ... from festival organizers (which was about as rhetorical as you could get. We half expected to see a sheaf of pink memo slips that would choke a Filofax crammed into the director's mail slot). We had no sooner cleared the lobby than the festival coordinator—the same woman who had patronized us with assurances of an interview—accosted us.

"Mr. Capra ... we were ... quite concerned when you didn't show up for your appointments today," she said, addressing Capra but shooting curare-dipped daggers at us with her eyes. Capra, with the classic timing of a silent film gagman, let us twist in the wind for about two beats short of three seconds and then said, with a crinkly twinkle: "I just spent a wonderful afternoon with a couple of first-rate tour guides."

It was a case of checkmate and exoneration in one fell swoop. Like a topper gag from a Harry Langdon silent comedy, there wasn't a comeback to be had. One man, one film and a helluva one-liner. Nearly a quarter century after he retired from directing films, Capra remained true to his credo of standing up for the little guy—this time via a timely, face-saving riposte delivered on our behalf.

We were about two miles, as the crow flies, from the Mississippi River and felt sure that at that moment Twain was smiling.

Stardust and Residuals

Hoagy Carmichael

The "Golden Age" of popular songwriting was brief, flowering roughly from the 1920s through the 1950s. Most of the composers and lyricists who filled the ranks of that elite fraternity and wrote for Broadway and Hollywood from Tin Pan Alley are gone now. However, as Irving Berlin once vamped: "The song is ended, but the melody lingers on."

More than half a century later the immutable words and tunes of men like Gershwin, Kern and Porter, and women like Dorothy Fields, are being rediscovered by new generations. Singers like Natalie Cole, Linda Ronstadt, Rod Stewart, Willie Nelson and now Michael Buble went "back to the basics" and struck gold with new recordings of old standards. Others, like Tony Bennett, Frank Sinatra and Ella Fitzgerald never strayed far from the Great American Songbook.

Neither, for that matter, did composer Howard Hoagland "Hoagy" Carmichael. His song "Georgia on My Mind" is a case in point; it first climbed hit parade charts in 1930, was reinvigorated by Ray Charles' definitive recording in 1960, and still gets mileage even today. As does "Stardust," "The Nearness of You," "Skylark" and "Heart and Soul." Together, the five tunes are among the most recorded songs in the entire American canon. And they're just a few of the hundreds of songs and 50 bonafide hits that he composed over a long career; hits that also include such out-and-out jazz standards as "Riverboat Shuffle," "Washboard Blues" and "Rockin' Chair" which has been covered by Louis Armstrong, Frank Sinatra, Bix Beiderbecke (Hoagy's idol) and even Hoagy himself.

"'Georgia on My Mind' slowly grew into a hit," Hoagy said. "I recorded it along with a couple of other people. Jazz bands took to it and it smashed out when Ray Charles did it."

We visited Hoagy in 1980, a year before he died just two days after Christmas. He was 82 at the time and lived in a hilltop condominium in La Costa, California that was cooled by a continuous breeze that vectored off the Pacific Ocean just down the hill. A slightly-built man, Hoagy was fastidiously dressed in a blue blazer and had a highball glass half full and well in hand when we walked up to his door.

"I never had any formal musical schooling," Hoagy said, sloshing the ice-cubes lackadaisically against the inside of his glass until they clinked in a kind of rhythmic cadence to his own loping stride as he led us to his backyard patio. "When I was a boy, I worked in a five and dime set in the shadow of the University of Indiana. A girl played a small instrument—an old hurdy gurdy we used to call it—and all the sheet music that would come in. I also listened to traveling song-pluggers who came through town.

"My mother played ragtime, and when I was about 12 years old she showed me some basic chord structures. I wish I would have studied fingering the piano. When I hear guys playing jazz now, they are well-trained and a helluva lot better than I ever was."

Hoagy developed his homespun, swinging piano technique at the Kappa Sigma fraternity dances at Indiana University, in Bloomington, Indiana. "Hot music" was a pleasant diversion, but certainly not substantial enough to build a career on. So, to please his father, Hoagy graduated with a law degree.

Bottoms up!

"I worked for a firm down in Florida in the early '20s, but kept my hand in on the piano—sort of on the sly," Hoagy said. "I first met Irving Berlin down there when I was playing a wealthy person's society party in Miami. Berlin was there with Florenz Ziegfeld. Someone asked Irving to sit down at the piano and play a couple of his songs. He did, and his touch was so feathery and lousy that I thought: if this guy can write songs, so can I.

The proper recording and handling of songs is an aspect of show business that some composers don't have much control over, and that was especially true for songwriters contracted to work in the movie studio "grist mills" in the 1930s and '40s.

"Songwriters should be consulted by the A&R man who is directing and recording a song," Hoagy said. "The songwriter knows the song better than anyone and should be present to see that it is being handled correctly. When I was working on tunes for films, I saw many songs that just missed becoming big hits because they were recorded at poor tempos. My song '(Up a) Lazy River' was recorded with the lyric: 'Up a lazy river, how happy we will be; up a lazy river with me.' It's stinky! It became public domain to sing 'how happy we will be' instead of 'how happy you will be,' which is the way I wrote it."

Quite apart from his iconic melodies, Hoagy contributed mightily to his own legend by appearing in many movies, and not just in cameo appearances but in full-fledged character roles. He even "appeared" in a *Flintstones* cartoon and sang a song he wrote especially for the episode ("Yabba-Dabba-Dabba-Dabba-Doo").

Hoagy's long face (a bony superstructure cleaved by an aquiline nose that seemed to go on for days), big ears and a receding hairline that at times, and from certain angles, looked like a skullcap, served him well as an actor. His physical features and nonchalant line delivery (halfway between hipster-speak and I-don't-give-a-shit) made him a memorable, unhurried presence in movies, usually as a laidback honky-tonk piano man adept at tickling the ivories with his own tunes. In fact, you might say as Hollywood's original piano man, he paved the road for telegenic performers like Elton John and Billy Joel who came along a half-century later.

Hoagy rode a mule, wore a stove pipe hat and sang his hit "Ole Buttermilk Sky" in *Canyon Passage*. As saloonkeeper "Butch," he taught double-amputee Harold Russell how to play "Chopsticks" with his hooks in the American classic of post–WWII readjustment, *The Best Years of Our Lives*. But his most memorable role was as the waterfront saloon piano player "Cricket," in *To Have and Have Not* starring Humphrey Bogart and Lauren Bacall in her movie debut.

"The wife of director Howard Hawks told him I'd be a good choice for the part of the piano player," Hoagy said. "I didn't know that Bogey was falling in love with Betty Bacall at the time. I had known Betty before he knew her, so when we were making the picture, I would go into her dressing room and we'd chat and talk and sometimes I'd get a little intimate with her, familiar, you know. Well, Bogey was sitting in the corner of her dressing room one day when I bounded in and patted Betty affectionately on the behind. Did Bogart's expression ever change! His chin just about dropped to the floor."

A footnote to the *To Have and Have Not* saga is that Hoagy suggested to Hawks that a kid singer named Andy Williams be allowed to dub Bacall's vocals in the film (she sings Hoagy's "How Little We Know"). It's become folklore that the voice people hear in the film singing for Bacall is actually Williams' smoky, low-register tenor, but Hoagy told us it's a myth.

"Andy had worked on my radio show with his brothers," Hoagy said, "but Hawks was a stickler for detail and wouldn't allow any dubbing."

Hoagy's recording career yielded a catalogue of 125–130 published songs (not including the hundreds he had "in his trunk"), a figure he described as "way low." In the 25 years that he diligently wrote songs and themes for films, Hoagy won only one Academy Award for Best Original Song in 1951 for "In the Cool, Cool, Cool of the Evening" from *Here Comes the Groom*.

"The title for the song came from a story a friend told me when I had been in college 30 years earlier," Hoagy said. "The story ended with a donkey saying: '...in the cool, cool, cool of the evening, tell him I'll be there.' I never forgot the story, or at least the last line of it. On my way to Palm Springs with (lyricist) Johnny Mercer, I mentioned that line and an hour later we had written the song.

"I love winning the Oscar," Hoagy added. "Mercer already had three and I was jealous."

Long-retired when we met him, Hoagy only marginally kept himself informed with trends in the music business. "I got lazy and the guy who merchandised my tunes got lazy too. I do like country music," he volunteered, taking a last sip of his drink and grinning impishly, "as long as Willie Nelson keeps recording my songs, that is. I get some nice residuals from his albums."

In his cups by the end of our visit, Hoagy bowed slightly and gallantly kissed both of us goodbye on the backs of our hands like he was Sir Lancelot paying boozy fealty to King Arthur. It had been a long day and scotch and soda-wise, Hoagy was a country mile ahead with no hope of us catching up.

The Gamine

Leslie Caron

gam·ine /ga ˈmēn/ *noun* **1.** a girl with mischievous or boyish charm.

In 1948, on a visit to Paris, Gene Kelly attended a performance of "La Rencontre," a ballet based on the classical theme of Oedipus and the Sphinx and staged by Roland Petit's company, *Ballet des Champs-Élysées*. Kelly was impressed with one 17-year-old dancer's "catlike" reflexes in the role of the "Sphinx." That dancer's name was Leslie Caron. A couple years later when MGM was readying for production a new musical called *An American in Paris*, Kelly remembered Caron for the role of "Lise," his love interest in the film. The part, as written, called for a slim, tomboyish girl with a pixish quality. It fit Caron to a T and a star was born when the Oscar-winning movie was released in 1951.

It was a damp fall day in London in 2013 when we paid a call on Caron. Her apartment in Chelsea was still cluttered with boxes from a recent move back to the United Kingdom from her native France where she had for several years owned a small hotel and restaurant—*Auberge La Lucarne aux Chouettes*—in the medieval town of *Villeneuve-sur-Yonne*, about 80 miles south of Paris in Burgundy. Wearing brown slacks, an olive-colored wool sweater with her eyeglasses wedged by one of the temples between the buttons of the sweater, Caron, ever the accommodating *propriétaire de l'hôtel*, poured us tea. More than 60 years had passed since Caron's debut in *An American in Paris*—the charming naïveté of her first role having long ago aged into elegant self-possession.

During her movie career, Caron could always be counted on to infuse her roles (*Lili*, *Gigi*, *An American in Paris*) with a kind of piquant Gallic charm, so we were surprised when she told us that she found herself back in London, a scorned refugee from

Moving day

her homeland. It stemmed from a bias that began when she became a Hollywood star with her first movie. It seems the French derided Caron's conversion from beloved local *danseuse* to movie celebrity as a blatant "sell-out."

"You know the moment I went to America, the French did not want to consider me French anymore," she told us in a Parisian accent tinged with slight sadness. "And from that point until the present, I was not French anymore. I could never convince people that I was born and raised in France and had a French family. So I finally just gave up and moved to London."

An American in Paris is the story of an ex–GI (Kelly), a starving artist living in a Paris garret, who falls in love with a young Parisian (Caron). The film, directed by Vincente Minnelli, is noted for its risky (at the time) 17-minute ballet to George Gershwin's "An American in Paris" orchestral tone poem.

"They (the French) were contemptuous," she said. "I think there was too much discrepancy between the way the French lived and this cute idea Hollywood had with the country. The French working class really had a hard time during those war and post-war years. There were the very rich, there was an okay middle-class, but the majority of France were hard-working poor. And to them a film like this was just cuckoo.

"I must admit that having arrived in America and having lived all my adult life in Anglo-Saxon countries, including England, I'm an Anglo-Saxon more than French," she continued. "And that extends to the politics, the social attitudes, democracy. I understand what goes on in America and in England and I'm forever frustrated in France because the French don't understand what's good for them."

Born in 1931, Caron and her family, including her American-born dancer mother had to endure the hardship of living in Nazi-occupied France, which she chronicled in her memoir aptly titled *Thank Heaven* from the song of the same name in *Gigi*. At her mother's urging Caron, still a teenager, became a ballerina with noted choreographer Roland Petit.

Like the title of a 2016 documentary on her life, one could say that Caron was a "reluctant star." As a young girl growing up in pre-war France, Caron said she had no exposure to American movies let alone musicals, although her mother had seen Fred Astaire on screen and often referenced to her young daughter his "genius about tempo." It was a story that Caron was too shy to repeat even when she had an opportunity to co-star with Astaire in the 1955 film, *Daddy Long Legs*.

"When he walked into the rehearsal hall, he was dancing already, just walking, that swing," Caron said of working with Astaire many years later. "I had never seen or heard of jazz, Gershwin or Gene Kelly for that matter," she confessed. "I didn't know or had ever seen a musical. The music of Stravinsky was the closest exposure I had to jazz because of his syncopation."

Caron's screen test for *An American in Paris* was performed in a Paris sound stage with Kelly improvising and feeding her dialogue from Alan Jay Lerner's screenplay. "The stage was very cavernous and I thought this was all really sinister," she said. "Gene was very polite and very sweet to me. I think he may have made me read the love scene that happens on the *Rue de France*. When it was done, I just went home and forgot all about it. To me it was just all nonsense."

Kelly and the MGM brass in Los Angeles, including the film's producer Arthur Freed, quickly agreed that they had found the fresh new talent with the gamine quality that they were looking for to play the part of Lise. With her mother in tow (Caron was still underage), and after three days of what Caron called "total turmoil," she landed in Los Angeles.

Caron's first day on the *American in Paris* set was an auspicious beginning. In fact, it almost became her last day in Hollywood. Just prior to reporting to work, Caron dramatically sheared her locks into a closely cropped tomboy look. It wasn't long before studio production head Dore Schary arrived on set with the equally stern trio of Kelly, Minnelli and Freed, along with the director of make-up.

"It was really like facing a firing squad," she said. "I had my back against the wall and somehow my sense of humor managed to poke through and I told them it looks like a firing squad. They didn't yell, but they were visibly upset. They were all breathing heavily and nodding, 'My God, what has she done?'"

Caron's cut was curiously prophetic because just a few months later a chorus girl named Shirley MacLaine copied the look and caught the attention of director Alfred Hitchcock who cast her in *The Trouble with Harry*. The close-cropped look was the start of a fashion trend.

"Unfortunately, Gene and the others didn't see it that way. They didn't get it," she said. "They postponed the start of shooting. It was just too brutal of a change and it's a real shame because imagine the fresh new look. It would have been absolutely sensational."

While Paris was being re-imagined "Tinseltown-style" on MGM's Culver City back lot, Caron found the idealization of her home country almost laughable. "The Paris street where Gene dances with the kids, that was phony as hell. The whole thing was like a pastiche of the real Paris. You must remember, to me, Paris was the war, the jackboots, the guns, the gray, sandbags, bombardment. The Paris you see now was not cleaned up until after 1960. Back then it was black with soot and a lot of poor, hungry and cold people."

Caron's introduction on film to the world came in a flashback montage early on the film, which showed through dance the many facets of her character's personality. The choreographed routine was worked out by Kelly's two dance assistants Carol Haney and Jeanne Coyne and included some droll variations on Caron's daily warm-up routine. Did Caron find any of the dance requirements particularly challenging? "Not a bit," she said without hesitation.

At MGM, the musical under the leadership of Freed had matured into a new phase of sophistication; in this case, a homage to end the picture danced against backdrops of the French painters via Gershwin's "An American in Paris."

"Between Freed, Minnelli and Kelly, they had the clout and good taste to get this ballet filmed," Caron said. "They had gumption and courage. It took a lot of courage because the word around the studio was, boy, are they making a mistake! This is going to be a catastrophe. You can't have a 17-minute ballet and no dialogue to end the film."

The doubters—and they were legion (among them, Irving Berlin)—were proven wrong.

You could say that Caron was the good luck charm for MGM's most notable producer of Hollywood musicals, Freed. In fact, she book-ended two of Freed's greatest triumphs in the 1950s, both Oscar-winners for best picture, *An American in Paris* and *Gigi*, in 1958, which ushered the end of the original Hollywood musical. Both films were directed by Vincente Minnelli, ex-husband of Judy Garland and father of Liza, whose impeccable color palate and attention to detail helped define the great MGM musical. A rather inarticulate person with a stutter, Minnelli gave minimal guidance to his actors, but would stop a scene cold if a vase of flowers or a swan swimming in a pond was not meticulously effective in the frame.

"That's absolutely true," said Caron. "And that was perfectly fine with me. I was completely attuned to his brain. I saw myself as the flower or the chair and would do various takes until I felt he was satisfied. This style annoyed some actors, but it did not annoy me at all because I knew even before we started. I just knew what he wanted without him having to say it. He was as you say extremely careful about the quality of the entire picture."

A couple of years earlier Kelly had come off his first directorial credit with the hit *On the Town*. But despite his aspirations as a director, he and Minnelli forged a successful collaboration. "Gene would be the one who would place me, turn me around and direct me. I don't remember Vincente saying much except, 'that looks good, angel.' I knew he was on the set, but he let Gene do the musical numbers."

In 1953, Caron was cast in the title role of *Lili*, which would earn her an Oscar nomination for best actress as a poor French orphan. "With my war experience, I knew what an orphan would look like—not exactly the glamorization the studio wanted," she said. "MGM wanted me in special clothes and wanted to make everything look new. They didn't want me to look like something the cat dragged in."

Rebellious and in search of more authenticity, Caron defied studio orders, took off her make-up and made her clothing look as rumpled as possible. Producer Freed (who did not produce *Lili*) made a rare appearance on set and offered up his apologies for her impoverished look.

"'Leslie, I'm really sorry with what they're doing to you,'" he told me. "'I brought you to America, made you this glamorous star and look at you now. This is so upsetting for me. I would like to make another film and rescue your career. Any ideas?'"

"I didn't hesitate for a second and I suggested *Gigi*, and he replied, 'Umm, I'll have to get back to you on that.'" It was 18 months before Caron heard back.

Gigi originated as a novella by the French author Colette and in 1951 was adapted for the Broadway stage as a non-musical that starred an unknown actress named Audrey Hepburn. Freed did not forget Caron's request and persuaded the songwriting team of Lerner and Loewe, fresh off their success in *My Fair Lady* to adapt the play into a big-budget film musical. He made good on his promise and cast Caron in the title role.

Caron felt obligated to set the record straight with us on one thing: "I get so mad when people think I stole the part from Audrey Hepburn," she said. "Audrey and her husband Mel Ferrer came to Freed's office and said, according to what Arthur told me, 'Audrey had this huge success in *Gigi* on the stage and we understand you bought the rights and are preparing a film. What about Audrey playing the part?' And Arthur said, 'I'm sorry, I promised the role to Leslie. But wait a second, if Audrey wants to play in a musical, hold on.' So he phoned Fred Astaire who was going to star in a new musical at Paramount. 'Hello Fred, I've got your next partner for you, she's right here.' And that's how Audrey was cast in *Funny Face* and it turned out well for everyone involved."

Gigi became the second film of the decade to win a Best Picture Oscar for Freed (*Paris* was the first), taking home a record nine statuettes. Caron had indeed become Freed's good luck charm. Shortly after our visit, a stage adaptation of Caron's first hit *An American in Paris* opened on Broadway to generally positive reviews. Caron called the show a "brilliant idea" and eventually traveled to New York City to see it and was feted by the cast and crew.

Although Caron remains the last living link to co-star in major films with the screen's most notable dancers, Gene Kelly and Fred Astaire, she wouldn't rise to the bait when we asked who she preferred as a partner. "It's not an apt comparison," she said. "Some people prefer Gene, some prefer Fred. They both had a distinctly different style. For me, Gene was paternal, fraternal and generous. He was a born father and protected and advanced the people he liked."

A life spent oscillating between her French birthright and life in "Anglo-Saxon" countries as an expatriate didn't really seem to trouble Caron. Whether her countrymen approved or not, in the interim, she had become an international star and citizen of the world. The important thing was that the gamine had become "game" for anything as she demonstrated when she bid us *adieu* and hurried us along with a comical "*vite, vite!*" At age 82, life was waiting and Caron had more boxes to unpack.

Jacked!

Jack Carter

Comedian Jack Carter passed away at 93, irascible and in a state of near-anonymity, something that galled him early on in his career and continued to bedevil him to the end of his days.

We should know. We interviewed Carter the year before he died in 2015 at his home in Beverly Hills where he puttered about with the aid of his ever-handy walker. His gait had slowed to an almost imperceptible forward momentum (he reminded us of Tim Conway's slow-moving "Mr. Tudball" character on *The Carol Burnett Show* who could be tripped up when living room carpeting gave way to kitchen linoleum). But Carter's rants about perceived slights (some going back a half-century) and the lack of accolades afforded to him during his long and varied career came faster than Usain Bolt in an Olympic sprint.

It's hard (and sad) to say that Carter hadn't possibly earned the right to his agitation. Where contemporaries such as Carl Reiner and Don Rickles are revered and other stars with lesser credentials make news, Carter and his formidable show business resume (TV pioneer, Broadway star and nightclub mainstay) has been largely chucked into the mildewy circular file of showbiz forgotten faces.

"Left out, lost, forgotten, it's the story of my life," he told us from the home he shared with his second wife Roxanne. "First of all, I never had a press agent. Never got on the Hollywood Walk of Fame, no picture on the wall at Sardi's (the venerable New York City showbiz hangout). Any television show or magazine article on old comedians, I'm never in it. It's like I never existed."

Even Carter's house seemed anachronistic to the times. It was one of those old pink, Spanish-style villas built in the 1920s and was so dark inside we practically needed a white cane to negotiate the severely-angled corners even at midday. Although located in a pricey part of town, the brickpile was a teardown, just like him.

Unsung and highstrung

Born in New York City, Carter grew up as vaudeville was wheezing its last gasps. Funny as a kid and with a knack for impressions, he decided on a career in show business after seeing the frenetic, no-holds-barred comedy of Milton Berle. "I first saw Berle at the Paramount Theater when I was a teenager," Carter said. "It was the wildest act. So many people hated Milton, but I loved the man." He also called comedian (and *Dick Van Dyke Show* cast member) Morey Amsterdam a "mentor."

Carter's show business breakthrough came when he went on the radio and twice won first prize on the *Major Bowes' Amateur Hour*, the precursor to today's *American Idol*. He later went on tour with the show along with another winner, a skinny kid from Hoboken, New Jersey named Frank Sinatra. "Frank was part of an act called the Hoboken Four at that time," said Carter.

Carter's impressions featured some of the more obscure stars of that era including many English actors such as C. Aubrey Smith, Basil Rathbone and Nigel Bruce (the movies' Sherlock Holmes and Watson, respectively), who later became frequent guests on Carter's TV show in the '50s.

After a stint in the Army during World War II, Carter continued to hone his night-club act by diversifying away from straight impressions ("mimicry," he called it) toward satire, without the benefit, he boasted, of employing any writers. "I realized I had to find a personality of my own so I mimicked classic Broadway shows from that period. Las Vegas required a joke act, whereas satire worked in the smarter nightclubs."

Carter reminisced about the glory days on the Las Vegas Strip, where he was pulling down $17,500 a week as one of the "kings of the lounges" along with other comics like Shecky Greene, Jan Murray and Don Rickles. "Before Howard Hughes came in and sterilized the city, it was magic," he said. "It was a glorious time. You were booked for a four-week engagement at top dollar. There weren't that many hotels and each one featured a headliner that was a household name."

As for the occasional heckler that would attempt to become part of the act, Carter said, "The mic was king. When you held the mic, you could out shout them. It wasn't really a major problem for me, except sometimes the third show in the early morning hours where some inebriated guy was out to impress his escort."

In 1949 Carter took the plunge in the newfangled medium known as television, serving as the first host of the *Cavalcade of Stars* variety show on the DuMont Television Network. The next year, NBC offered him his own variety show (*The Jack Carter Show*), part of a two-hour block called "Saturday Night Revue," which also featured *Your Show of Shows* with Sid Caesar. Carter bolted, but not before handing the *Cavalcade* off to another television up-and-comer, Jackie Gleason.

The early days of television were unchartered waters for pioneers such as Carter. "Live TV was furious," he said. "On one show we were caught eight minutes short and I had to ad lib to fill the time."

Carter also had a taste of Broadway success starring with Sammy Davis Jr. in the 1956 Broadway musical, *Mr. Wonderful*. He was also a TV guest star staple, appearing on *Ed Sullivan*, *Merv Griffin*, the *Dean Martin Roasts* and dozens of sitcoms.

Although slowed from a serious car accident that happened a few years before (one that claimed the life of another passenger, Toni Murray, Jan Murray's widow), Carter was adamant in his desire to stay active and continued to book guest spots on TV shows like *Desperate Housewives*, *iCarly*, *New Girl* and as a voice talent on *Family Guy*, where he famously mispronounced Sigourney Weaver's name. His last showbiz appearances before he died were in an infinitesimal recurring role as the owner (suffering from dementia) of a bar in *Shameless*. Adhering to the raunchy, dysfunctional theme of the TV series, Carter went out incontinent, his untethered jumbo-sized ass photographed so that it looked like a partially deflated Takata airbag. Oh the humanity!

As we got up to leave, Carter commanded, "Sit down, I'm not finished!" Here now, a smattering of Carter's acid reflux—some hates with a couple likes he threw in for a salve, like Pepto-Bismol.

… "I got to know Groucho. I admired him and used to go to his house. I loved Jimmy Durante. It would take him a week to learn a joke. When Jimmy was dying at home, Groucho would go over there and say, 'Die already! Why do you have that stupid hat on?'"

… "When someone dies out here, who do they call? Phyllis Diller and Red Buttons. Before the Dean Martin 'Roasts,' Buttons couldn't get a job; he was a bum. I worked Vegas for years but I'm a total unknown. I see articles on Vegas in the paper and I'm not even mentioned."

… "Buddy Hackett was not dirty originally. He was a flop. He had no act. Redd Foxx was funny filthy and nobody was funny filthy more than Lenny Bruce. The king was Richard Pryor. He was brilliant."

… "George Burns was the nicest man that ever lived and he loved the young ladies. I asked him how he did it with young girls and George said: 'I got a strobe light in the bathroom, makes it look like I'm moving, but sex at my age now is like trying to shoot pool with a rope. When the girl says 'no,' I say, 'Thank you.'"

… "Carol Burnett is vicious; nasty. Lucy was only funny with shtick, otherwise she was very stern." (We vouched for that.)

… "I was never a (Johnny) Carson fan; never did the show. He was a terrible anti–Semite and he drank. One night in New York City, Jan Murray and I were leaving a restaurant and Carson came out and said: 'Fucking Jews, are you going to eat here?' Jan slapped the shit out of him. I did 85 Merv Griffin's—adored Merv. I'm still close with Carl Reiner and I talk to Shecky Greene a lot. He doesn't do anything. Nobody's left."

As we departed, Carter offered one final fillip on his ill-fame: "Joey Bishop used to live next door," he told us. "The tour buses still come by and point that out. They don't stop here. Nobody cares."

Why would they? It was a teardown anyway.

(A few weeks later)

Tom got a phone call at home. It was Carter. He wanted to know if we'd be interested in ghostwriting his autobiography. "I want to set the record straight and settle a few old scores," he rasped.

Tom let him down as easily as he could. We just didn't have the time.

Anonymity can be a bitch!

"Beautiful Dynamite"

Cyd Charisse

"She came at me in sections,
more curves than a scenic railway.
She was bad. She was dangerous.
But she was my kind of woman."
—*Fred Astaire upon first encountering Cyd Charisse,
"Girl Hunt Ballet" from the film,* The Band Wagon

Cyd Charisse, with legs that stretched into infinity and a smoldering sensuality that no other dancer in Hollywood could match, became a reigning icon of the Golden Age of MGM musicals that peaked in popularity in the early 1950s. Nicknamed "Beautiful Dynamite" by Astaire, Charisse proved to be a perfect duet partner for Fred in *The Band Wagon* and later in her favorite role as "Ninotchka" in the musical version of that film, *Silk Stockings*.

It's true; MGM had no shortage of talented dancing ladies in those days. Ann Miller's tap dancing could approximate a pneumatic drill gone berserk; Leslie Caron was ballet-trained and had a certain pixyish gamine quality; and Vera-Ellen could tap or toe-dance with equal aplomb. But Charisse's routines had an added dimension guaranteed to appeal to red-blooded American males in theaters across the country. In the "Broadway Ballet" from *Singin' in the Rain* for instance, when Charisse sinuously wrapped her legs around Gene Kelly's torso and then rubbed his steamed-up eyeglasses on her inner thigh to the muted, smokey cornet glissando of "Broadway Rhythm," enough sexual heat was generated to melt granite. More than 60 years later, the effect on movie audiences is still the same.

When we met Charisse in April 1996, she was 76 and lived on the top floor of a luxury high-rise apartment building along the "Wilshire Corridor," a stretch of Wilshire Boulevard lined with plush condos that bisect some of the priciest real estate in Los Angeles. At the time, Charisse had been married to debonair MGM baritone Tony Martin for 48 years. They would be married another 12 until Charisse's death in 2008. Martin would follow her four years later at the age of 98. Although Martin never appeared from his bedroom (Charisse said he was nursing a bad case of bronchitis), we did intermittently hear his hacking cough throughout our visit.

Slim and chicly dressed, Charisse greeted us at the front door with a "Hello, darlings" that oddly seemed anything but perfunctory. In making her way from the entryway to a sitting room, she still displayed an effortless grace that was as natural as a prima ballerina's classical walk. But in reality, such equipoise did not historically come easily. From the age of six, the practical considerations of overcoming a handicap were the motivating factor in Charisse's decision to dance.

"Growing up in Amarillo, Texas, I had a slight case of polio which resulted in an atrophied shoulder and me being very skinny," she said. "People were afraid to touch me. So in order to exercise my muscles and become part of the community again, I took dance lessons." It helped that Charisse's father, a jeweler, was also a self-professed

Lovely Cyd

"balletomane" who loved to see his daughter dance and encouraged her every step of the way.

Before long, Charisse's precocious talent required an outlet beyond what her West Texas hometown could provide. She began studying dance in earnest in Los Angeles, California, with a former partner of the great "danseuse" of Diaghilev's *Ballets Russes*, Anna Pavlova. It was during the strict regimen of daily classes that the ballet master of the *Ballet Russe de Monte Carlo* saw Charisse. The world-renowned troupe was performing at the Los Angeles Philharmonic Hall. In short order, she was offered a spot in the company.

After journeying home to Texas to receive her father's blessing, the teenage Charisse joined the company in Cincinnati. However tragedy struck, and Charisse's father fell gravely ill. She left the troupe to be with him when he died. Then, at the age of 16, Charisse got a second chance to join the company during another stopover in Los Angeles. Proceeding to Europe, the *Ballet Russe de Monte Carlo* was about to embark on a tour of the great capitols starting with Berlin. "We were schedule to perform there on Sept. 1, 1939," Charisse said. "Unfortunately, Hitler chose that day to invade Poland and begin World War II. At the urging of the U.S. State Department, I found myself on a steamship back to the United States."

Back for a third time in Los Angeles, Charisse auditioned for the MGM film *Ziegfeld Follies* which starred just about all the high-octane musical talent the studio could muster.

"Arthur Freed, the producer of the picture, became my mentor," Charisse said. "He needed someone who could dance '*en pointe*' in the opening 'Here's to the Ladies' sequence that featured—portentously—Fred Astaire." In the number, Charisse dances tantalizing close to Astaire. "Fred was in top hat and tails and I did this tentative little toe dance around him but not with him."

Charisse had another chance in the finale of the film to the song "There's Beauty Everywhere" sung by Kathryn Grayson. "The problem was these huge mountains of soap suds that were part of the number. Showgirls were gathered on a big staircase that I was supposed to pirouette down. But the bubble machine went crazy and started to cover the girls with suds. They started to scream and pass out and ambulances were called. In the final print all you see is one small shot of me pirouetting through the mess."

Her movie debut opposite "Mr. Bubble" notwithstanding, Arthur Freed liked what he saw and signed Charisse to a standard seven-year contract at $350 a week. In one fell swoop of a pen, Charisse became a cog in the greatest dream factory in movie history.

"It was fabulous," she said. "I took singing lessons, acting lessons and had a vocal coach who worked with me to get rid of my Texas twang. MGM in those days had the greatest writers, directors, costume designers—you name it. Everything was at your fingertips, and everything was done in-house.

"They turned out musicals in those days as if they were water," she continued. "The studio would think nothing of having Freed produce two or three; Joe Pasternak produce a couple more and the same for Jack Cummings. Musicals were a cinch in those days to turn out."

According to Charisse, MGM "built stars to last." "Today," she said, "an actor is lucky if they're in a film big enough to sustain them to stardom. In my day, you had an army of gifted people, all experts in their fields, tailoring parts for your particular talent."

Charisse's breakout role was as the object of Gene Kelly's affection in the "Broadway Ballet," the 15-minute dream sequence near the end of *Singin' in the Rain*.

"Gene was going to use his dance assistant, Carol Haney, in the role," Charisse said. "Carol was a wonderful dancer, but Freed didn't think she photographed well. All the moves were already blocked out by the time I was brought in. The 'vamp' part of the ballet was hard to do because of all the nuances. It was really like a mini-drama within a number. We rehearsed the Salvador Daliesque 'Crazy Veil' sequence until my shoulders were chapped—they had to blow so much wind on me in order to make the veil go up into the air. And then it took all my strength to run the length of the stage against that wind."

When queried about her favorite dance number, Charisse spoke without a moment's hesitation: "'Dancing in the Dark' with Fred Astaire from *The Band Wagon* was so simple, yet so lovely," she said. "I loved Astaire's style. He had a quality when he walked into a room that was his and nobody else's in the world; a charm, elegance. He was also extraordinarily gentle. He would never confront you with a criticism directly for fear that he would embarrass you. But he wasn't a pushover. With Fred, you would invariably come in early and work late. You had to have stamina. Some girls who weren't trained dancers would be in tears because Fred would work them so hard to get the routines right. But it wasn't Fred's fault that their muscles ached at the end of a rehearsal day. He liked to work hard and I like to work hard, so we got along famously."

To Charisse, comparing Astaire and Kelly was a specious, ultimately futile exercise in empty rhetoric; like comparing an apple to an orange. "Gene was more the creative type and not shy and retiring at all," she said. "Fred created his own dances, but Gene's ambition extended far beyond the dance numbers, to directing pictures—like *Singin' in the Rain* and *It's Always Fair Weather*—two of the pictures we did together. Gene wanted to be behind the camera as well as in front of the camera. It was more of a difference in personality; they were both geniuses as far as talent went."

Another favorite dance from Charisse's favorite picture in fact, is the title number from *Silk Stockings*. She dance/acts the number with a tenderness that adds real poignancy to the scene and underscores her transformation into a beautiful butterfly from the drab "apparatchik" chrysalis in which she had been confined all her life.

"It was a good role for me," she said. "Eugene Loring (the film's choreographer) staged that solo for me. It was a pivot point in the plot where I shed my proletarian garb for silk stockings and *haute couture* that exemplified western styles. No lines were needed. The dance itself told the story of my change more effectively than any lines in the script would have."

Despite surviving grueling rehearsals, Charisse wasn't the bolt of lightning she often appeared to be when she danced. "She's not strong—she's not a powerhouse, she just looks that way," said Loring. "In the 'Red Blues' number (from that film), she looks like a dynamo. She has bursts of energy, not for long and then she gives up."

Thank heavens for the magical intercession of multiple takes and seamless editing which delivers a "*trompe l'oeil*" effect to most movies and particularly musicals. "I was never very interested in doing my own choreography," Charisse said. "When you work with a gifted choreographer, they always take the best of what you do. They use your strengths."

At that time, Charisse lamented that interest in film musicals as a popular staple had ebbed and that the genre was for all practical purposes on life-support. "It's so difficult to do them because not only did we lose the studio system, but also the technical knowl-edge which was considerable," she said. "The armies of people who specialized in specific, important and intricate aspects that went into making top-notch musicals are gone. You need writers like Alan Jay Lerner and composers like Cole Porter and Roger Edens and Saul Chaplin. All those kinds of people were around when we did a musical. Cole Porter was on the set when we did *Silk Stockings* and Lerner was on the set during the shooting of *Brigadoon*. They were all interested in how their work would be portrayed. You can't just get a script and do a musical."

It was logical to assume when we met Charisse that she might want to relax a bit and accept the plaudits her talents had earned her over decades spent in front of the camera. It was logical, but it was wrong. A couple of years before we visited, to help her mother combat a severe case of arthritis, Charisse in tandem with a chemist friend of hers, developed a product they dubbed Arctic Spray. The "liquid ice" curative is still sold online.

We thought at the time Charisse may have been driven by a work ethic underscored by arduous hours spent rehearsing in drafty soundstages, or possibly that her newfound career owed its provenance to memories of a little girl born Tula Ellice Finklea in Amar-illo, Texas, who triumphed over some tough odds of her own. In any case, Charisse told us with a hint of astonishment, "I now find myself a business executive."

For her, it was a whole new dance.

"Mannix": The Last Interview

Mike Connors

Mike Connors, known to millions of his TV fans as canny private investigator, "Joe Mannix" (and to his Armenian-American parents as Krekor Ohanian), died of Leukemia in January 2017 at the age of 91. Less than 10 months before, we sat down with Connors for what was likely the last interview he ever gave.

Connors' "compound" took up a fairly sizable corner lot on a street a couple of blocks south of Ventura Boulevard in Encino in the San Fernando Valley. In addition to the main house, there was a tennis court carpeted with sycamore and white alder leaves and a swimming pool. Connors, old school that he literally was, greeted us outside as we pulled into the parking area after being given the right of way by his electronic gate.

"I haven't played tennis in a long time," he said, rightly anticipating our first question as we exited the car. "I haven't played golf in about eight months either. I had a kneecap replaced. You know, I'm probably the oldest guy you ever interviewed."

"George Burns had you beat by a few years," Dave said.

We met with Connors the morning after one of those storied El Niño dumps that hit SoCal from time to time and make the national nightly news. "It woke us up like a nuclear blast," Connors said in a calming voice that, juxtaposed with what he just described, sounded like grains of sand sifted through an hourglass. He led us by way of his den to a patio where the light fully engulfed us. Along the way, we noticed Golden Globe Awards bookending volumes on a shelf, and photos of Connors with Frank Sinatra and Dean Martin. In the Martin photo, from an appearance on Dean's TV show, Connors was giving the crooner a piggyback ride.

"Frank told me once that just hanging out with Dean in a steam room, he could be funnier in 10 minutes than most professional comics can be in an hour on stage," Connors said.

The most famous American of Armenian descent (after William Saroyan and before the onset of the Kardashian clan), Connors had us read a letter he received from Saroyan, author of *The*

Armed and dangerous

Human Comedy and *My Name is Aram*. It was a long, chatty block of type-written text without paragraph breaks that looked like a giant ink smudge about the goings-on in Fresno, California where Saroyan lived and where Connors was born.

"He was quite a character and a great writer," Connors said. "When I was a kid, the family would go out and play bridge at night and take us kids with them to the Saroyans. My father was a great friend of Bill's uncle Aram, the guy Bill's book was about. They'd put us to sleep in another room. Now pistachio nuts in those days were very precious. When we kids would try to grab them, they'd say, 'Those are for the adults. Stay away from them!' When we were sleeping, Bill would come in and put the pistachios in our pockets so that when we woke up, we'd find pistachio nuts there."

Like most showbiz veterans, Connors was a good interview subject, but what he loved best in answering questions was to wend dramatic tales often with a humorous twist. In that, he seemed linked to the storytelling legacy of Saroyan and his own Armenian roots in Fresno, a couple hundred miles up north in the Central Valley. (Apparently, the pistachio doesn't fall very far from the tree.)

The person who introduced Connors to the acting profession was William Wellman, the director of *Wings*, the first movie to win an Academy Award for Best Picture in 1927. Wellman discovered Connors at a UCLA basketball game where he was a freshman guard with such a light shooting hand he had acquired the nickname, "Touch" and was billed as such in some of his early film work.

Connors said some of the most important life lessons he ever learned were at UCLA from legendary basketball coach John Wooden. "He's probably one of the best men I've ever known. He said your primary job here is to get an education not play basketball. He used to say, 'If you don't get the grades, you're not going to play.' I never heard him use a cuss word."

We had always heard the story that Lucille Ball, operating out of her Desilu Productions, gave Connors his seminal role as "Mannix," but Connors begged to differ. "A 1937 Bentley convertible got me 'Mannix,'" he said.

It was while filming a remake of *Stagecoach* in Boulder, Colorado in 1966 that Connors noticed a couple of young Brits drive a Bentley onto the location. A lover of cars, especially older cars, Connors asked them what on earth they were doing in Colorado driving that car. They told him that each year they bought an old car, shipped it from England to New York City, drove it across the U.S. and then sold it in Los Angeles, using the money to travel back to England. On the spot, Connors made a deal to buy the car for $4,000 with the proviso that they drop it off to him in Los Angeles.

The next year, Connors said he drove the Bentley onto the Desilu lot for an interview. "As I got into the car, I heard a voice yell, "Mike Connors, wait a minute. I want to talk to you.' It was Gary Morton, Lucille Ball's husband at the time. He said, 'Goddammit, if you want to sell it, let me know. Hey, wait a minute! I've got a script you'd be perfect for. Let me go get it and see if you like it.' I took it home, read it and that was *Mannix*."

The show, like *Tightrope*, an earlier TV series in which Connors starred, was considered violent for its time—the late 1960s to the mid–'70s. "But they considered car chases violent back then," Connors said. "We were so tame compared to what there is now."

The original clunky concept of the series was that Joe Mannix worked for a computer company called Intertect, but when the show began to tank, CBS was ready to cancel it. That's when Lucille Ball stepped in. According to Connors, Ball said, "'I like Mike Connors and I like the idea of the show. I think you ought to give it another crack.' She was the biggest star at that time and they would do anything for her."

The show was revamped (and renamed) with Connors freelancing as a detective and working from "his heart and his mind." A catchy theme song was added along with split-screen action shots over the credits that conjured *The Thomas Crown Affair* and *Mannix* began to gain traction in the ratings.

Mannix was also one of the first TV shows to cast a black woman, Gail Fisher, in a regular role that wasn't subservient. "Bruce Geller, one of the show's creators came to me and asked if I'd be OK with Gail playing my secretary, Peggy Fair," Connors said. "I was fine with it but the network didn't want her. Bruce said that if I'd back him up, she could be cast."

Joe Mannix's wardrobe on the show each week was invariably anchored by a checkered sport coat from Botany 500 with a pattern that any vigilant perp could see coming a mile away. Inexplicably, Tom wondered aloud about the coats.

"I still have about three or four of them in my closet," Connors said, brightening. "Funny story, one day I get a letter from Bill Gates' secretary. And she said, 'Mike, would you call me? I'd like to talk to you.' So I called her and she said, 'Bill Gates and his wife are such big fans of your show. It's his birthday and we'd love to give him an autographed picture. Would you send one to Bill?' I said, 'Sure. How big a fan is he really?' She said, 'Well, he's saved stuff. He's got a whole big room of memorabilia.' I said, 'Would you like to have a *Mannix* sport coat for him?' She said, 'Are you kidding?' I said, 'No, because I brought home a whole bunch with me.' So along with the picture, I sent a sport coat. It's probably hanging on a wall up in Seattle."

After eight years, *Mannix*, which was still in the top 20, was cancelled. "Paramount Television co-produced the show with Desilu and one of the distributors was CBS," Connors said. "Paramount wanted to rerun the show on some channels late at night while it was still on first-run on CBS. CBS vetoed the idea and Paramount—which wanted to start syndication—pulled the plug on the show. It turned out that within 10 years, broadcasting a show concurrently with reruns became the most common thing in the world."

Connors had a famously long marriage, one that endured 68 years despite "tremendous temptations," he said. And to prove that wasn't just a rote answer he peeled off to interviewers, he told us a story of when he and his wife Mary Lou lived in a tiny apartment just off Sunset Boulevard and right behind a haberdashery owned by L.A. gangster Mickey Cohen. Connors had made his film debut with *Sudden Fear* (1952) as "Touch Connors" with Joan Crawford and Jack Palance, and as an eager up-and-comer, he said he used to visit an actor friend at MGM and then troll various sets networking with whoever would give him the time of day.

"MGM was shooting a picture (*Latin Lovers*) that starred Lana Turner and Ricardo Montalban," Connors said, "and I thought I'd visit the set and watch them shoot a scene. There was a hairdresser that had been a hairdresser for a picture I'd done and we were standing there talking and all, and this cute little blonde comes up to me and says, 'Miss Turner would like to know your name.' And I say, 'My name's Mike Connors.' She says, 'Thank you' and disappears and I keep talking to the hairdresser. She comes back and says, 'Miss Turner would like to know if you would like to stop by and have a drink with her in her dressing room.' And I say, 'Tell her thank you very much but I have an appointment and I can't stay.'

He continued. "After the girl left, the hairdresser says to me, 'What are you a fucking idiot? How do you think you get ahead in this business?' I say, 'Hey, I haven't been married that long and I'm in love and all.' And she says, 'Well, you're an idiot, go have a drink.' As we were talking, Lana Turner comes walking by and says, 'Coward! It could've been fun.' Now here's the part of the story that's scary. I left, got in my car and drove home which took me approximately 40 minutes at the most. I walk in the door and my wife says to me, 'How's Lana Turner?' I said, 'What the...' She said, 'I got the word on it.'"

Connors explained that a bit player on the set—a woman both Connors and his wife knew—had called and told Mary Lou that Turner was "making a move" on Mike. "If I had stayed to have that drink, we wouldn't be sitting here now in my home," Connors said. "My wife would've said, 'Fuck you!' So, anyway, we were right for each other."

Enter stage left as if on cue, Mary Lou. "He usually keeps me locked in the closet until the interviewers have left," she deadpanned. We looked at Mike who chuckled while at the same time flashing his wife a beatific look that telegraphed all we needed to know about their relationship. Despite Connors' rather flimsy excuse to the contrary, it was easy to see why he remained faithful to her (fidelity that even a siren like Lana Turner couldn't disrupt) and why they stayed together for almost seven decades until her own death the same year as his. Humor is the best coping mechanism there is and it binds like superglue.

"Most of our friends that we go to dinner with are all people with great humor," Connors said. "They are very successful people in the business and the nights are a lot of laughs. We recently attended a small dinner party and it was Bob Newhart, Tim Conway, Jimmy Fallon, Don Rickles, Steve Lawrence and laughs. We have a lot of those nights and they keep you young."

From our vantage point, it kept Connors approximately 91 years young. "I think Saroyan once said something along the lines of, 'It takes a lot of rehearsing for a man to be himself,'" Tom said. "But we don't think you've had to rehearse much."

"I'm just a regular guy; an average *Joe*," Connors replied, flashing us a punny wink. Far from average we thought, but, alright.

Festering

Jackie Coogan

JACKIE COOGAN: "Gomez, I'm so hungry I could eat a horse."
JOHN ASTIN: "Come, come, Fester, you had one for lunch."
                                        —*The Addams Family* (1964)

In a show business career that spanned more than 60 years—from silent films to television—Jackie Coogan is best remembered for one role: Uncle Fester on TV's wackadoodle *The Addams Family* which has enjoyed more than 50 years in syndication since the comedy first aired in 1964.

It didn't seem to matter that Coogan worked in just about every entertainment medium including vaudeville, movies, radio and the stage. For millions of Baby Boomers who have seen *The Addams Family* in reruns, Coogan will always be the bald, fat man in a dark coat with fur collar who likes to ride his motorcycle through the house, sleeps on a bed of nails, puts his cranium in a metal vice to cure headaches, plays with dynamite caps and has the knack of illuminating light bulbs in his mouth.

Creepy and kooky

We met Coogan in 1980 (he died in 1984) at the Trancas Restaurant in Malibu Canyon. And no, we didn't eat "eye of newt," eels or fillet of lizard. Coogan ordered a ham, cheese and mushroom omelet with potatoes and an ice-tea. After the waitress had taken our order, Coogan leered after her: "I'd like to rent her butt as a neon sign." No doubt about it, Fester had an acid wit—pass the Prevacid!

Although we were steps from the ocean, it was hot

out that morning. Coogan was dressed in a Hawaiian shirt, had a few localized strands of long hair falling haphazardly from his mostly bald head and enunciated in a high-pitched squawk through a zeppelin-sized red nose that looked as if it had recently seen service as a Doberman's chew-toy.

Coogan was born October 26, 1914, in Los Angeles. Both of his parents traveled throughout the country in vaudeville and during his first few years, Coogan stayed with his grandmother in San Francisco or his other grandmother in Syracuse, New York. "I guess that's where I learned to hate snow," he said. His earliest recollection of performing was in 1918.

"I became part of the act. We only made it look like a surprise. I was a four-year-old kid. I could do imitations, dance and sing. Of course, there weren't many of those types back then and there still aren't."

Besides Coogan's three-year stint on *The Addams Family*, his most noteworthy show business accomplishment was his career as a child actor in silent pictures. His most famous role came early, in 1920, when he played an orphan who tugged mightily on Charlie Chaplin's paternal heartstrings in *The Kid*.

It was while Coogan was performing with his father, Jack Sr., at the Los Angeles Orpheum Theater that Charlie Chaplin got a glimpse of the little kid who would co-star with him in the movie—one of the great tearjerkers of the silent era. *The Kid* became a milestone for Chaplin. It was his first film that was not total slapstick, and he proved that pathos could sell. Jerry Lewis, Red Skelton and Jackie Gleason would all go on to interject pathos (to varying degrees and varying degrees of success) into their films and TV shows.

"About 90 percent of the people in motion pictures came from vaudeville," Coogan said. "Every Thursday night at the Orpheum was like old home week. The film actors would come to the theater to see their friends from vaudeville—to shoot the shit and bring themselves up to date with the latest dirt. Chaplin liked what he saw and signed me to a contract at the magnificent (then) sum of $75 a week."

Coogan recalled how difficult it was for Chaplin to get the film made. "He had a deal with First National to produce and direct a picture of his choosing. When these backers found out what he had in mind, they blew up. They thought he was crazy for wanting to make a drama. But Chaplin had an ironclad contract and got his way.

"We never worked from any kind of script," Coogan added. "So, consequently, he would sit and think. We wouldn't turn a camera on sometimes for two weeks. When he came up with an idea he would put it together. You were never conscious of his direction. He showed me what to do and I did it. I can't remember him ever losing his temper. He was so far and above what we know today. Who have we got now, Chevy Chase, who can't even fall funny!"

A year and three days later the picture was completed at a cost of almost $500,000, which was a fortune in 1920 (and ain't half bad today!). The film opened to rave reviews and huge box office grosses and Coogan was an overnight child sensation.

After *The Kid*, Coogan went on to make 29 silent films including *The Adventures of Tom Sawyer*, *Oliver Twist* and *Peck's Bad Boy*. Careerwise, things went well for Coogan until 1938 when he was involved in a bitter lawsuit with his mother over money he had amassed as a child performer (as his guardian, his mother had spent all his earnings). The law that resulted was dubbed (and is still known today as) the "Coogan Law" and has since protected the earnings of minors who work in the show business salt mines.

The repercussions from the highly publicized trial had a negative effect on Coogan's career (he was blackballed by producers all over town) and for a quarter century he struggled until casting in *The Addams Family* made him a household oddity if not exactly a name.

"I had read Charles Addams' cartoons and really enjoyed them," he said. "So when I read they were going to do a show, I told my agent I wanted to try out. He didn't want me to because when you do something weird like that it tends to typecast you for life. But I knew exactly what I wanted to do. I shaved my head and made the test using the high voice. The show lasted three years on ABC. All they had to do was go in color with that impressive set and the show would have stayed on TV much longer."

The only thing Coogan didn't like about the show was that he felt the character of Gomez as played by John Astin was a copy of Groucho Marx. To us, Coogan's comment seemed like a case of the potbelly calling the kettle black since his portly character of Uncle Fester was a direct rip-off of (or maybe ode to) Curly Howard of Three Stooges fame.

Regardless, we were utterly relieved when Coogan told us that he still owned his Fester fur-lined coat. Next stop the Smithsonian?

Since cancellation of *The Addams Family*, Coogan had managed to pick up a steady stream of character roles (he specialized in sweaty, small-time operators one step ahead of the Bunco squad) in films and TV. He also had a memorable voiceover stint as a product pitchman projecting his Fester screech into Mattel's Creepy Crawlers commercials.

In assessing his life, Coogan said: "I have very few friends. I've always kept apart from the establishment. I've always been a loner. The only people I still see are my old nightclub and vaudeville partner, Jimmy Cross and Gabe Dell, who was one of the Bowery Boys."

The conversation—which we thought was winding up—then took a fatal header when Coogan (apparently tired of talking about his status as an icon of the bizarre) launched into a self-serving panegyric about his World War II experiences in Burma. It was an endless tale of midnight parachute drops and all-out heroics that made Audie Murphy, by comparison, seem like a rear-echelon loafer. It was almost as if Coogan was trying to put some Svengali-like spin on how we handled his story by trying to minimize our embedded perception of him as a pot-bellied guy in a long black coat who had dark circles under his eyes and who never left the Addams house. Fat chance, but we listened to his ramble anyway.

Two hours and six iced-teas later, Coogan was almost done pontificating. "You know the good thing now is that I'm in a financial position where I never had to work again if I don't want to," he told us. On that discordant note, he handed us the luncheon tab and traipsed out of the joint. "Coogan's Law" or not, he wasn't taking any chances.

We were left with a creepy, kooky, altogether ooky feeling, but we didn't have the heart to accost Coogan out in the parking lot where he was having trouble backing out from a tight space. Not the cleanest getaway, for sure. That said, for a brief moment, we felt like calling in some paratroopers of our own for retribution, but we let the moment pass. Where's Lurch when you need him!

Fred and Ed (and Johnny)

Fred de Cordova and *Ed McMahon*

It was a troubling sight and prelude to a sad ending: Early in the tenure of Jay Leno's *Tonight Show*, in the mid–'90s, we were lolling around the green room just prior to interviewing Johnny Carson's controversial replacement when in walked a blast from the past—Carson's producer of almost 25 years, Fred de Cordova.

Instead of walking off the set and into television history arm-in-arm with Carson, Ed McMahon and bandleader Doc Severinsen when they taped their last show together on May 22, 1992, de Cordova, "hung around" as an "advisor" to Leno for a couple of years at a reported lowly $500 a week; a token stipend compared to the salaries he had commanded in his 40-year career as a film and television director and as Carson's longtime producer.

Twelve years earlier, we had interviewed de Cordova in his *Tonight Show* office bungalow when he was dialed in to the most rarified strata of show business heavyweights. At that time, he and his wife Janet were the toast of the town, hosting Hollywood's old-guard at glittering parties in their Beverly Hills home on Carla Ridge. The present for de Cordova had become much harsher. Nice guy Leno had taken him on as a de facto charity case.

Our "reunion" in the green room became awkward as de Cordova unconvincingly feigned recalling our interview years earlier when we were two college students and he was in his *Tonight Show* prime. De Cordova was cordial—politely but formally reserved you might say, just like he was a decade and a half earlier when we first met—but he seemed strangely out of sorts as if he knew on some level that he was a fossil, a grudging legacy fighting a losing battle to maintain relevance at a network that had become a house of cards for him.

We weren't aware of it then, but it was a juncture in a long downhill slide that began when de Cordova became estranged from Carson as the show completed its 30-year run. It ended when de Cordova died broke at the age of 90 in 2001 at the Motion Picture Country Home and Hospital.

Fred pontificating

De Cordova's final years were chronicled in a 2001 *Vanity Fair* feature where it was reported that former boss Carson contributed $100,000 for the destitute producer's funeral. The estrangement that started it all occurred in 1991 when Johnny's son Richard died in a car accident. During an uncharacteristically personal on-air tribute from a bereaved Carson, de Cordova just off-camera (his nightly perch) signaled for the "King of Late Night" to "wrap it up," a move that permanently severed what had been a strong professional partnership.

It was a steep drop for a man who at the time of our visit was personal advisor to two of America's most powerful men—President Ronald Reagan and Johnny Carson. De Cordova directed Reagan in a modest (and maligned) comedy called *Bedtime for Bonzo*, a 1951 film about a university professor (Reagan) and his chimpanzee roommate. De Cordova signed on as the producer of *The Tonight Show Starring Johnny Carson*, in 1970, when he was already 60.

"I go back in show business a long way, about a half-hour after I was born," de Cordova told us during our 1980 interview. Dressed in a white linen sport coat, de Cordova's cluttered office served as the show's nerve center with a bulletin board behind his desk that had note cards thumbtacked onto it of guest names slotted for each installment of *The Tonight Show*.

"Both of my parents worked in show business in New York City. When I was young I saw Al Jolson, W.C. Fields and dozens of Broadway shows," he said. De Cordova was educated at Chicago's Northwestern University and then attended law school at Harvard. It was there that he became a close friend of Johnny Schubert, the son of Broadway impresario J.J. Schubert.

"My mother knew his mother, and after we graduated from Harvard together I went to work in the Schubert's New York office," de Cordova said. "I worked as a 'gofer,' and then as a stage manager for Beatrice Lillie. My first direction of a musical was with Bob Hope, Josephine Baker and Fanny Brice. I go back a long way. There were a lot of performers I worked with who are now under the bridge."

Michael Curtiz (nicknamed the "Mad Hungarian"), director of such screen classics as *Casablanca*, *Robin Hood* and *Yankee Doodle Dandy* gave de Cordova his first big break in Hollywood. It was a red-letter date forever etched in de Cordova's memory.

"I worked for Curtiz as a dialogue director at Warner Brothers. He spoke with a very thick *Mitteleuropa* accent. I had a good education under him except for the flow of the language. He had a notorious temper and one day he called me over and said, 'You're through here, Jack Warner wants to see you, get off the set.' I had no idea what I had done, so I went to see Warner. He said, 'You're no longer a dialogue director. Curtiz says you're good enough to be a director.' Warner then handed me my first full-fledged assignment. What an exciting way to start. Curtiz certainly earned his nickname."

De Cordova remembered his years as a director at Warner Brothers as a "young orientation," assigned to B-pictures that usually played neighborhood theaters as part of a double feature.

"I was primarily a director of young people in pictures," he said. "They were not your blockbusters, but they were pleasant and all films at that time were fairly successful. I made pictures with Deanna Durbin, whom I adored, Shelley Winters, Yvonne De Carlo and skating star Sonja Henie."

One of those young performers that de Cordova so deftly handled was Ronald Reagan. "Ronnie was as he is, charming," de Cordova told us. "He was an efficient and totally likable professional performer. I don't think at that time that anybody thought he was another Spencer Tracy or Brando, but he was a successful leading man."

As far as the camp status *Bedtime for Bonzo* had acquired, de Cordova had this to say: "Its title makes it a figure of fun, but it was a rather good movie. We did two sequels to it which were of diminishing value, but the first one with Ronnie was pretty good in fact, now it's a class act! There was *Bedtime for Bonzo, Bonzo Goes to College* and *Bonzo Private-Eye*, after which time I thought that was enough of me with chimpanzees."

The TV producing and directing career of de Cordova reads like a Who's Who of iconic comedians, including George Burns and Gracie Allen, Jack Benny, *My Three Sons*, the Smothers Brothers and finally the "top man in the business," Johnny Carson.

These plum assignments, de Cordova said, came from "a combination of good luck and the fact that most of the important people in the business know the other important people in the business. After a while, I was well enough known in the community so when an opportunity comes up, it often came my way.

"This might sound like a stupid remark," de Cordova continued, "but I believe to work well with comedians one must have a sense of humor, and a sense of humor does not necessarily mean making jokes all the time, but an awareness of what will and will not work."

Before his rift with Carson, de Cordova never had a serious falling out with any of the comedians he directed. "At least nothing long or drawn out," he said. "George Burns used to fire me regularly, but by the time I got home there would be flowers for my mother with a note saying 'I apologize.'"

In an eerie foreshadowing (certainly not precognition on our part), we asked de Cordova about scuttlebutt that painted Johnny Carson as an unpredictable and intemperate slave driver.

"He is anything but that," de Cordova said instantly springing to Carson's defense. "Johnny is a totally dedicated man whose professional life is culminated each evening on *The Tonight Show*. It is very important to him to do each night's show as well as that show can possibly be done. That is what he cares about from the moment he comes into work until the moment he leaves. We have a little talk after each show to evaluate it. He is no slave driver in the tantrum sense like Jackie Gleason was. Johnny will say, 'That joke didn't work; why didn't it work?'"

The irony increased ten-fold (the foreshadowing growing until it could have darkened half of downtown Burbank) as de Cordova dispelled any myth concerning the hiring and firing practices at *The Tonight Show*.

"There have been four producers of *The Tonight Show*, I am the fifth," he said. "I have a much cherished photograph of Johnny at home which is inscribed: 'To my favorite producer' with the names of the previous producers crossed off underneath. There is no rancor. The producer that preceded me was actually of enormous help. Instead of leaving me adrift in this new job when I was first hired, he gave me three weeks of intensive training."

De Cordova gave us a rundown of his daily duties. "In the morning the staff meets in my office to go over what we have learned since yesterday. Through newspapers, magazines and press agents we see who will be available for future bookings. We try to book the show as far in advance as possible. We evaluate perspective guests—good or bad, mediocre or wonderful, and how they might fit in with Johnny's personality. Then there is a production meeting with all the people involved in the show. We discuss who is going to sing that night, how many musicians are needed, etc. Next we go into rehearsal. After that there is another meeting in my office to discuss the details of the rehearsal. Then comes the actual taping of the show. In the meantime, Johnny has had discussions on his written material and monologue. Is it okay to make a joke about a bomb explosion? Yes, if no one was hurt. We welcome presidential campaign years even at their dullest. They always provide humorous fodder. We go home happy if the show was a hit that night, or dejected if it wasn't."

We asked de Cordova how long he planned to stay with the show. "I'm going to stay with *The Tonight Show* until I die—I don't care so much about Johnny staying with it," he laughed.

Foreshadowing notwithstanding, de Cordova was a man of his word. His self-fulfilling prophecy came true—sadly so. Some people just don't know when to quit.

(A short stroll then ensued)

After interviewing de Cordova back in 1980, our next interview was the shortest commute we ever made; 100 ft. down the hall to *The Tonight Show* office that housed Carson's indispensable "second banana," Ed McMahon. He was waiting for us his feet propped up in the middle of his weekly manicure/pedicure. The improbable scenario of being interviewed sitting in a recliner with a notepad in one hand and a telephone in the other, his feet elevated while a manicurist filed his nails with the delicacy of a surgeon stitching a ruptured vessel, was not lost on McMahon who greeted us with a bellowing laugh that could be measured on the Richter scale.

Ed's pedicure

And it's precisely that laugh that became a key ingredient in the show's success acting as a life-saving silence-breaker when Carson's jokes occasionally bombed.

"Johnny made a joke about a naked man standing with a boulder covering his private parts, and he said: 'Here's a shot from a new movie, "A Hatful of Ralph." Not a sound from the audience. I started to laugh and he started to laugh and from that point on we gave each other this special look and called it our "Hatful of Ralph" category for anything that has a nonsensical feel. Another example was a sketch we did ('The Edge of Wetness') featuring a deodorant that makes you smell like Fred MacMurray. It makes no sense!"

The Tonight Show from its earliest roots with original host Steve Allen has endured as the epicenter of late-night television entertainment. At the historical center of its success were Carson and McMahon. For millions of Americans, they were welcome guests into darkened bedrooms—a reassuring nightlight of comedy shtick and guest interviews.

"We have worked together now for almost 23 years," McMahon told us at the time. "So that's every single day minus weekends and vacations. Most people who work together don't see each other on a daily basis. Laurel & Hardy didn't see each other every day. How many films did Abbott & Costello make? We've been doing this so long so you really get to know that person, like you're wired into their mind."

McMahon expounded further on his synergy with Carson: "I'm able to read him," he said in that tuba-like voice, graveled by a few too many Pepe's Martinis (a McMahon favorite served up by bartender Pepe Ruiz at Chasen's Restaurant which he referred to often on the show). "There's a look that he gives me when there's something that really pleases him coming up. Now I'm psyched up to like this. It's usually something that the writers bring in and he starts laughing uncontrollably. But there's a feeling, a thing that you get over the years and that's just from being around someone for so long."

McMahon and Carson's relationship predated *The Tonight Show* and extended back to 1958 and a television game show Carson emceed in New York City called *Who Do You Trust?* A year into the show, McMahon replaced the show's original announcer, Bill Nimmo.

"I went up to see Johnny for the job and we spent five minutes together in his office dressing room," McMahon said. "He stood at one window and I stood at another and we watched as they changed the Schubert Theater's marquee for *Bells Are Ringing* starring Judy Holliday. We were watching them lift this monstrous marquee into place. It was a fascinating thing and that's all we did—watched. We didn't even look at each other."

Convinced he'd blown the "audition," McMahon later found out that Carson and the show's producer had already decided they wanted him for the job. "So, our first meeting was impressive by being so unimpressive," he said.

It was during their first teaming on *Who Do You Trust?* that McMahon's reputation as a heavy imbiber began (a conceit that became an integral part of the TV banter between Carson and McMahon for decades).

"Johnny is not a good drinker by his own admission," McMahon said. "He has three drinks of anything and he thinks every day is Wednesday. Years ago when he was having marital problems, we would go out drinking because he didn't want to go home. After the third drink I was leading him from bar to bar. It didn't affect me because I'm a big guy. I'm a good drinker, not a heavy drinker. So, the next day he would say on the show, 'Boy, did we go to town last night. That Ed, boy, is he something!' The image of me being a boozer started because he thought I was in the same condition as he was."

A true-blue sidekick, McMahon was a staunch loyalist to Carson and *The Tonight Show* to the very end. In 1980 the show was still a ratings giant for NBC. Still, we asked him if he had any definitive plans of clocking out.

"I want to let the show run its course," McMahon said, the manicurist now working over the cuticles on his toenails. "I'll stay with it as long as Johnny does. My deal is that I leave the night he leaves. He picks up his pencils, I get my cup and we split into the night."

And that's just what they did on May 22, 1992—Johnny and Ed, anyway. Hey, two out of three ain't bad.

Angie

Angie Dickinson

Who knew that the most direct route to Angie Dickinson's heart—and an interview—was a cup of coffee?

Prerequisites are an onerous fact of life for reporters trying to schedule interviews with celebrities. They're usually funneled through obstructive "third person" public relations flaks who let the reporters know how long the visit will be, if photos will be permitted and sometimes even subject matter areas that are taboo and not to be discussed. "Don'ts" always vastly outnumber the allowable "do's" on the prerequisite agenda with coming to terms nearly always a Sisyphean struggle that frays nerves and puts patience to the ultimate test. Overlaying it all (if the interview is conducted with the flak in the room) are insistent reminders to "stay on topic" and plug the star's latest project. These nudges usually occur with the droning frequency of a tripped car alarm that repeats its pattern incessantly.

So, we were caught delightedly flat-footed when the only condition Angie made before granting our interview was that we pick up a Grand Latte decaf from Starbucks on the drive up to her house. She even told us which Starbucks on Ventura Blvd. to go to get the drink. "I know all the Starbucks locations in L.A.," she said. "One thing about me is that I don't like to leave my home unless I really have to. I'm a total homebody."

Angie was waiting for us outside the door of her house which is perched on a mountaintop in the highest reaches of Beverly Hills and from which you can see all the way south to Long Beach on a clear day. "You bring the coffee?" she asked, giving us hugs, grinning and still with that breathy timbre in her voice that was catnip to "Rat Packers" like Frank Sinatra and Dean Martin—and JFK.

Here's the thing: Angie's voice, and how she carried a conversation, had a kind of cognitive dissonance to it like she was caught between sly bemusement at the ridiculousness of most, even small, things but was also utterly sincere about discussing them. We never knew from one moment to the next which element was in play. We only knew that the full effect was bewitching—a charm onslaught—and that if Angie narrated audiobooks, untold numbers of drivers would hit the guardrail lulled by her purr into a state of tranquil, somnambulistic bliss.

"Growing older doesn't bother me," she said. "Would you prefer to see me play opposite Robert Redford or Michelle Pfeiffer? As a moviegoer, I wouldn't want to see me in that kind of part. I don't resent this type of casting at all. I understand it. What I'd like to do is play Al Pacino's mother. That's what I'd like—really hot and hip mothers, or even grandmothers. I just don't want to play stereotypical, boring mother roles."

When we visited Angie (star of such movies as *Rio Bravo* with John Wayne, *Ocean's 11* with Sinatra and the "Rat Pack" and *Point Blank* with Lee Marvin), it was hazy. Long Beach (or any beach) wasn't in sight so we consoled ourselves by popping the cork of (or was it twisting the metal cap off) a bottle of Sauvignon Blanc from Trader Joe's.

"I can see in your eyes that you think this'll be rotgut," she laughed, "but trust me."

Although "two-buck Chuck" is a vintner's country mile from *Chateauneuf-du-Pape*, it didn't exactly rot the palate either, but then that probably speaks volumes about the remedial education of our particular taste buds. You see, Angie at 81, doesn't put on airs. She likes what she likes, speaks her mind and makes no excuses about any of it. And no one appreciates unadorned directness more than a reporter. As Sinatra might have said back in the day, "She's a gas!"

Looking around, it was easy to see why Angie rarely leaves her mountaintop hermitage. It has a wrap-around terrace that affords a 180-degree view and the house is filled with personal mementos: photos of when she was married to composer Burt Bacharach; a framed candid of when she attended President Kennedy's 1960 inaugural and then a follow-up letter from JFK's personal secretary, Evelyn Lincoln, thanking her on behalf of the new president for attending; inscribed pictures of Frank with and without his King Charles Spaniel.

Angie likes to say that her mid-century modern (formerly owned by cartoonist Walter Lantz) is the house "Woody Woodpecker" built (we noticed it did have a lot of wood paneling). But it was another home that Angie wanted to reminisce about during our visit—Ira (brother of George) and Lee Gershwin's home at 1021 North Roxbury Drive. (Angie said she wanted to buy the house after Lee Gershwin died but couldn't afford it.) She was a young starlet—"maybe 24 at the time"—and new to Hollywood when she was invited to be part of a weekly poker game (Seven Card Stud and Five Card Draw) that typically began Saturday evening and ended the next morning as early risers made their way to church services. Mandatory buy-in was $500 for a stack of chips with a settlement of one-tenth of the total or $50.

"I also used to go to the racetrack with Ira because Lee didn't like to. He was so low-key and made doubly so by the death of his brother, George. It was a veil over him forever," Angie lamented. "The things I missed out asking Ira—he would've been my Google."

Angie said that MGM film producer Arthur Freed and his wife were regulars on poker night as was Oscar Levant and Richard Conte. "I played for years in those games and they were so much fun, all the banter, especially from Oscar," she said. "I just wish I had paid more attention to what was being said, but you never do when you're that young. During an 11 p.m. break we'd feast on deli that had been catered in from Nate 'n' Al's. I remember Arthur had a stock line that he'd say after coming back from the buffet table. He'd say: 'This is the best sandwich I've ever had … in my mouth!'"

John Cheever, in the preface to his Pulitzer Prize–winning collection of short stories, wrote about "the last generation of chain smokers who woke the world in the morning with their coughing, who used to get stoned at cocktail parties and whose Gods were as ancient as yours and mine." He might as well have had Angie and her card-playing cronies in mind. To wit: she asked us if we knew what a "silent butler" was. "It's an ashtray with a lid over it," she said, "and about every 45 minutes someone at poker night would come around to empty it because it would be full of ashes and butts. We all smoked like chimneys then.

"Arthur would always talk with a cigarette dangling from his mouth," she continued. "And the ash would grow and grow and we'd wonder when it would drop. It was about the only thing we didn't bet on. He loved to win; had to come out a winner and he won a lot."

It was Freed who invited Angie to an early screening of his picture *Gigi* which would go on to win nine Academy Awards including the Best Picture Oscar in 1958. "Cary Grant was at the screening and I had brought my mother, because she loved him in all his movies and she literally almost fainted," Angie said. "Later our paths crossed several times. He called me on the set of *Police Woman* and I could tell he was asking me out but I wasn't dating at that time. But actually, if we had had TV as we have it today, pulling up all those great movies of his, I'm pretty sure I would've fallen hard. Cary Grant aside, those were my earliest days in the show business world, so I had a good start."

A native of Kulm, North Dakota, Angeline Brown (she took the name Dickinson from her first husband), and her family moved when she was a child to Burbank, California. While working as a secretary near Lockheed Aircraft, some friends urged her to enter a local television beauty pageant.

"Since I was in an 'oil and water' marriage that wasn't working and never should have been," she said, "I entered the contest simply as something to do on the way home from my job. I was one of six winners. And I was thrilled to death except when I learned that the prize was … nothing!"

A few days later a talent coordinator for the *The Colgate Comedy Hour* called Angie and asked if she'd like to perform on the show. "I told him that I couldn't act," she said. "He replied: 'Can you walk?' The show was taped in Hollywood at the Masonic Lodge (where Jimmy Kimmel now opens his late-night talk show each night) and when I walked in, Frank Sinatra and Jimmy Durante were rehearsing a number. It was an injection for me. I knew I wanted to be in show business."

Although bitten by the acting bug, Angie, in keeping with her Midwestern sensibilities, held on to her secretarial job while pursuing work in film and TV. She got divorced and soon the parts became more steady and substantial, "Enough for my mother not to worry about me," she said.

Angie's first film role in the 1954 Doris Day/Bob Cummings trifle, *Lucky Me*, consisted of a single line: "Happy birthday, Uncle Otis." A number of other walk-on parts followed before she slowly began to edge her way into meatier roles such as the gun moll in *Cry Terror!* (1958), starring Rod Steiger and James Mason.

"In that film I came to the realization that I could work and succeed in this business," she said. "I didn't care about being a star. I just wanted to make a living and have a career."

That fond hope would have been dashed if it wasn't for legendary director/producer Howard Hawks, a man with a roving eye and propensity for discovering "fresh, young talent." More than a decade earlier, Hawks had cast an unknown Lauren Bacall to play opposite Humphrey Bogart in *To Have and Have Not.* Hawks signed Angie to a seven-year contract after seeing her in an episode of *Perry Mason*, and played Svengali to Angie's Trilby for the 1959 Western classic, *Rio Bravo*, starring John Wayne, Dean Martin and Ricky Nelson. Angie's yearning "cool-cat" performance as "Feathers" in the movie has often been compared to Bacall's enigmatic unflappability in *To Have and Have Not*. Both actresses oozed sex-appeal without taking a stitch of clothing off.

"I think it was sexier when you didn't have to take it all off," Angie said. "In *Rio Bravo*, when Duke finally makes love to Feathers, the scene dissolves to the next morning where we see him putting on his vest and almost humming. It was subtle, but you knew what happened. Give me a towel and some blankets any day."

Angie didn't remain part of Hawks' stable of stars for long. He soon sold her contract to Warner Brothers. "Howard had a track record of launching careers—especially those of women—and then casting them off," Angie said. "I can't explain it. All I know is that I never worked for him again." (When Hawks died, the only two stars in attendance were John Wayne and Angie.)

After some roles in mostly "B" pictures, Angie jettisoned her Warners contract in favor of a similar pact with Universal. The carrot was the opportunity to work with Gregory Peck in the Army hospital drama, *Captain Newman, M.D.* After that, Angie starred as the deceitful "Sheila Farr" in the 1964 remake of *The Killers*, costarring Lee Marvin and in his last screen role (and his first as a heavy), Ronald Reagan.

"He (Reagan) was so bad at playing a heavy," Angie said. "That's why it's such a cult film today. He was so nice personally and that's why he was so bad at playing an evil man. Audiences just couldn't accept it. Every time we'd meet socially after that, he would joke how pleased he was that he really didn't have to hit me, although in the film, his character gives me a good slap. Reagan was fulfilling his final contract commitment; he was more preoccupied with launching a political career. No one at the time would've guessed where that would take him."

From taking a slap in *The Killers* to getting sliced and diced by a straight razor in an elevator in *Dressed to Kill*, Angie, throughout her career, was game for just about anything. However, she told us that she had to be convinced by Director Brian DePalma to appear in *Dressed to Kill*.

"I told him I can't do this," she said. "Brian asked why and I told him it was because of my *Police Woman* image (Angie had made a huge impression a few years earlier starring in the TV series). People love me, I'm a heroine. Brian said he would use a body double for me but that he needed an actor who was very recognizable; very likeable immediately. He told me he didn't have time to build the character up. 'I have to lose her in the first half hour,' he said, 'and you're not going to expect that she's going to die because she's one of the stars. I have to have *you*.'"

As indelible as her screen performances are, from 1974–78, Angie starred on television as sexy undercover cop "Pepper" Anderson in *Police Woman* and she might be best remembered for that. She told us the idea for the series was a spin-off from her role that same year in an episode of *Police Story*, a TV series created by real-life former cop, Joseph Wambaugh. Angie especially loved that *Police Woman* made an impact on the nascent women's movement.

Angie said that without *Police Woman* she wouldn't have had a career. "The show started about the same time the women's movement was taking off. Ours was the first primetime one-hour show featuring a strong, professional woman. It paved the way for other series to follow.

"You know, a few weeks ago, Earl (Earl Holliman, Angie's boss, Lt. Bill Crowley in the series) and I finally got together for a reunion," she continued. "It had been more than 30 years since we got together to spend some time—and he lives in Studio City which is about six miles from here as the crow flies. "We had such a great time laughing and remembering, it was like we were just back from hiatus."

Three decades to come down the hill for a reunion; proof positive that Angie walks the walk and that she is perhaps the ultimate homebody. We cracked that Holliman must've had some Starbucks brew on hand as an enticement.

"Funny to find out that a cuppa joe is all it takes to get me down to the flatlands," Angie said. "You want a refill on the wine?"

In Angie's estimation, everything that happened in her life—even the parts big and small that she earned or cadged in her career—are contributory to what she became. "They add up," she said. "They're all elemental, part of the puzzle. They take away or add onto the place at which you eventually arrive. I've been cheated on and I've been the culprit. It's so dumb, but that's life. To learn, to be exposed, to dare, to be brave, to not faint, it's all part of the same deal."

Angie likes to say that she was "an innocent bystander that just got lucky." But really it's much more than that; like her friend Sinatra, from the "Rat Pack" to rotgut, Angie did it her way.

Testy(monial)

Sparring with Stanley Donen

Time and distance.

It took 34 years and 3,000 miles between our first and second interviews with the director Stanley Donen to get it right. And we needed every bit of that thick margin.

Our first visit in 1980 with the co-director (with Gene Kelly) of *Singin' in the Rain*, *On the Town* and *It's Always Fair Weather* was, on balance and minus any hyperbole, a disaster, and one that is only partially redeemed in the retelling.

Artistic temperament is a catch-all used to describe the vagaries—sometimes rankling—of talented people. Donen possessed it in spades. But while millions of movie-goers (us included) have benefited from his brilliant film work as director in his own right (*Charade, Funny Face, Seven Brides for Seven Brothers, Two for the Road*), artistry wasn't part of the conversation on that early summer morning when we drove up to the gate in Bel Air off Stone Canyon Road. The full fury of his temperament, however, couldn't be quelled.

Mulling it all over in the intervening decades, Donen's state of high dudgeon during the interview could've been due to:

A. The 9 a.m. appointment (early for L.A. creatives)

B. The fact that his two boisterous collies had shed fur all over the furniture in his den (they had all over us)

C. The galling idea, perhaps, that he had ceded undue credit and acclaim to "senior partner" Kelly

D. Or, just maybe, an incident that happened between us and Donen's then-wife, actress Yvette Mimieux, a few seconds before we met him

Mimieux ("Weena" in *The Time Machine, Inside Daisy Clover, Toys in the Attic, Light in the Piazza*) was about two decades younger than Donen and the subject of a long-standing crush of Tom's. We hoped that possibly meeting her would turn out to be a bonus for us. Be careful what you wish for.

We had been shown to Donen's study which was decorated with framed lobby cards from his movies hung right below the crown molding along all four walls of the room, as well as a glossy of Kelly swinging from the iconic lamppost in *Singin' in the Rain*.

No sooner had we hustled the collies off our laps than Mimieux burst through the casement doors. She was smiling. She was beautiful. She was buck naked with hair wet from the shower! Mimieux emitted a shriek that startled the dogs (we were mesmerized) and then sprinted from the room. We heard her quarreling with Donen and although we couldn't make out actual words or phrases, Mimieux seemed to be getting the better of the donnybrook.

Donen, dead serious and wearing slightly tinted oversized glasses that failed to mask his unfunny face, soon entered the study, sat down in a chair right next to his exercise bike and distractedly began flipping a paperweight from one hand to the other. It didn't take a mentalist to figure out what he wanted to do at that precise moment—from dudgeon to bludgeon! And from an anticipated scenario of conversing about sunny musicals, we instead found ourselves thrust into a netherworld of snark—more *Who's Afraid of Virginia Woolf* than *Singin' in the Rain*.

"O.K., let's start," Donen snapped, dispensing with pleasantries. For our part, we had to willfully ignore what we had just seen, recalibrate, and proceed as if nothing had happened. Ours was an Oscar-worthy performance that made Albert Finney's theatrics in *Two for the Road* seem like amateur emoting from a high school stage.

Prickly in 1980

A protégé of Kelly's before Gene headed to Hollywood from Broadway, we asked Donen how he came to be cast as a chorus boy in *Pal Joey*, the Rodgers and Hart show that made Kelly a Broadway star in 1940.

"I just auditioned and got the job," he said.

"You followed Kelly west fairly soon afterward," Dave remarked. "How did you wangle a contract at MGM?"

"I auditioned and they said, 'fine.'"

The less-is-more axiom rarely applies when conducting an interview, to say nothing of the sense of *déjà vu* we were beginning to feel about Donen's last two answers, but we pressed on and asked Donen his opinion of Kelly during those early days at MGM.

"Gene was ambitious, experienced and single-minded, but probably less narrow in what he thought was good or bad in the theater and movies than I was," Donen said.

Three's the charm, we thought. Jackpot!

"At the same time, I was extremely certain of what was good or bad. I was much less accepting or appreciative. I'm less certain now. For example, I hated the work of Busby Berkeley when I was younger; I don't anymore.

"I have enormous respect for Kelly in many ways," Donen continued, "but we had disagreements over the way certain parts of films should be directed. Neither of us are good compromisers. Rodgers and Hart used to fight; Gilbert and Sullivan didn't speak to each other. Gene and I got along well compared to those people."

Latching onto Donen's comment about disagreement over which way "certain parts of films should be directed," we asked if he could extrapolate on that idea regarding any scenes he personally directed in *Singin' in the Rain*.

"There is no way I can answer that question," he said. "Gene and I were co-directors and you can't divide that up anymore than you could ask Hecht or MacArthur who wrote what in *The Front Page*."

Donen followed Kelly over to Columbia Studios when he was loaned out by MGM in 1944 to do *Cover Girl* with Rita Hayworth. Kelly's "Alter Ego" solo in that film where he dances in perfect synchronicity with a mirror image of himself is a screen classic.

"I did everything. It was my idea, I directed it and I organized the shots," Donen said.

"Everything but dance the number," Dave said.

"Well, Gene danced it. I mean, we worked it out together."

After directing the screen version of *Damn Yankees* in 1958, Donen abandoned musicals for light comedies, thrillers and finally science fiction films. We asked him why he stopped directing musicals. "I didn't," he snapped, "they stopped being made. I don't like to direct thin air."

That seemed to be the ideal abrupt segue into inquiring about *Saturn 3* which, in addition to being a departure for Donen thematically, starred Farrah Fawcett Majors battling a malevolent robot in a faraway space station. Fawcett at that time (a couple years before her revelatory breakout role in *The Burning Bed*) came from the *Charlie's Angels* cheerleader school of acting with teeth so white you could go snow-blind when she smiled. Film critics reacting to Fawcett's performance and perhaps her dubious TV pedigree, had savaged the movie and it tanked at the box-office.

"I don't accept that!" Donen said, his gorge visibly rising. "Who is this person that decides someone is box-office poison? Is it a person ... six people ... or do they have a seal of approval?

"Maybe it relates to the financial ledger," Tom interjected.

"Where is it, show it to me, where is it?" Donen insisted.

"It was in *Variety*," Dave said. "We could send you the clipping."

"Do you believe Katharine Hepburn is box-office poison? She was considered that by some asshole ... by numbers of assholes and other people who thought that was true." What followed was an irksome period of question-dodging by Donen—the effective technique of intentionally avoiding giving answers by throwing the questions back us.

"Are you happy with how the film turned out?" we asked.

"Are you happy with how it turned out?" Donen parried.

We told Donen that since he directed the movie, we and our readers would be more interested in how he felt about the film."

"That's neither here nor there," he said. "I'm not happy with your questions."

Mea culpa, mea maxima culpa.

Soon after, we beat a hasty retreat. In fact, it wouldn't be an overstatement to say we moved out of there with more celerity than Donen's dog exhibited earlier in humping Dave's leg.

For years, that visit stood unchallenged as the most belligerent and disputatious interview we ever did; and Donen the apotheosis of feisty interviewees, our *bête noire*. But truthfully we didn't ameliorate matters much by meeting Donen's curtness with obstinacy as entrenched as the subjective truths mewled by Trump and Hillary during their round of presidential debates. Still, our pugilistic visit was memorable for all the wrong reasons and we always regretted that.

In 2014, we got a chance to make amends of sorts. We had been researching a planned biography of Donen's boss at MGM, producer Arthur Freed, head of the legendary musical Freed Unit at the studio. As an integral part of the Unit and one of a dwindling few still alive that made musicals during MGM's golden era, we reached out again to Donen for an interview that would trod some of the ground we had tried to cover three decades before.

He agreed and we scheduled what we hoped would be a conciliatory visit.

On the appointed day we were early for our "rematch" which was to take place at Donen's office on the ground floor of the San Remo, a luxury co-op building on Central Park West at 74th Street in New York City. Years before, Donen had relocated from his home in Bel Air to Manhattan and, since 1999, had been in a relationship with actress-comedian-director Elaine May.

As we milled about the San Remo's lobby marking time, Dave grew skittish that Donen might recall our previous interview. "What if he remembers?" Dave said shooting Tom a worried look. "No chance," Tom said. "He's 90 and the interview happened 30 years ago. Unless you jog his memory about Mimieux—and I wouldn't recommend that— there's no way." The fact that Dave had brought along a snapshot we had taken of Donen looking austere from when we had visited him in Bel Air didn't exactly allay our fears any.

"Yeah," Dave said, reassuring himself. "Duh, he wouldn't have agreed to this visit if he remembered ... unless ... he's a sadistic gadfly that loves fucking with reporters."

"That's not off the table," Tom muttered adding that no matter how it goes we can't end up oafishly trading salvos this time like two battlewagons at the Battle of Jutland or words probably not even remotely to that effect.

Donen's various factotums manned phones and scurried purposefully about, telling us that the director was in the process of moving his office out of the building to space

Pleasant in 2014

nearby. An oversized portrait of Fred Astaire looking debonair in white tie and tails from the 1930s hung on one wall over a table where a pair of old iron manacles rested. Donen's bookcase contained a copy of the authorized biography (*Dancing on the Ceiling: Stanley Donen and His Movies*) written about him by Stephen Silverman as well as Donen's Oscar for Lifetime Achievement given to him in 1998.

After a few minutes the director entered haltingly with the aid of a cane and plopped down on a couch.

"Great photo of Fred you have there. He was your idol wasn't he?" Tom said.

"I admired him enormously," Donen said. "He was obviously one of the major influences. That's why I wanted to be in show business; to be connected with that. I suppose Fred was the largest magnet to show business that I ever had. I got great joy from his numbers. When Arthur Freed asked me if I wanted to direct *Royal Wedding* with Fred, I said: 'You're fucking right I do.'"

After 30 years, Donen had grown more saturnine in appearance and aspect with expletive-laced answers that were as short as they were sardonic and declarative. We felt right at home.

"I absolutely don't recall my first encounter with Arthur Freed," he told us. "And I want to tell you something: there was no such thing as the Freed Unit. It was just an idea. Nobody talked about it back then. You worked with Freed or you worked with Joe Pasternak or you worked with that *schmuck* Jack Cummings (the troika of producers specializing in musicals at MGM). Arthur loved musicals. For him, it was like being in love with a woman. And that's all there is to it. He didn't know exactly how to 'do' them; that would've fucked everything up. He just got the right people for the job."

"You didn't like Jack Cummings as a person or as a producer?" Dave asked.

"I don't remember him as a person," Donen said. "As a producer, he didn't know his ass from his elbow. In *Seven Brides for Seven Brothers* he said: 'You're gonna have a bunch of men dancers here; you're gonna have fags dancing around on screen.' I said, 'What are you talking about? Dancing can be very masculine.' 'No,' he said. 'They're all fags.' He was a shit-heel and an idiot."

In addition to being an indispensible member of the Freed Unit, Donen told us that he was also the youngest member by 10 years or more. "I was a baby," he said, "and that was pure luck. I didn't know anything; I just knew what I thought was good. That's all. I didn't try to figure out if the numbers or scenes or pictures I was working on were the right thing or not. You just do what feels right.

"It sounds so simple," Donen continued. "The thing is; you get lost if you're trying to make something up. Do you really like it or have you settled? That's where you get screwed up. Are you telling the real truth about how you feel or are you fudging?"

Donen never fudged. His storied career studded with iconic cinematic moments is proof of that: the exhilarating overhead boom shot of Gene Kelly swinging his umbrella in circles while singin' and dancin' in the rain; Fred Astaire defying gravity tapping across the walls and ceiling of his hotel room in *Royal Wedding*; and some especially limber brothers performing an acrobatic barn-raising in *Seven Brides for Seven Brothers*. To name just a few.

"I don't want to shock you as we're concluding this interview, but I have a photo of you that I want you to autograph," Dave said, pulling out the 8 × 10 hidden among his notes.

"What's this? I look 12 years old," Donen said squinting at the picture.

"Do you recognize where it was taken?" Tom asked.

"I have no idea," Donen said. "Was this when I had returned to America from living in Europe?"

"Yes," Dave said. "It's from 1980, your house on Stone Canyon Road."

"That's my house?" Donen said somewhat bemused at the pictorial trip down memory lane, "I don't remember this at all, you guys were there?"

"Indeed we were," Tom said.

In that moment we learned a penetrating lesson: time does heal some wounds. Time and distance … and forgetfulness.

You Must Remember This

Julius Epstein

At Penn State University, the Epstein twins, Philip and Julius, gained a reputation as pugilists with Julius earning a title of NCAA Bantamweight Champion. That was in

1931. Half a century later Epstein, 72, consented to go a few rounds with us, and he proved instantly that he had not lost his ability to weave and jab just like he did when he substituted pounding heads for pounding out repartee for *Casablanca*.

The 1942 Oscar winner for best motion picture, *Casablanca* stands among the most venerated productions of the Golden Age studio system with historians oscillating between it and *Citizen Kane* as America's greatest film. The film has the perfect, and somewhat accidental confluence of a great cast, Humphrey Bogart, Ingrid Bergman, Paul Henreid and Claude Rains, a solid director (Michael Curtiz, nicknamed the "Mad Hungarian" who also won an Oscar) and a witty screenplay sprinkled with more immortal lines ("Here's looking at you kid," "We'll always have Paris") than any other film before or since with the possible exception of *The Godfather*.

Epstein's home, just up a verdant hill plush with greenery from the Bel-Air Hotel, wasn't as palatial as many of the gated estates in that show business enclave, but it had the warm, intimate feel of a writer's bungalow, although one considerably roomier than the cramped garret afforded him during his 14 years as a Warner Brothers contract screenwriter.

He greeted us in his office adorned with books, awards and his career-defining Oscar for co-writing *Casablanca* with his brother and Howard Koch. Dressed in a tan-short-sleeved shirt, Epstein, with his bony cranium, looked like something Darwin might've noted on a trip to the Galapagos Islands. He nestled himself comfortably at his desk behind a small portable Royal typewriter and we began with the questions about his most famous film.

It was a bit surprising then that at the outset we learned even a furtive gesture of praise about *Casablanca* was as lost on Epstein as, well, Ugarte trying to impress Rick

Here's looking at Julius

Blaine by boasting he had stolen the letters of transit. "Personally, I don't understand it (the film's reputation)," Epstein snapped. "The movie was almost camp when it came out. I thought it was camp. You're not going be very proud of something that's camp. I'd be perfectly all right if all this adulation died down. I've done so many of these (interviews). I always say, 'This is the last one.' Everybody's writing a book; they come out two or three a week. Nobody reads them, either!"

Epstein came out swinging, that's for sure. The response threw us for a loop but we came back with a query that turned the tables (not unlike Victor Lazlo one upping the hated Major Heinrich Strasser at their first meeting). With the Reagan Administration in full flower, we asked if there was any truth that Ronnie was considered for the role of *Café Américain* owner, Rick Blaine. "Baloney! He was never considered for anything important. He's a lousy president and he was a lousy actor you know," Epstein exploded with the same outrage Captain Louis Renault exhibited when, to his shock, he found out there had been illicit gambling going on in Rick's café.

It was at that point that we had our "ta-da!" moment. It dawned on us that quite possibly Epstein didn't really want to talk about his most famous screen accomplishment. We were crestfallen just like Rick is when Ilsa Lund stands him up at the train station. Looking at Epstein's Oscar on a shelf a few feet away, we wondered if he was all bluff and bluster and if the statue—the stuff that dreams are made of (apologies for the *Maltese Falcon* interjection)—had real significance for him. "It really doesn't mean much to me," he sniffed convincingly. About working with director Curtiz, Epstein volunteered, "He was a good pictorial director. He didn't know what the hell the actors were saying in the English language."

Taking a break from all the negativity (like Sam the piano player tried to do, when he attempted to sway Rick to go fishing all night to get away from Ilsa), Epstein admitted that two of his favorite lines from *Casablanca* came off *his* typewriter. "When Bogart had the gun pointed at Claude Rains and he said, 'I'm aiming at your heart.' And Rains replied, 'That's my least vulnerable spot.' That's my line," Epstein said. "The other line is when Rains asks Bogart, 'What in heaven's name brought you to Casablanca?' and Bogart said, 'My health. I came to Casablanca for the waters.' Rains replied, 'The waters. What waters? This is the desert' to which Bogart said, 'I was misinformed.'"

From about 1939 until Philip's untimely death in 1952 at age 42 from cancer, the Epstein brothers almost exclusively collaborated. In addition to their credited work, the brothers worked as "script doctors" receiving no credit on several films, most notably *Yankee Doodle Dandy* in 1942.

In the assembly line of the studio system, Epstein said he was required to produce anywhere from 4–5 screenplays a year. Once a script was submitted, control and ownership became the rightful property of Warner Brothers. "We didn't have any rights of ownership," he said. "But creative control also depended on who you were working with and how much clout you had at the moment. What was your relationship like with the lead actors? Sometimes you had no control, other times a lot, and sometimes you had medium control. But legally we never had total control of our work.

"When you're under contract with the studio, which doesn't exist anymore, you were always on-call. I would go down to the set once in a while and look at the pretty girls. It made sense to be on call because if they needed you, we could respond quickly. (Kind of like everyone in Rick's Café when they responded *en masse* to sing the "Marseillaise," effectively drowning out the Nazi's caterwauling.)

Epstein died in 2000 at the age of 91 stubbornly unreconciled to the changes that had taken place in the movie business. (His head would've spun at recent news that an Italian issue movie poster of *Casablanca* sold for $478,000. Bogart's salary on the film was $36,667 and Epstein himself earned $15,208 for his work on the screenplay.)

"Right now I think it's the most disgraceful time in the motion picture industry," he said to us back in 1980. "When two-thirds of the pictures are horror movies, ghost pictures or sci-fi—there's no writing in those films. There are no people in the movies anymore, it's all special effects. To find a recent film that I liked I would have to go to an Australian picture, *Breaker Morant* or a few other foreign films. I can't think of any American picture whose screenplay has knocked me off my feet in the past couple of years."

More's the pity, but thanks to Epstein, "We'll always have Paris"—and *Casablanca*.

Common and Preferred

Peter Falk

"You can't use an umbrella as a prop when the sun is out, but you can use a cigar under almost any circumstances," Peter Falk announced in that gravelly, clutched rasp known to millions worldwide as the voice of "Columbo"—everyone's favorite, rumpled television detective.

In 1996, when we sat down with him in at his home in the Beverly Hills flatlands, Falk was a spry 71. And he imparted that bit of actorly wisdom not while chomping on a cheap stogie (Columbo smoked cigars, but Falk told us he never did), but in between puffs on a True 100 cigarette which was seldom out of his hand.

"I've been chain-smoking cigarettes for 55 years," he said, hunched in a chair in his office/painting studio. "My mother is 91 years old and still lights up. I'm trusting to luck that I'm blessed with her constitution." (Falk made it to 83, dying of pneumonia in 2011.) Throughout our interview, so many ashes accumulated in the folds of Falk's paint-smeared Oxford shirt and chinos that by visit's end he seemed to have morphed into a walking, talking pewter-colored ashtray. The overall effect was as charming as it was unassuming and very much akin to his Columbo character.

Indeed, Falk belongs in that rare pantheon of TV actors who have originated truly unique personas. Don Knotts as deputy "Barney Fife" on *The Andy Griffith Show* was another complete original although the only thing the two characters had in common were "careers" in law enforcement and large Emmy hauls (Falk won four as Columbo; Knotts won five as Fife.)

As Columbo, Falk played the shambling hayseed to perfection; a seemingly hapless, absent-minded detective that lulled adversaries into thinking they had the upper hand while he implacably pieced the jigsaw evidence of a case together toward a final reveal. And it wasn't just stagecraft that made Falk's eight-year run in the series so indelible. Even his physical attributes played a part in deepening his TV character. Falk's right eye was surgically removed when he was three because of a retinoblastoma; he wore an artificial eye for most of his life and it was the cause of his trademark squint. Falk also incorporated into the role his speech impediment—the same nasal "L" that anchorman Tom Brokaw swallowed into the back of his throat during newscasts—to lull criminals into thinking he was flawed right down to his pattern of speech.

Perhaps more than anything else, meeting Falk face to face was like running into a Damon Runyon character fresh off a three-day poker bender. Following him as he padded around his beautifully-appointed studio, we wouldn't have been overly surprised if he decided to launch into an impromptu version of "Luck Be a Lady" from *Guys and Dolls.*

As Falk pointed to a low shelf where those four *Columbo* Emmys rested, it became apparent that the actor and his most famous character *are* intrinsic and not an affectation. However, something seemed amiss. We finally realized it was Falk's house; the kind of Beverly Hills brickpile that the intrepid police lieutenant (dressed in his shapeless raincoat and rayon tie) would fearlessly invade searching for clues, armed with just the tiniest pin to deflate the ego of its cocky owner. It was a spread that would've dazzled "everyman" Columbo, but Falk seemed right at home. (At that time, he lived there with his actress/wife Shera Danese.)

"I'm a Virgo Jew, and that means I have an obsessive thoroughness," Falk said, making the correlation between himself and Colombo. "It's not enough to get most of the details, it's necessary to get them all. I've been accused of perfectionism. When Lew Wasserman (legendary Hollywood powerbroker, Steven Spielberg's mentor, and, back then, head of Universal Studios) said that I am a perfectionist, I don't know whether it was out of affection or because he felt I was a monumental pain in the ass."

However, Falk's mania to excel was tempered in the sweet-natured TV detective. "Colombo has a genuine mistiness about him. It seems to hang in the air," Falk said. "He's capable of being distracted. I remember one case where it was 20 minutes into the teleplay before he realized he hadn't taken off his pajamas. Colombo is an ass-backward Sherlock Holmes. Holmes had a long neck, Colombo has no neck; Holmes smoked a Meerschaum pipe, Colombo chews up six cigars a day at a quarter a piece."

The connection Falk feels—that Colombo is some sort of tattered stateside reincarnation of the famous Baker Street sleuth—is underscored by the fact that in a position of prominence, on a bookshelf right next to a copy of *The Colombo Phile*, was the *Complete Sherlock Holmes* by Arthur Conan Doyle. Volumes that speak volumes about where the poor man's Hercule Poirot ranks in the crime-solver firmament.

"The show is all over the world," Falk said with genuine amazement. "I've been to little villages in Africa with maybe one TV set, and little kids will run up to me shouting: 'Colombo, Colombo!'" When people weren't calling out the name of their favorite shamus, strangers invariably yelled to him, "serpentine," in reference to a hilarious, bullet-dodging scene in the 1979 film, *The In-Laws.* Director Arthur Hiller and costar Alan Arkin had to convince a reticent Falk that the scene would work comically. He said he was thankful that he capitulated.

Curiously, Falk wasn't particularly enamored by his unique voice which was as much a signature as the trench coat he wore that never saw the inside of a dry cleaners. "I never considered my voice part of my acting arsenal," he told us. In fact, he believed his performances played much better when they were dubbed into foreign languages—especially French.

Whatever the combination, the voice allied to Falk's peculiar brand of American unpretentiousness caught the eye of director Frank Capra who cast him in *A Pocketful of Miracles* (1961). The film, Capra's last feature, was not the critical or commercial success he had hoped it would be, but in his autobiography, *The Name Above the Title*, Capra gushed about Falk's performance.

"The entire production was agony ... except for Peter Falk," Capra wrote. "He was my joy, my anchor to reality. Introducing that remarkable talent to the techniques of comedy made me forget pains, tired blood, and maniacal hankerings to murder Glenn Ford (the film's star). Thank you, Peter Falk."

For his part, Falk said that he never worked with a director who showed greater enjoyment of actors and the acting craft. "You could see his shoulders shaking with laughter when we nailed a scene," Falk said. "And there is nothing more important to an actor than to know that the one person who represents the audience to you, the director, is responding well to what you are trying to do.

"One time I remember we kept doing a scene after Frank had yelled, 'Cut and print,'" Falk continued. "I asked him why, and he laughed and said that he loved the scene so much, he just wanted to see us do it again. How's that for support?"

During another scene in the movie, Falk said he learned a valuable object lesson from Capra about playing comedy.

"I had a scene where I was mad and had to rather distractedly put on my overcoat and leave a room. The scene called for me to have trouble putting on the coat with the idea of mining a few laughs out of it. We did several takes but it never seemed to come off right. It looked too much like I was faking having trouble putting on the coat. Frank called for a five-minute break and during that time had some crew member sew shut one of the sleeves of the coat—unbeknownst to me. Well, when we did the scene again, I went crazy trying to put the damn thing on. Frank's solution was perfect and truth came to the scene. His films are filled with moments like that. They are what you remember. After the scene was over and I realized what Frank had done, I went over and hugged him."

For Falk, art was always in the details and not just in an astrological sense or as the lever that makes a scene succeed in a

A Falk charcoal given to the authors by his publicist at the time of the interview

movie. Until he was in his mid–'20s he pursued a career in public administration as an efficiency expert for the Connecticut Budget Bureau. But he soon grew tired of bottom lines and balance sheets and became involved in amateur theatricals. In 1955, with the encouragement of stage actress Eva Le Gallienne, he turned professional and his performance in the Off Broadway production of *The Iceman Cometh* led to more work on Broadway, in television and films.

During the filming of *Castle Keep* with Burt Lancaster in 1969, Falk broadened his artistic horizons in an area that seemed to take him by surprise. "I was holed up in this cell-like hotel room after the day's shooting and I noticed an Italian leather valise on the floor half hidden under my bed," Falk said. "I picked up a pencil and began to draw it. Instantly I became a compulsive sketcher."

Although Falk admitted that a couple of years could pass before he approached an easel, his devotion to charcoal sketching (primarily nude figure studies) had been as constant in his life as, well, the ratty trenchcoat Columbo wore and which then hung in Falk's upstairs bedroom. Falk told us that he had sold his work at galleries on just two prior occasions and that his sketches sold for about $400.

"They command a certain price because Columbo drew them," he laughed "If *you* drew them, they wouldn't be worth shit!"

All things considered, Falk said, as he showed us some several sketches on buff-colored paper, that he preferred regular movie work with a bit of "Columbo" thrown into the mixture but with ample time in between to be spent in his airy studio trying to fathom the confounding beauty of the human form.

As a parting shot, we tried to bait him out of his artistic reverie with a question about what it was like to work with Frank Sinatra and the rest of the "Rat Pack" during their heyday in the film, *Robin and the Seven Hoods*. (The whole "Swinger" scene was very retro-hip in the mid–'90s.)

Falk stiffened us with a glassy stare as if perhaps we had spent too much time confined in our own castle keep somewhere and said: "I don't know or care about all that crap, I just like to draw."

Straight to the point. For Falk as for Columbo, bullshit came in various advanced degrees and from many quadrants. And on those occasions, he was ready with that tiny pin!

With a Song in Her Heart

Kathryn Grayson

We dressed to the nines for this one.

Dressing up (or down) often seemed to be the prime difference between hip, young, backwards baseball cap-wearing Tinseltown circa 1995, and the more staid adherents to old Hollywood rules of sartorial decorum governing press interviews. So, for us, it was suits, ties and Cole Haans buffed to a high sheen. After all, we had a date with a diva.

Kathryn Grayson, then 73, and once Metro-Goldwyn-Mayer's reigning thrush in musicals and operettas of the '40s and '50s, commanded that token of respect. At least that's what we figured, and we weren't far off.

Under what she said was Louis B. Mayer's benevolent and encompassing eye, Grayson literally grew up at MGM, engulfed and protected by the all-powerful studio system. Grayson came to believe she was special because everyone in MGM's "extended family" was special.

The grounding Grayson managed to get at MGM was evident even back then. In a town where fame can be as fickle as it is fleeting, she had lived serenely in the same rambling mansion in Santa Monica for 50 years.

And that's where we found her.

A longtime housekeeper led us from the foyer through a darkly paneled corridor and into a small library anteroom. There, Grayson, a bit pulpy with age, reclined in a highback chair. She was in a flowing red dress that pulsated; its bright red hue looking like a feathered ladies chapeau in a painting by Renoir. To add to the dramatic effect, Grayson was suffused in what could only be described as a weird theatrical glow. It was a couple of seconds before we realized she was benefiting from an uplight hidden from view on the floor behind the chair, one that beamed her shadow against the volumes lined tidily on the shelves. It was as if for old time's sake, MGM cinematographer George Folsey himself had dropped by to do one last solid for a Metro alumnus.

To this day, Grayson is the only star we ever interviewed that could make an entrance just by sitting down.

"Ah, the gentlemen from the press," she archaically exclaimed on seeing us, and in that instant we couldn't help but be faintly reminded of the character of "Miss Havisham" from Charles Dickens's *Great Expectations* lost in time and living alone in her mansion, Satis House.

"I moved here from Bel Air with my husband (actor/singer John Shelton) just after World War II," Grayson said. "He had been shot down over the Solomons and was rescued by a submarine off a Japanese-held island. After getting back stateside, our old house made him feel claustrophobic."

In addition to neighbors Julie Andrews and Michael Crichton, Grayson said Mel Brooks and his wife Anne Bancroft had recently moved next door.

"A few days ago there was a knock at the door and I answered it," Grayson said. "And what would you know but Mel Brooks was there. He asked me if Mario Lanza could come out and play. The guy's hysterical."

Grayson came by her singing early, perhaps even genetically. Surrounded by brothers and sisters with four octave ranges, Grayson would sing coloratura soprano to RCA Red Seal recordings of Enrico Caruso (she would later record for that label), and with her siblings perform impromptu quartets from *Rigoletto* and *Lucia di Lammermoor*.

"A friend and I used to climb over the fence at the St. Louis Municipal Opera Amphitheater in Forest Park," Grayson said. "We would sing arias for the janitor who worked there. He always applauded and said we were as good as the singers who performed there on tour. Well, we thought we were pretty hot stuff until we learned that the janitor was stone deaf!"

Grayson was in California studying to be an opera singer when MGM expressed interest in signing her to a contract. On Saturday afternoon (so as not to conflict with high school), Grayson and her singing teacher visited the studio for an audition. "I sang

MGM's operatic songbird

Deanna Durbin's songs, Judy Garland's songs, Jeanette MacDonald's songs and even Grace Moore's songs," Grayson said. "I must have sung for two or three hours."

She made the cut and was signed to a standard contract with an option for renewal and a salary increase at year's end.

In addition to her singing ability and rather delicate facial features—large pellucid eyes, a pert nose and high cheeks that tapered to a slightly jutting chin—Grayson had another fabled asset. Fellow contract player at MGM, Ava Gardner, once said that Grayson had the biggest tits on the lot. Regardless, Grayson didn't think she was pretty enough for pictures.

"Edward Johnson, who was head of the Metropolitan Opera in those days, approached me and asked if I wanted to sing *Lucia* on stage. I loved the opera and wanted to do it desperately, but Mr. Mayer said no. He told me that if I made my operatic debut before the release of my first picture, I would be known forever after as an opera singer. However, if I was a hit in the movies, then I'd be internationally famous for the rest of my life."

Grayson, who was the self-styled "spoiled brat of the lot" at MGM (she used to make the commute from home to studio on her Harley-Davidson motorcycle, against the advice of studio executives), didn't agree with Mayer's plan.

"I was still furious," she said. "We had this tremendous row, until finally he said: 'Kathryn, you're such a little rebel, I want you to go to a mountaintop and yell, 'Go to hell!' and then I want you to listen to the echo coming back at you. I then want you to yell, 'God bless you!' and listen to that echo.'"

That's when Mayer's philosophy sunk in. "He saw the big picture; he wanted us all to have happy lives," Grayson said, her voice clutching a bit.

Throughout our visit, Grayson proved to be one of Mayer's biggest boosters, deferentially referring to him as "Mr. Mayer." It was a token of respect echoed by many (but not all) of the MGM leading ladies we interviewed over the years. Understandably, the studio was a finishing school for many young women who never had time to pursue a formal education and Mayer was the *pater familias* who lorded over all of it.

Grayson made her film debut in 1941 opposite Mickey Rooney in *Andy Hardy's Private Secretary*. "Those *Andy Hardy* films were a training ground for MGM starlets," Grayson remembered. "Judy Garland, Lana Turner, Donna Reed and Esther Williams all got their start in those pictures. I didn't realize until quite recently that my *Andy Hardy* movie was one of the top-ten moneymakers in 1941."

Grayson's initial success was followed up with starring roles in a series of lighthearted musicals including *Anchors Aweigh*, co-starring Gene Kelly and Frank Sinatra. "Frank was one of the sweetest people with whom I've ever worked," she said. "During *Anchors* we would do our close-up shots at the end of the day. Frank and I would feed lines to Gene during his close-ups, but Gene would be mysteriously AWOL when it came time to feed lines to us for our close-ups. Gene was very ambitious about all aspects of filmmaking and would be off somewhere learning about cameras or some such thing (actually, Kelly was often engaged laying out the choreography for the film). Frank, on the other hand, didn't have to be ambitious. He was Frank Sinatra—already a star."

Grayson remembered recording the whole score of the film in one or two days. "Sometimes the music would come into our hands wet, still smelling of ink," she said.

Living under a strict dietary regimen of steak and tomatoes for lunch (high-energy protein) and soup and salad for dinner, Grayson starred in and recorded the soundtracks for *Kiss Me Kate*, *Show Boat* and two films starring another operatic sensation, former Philadelphia truck driver Mario Lanza.

"I went to the Hollywood Bowl in 1948 with Mr. Mayer, his secretary Ida Koverman and my husband to hear Mario sing with the Bel Canto Trio," Grayson recalled. "He had such a beautiful voice. He came to the studio the next day and we sang together for the benefit of the sound technicians. Their verdict was that we sounded great together. The only problem was Mario's weight. He was heavyset."

But trimming a few stone from a leading man wasn't much of a hurdle for a studio that boasted of creating "more stars than there are in the heavens."

"I lent Mario my masseuse to help him trim down, and in a few months we were ready to start filming our first picture, *That Midnight Kiss*, which was followed soon after by *The Toast of New Orleans*."

The only memorabilia from those halcyon days that Grayson ever kept was a dress she wore in that first film with Lanza. "Everything is gone now," she said wistfully as if the Golden Age had been nothing more than a castle in the air; a chimera lost in time. "The MGM backlot is leveled. The whole studio system fell apart when Mr. Mayer left MGM. He loved quality. I hear the Sony people who now own the former MGM studio have beautiful gardens there; I wish they'd make beautiful pictures instead."

A lyrical lament from one of MGM's storied songbirds.

Man Tan

George Hamilton

George Hamilton first experienced Tinseltown when it was still golden, or in his case, the same hue as his vaunted butterscotch complexion.

"I was just a kid, but I lived in Hollywood from 1947 to 49 when my mother (Anne Stevens) was trying to break into movies," he told us. "It was my first taste of the town, but I was very comfortable in Beverly Hills. It was a sleepy little hamlet with a path going down Sunset Boulevard all the way to the beach. We'd go to a little theater called The Hitching Post on Hollywood Boulevard to see Westerns and you'd just see the movie stars on the street. My mother dated and knew stars like Ronald Reagan and Clark Gable."

Hamilton had no idea when he subsequently moved to Florida (he was born in Memphis, Tennessee), that one day he would come back and become one of the last stars to sign a long-term contract during the waning days of the studio system.

Then as now, Tinseltown's measure of beauty is in a state of constant flux (like the surface of an ever-churning ocean) and is governed by ineffable standards which often come down to the tricky consensus of what is considered "hot" at the moment as defined by a few key tastemakers or sometimes the *vox populi* at large (marketing hype is a crucial factor in this).

In his acting heyday, Hamilton, much like his contemporaries the two Roberts—Wagner and Evans—was eye candy for the ladies (and doubtless quite a few boys). But his matinee-idol good looks really harkened back to an earlier movie era—"The Silents"—and the unblemished darkly handsome profile of Rudolph Valentino, a visage silky smooth as an infant's tush. There were no crags, welts or other protuberances to mar Hamilton's well-favored countenance. For him still, the Bronze Age isn't a term from antiquity; it's a jokey reality that's lasted Hamilton's entire life and continues unabated with his appearance as an "extra-crispy" chicken "Col. Sanders" spokesman in KFC's latest round of television ads. Clearly, the man has never met a bottle of sunscreen he's ever liked!

In 2013, we paid a visit to Hamilton's penthouse on the West Side of Los Angeles. At 74, tanned and toothy, he flashed us pearly whites that illuminated the room like a halogen bulb and were of a piece with his white hair and white slacks.

A natural athlete in his youth, Hamilton began acting in high school theater productions winning several statewide awards for his stage performances. "I had no real desire to work in films, but I thought this was a lot easier than going to school and doing all that math and stuff," he said. "I also liked the idea that I had a lot of girls, as many as the football captain had, so I thought there is something to be said about this acting."

About 10 years after his first taste of Hollywood, and right after graduating from high school in 1957, Hamilton cajoled two buddies into joining him on a road trip back to Los Angeles. "I figured we'll just go out there for the summer," he said. "I convinced them to come with me, it was sort of safety in numbers. I had $90 bucks and one of the boys had a Ford with a stick shift, which I didn't know how to drive. I drove in low gear pretty much from Florida through New Orleans."

Golden boy

The almost 10-year absence since Hamilton had last been in Hollywood had brought significant changes, most notably the emergence of television and the steady disintegration of the studio system. The changes were at first jarring to Hamilton. "The first few days I took stock of the town and things were starting to change," he said. "Hollywood and Vine was a state of mind, it wasn't a place. I was drawn back to what was, not what was going to be. I kind of wandered around town with my two buddies; none of us had any money. We were tapped out and pretty much living on what was left in the refrigerator."

Hamilton's ascension in Hollywood in the 1950s came at a time when he was competing for work with a new crop of handsome leading men such as John Derek, Robert Evans and Warren Beatty in an environment of dwindling roles as the studios began paring down their annual slate of feature film releases.

As the decade drew to a close, Hamilton said the nation was still basking in a postwar naïveté where "Everything was kind of wonderful. We all felt that we could do anything and I was no different. I thought if movies were what I want to do, why not? Everybody around town at that time was either a Marlon Brando or a James Dean. I was different or as Burt Reynolds said, 'Only George Hamilton wanted to be David Niven.'"

While Hamilton's buddies had no intention of pursuing show business stardom ("They were just trying to get some booze and meet some girls"), he embarked on a savvy, if not totally original form of self-promotion that would provide him visibility with industry executives and—in the process—a nice tan.

"I started hanging around the pool of the Beverly Hills Hotel and having myself paged," he said. "In those days you would page yourself—'Mr. Hamilton, please come to the cabana or Mr. Hamilton, please pick up the phone.' It would go on all day and people would say, 'Who the hell is George Hamilton?' Then, I noticed that there was another guy doing the same thing. It was Robert Evans. I started laughing; we were both playing the same game.

"I actually backed into stardom," Hamilton added. "I had to learn about the film business from the ground up, but landed the lead in my first movie."

That first film, *Crime and Punishment, U.S.A.*, a contemporary Beat Generation retelling of the Dostoyevsky novel was the ideal first vehicle for a neophyte like Hamilton. Shot in 1958, it was not released until the following year. "I went in and shot a screen test with Marian Seldes," he recalled. "She was such a commanding actress I only had to react to her. Another co-star of the film, Frank Silvera told me, 'Look, you've got to put more pain into it so take a rock and put it into your shoe and walk with it.' And I thought, 'God is this what acting is really about?'"

The film was made by the Sanders brothers, shot in 13 days and afforded Hamilton an opportunity to "carry around the camera equipment" and learn the business. He also earned the princely sum of $1,800 for his work. One of the fortunate consequences of this low-budget shoot, he said, was an opportunity to meet Jack Lemmon, a friend of the Sanders.'

"He happened to know my mother," Hamilton said. "I just started asking him everything about acting in Hollywood. He was an interesting guy and he could drink a lot. One night I saw him on the Sunset Strip completely wiped out, just wandering around. He was just completely blitzed."

After the film wrapped, Hamilton said that as a virtual unknown he had to bide his time taking a few TV roles before his eventual break came. "I had already made a movie, but I couldn't get arrested in this town and just kind of hung around until a few people saw me in the film. I was also running out of money ... again."

By the time *Crime and Punishment U.S.A.* was finally released in 1959, Hamilton, with no offers pending, took a flyer to South America where he sunbathed and made time to date a Miss Venezuela pageant winner (one in a series of beauties Hamilton would squire through the years). While living *la vida loca*, Hamilton's agent called to inform him that he had picked up a BAFTA nomination (the British version of the Academy Awards) for *Crime and Punishment, U.S.A.*

The film caught the attention of director Vincente Minnelli, fresh off an Oscar win for *Gigi*, who was eying Hamilton for a role in his dramatic film, *Home from the Hill*. MGM also wanted to sign their new find to a standard seven-year studio contract. "I started traveling back from South America with a friend, but got caught up in Havana the day Castro came in," Hamilton said. "The place was in total turmoil and nobody had any idea what was going on."

Finally back in Hollywood, Hamilton reported to MGM and the set of *Home from the Hill*.

"Minnelli could do no wrong," said Hamilton. "He could do any type of film he wanted. *Home from the Hill* was a departure for him, an intense story about the patriarch of a Texas family, along the lines of *Giant*. George Peppard played my illegitimate brother as I was being thought of as this new, young, intense James Dean–like actor. I thought to myself, 'oh geez,' I didn't really want to be James Dean."

On the Culver City lot, Hamilton caught one of the last freeze-frames of Hollywood's Golden Age. "I walked into the commissary and there were producers Arthur Freed, Joe Pasternak and Pandro Berman and sitting at another table was Cary Grant, Gary Cooper and Fred Astaire."

His new co-star, Robert Mitchum, was off in a corner at his own table wearing a cowboy hat and boots. "'Mr. Mitchum,' I said as I shook his hand, 'I'm working in a movie with you and they suggested I come over and say hello and meet you.' He said, 'Just sit down and forget the speech.' I asked him if he wanted to run through some lines and he replied, 'I know the lines, I'm just too drunk to say 'em.' Mitchum was not one of those guys you could move. You could try and move him with a certain charm, but don't try to hustle him and don't try to fight him. He and I became the best of friends. He was just incredible to me, and he gave me so much advice."

Hamilton's late studio-era contract had its limitations as most actors by that time were working as freelancers which gave them the flexibility to compete for a larger pool of roles. "I found that there was an influx of actors reading for every role I was up for, but they weren't under contract," he said.

A breakout film for Hamilton came in 1960 with the release of *Where the Boys Are*, a coming-of-age-comedy best remembered for the Connie Francis hit recording of the title number. The film was a box-office success and served as the inspiration for the *Beach Party* series of films starring Frankie Avalon and Annette Funicello. While Hamilton didn't catch this wave, his tenure at MGM was launched. His next three films (two loan-outs to other studios) received tepid responses from audiences and Hamilton determined that his next project would be more successful.

In film lore, perhaps the most storied case of an actor lobbying for a role is Frank Sinatra, who (with the inestimable help of Ava Gardner) pulled out all the stops to be cast as the Army hothead "Maggio" in *From Here to Eternity* winning a Best Supporting Actor Oscar in 1954 and resuscitating his career. Not to be outdone, Hamilton embarked on a similar effort to play the lead role of an Italian playboy in Arthur Freed's production of *Light in the Piazza*.

"Every night when we were watching the dailies I'd wait until the others went to the bathroom and then I'd jump the script cage," he said. "All the scripts that were coming out would be dispersed to the producers the next day, sometimes weeks in advance before anyone else received them. So I read *Light in the Piazza* and thought, God, that guy's an interesting character, but he's Italian. I thought, why couldn't I do that? I'm an actor. Isn't that what I'm supposed to be doing?"

MGM was hell-bent on giving the role to a Cuban actor, Tomas Milian. But by 1962 the studio had been considerably reduced in stature from its Golden Age heyday under the watchful eye of Louis B. Mayer. Enter Benny Thau, a long-time studio executive who had a short tenure as studio head wedged between Dore Schary and Sol C. Siegel on the MGM timeline. Thau, a dutiful studio employee had through the years gained the reputation of having the "busiest casting couch in Hollywood." Although no longer running MGM, Thau was still a power player who wielded significant influence at the studio.

In an act he put down to youthful impertinence, Hamilton thought he'd go directly to Thau's office in the Thalberg Building to personally lobby for the role. "It was late afternoon and I went up there and he was having a little dinner," Hamilton said. "I walked in, peeked my head around and I caught his eye. He said, 'Jesus Christ, what in the world are you doing—you knock on the God-damned door!' He asked me what I wanted and I could see there was a girl under his desk, and I thought, 'Well, George, this is your chance.' I said, 'Mr. Thau, I really want to test for this movie.' He said, 'Just get the fuck out of my office, will you!'"

Breaking the fourth wall in his story about Thau, Hamilton schooled us on the *art* of the casting couch. "You either made love to everyone, or none, but you couldn't do it in-between," he explained. "In fact, when I went under contract they said, 'Don't date other women. We have plenty here. When you want to go out, call Publicity, tell them where you want to go and take a contract girl with you. We'll send a car and take care of everything.'"

Thau remained recalcitrant, but Hamilton had another plan (a Machiavellian one worthy of Thau himself) to circumvent him, break the stalemate and secure a screen test for *Light in the Piazza*.

"There was a guy by the name of Nate Cummings, who ran Consolidated Foods in Chicago and he was a friend of my mothers and I knew that they were major shareholders in MGM. So I wrote him a letter. 'Dear Mr. Cummings. I understand you are a major stockholder in MGM. It seems to me that good business starts with economy at home. Why would a studio put you under contract and not use you, not even test you?' He forwarded my letter to MGM and Benny Thau said, 'Listen, just stay out of this. You're all over the place.' For my part, I wasn't going to give up."

Light in the Piazza was based on a 1960 novel by Elizabeth Spencer, about a young lady with a cognitive disability (Yvette Mimieux) who travels to Italy on holiday with her mother (Olivia de Havilland) only to meet a handsome young Italian (the role Hamilton was vying for). Arthur Freed was the producer on what would become his final film. Upon meeting Mimieux, Freed was not overly impressed. Guy Green, the director, was also reticent in casting Mimieux for the film, but, according to Hamilton, he (Green) had a crush on her.

With the cast and crew preparing to head to Florence for the shoot, Hamilton knew the clock was ticking. "I was studying Rossano Brazzi's (who was also in the film) voice pattern and learning his accent, I learned all the lines in Italian. I'd known the script way before anyone else so I was well-prepared."

Hamilton soon found the perfect opportunity to put his new-found dialectician skills to use—in this case, French. He hopped a plane to the South of France so he could again stalk Thau, who he heard was holed up in a luxury Monte Carlo hotel with his girlfriend.

After bribing a room service waiter with a few Francs, Hamilton donned the uniform to deliver Thau his breakfast. "I walked in and he was in a silk robe reading the trade papers and his girlfriend was either in the bathroom or still in the bed under the covers. And I said, '*Bonjour!*' He replied, 'Just put it over there.' I said, 'Would you like me to pour more coffee for you?' I'm going through this whole thing and finally I pushed the tray right up to him and said, 'Sir, would you please sign your name?' He said, 'Yeah, all right, no problem.' And I backed out of the room and as I got to the door, I said, 'Pretty good accent, don't you think?' He said, 'What?' And I said, 'That was a pretty good accent for a guy from Hollywood.'"

Recognizing Hamilton from his earlier intrusion in Culver City, Thau said, "Oh Jesus Christ, not you again!"

"Then I said, 'Mr. Thau, just give me this damn test. I came all the way over here and you didn't even know it was me.'" Thau finally caved and OK'd Hamilton's screen test which was shot with Mimieux under the watchful eye of Freed.

Hamilton's fondest memory of the film was working with de Havilland who is one of the last Golden Age stars remaining (she celebrated her 101st birthday in 2017). "We laughed about everything," he said. "We talked about everyone from Howard Hughes to Errol Flynn. Olivia never seemed to be serious, but she is *so* serious as an actress. She was always bemused by me. She always thought I was kind of a scamp and that was good for the character. She showed me little tricks and how to cry, just look into that arc light over there and just hold your eyes. I thought 'God, it's burning my retina, but I would do it. She was an old-time pro."

Outside the notoriety of his tan, what has perhaps best defined Hamilton's career, are two biopics he made depicting the lives of country music legend Hank Williams and motorcycle daredevil Evel Knievel, respectively. Initially, the studio balked—again—at casting Hamilton in the role of Williams, bantering about other names, including Elvis Presley, Steve McQueen and Nick Adams. Hamilton had been a fan of Williams and was familiar with his songbook. He was also a buddy of Col. Tom Parker, Elvis's manager.

"The Colonel told me that there was a picture Elvis turned down and I'd be great for," he said. "He encouraged me to go down to Nashville and meet William's widow, Audrey. She originally didn't want me for the picture. I spent a month in Nashville drinking Jack Daniels with her, going out every night with Faron Young and other country singers. Finally she said, 'You're the only guy that's going to play this.' I said, 'really?' and she said, 'Yeah, I'll tell 'em' and she did."

By the time the film was shot it was relegated to B-Picture status and directed by former screen hoofer Gene Nelson. *Your Cheatin' Heart* was released in 1964 and has the distinction of being the last MGM musical shot in black and white.

When MGM celebrated its 50th anniversary in 1974 with the release of *That's Entertainment!*, a group portrait was taken at the opening night gala with as many stars as possible that could be herded on stage. Dressed in a black tuxedo, Hamilton proudly stood next to Charlton Heston on the very back riser that also supported Dan Dailey, Buddy Ebsen, June Allyson, Glenn Ford and the "Tin Man" from *Oz*, Jack Haley. It was the last and largest convocation of stars from that bygone age and its moment was not lost on Hamilton.

"The thing about entertainment from that era is that it took you out of your seat, took you somewhere and gave you permission not to envy people, but to admire them for being wealthy and glamorous. MGM was a wonderful family," he said.

An epilogue fitting for the Golden Age straight from the Golden Boy himself.

This One's for the Birds

Tippi Hedren

The godforsaken edge of the Mojave Desert, north and west of Los Angeles near Acton, California, is hardly the habitat of choice for most movie stars (unless you're Steve McQueen on a dirt bike). But, then again, Tippi Hedren in 1997 was not your garden-variety leading lady.

Hedren, then 62, the stunning blonde with the icy reserve of Alfred Hitchcock's *The Birds* and *Marnie*, didn't give a whit about the Hollywood fast lane. And she didn't "do lunch" unless the end result benefited her one consuming passion—Shambala Preserve, a wildlife sanctuary of more than 70 exotic animals (64 of them big cats the day we visited) that roamed over 60 acres of Soledad Canyon that she and her ex-husband Noel Marshall set aside for that purpose in 1972.

"I think we were put on this earth to do more than just watch television and stuff our faces," she offered in a tone that suggests she does little of either. Hedren, for one, lives by that platitude telling us that if she can't zip up her bluejeans in the morning, she doesn't eat that day. Dressed in a leopard-print shirt and wearing a lion head ring and "Shambala" chain around her neck, Hedren seemed every bit as sleekly feline as the cheetahs and leopards that stalk her menagerie. The cats themselves didn't have to worry about bulging waistlines. "They're fed 700 lbs. of beef a day," she said.

"You don't become a fat bunny overnight," she said. "Suddenly you're another size and then you're fat. It really bothers me that Americans are so fat. It's obscene."

The day started early for Shambala's 11 staff (the word is Sanskrit for "A meeting place of peace and harmony for all beings, animal and human"). Hedren, who lived in a house on the grounds, told us she'd been up since 4 a.m., attending to business. In the house itself, wildlife art ("Art Ducko") was everywhere with an overage of cat pictures and sculptures. She pointed with pride to a plexiglass cube sheltering a bird's nest made entirely of lion's mane. It reminded us (though less unsettlingly) of the famous Texas Dust Bowl photo of a crow's nest that had been constructed entirely of barbed wire.

"Back in '72 there was nothing here," she said, giving the preserve a rather desultory scan. "We planted 800 trees, redirected the creek and dredged the pond over there." Hedren motioned to a marshy slough where Muscovy ducks and Mallards were busily paddling around. In stark contrast, across the creek, Shambala's two resident elephants were giving themselves the dustiest mud bath this side of a Tarzan movie.

"All of Hollywood thinks this is what I do," she protested, "but I need to work in movies because Shambala doesn't provide me with an income. It's strictly a nonprofit enterprise that gives sanctuary to animals that need a home—mainly the big cats; the predators."

Some of those cats, Hedren said, came to Shambala as rejected "pets" that grew too large and ominous for their human caretakers. "You can get a lion or tiger easier than getting a dog. They were never meant to be a house pet and never meant to be domesticated, never," she said about as emphatically as possible without shouting. "Anyone that thinks that is in for a rude awakening, a destroyed home and possibly death. That's the bottom line. We don't ever take these animals for granted. We don't think of them as pets even though there are some that we can walk alongside."

Shambala hadn't usurped Hedren's interest in movies at all but the preserve and its attending foundation, The Roar Foundation, are run entirely on donations, including her own substantial financial contributions. When we visited, Hedren's daughter Melanie Griffith and her (then) husband Antonio Banderas, were on the Foundation's advisory board, along with Betty White, Linda Blair, Loretta Swit and many other actors and non-actors.

Since starting the preserve, Hedren had put a couple of her homes and at least one large piece of commercial real estate on the auction block to keep the Chapter 11 creditors at bay. After nearly 25 years, her enthusiasm—her call of the wild—for providing a refuge for animals remained unabated. "None of the animals at Shambala have ever been in the wild," she said. "All of them depend on human care. Many arrived having suffered from gross mistreatment and neglect. With the expert care we provide, they are brought back to health and live out their lives in dignity."

Hedren referred to her life-long love of animals as a "birth affect"—something she'd harbored since she was a little girl growing up in the tiny farm town of Lafayette in southwestern Minnesota. Back then she also dreamed of becoming a champion figure skater with the Ice Capades, and practiced incessantly on area ponds and, later, on frozen lakes after the family moved to Minneapolis.

"Like most natives, I love Minnesota in the fall and spring, but you can have it the rest of the time," she laughed, referring to the bleak, exhausting winters and summers so humid it sometimes seems there's an anvil resting on your chest when you venture outside.

Hedren began her career modeling at Dayton's and Donaldson's Department Store fashion shows. "I got off the bus coming home from West High School (in Minneapolis) and this lady handed me a card and said, 'Would you have your mother bring you to Donaldson's Department Store? We'd like you to be a model in our Saturday fashion show.' Her name was Ella Knott. My mother brought me down there and that started my whole career."

Modeling led to commercial work—a lot of commercial work—for Hedren. "At one point I had 12 commercials running at one time," she said. "I made so much money that I took a trip around the world for four months." With her father ailing, the family decided to relocate from Minnesota to California. "It was so miserable to move during my teenage years," Hedren said. "It was so traumatic for me. The train station had never seen anything like it; 200 of my friends came down to say goodbye. My mother said I cried from Minneapolis to Omaha—about 250 miles, sobbing."

Hedren was in Los Angeles when a commercial of hers for Sego Milk aired during *The Today Show*. Sego Milk was a product with a high concentrate of Vitamin D, something Hedren said she herself needed badly at the time. "I weighed all of 100 lbs. when I did the commercial," she said. "I don't weigh much more than that now."

After seeing the commercial which aired for days on *The Today Show*, Hitchcock called Hedren and asked whether she'd like to appear in an animal movie—of sorts. Hedren, who felt her modeling career was waning, accepted. "I had rented an expensive home and was getting a little bit worried as to how I was going to pay for it, and that solved the problem which was great," she said.

Following the most expensive screen test in Hollywood history (it was shot over three days and featured script readings from such Hitchcock films as *Rebecca*, *Notorious* and *To Catch a Thief*), she was offered the role of "Melanie Daniels," the chic mantrap who fatefully pays a call on Rod Taylor in Bodega Bay just as the birds are massing to attack.

"I loved doing the tests," Hedren said. "Then we did extemporaneous stuff with Hitch and me talking. It was crazy. Two of them (tests) *Notorious* and *Rebecca*, had to be destroyed because Hitch didn't own the rights, but I heard that they do exist. I would love to find them and I don't know how to do it."

Hedren said that the bird trainer on set, Ray Berwick, was the irreplaceable conduit between her and all the avian extras. We mentioned the famous series of campy publicity stills that featured a puffy raven about the size of a pterodactyl perched on Hedren's arm. In one shot she's dressed in a formal ball gown and in another she's seated in a chair, the raven lighting her cigarette from a match in its beak.

"Say what you want about Hitchcock, those stills are pretty funny," Tom said.

"That was 'Buddy,'" Hedren grinned, identifying the bird. "He was slick."

Hedren said that everything culminated with the last scene where she goes to the attic to investigate a strange noise she hears, this after a bird attack on the house that makes the London Blitz look like Styrofoam gliders thrown at a kid's birthday party (suspension of disbelief for the scene is as mandatory now as it was in 1963). For the scene in which Hedren is attacked, she had been assured that mechanical birds were going to be used.

"The morning, Monday, we started shooting it, I was in my dressing room on set, the assistant director, Jim Brown, came in. I said, 'Jim, what's the matter with you?' He looked at the ceiling and the wall and the floor and I said, 'What's the matter with you?' He said, 'The mechanical birds don't work. We have to use real ones.' I just went, 'Oh, Jesus!'"

A cage had been built around the attic door that Hedren opens, and three prop men were there wearing leather gauntlets with huge cartons filled with ravens and seagulls which they hurled at her. The scene took five days to shoot.

"On Wednesday, Cary Grant visited the set and told me I was the bravest woman he ever met," Hedren said. "By Friday they had me on the floor of the attic, my dress torn to shreds from the talons of the birds."

According to Hedren, to achieve a more realistic effect, her dress was fitted with elastic bands that were then tied to the legs of some of the birds. "One broke loose and scratched me right under the eye," she said. "I started to cry from sheer exhaustion. Everybody left the set, they just left me there. I somehow got home that night. I met a friend for a drink and he later said that he never saw anyone as exhausted as I was. I got home and had to take care of my little girl, Melanie, because the nanny was off."

Hedren did suffer a sort of nervous shutdown after that scene. "On Monday morning I don't remember driving to work," she said. "I got into my dressing room and laid down on the couch. The makeup man couldn't wake me; the hairdresser couldn't wake me; the assistant director couldn't wake me. They got me home and the doctor called the studio and said I couldn't work. Hitch said, 'She has to, we have nothing else. She's the only thing in the movie.'"

Oblivious to Hitchcock's protestations, Hedren remembered sleeping for a solid week.

"It's so wonderful to be in a film that almost everyone has seen," Hedren said. "Now I'm running into people that haven't seen it—they're basically young kids. It's amazing how many young people come saying, "God, I saw it and it's scary!' It's still scary."

That said, Hedren took Hitchcock to task for hampering her career before it really got started, a movie debut that was sullied by his intractability and possessiveness. "After awhile I couldn't stand it anymore, but he wouldn't release me from my contract and so for two years (after *Marnie*) I didn't make a movie; I just sat around drawing my $500-a-week salary. After that, we never spoke to each other again.

"My advice to anyone contemplating acting as a profession is to be independently wealthy or have another vocation as a backup," Hedren continued. "Most actors make a pittance."

A word to the wise from an actress who had to stretch every dime to follow her true vocation; an animal sanctuary that became, in time, her sanctuary too—her pride and joy.

Holy Moses!—Heston on High

Charlton Heston

It's strangely appropriate that the actor who portrayed Moses and other historical heavyweights during an illustrious 60-year movie career would himself have lived atop a mountain. That was the case with Charlton Heston when we interviewed him first in 1980 and again in 1996. For more than 30 years, his piece of the rock had been a secluded parcel of real estate perched on top of Coldwater Canyon in Beverly Hills. Heston's land adjoined undeveloped acreage managed by the Los Angeles Water Department, thus furthering the illusion of a pastoral retreat, albeit a hideaway set against one of the largest urban areas in the U.S.—greater Los Angeles—that recedes endlessly in either direction from Heston's aerie.

It's the same house documentarian Michael Moore visited a few years later when he ambushed Heston (who may have been exhibiting early symptoms of subsequently diagnosed Alzheimer's disease) with questions about gun violence in *Bowling for Columbine*. Heston, a bulwark of conservative values, was the president and spokesman of the National Rifle Association from 1998 until he resigned in 2003. He died in 2008 at the age of 84.

For us, ascending to Heston's hilltop retreat didn't come close to approximating his biblical journey up Mt. Horeb under the watchful eye of Cecil B. DeMille, but it did require all the torque our sub-compact could muster. Still imposing at 73 when we met

Welcome to the gun show

him, Heston sported an Adidas polo shirt and shorts when he greeted us at the door. His broad shoulders and barrel chest tapered down to a thin waist and muscular (although slightly knock-kneed) legs—the product, no doubt, of hoisting cast-iron broadswords overhead and the dead weight of flintlock rifles to the ready position in scores of films over more than a half century.

Since screen images are so indelibly linked in the public's collective consciousness, for just an instant, we half expected Heston to perform a miracle and part his swimming pool for us as we moved to a workout room located just a punch volley away from his tennis court. Sadly, his binding pole/staff was not on the premises and the pool, although Olympic sized, was no Red Sea.

"Those Wood Ducks you see paddling around are always there," he said. "They'll probably never get to Canada."

Heston proved to be a mere mortal, humbly admitting that lucky casting afforded him the opportunity to play "larger than life" characters on the screen—Moses, Andrew Jackson, Judah Ben-Hur, John the Baptist and Michelangelo, to name just a few. "I've been a public face for more than 40 years," he said. "It has advantages and disadvantages. But don't get me wrong, the positives far outweigh the negatives."

The interview took place in a glass-enclosed hallway that afforded a grandstand view of the action on Heston's court. The hallway was stocked with buckets of tennis balls, a wealth of rackets, even a Universal Gym for weight training. In what seemed an unconscious attempt to dispel any thought that he might be guilty of conspicuous consumption, Heston said he was fully aware his hard-earned good fortune as an actor allowed him to indulge in the pleasures of the good life.

"The time I spent as president of the Screen Actors Guild gave me a wide and embittering understanding of the mortality rate in the acting profession in Hollywood," he said. "More than three-fourths of the members of the Guild made less than $2,500 last year. The brutal fact is that the overwhelming majority of actors don't act at all. To be in a tiny band of perhaps a dozen men and five women who can choose what film projects they want to do is a shining stroke of good fortune."

Heston fervently believed (he was fervent about many things) that the rampant unemployment among actors was a problem that could be credited to a historical lack of autonomy in the entertainment profession.

"The actor alone among artists can work only if someone gives him a job," he said. "A painter can pump gas all week for a living and then paint masterpieces in his furnished room or backyard. The novelist needs only to earn enough money outside his living to be able to buy pen and paper. But the actor cannot act at all unless someone volunteers, 'Here's a part, there's a stage, go do it!' It's a unique frustration."

The concern Heston felt for his fellow thespians wasn't blind sympathy. He served a stint as co-chairman of President Reagan's task force on the arts and humanities and in accordance with the tighten-the-belt doctrine of Reaganomics and Republican mandarins of the time, Heston believed arts funding shouldn't be exempt from cutbacks.

"If you're cutting school lunches then you'd better cut support for the San Francisco Ballet," he said. "I think the public marketplace has to be an appropriate factor in judging the validity of art. While some creative undertakings are less well-equipped to thrive in the marketplace than others, they all have to accept the responsibility to test themselves there. I understand that ballet productions are expensive to mount and that grand opera with a full house can't break even. If you can't break even, then what's happening? Theaters, orchestras, or any artistic endeavor that seeks to insulate itself entirely from mass public consumption can't make a very good case for itself for government funding."

Throughout his career, Heston showed a penchant for starring in epic box-office winners. He practically cornered the market in adaptations of stories from the Old and New Testaments. *Ben Hur* and *The Ten Commandments* are two biblical opuses that Heston admitted profoundly influenced his career. Working with DeMille (on *The Ten Commandments* and the Oscar-winning circus epic *The Greatest Show on Earth*) made an equally strong impression.

From the religious prophets of the ancient world to Elizabethan England and the tragedies of William Shakespeare, Heston always had an unerring eye for quality scriptwriters. "I've had the supreme satisfaction an actor can have, and that's the chance to try the great parts over and over again. I first performed *Macbeth* in school and I've done it five times since then. I figure I have one more left in me. Those combats at the end are the toughest fights in Shakespeare. They absolutely drain you. I fight with a broadsword and shield and sometimes with heavy war clubs—none of that light foil stuff like in *Hamlet*. Any actor properly trained can do combat, but the problem with the great roles is that you are already pouring on the energy knocking the bottom out of the barrel and then to come to the fifth act of *Macbeth* and say, 'OK, now the fights.'"

The great roles notwithstanding, Heston believed that creating art (like navigating the world of politics) also meant compromise and frustration. "I have never made a film or done a play where I felt the potential was realized," he said. "The whole creative process is one of failure, that's why you can spend a lifetime in quest of perfection. It is like Michelangelo (whom Heston played in *The Agony and the Ecstasy*) standing back from the Moses statue after working on it for two years, then throwing his hammer at it and saying, 'Why don't you speak?' If Michelangelo could be dissatisfied with his work, then the rest of us bloody well better be."

While younger audiences may not know him as Moses, despite the regular Easter-time TV airing of *The Ten Commandments*, Heston's continued appearances in films, such as the 1994 hit *True Lies*, in which he played Arnold Schwarzenegger's menacing, eye-patch wearing boss, introduced him to a new generation of filmgoers. Add to that his portrayal of a nefarious poacher in the 1996 film *Alaska* directed by his son Fraser, and a co-starring role in Kenneth Branagh's *Hamlet*, it's no wonder when we pressed him to name his favorite film, Heston replied, "I don't know, I'm not through yet!"

In order to get a fuller perspective of Heston, we called up Fraser at his L.A. office. Heston's son, you could say, was a "born" movie actor, who made an auspicious movie debut as the baby Moses cast adrift into the Nile by his mother to save him from Pharaoh's death decree to the Hebrews in *The Ten Commandments*.

"Dad told me that DeMille was a real stickler for detail," Fraser said. "They cast me off in a real pauper's basket lined with pitch. Unfortunately, no one checked to see if the basket could even float. I quickly sank to the bottom of what is now the executive parking lot at Paramount. My father had to jump in and rescue me."

Fraser recalled that his father encouraged his wish to become a writer and later a director. "He realized very much that I wanted to be a storyteller," Fraser said. "And a director is the ultimate storyteller. However, he did discourage me from becoming an actor. He was very circumspect about it and said its tough work; further, that being the son of a famous movie actor doesn't guarantee success."

* * *

Fantle & Johnson: *In the movie* Alaska, *Fraser, directed you. How would you assess him as a director, especially vis-à-vis some of the all-time greats with whom you've worked?*

Heston: Fraser is a good director. He also has the enormous advantage in directing me because he knows me very well and he knows that I like to be pressed. Nowadays I almost always work for directors who are younger than me, and dare I say, greener in reputation. This situation usually results in an extraordinary deference, which is not useful to me as an actor. They'll say, "Chuck, that take was marvelous. Could we just do one more to be sure." I'll reply, "Hell, let's do five takes until I give you exactly what you want!" Fraser understands that those niceties are trivial and he gives me a frank assessment."

You've even taken a turn at the helm, directing such actors as Sir John Gielgud in a TV version of A Man of All Seasons.

My major flaw is that I am too kind to actors. Being an actor myself, I know it is hard when you are striving to get something that by definition is probably unattainable. I tend to praise actors too much—and some need a lot of coddling. Gielgud, for one, was not interested in praise. He presumed he would be good, and he was. Many directors and actors like to talk endlessly about their scenes. It's like jacking-off; it's fun, but it really doesn't accomplish anything. If you have questions, explore them, but the time to talk about a scene is on your own time with the director, over a beer. Shooting time is too important.

You worked with directors William Wyler and Cecil B. DeMille on two biblical blockbusters, Ben-Hur *and* The Ten Commandments. *What were their particular styles like?*

Wyler's instinct for performance was the best I've ever seen. He would shoot several takes, but he wouldn't tell you what he wanted done differently because he really didn't know himself. He was just probing and searching for the best performance he could extract. DeMille was always very courteous to me and especially to actors at a time when it wasn't very fashionable to be polite to actors. He would always address them as ladies and gentlemen, not, "Hey you!" If he shot in the fall of the year, he would take great pains to shoot long and elaborate sequences that required a lot of extras. That way, he felt these people would be employed at a time when they could use a little extra money for the holidays. He gave me my first big break as the circus manager in *The Greatest Show on Earth*. If you can't make it fly with two DeMille pictures, it ain't gonna get off the ground.

Your recollections of DeMille don't jibe with some reports that he was a real fire-eater!

I think he earned that reputation in his younger days. The two pictures I made with him were the last films he ever directed. He was in his 70s then. Don't get me wrong, he was quite authoritative. You've got to remember that for more than 40 years he had been one of the best known directors in the business and that shaped his personality. He was formal and really quite magisterial, I guess you could say.

Have you ever not taken on a Shakespearean role? You always seem to jump at the chance to play the great parts, the latest being your role in Branagh's Hamlet.

Every time you get a chance to waltz with the old gentlemen, you have to do it, especially as an American actor, you don't get that many chances. Obviously, I was never right for the title role in *Hamlet*: bass voice, 6 ft. 3, broken nose—that's not right. It would be a one-act play. The great parts are all unachievable, really. I've done *Macbeth* five times and still have not gotten it right. I'm striving in roles that other actors have been trying to whip for four fucking centuries! As far as Shakespeare is concerned, I was attracted to parts that I was physically right for—Henry the V, Macbeth and Marc Anthony. I first played Macbeth—badly, no doubt—in high school. I got the part because even at 14, I had a bass voice.

In The Big Country, *another Wyler film from 1958, you had to be persuaded to take a supporting role as the hot-headed ranch foreman. Cut to 1994 and your small part in* True Lies; *are you comfortable at this stage of your career to cede the leads and assume character parts?*

Of course. Jim Cameron (the director of *Titanic* and *The Terminator*) offered me the part and I asked him, as I ask every director, "Why do you want me to take this role?" He said that he needed me for the role because he required someone who could intimidate Arnold Schwarzenegger in his agent role. I told Cameron I could do that because I've been playing those kinds of parts all my life. To make the guy more menacing I came up with the idea of wearing the eye patch. I figured the guy had probably been an OSS guy during World War II, parachuting into Yugoslavia to cut German throats. Along the way, it's conceivable that he lost an eye.

You are perhaps Hollywood's best-known political conservative. What do you see as your role in political campaigns?

I think the role of surrogate, which I play in political campaigns, is widely misunderstood. Happily, it's most often misunderstood by Hollywood liberals who think they're contributing to a campaign by hitching a ride on Air Force One, or going to a White House dinner. That has nothing to do with a campaign. A president or presidential candidate really feels perfectly capable of electing himself—and he'd better believe that. They sometimes want you to show up at the big rallies. I think I can make more of an impact on behalf of congressional and senatorial candidates. I do two things for a campaign—I get people to show up at fundraisers, and I can usually turn out the media to cover an event.

Liberal causes have always been de rigueur in Hollywood. Do you think your outspoken stance on such issues as less government and the right to bear arms has had an adverse effect on your ability to land certain film roles?

The obvious presumption is that I lose roles because I'm a conservative. I refuse to accept that. I would be deeply distressed if that were true. It's different for younger filmmakers who happen to be conservative. They tell me, "Chuck, nobody's *not* going to hire you because everybody knows you are a political conservative, you've always been a conservative like John Wayne. But it's different for us." If they think that is true for them, O.K., but I have never had that feeling about myself.

Many people don't realize that you were active in the early Civil Rights Movement.

That fact insulates me from some criticism. There are certain things that political opponents dare not say about me—for instance, that I am a racist. The Democratic Party shifted to the left in the 1960s after Jack Kennedy was killed. I don't think that's why the shift occurred, but nonetheless it happened. My politics are exactly the same as they were at the beginning.

You met your wife Lydia while attending Northwestern University outside Chicago and have been married for more than 50 years now. Can such a long and exclusive run be chocked up, perhaps, to Midwestern family values?

It really depends on picking the right girl in the first place. I suppose you could say, though, that I believe in the strength of Midwestern values. I am a Midwesterner. It's the center of the country—it really is.

* * *

We descended from Heston's high place the way we came, *sans* any inscribed stone tablets but enlightened by what we felt were a few elemental verities about the man and his profession, all delivered without the faintest aromatic hint of bullshit attached. Just straight talk from one Midwesterner to a couple of others. Thank God!

All the Best Lines

Al Hirschfeld

Al Hirschfeld, late caricaturist of *The New York Times,* spoke volumes with a single, sinuous line. And he did it continuously—every week, in fact—in a career that spanned an astonishing 80 years.

The inveterate New Yorker came from a rich tradition of distinguished theatrical caricaturists that include Ralph Barton, Al Frueh, Miguel Covarrubias (who had the greatest influence on Al's style), all the way back to English caricaturist Max Beerbohm in the late 1800s. Hirschfeld's economical drawing style of pure, calligraphic line in black ink is inimitable, classic and as instantly recognizable in its own right as a ballad by Sinatra or a dance by Astaire.

With work enshrined in the permanent collections of the Metropolitan Museum of Art and the Museum of Modern Art, Hirschfeld has become a certifiable national treasure and is considered one of the most important figures in contemporary drawing and caricature, having influenced just about anyone who ever picked up a pen with the intent to doodle.

For generations of *Times* "Arts and Leisure" Sunday supplement readers, finding Hirschfeld's "Nina's" craftily camouflaged in his drawings was as revered a tradition as grappling with the iconic, diabolically difficult crossword puzzle.

A couple years back, the New-York Historical Society (NYHS) presented an exhibition called "The Hirschfeld Century: The Art of Al Hirschfeld" which was apropos since the artist chronicled much of the 20th Century. We took in the exhibition which featured a trove of more than 100 of Al's original works shortly after it opened.

The exhibition explored Hirschfeld's career chronologically beginning with his pre-caricature days at Selznick Pictures in the early 1920s to his last drawings in theater, film, television, music and dance in 2002. We then spoke with David Leopold who curated the NYHS exhibition and has written the definitive book (*The Hirschfeld Century: Portrait of an Artist and His Age*) chronicling Al's life and career.

"It was good to put 25 years of research into one place," Leopold said about his book. "I started working with Hirschfeld in 1990 on an exhibition for the New York Public Library about theatrical illustration. We hit it off and I was asked to organize his archive. He was 86 at the time; I was 25 and thought, 'Well, the job will last about two years at most because, after all, who lives that long?' It went on for 13 years."

According to Leopold, Hirschfeld didn't draw for immortality but in order to solve graphic questions that he himself created. "When it gets down to it, people look at Hirschfeld drawings because of the drawing itself," he said. "Al really created a vocabulary all of his own. He's not the best at what he does; he's the only one who does it.

"When we talk about caricature in the 20th century, we don't talk about anyone else; he is the field," Leopold continued. "Because his work wasn't limited to one entertainment genre exclusively (Hirschfeld did movie posters and advertisements as well as theatrical caricatures), it's a much shorter list of who he *didn't* draw."

The potential endurance of Hirschfeld's fame can perhaps best be seen in the way millennials react to his drawings. "They don't have a visceral response to Carol Channing or Zero Mostel or even Katharine Hepburn or the Marx Brothers," Leopold said. "Those stars are names to them but they don't have the personal experience that you or I have and yet they are responding to Al's drawings in a way that perhaps you and I can't because they are looking at just the drawing and they aren't clouded by their recollections of seeing the stars on stage or in film when they were younger."

Back in the late 1970s, we had lunch with Al and his wife, former German actress Dolly Haas, at their Manhattan brownstone on East 95th street off Lexington Avenue. In the months prior, we had written to Hirschfeld saying that we would like to meet him; and added almost as a postscript that we also had plans to travel up the Connecticut coast to Old Saybrook to interview Maggie Held, cartoonist John Held Jr.'s widow, for a story later to appear in the arts section of the *Minnesota Daily*, the student newspaper of the University of Minnesota.

More than any other pop culture artifact, the caricatures and cartoons of Held personified the 1920s—an era of hot jazz and all-night, booze-filled parties where gold-digging flappers Charlestoned their way into sugar daddies' hearts. Held's whimsical watercolors of ship launchings, society parties and the collegiate life of "Joe College and Betty Co-ed" appeared in magazines such as *Smart Set, Life, Judge* and *Vanity Fair* and had a flitting resonance that perfectly suited the "live it up now" philosophy of that roaring decade.

"Why don't you come 'round for lunch before you go up and see Maggie," Al said over the telephone in a sonorous voice that betrayed his St. Louis, Missouri roots. "I have something to say about John that you might find interesting for your article."

A cross between a Sephardic Santa Claus and a majorly cute garden gnome, Al had a pointy beard that looked like it had just been dipped in a can of silver spray paint. It reminded us of the scene in the Marx Brothers movie *A Day at the Races* when Groucho says to a glowering Sig Ruman who towers over him with a similar tapered goatee: "Don't point that beard at me, it might go off!" Al's wife Dolly who had her hair cinched so tightly in a perfectly formed bun the hairdo could've come straight from the counter at Entenmann's, was given to theatrical flourishes that included even the way she poured Italian red into the wine glasses.

At the lunch was Edward Chodorov, an old friend of Al's, and his wife. Chodorov was a Hollywood screenwriter (*Undercurrent* with Katharine Hepburn and Robert Mitchum; *Road House* with Ida Lupino and Richard Widmark) who was blacklisted in 1953 after being outed as a Communist Party member by choreographer Jerome Robbins.

Al and Dolly really seemed to enjoy the strange bedfellows' game of mixing two college entertainment journalists with a Hollywood veteran. In fact, lunch was a real *gemütlich* affair, rollicking with anecdotes about the Broadway Theater, movies and just the everyday theatrics of living in New York City. (Dolly's dramatic soliloquy of the strategy needed to cadge a seat on a crowded cross-town bus during rush hour seemed to rival in meticulous planning the preparations for storming the Normandy beaches on D-Day.)

All the while, Hirschfeld just leaned back in his dining room chair, an impish gleam in his eyes, and observed; something he had been doing, sketchbook in hand, for a half-century from orchestra seats in countless theaters.

Al told us that John Held's eventual toppling from glory in the 1930s as the country's most popular cartoonist was due to a technical Achilles' heel. "John couldn't sketch full-length dresses," Al said. "He was unparalleled in his ability to draw young girls in short skirts, but in the 1930s when long dresses were in vogue, Russell Patterson took over from John as the cartoonist *du jour*.

"Say," he suddenly brightened, "would you guys like to see where I work?"

We followed Al from the dining room up several flights of stairs to where he worked on the top (fourth) floor. Along the way we passed a living room that had a fireplace bordered with color tiles of caricatures that Hirschfeld had painted and possibly fired himself in a kiln. On one wall, adjacent to the stairway and partially obscured by a grand piano, was an eight-foot tall mural that Al had painted; a brilliant jumble of stars including, Charlie Chaplin, Frank Sinatra, Louis Armstrong, Marilyn Monroe and Stan Laurel and Oliver Hardy.

Laurel & Hardy caught napping (1928) (© The Al Hirschfeld Foundation. www.AlHirshfeld Foundation.org)

We finally made to the fourth-floor studio where Al's easel seemed to swallow the room. Pushed up to it was a barber chair that he sat in while working. We thought the odd pairing of an artist's easel with a barber chair was the kind of thing another famed cartoonist might have conjured—Rube Goldberg to be exact—but Al explained.

"I just find it works best for me especially for large sketches," he said. "Using the lever on the side of the chair, I can adjust my position whenever I need to and don't even have to get up."

One of the highlights of the "Hirschfeld Century" exhibition was Al's famous mixed-media drawing for MGM Studios of Laurel and Hardy in bed covered by a riotously-colored blanket made from a collage of wallpaper samples. The effect is stunning and to our minds a zany reimagining of another famous picture: Klimt's "Lady in Gold" portrait of Adele Bloch-Bauer which hangs in the Neue Galerie just across Central Park from the NYHS. To give his portrait texture, Klimt labored tirelessly applying gold leaf; for Hirschfeld, it was wallpaper samples. Refined or rough-hewn, beauty is in the eye of the beholder and supreme artistry, wit, and the ability to capture character via caricature is in every Hirschfeld rendering. It was his genius.

In trying to encapsulate Hirschfeld's legacy, Leopold said: "The names and the shows will fall away, but the drawings won't."

Al died at the age of 99 in 2003 at home in his beloved New York City—the end of a long line.

On the Road with "Old Ski Nose"

Bob Hope

In 1980, when we had our first interview with Bob Hope, he was long established as one of show business' most venerated performers. Yet, at the mere mention of his "legendary" status, Hope blanched and squirmed uncomfortably on the couch on which he was sitting.

"Oh Christ!" he told us, "A legend is someone who had a great past, and I just don't like to think about that. I look forward to what I'll be doing tomorrow. I'm an entertainer. I have to worry about my next show. If you start believing this legend stuff, you're in trouble."

There's no doubt that his name conjures up different emotions among the several generations he touched. For the veterans of every American conflict from World War II to the Gulf War, Hope and his band of show business gypsies brought humor and a bit of home to war-weary troops stationed in all corners of the world. To the anti–Vietnam War protesters of the 1960s, Hope represented a right wing hawk who never met a conflict he didn't like; and to the people who grew up in the '80s and '90s, he was an elderly, cue-card-reading comedian who sleep-walked through cornball sketches with the likes of Brooke Shields and Connie Stevens as comic foils.

Throughout his career, Hope publicly paid credit and expressed deep appreciation to his "army" of writers who—at a moment's notice—provided him with topical gags tailored to meet any occasion. A comedian performing without good material is like being exposed to an audience naked. And throughout his career, thanks to his gagmen, Hope was fully clothed. To his enduring credit, Hope brought something else to the equation that rivals the importance of the material itself—masterful timing. Like two of his contemporaries, George Burns and Jack Benny, Hope had impeccable sense about when to unload the kicker. His gags often had the speed of a machine gun ("Rapid Robert" was a nickname of his) delivered with the insouciance of a Saturday night drunk.

Because of his continually booked calendar, Hope even then didn't figure on anyone's list of most accessible movie stars. Yet during a week of performances at the Carlton Celebrity Room in Bloomington, Minnesota, he sat down with us in his hotel suite for a few minutes of supervised (by his wife) chat.

Hope's dinner show at the Carlton presented a patriotic medley of songs, jokes, a couple of tunes sung by his wife Dolores and a cameo appearance by his poodle, Tobey, who scampered onstage and ate off the dinner plates nearest the stage. Dolores and Bob were married 69 years up until Hope's death at age 100 in 2003. Dolores died eight years later at age 102.

After a quick change, we met Hope who was dressed in khakis, a short-sleeved sport shirt and wearing Sperry Topsiders. In tune with Minnesota's sweltering summer, Hope looked as though he could have just docked a Starcraft boat at Lord Fletcher's on Lake Minnetonka on the way to quaffing a few Grain Belt Premiums.

With him was Dolores, a muscle-bound bodyguard (a former "Mr. Minnesota" we later learned), and their ravenous pooch that Hope cradled like a new-born infant during much of the interview. Off to the side of the room was an aluminum portable massage table that doubtless performed yeoman's service in keeping Hope's posture ramrod straight as well as facilitating his classic gliding saunter on- and offstage.

"Hi guys, how ya doin'?" Hope greeted us in that nasally high-pitched voice familiar to generations of moviegoers and TV viewers. That nose, the septum source of the piercing decibel level and one of the most famously caricatured facial features of any comedian, dropped precipitously and then arched up infinitesimally at the end so much so that Tom whispered he hadn't seen a slope that dramatic since he had last skied Afton Alps.

Hope springs eternal

An odd thing about Hope, perhaps because he had been asked (and had answered) every conceivable question about his career over the past 50 years, he had become a master of false verbal transitions. Journalistically speaking, transitions are the setups between paragraphs or ideas that make a story flow; in essence, the connectivity that helps to make a story a story. At the end of Hope's discourse about various aspects of his career, he'd "transition" into new topics with such lines as: "No, but I enjoy it," or "I wanna tell ya..." The throwaway lines really were apropos of nothing and weren't germane to what had just been discussed but they served their purpose in keeping Hope semi-interested and the conversation flowing.

We wanna tell ya, we were thankful for that!

* * *

Fantle & Johnson: *You have such a constant lack of privacy. How do you deal with it?*

Hope: Dolores and I have so much privacy in our schedule, my goodness. We go down to Palm Springs and stay there 10 days. Nobody bothers us. We live high up on a hill, and we get to the golf course and meet just the people we want to meet. It's only when I travel that I get so many requests to meet people.

How did you first get involved with the United Service Organizations (USO)?

I started working for it at its inception in 1941. I went to an Air Force base not knowing what I was doing. The audiences were so great that I decided to do more and kept doing it and doing it. When war was declared, it became very dramatic. We went and did our radio shows for five years at military bases. We did only two shows in those five years back in Hollywood. Then we quit for two years and did the Berlin Airlift. We did USO shows for 31 years and it's the most gratifying experience I've ever had. I get letters every day from people I entertained at those shows. Tonight somebody brought back a USO picture of all of us in Africa for me to autograph.

How did you land your first motion picture contract?

I was in *The Ziegfeld Follies* singing, "I Can't Get Started (with You)," which I introduced. I was singing it to a redheaded showgal who later turned out to be Eve Arden. A producer and director saw me, and they said, "We want you for *The Big Broadcast of 1938.*"

How long did it take before you realized that "Thanks for the Memory" was going to be your signature song?

I got a pretty good idea of it when the song was voted an Oscar and BMI named it the song of the year. I adopted it immediately for my radio show—*The Pepsodent Show*—way before you guys were born. It turned into something … I wanna tell you.

What are your remembrances of working with W.C. Fields in The Big Broadcast of 1938?

W.C. Fields was something else. He was tremendous and a great ad-libber. They used to let the camera run on him hoping he'd say something brilliant. After a scene, they wouldn't yell cut, they'd just keep rolling. I remember a shipwreck scene when he ad-libbed, "Ah, they're jumpin' overboard. There go the women, the women are jumpin' before the kids; the men are jumpin' before women…" He kept talking. Finally he looked into the camera and said, "They'll run out of film pretty soon."

How did you first get teamed with Bing Crosby?

We worked together for two weeks in 1932 at the Capitol Theater in New York. I was master of ceremonies and Bing was singing. We got to fooling around and doing bits together. When I was contracted to Paramount Studios in 1937, Bing owned a piece of the Del Mar racetrack and he invited me down for the Saturday night gala. We did the bit that we had done five years earlier at the Capitol. There was a producer there, in fact, the same producer who hired me for *The Big Broadcast of 1938*. He saw us work together and exclaimed, "Those guys really hit it off!" That's how *Road to Singapore* came about, and we were on our way. We made seven *Road* pictures together and were due to make the eighth when Bing died. I would like to do the eighth with George Burns.

How much, if any, were the Road *pictures ad-libbed?*

I would say 20 percent. Those writers were marvelous; they knew construction so well. They knew how to get us into trouble and how to get us out. I had just started a radio show with 13 of the best writers who ever lived—now they're all producers and directors; Mel Frank, Norman Panama, Jack Rose, Jack Douglas. I would give them the script and they would dash off material for me. I would then go to Bing and say, "What do you think of this, and this…" He'd say, "Oh, that's marvelous." So we would use the lines. Now the first picture, we ad-libbed so much, and they laughed so much on the set that *TIME* magazine said we had ad-libbed the entire script. It hurt Don Hartman, one of the original writers. He was really wounded. He came onto the set one day during the filming of *Road to Zanzibar* and was listening to the dialogue. I shouted to him, "If you hear one of your lines, yell bingo." That made him furious. But when the picture was selected for the New York Film Critics Award, he started smiling and saying that our spontaneity was what made the films so successful. Audiences used to die, they didn't hear half the jokes they laughed so much.

How do you think comedy has changed through the years, if at all?

Comedy has changed in the last 25 years. They're doing things in person and on the screen that I would never have dreamed they'd get away with. I think it is a sad commentary to see total crudity in comedy. I hate to see it in pictures or anywhere, but especially in pictures because they are endorsements and documents that we send around the world. People must think Americans are a bunch of dirty-mouthed, oversexed people. But thank God you can see pictures like *Raiders of the Lost Ark*, *Superman II* and *Star Wars*, which make all the money. It's shaking up a lot of people. I remember when *I Am Curious (Yellow)* came out. That dirty stag film cost about $35,000 to make and they grossed $15 million. That was the start of all those dirty pictures. The producers said, "Oh, we can get away with it," then everybody started hopping into bed. There was a film I went to see when I performed here last year called *North Dallas Forty*. I love football. Mac Davis was in it, and he's a good friend of mine. We play golf together so I had to see it. I took a cab out to a neighborhood theater, the Roseville IV. Let me tell you the filth in that picture. At the finish there was one word on the screen that I had never heard before. I walked out disgusted.

What do you think of President Reagan's budget cuts for the arts?

I'm baffled by it all. I just don't know how he is going to make it work. He's got the confidence of the people, thank God. And the polls show that they're going to give him a great chance, which is something new. He's got a wonderful group of guys around him, so I think they'll work it out some way. He's got more guts than any president I've seen. To stand up in front of the air traffic controllers union, say what he thinks, and get away with it.

Do Asian countries that you perform in really appreciate your brand of humor? Can they understand it?

In China I had a good interpreter at the Peking College. I showed them my picture *Monsieur Beaucaire*, and I went around back to listen to them. They laughed like hell at it. I mean they really dug it. Because it was about a poor barber fighting the system. I was amazed at how fast they caught on to my humor.

Working on a film doesn't allow you the luxury of immediate audience feedback. Is that why you haven't made more movies lately?

Not at all. The reason I haven't made so many films is because I haven't seen anything I've wanted to make. A movie is a document that lives forever—I have 60 of them out. I was performing in a little town called Owensboro, Kentucky recently, so Sunday morning I turned on the television. *My Favorite Brunette* was showing with Peter Lorre and Dorothy Lamour. Dolores and I were enjoying it I must say, when on comes a commercial and right after that they started to repeat the previous reel of the movie. I tried to get hold of the station manager, but it was being broadcast out of Indianapolis. The guy in charge probably pushed the button twice and then went back to sleep. At the finish of *Brunette*, I'm about to be executed in the electric chair, but I get a last-minute reprieve. Bing did a cameo as the warden. He was heartbroken that I got off scot-free.

Have you ever been asked to run for public office?

Yes I have. There was a radio poll held up in Seattle asking if they'd vote for me if I ran for the presidency. I didn't know anything about it, but 81 percent of the people said yes. The news got back to Washington and a couple of senators came out to see me about it. One was Senator John Tower of Texas.

Last political question. You supported Reagan for the presidency, yet came out in favor of gun control. Why?

I asked him about it, and I think his argument is very weak, especially since he's been shot. You know, a lot of states have gun control. California has gun control. I wish they would get real tough about it. I don't know why a guy can get doped up, buy a gun and then shoot up a town. If there would have been gun control in Memphis when they first found (John) Hinckley with those three guns, they might have grabbed him and looked into his head—there were a few things mixed up there. I don't know why the hell they ever let him go. Jim Brady looks like he's ruined forever. Reagan is damn lucky.

I guess it's a reflection of the times. It does seem a sad state of affairs when you now see police on horseback patrolling Hollywood Boulevard at night.

Hollywood Boulevard is a real zoo. I hate to think what those loonies are doing to my cement star on the Walk of Fame. They're probably cleaning their feet on it!

It's no secret that you've been an outspoken conservative, yet you remain extremely popular on college campuses. How do you account for that?

That's easy to understand. Students are very fair about everything. They look for ideals. They told me Columbia University was a nest of liberals. I did a show there and they turned out to be one of my best audiences ever. I've found that students have the ability to separate my personal political beliefs from the bipartisan comedy I perform on stage.

How do you account for your amazing longevity?

It's a tough, tough business. You have to keep coming up with things all the time. When I started at Paramount in 1938 I had the invaluable grounding of stage and radio behind me. I worked my way up until I was number one. From that time on I had a pretty solid rock to stand on.

Why is it that after the 1960s you, for all intents and purposes, stopped making films?

I haven't read anything I've liked. First of all, my television and personal appearance schedule has been tremendous. I am doing a film on newspaperman Walter Winchell, which should be released in April or November of 1981. The picture will be along the lines of *The Seven Little Foys*, a film I made about 25 years ago. I'll enjoy doing this because the story will have a lot of everything—drama, comedy, music, show business and journalism. (Hope never made the Winchell movie.)

What's your secret for staying so active and vital?

The secret to staying youthful is to have fun. If people could only get a laugh every day, I think it's the most important thing in the world because many people never exercise their laugh lines. They stay grumpy. When an audience laughs at one of my jokes I get a good feeling inside. My wife once said to me, "Boy, this is a lot of work." This isn't work to me. It's fun. When you do one show a night and play golf every day and meet a lot of friends, you're having a ball.

* * *

In the 15 years since Hope's death, his fame which was all-encompassing, even gargantuan in his heyday, has slowly dimmed, especially among younger generations. Perhaps it's due to the fact that his chief legacy is a decades-long run of almost continuous radio and TV shows in which he starred or appeared. The indefatigable Hope even hosted the Oscars a record 19 times between 1939 and 1977 (distant runner-up Billy Crystal has just nine emcee stints under his cummerbund). But radio stardom isn't what it once was before the advent of television and TV notoriety is itself fleeting. Out of sight, out of mind.

It seems inevitable then that Hope's once impermeable legacy is destined to fade until only vestigial traces will be available on view in digital archives, at vintage film festivals or in the hearts and minds of a dwindling pool of fans.

Eighteen years after we sat with Hope, Delores, Tobey and Mr. Minnesota, on the occasion of Hope's 95th birthday, we received an email out of the blue from one of those fans, a veteran who preferred to remain anonymous. He had been surfing the Net and had seen an old story we'd written about the comedian so he sent us a poem that he fervently wished Hope would read because, he said, it came "straight from the heart."

Happy birthday, Mr. Hope,
You had a life like a kaleidoscope.
You changed your life for
*   a special reason,*
Giving us pleasure
*   from season to season.*
I hear your name and a smile is seen,
One a prince would give
*   his king and queen.*
You see, I saw you one holiday,
*   in a faraway land on Christmas Day.*
My mother would sit by the TV and cry,
*   praying to God that I would not die.*
But I told her of my seeing your show,
And it was a special memento.
For a man to leave his
*   family and love,*

Will get special treatment
from God above.
Yes, your name brings a smile
and I do not mope.
God bless you and happy birthday,
Mr. Hope.

And thanks for the memory.

"To the Greats Without a Microphone"

George Jessel

We'd heard of Georgie Jessel but never quite knew exactly why he had once been famous. To us, he was the self-proclaimed "Toastmaster General of the U.S.A."; an old geezer who wore a Purple Heart medal on his tuxedo, hosted social affairs at the Friar's Club for other stars that hailed from his own era (vaudeville of the early teens and Broadway of the 1920s) and delivered eulogies at their funerals—often in quick succession.

Definitely old school.

Our earliest recollections of Jessel—or Jessel by proxy—included a hilarious late-night television sketch that Rob Reiner did before he attained larger fame as a movie director. Reiner lampooned the comedian, portraying him as the oblivious host of a telethon called: "Stop Death in Our Lifetime." His characterization was on the mark, right down to Jessel's toupee, be-ribboned tuxedo and thick, Lower East Side dialect which was a spot-on match to the marble-mouthed voice of the Carvel ice cream pitchman exhorting TV viewers to buy "Fudgie the Whale" cakes.

All in all, Jessel's existence, or at least the reality of how he lived when we met him in 1980 (he was 82 then), reminded us of one of Norma Desmond's "waxworks" dinner party guests in *Sunset Boulevard*.

However, due to our ongoing interest in the extinct American art form known as vaudeville, we had a desire to interview Jessel, who—forgotten relic or not—was a staple in that form of entertainment from the time he was a mere 10 years old. He performed along with fellow kids Eddie Cantor and Walter Winchell in an act staged by impresario and songwriter Gus Edwards called "Gus Edwards' Kid Kabaret."

During our visit with Jessel in his Los Angeles–area home (Reseda in the San Fernando Valley, to be exact), his eccentricity was in full flower. Attired in a black beret that would have made Albert Camus feel at home, bathrobe and slippers and sitting in a recliner, Jessel played us like we were a couple of wide-eyed rubes sitting front row center at the Palace Theater 70 years ago.

Jessel's housekeeper seemed nonplussed by our presence although we guessed visitors to Jessel's home must have been few and far between. She perched herself on a kitchen stool and didn't once shift her gaze from the Sunday *Los Angeles Times*. Flies buzzed around her, and the smoke from her cigarette curled lazily upward creating a smudge pot protective zone around her from the bothersome insects.

"I just talked with Burns [George]," Jessel bellowed from his La-Z-Boy. "How is he?" we asked. "Making millions," he replied nonchalantly, betraying just a trace of envy, we thought.

What attracted our attention even more than Jessel's less-than-formal attire was his home. He was a living endorsement for Swanson TV dinners with half-eaten meals encrusted on aluminum trays that were splayed all over the kitchen counter. We noticed a few of his cats making quick work of the leftovers that were beginning to spoil in the mid-day heat of the Valley and waft their odors over to us. Aside from the mess, the house was a veritable museum of show business artifacts. And Jessel took great delight in directing us to strategic points on the wall where autographed photos of the queen of England, Golda Meir, Eleanor

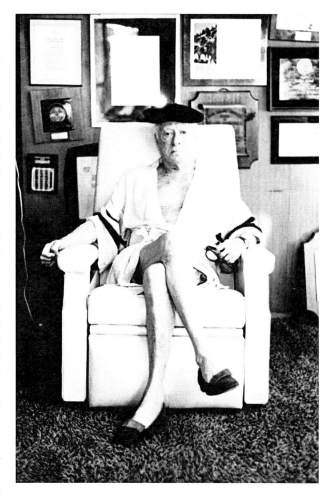

Jessel among his souvenirs

Roosevelt, several U.S. presidents and dozens of show business celebrities reposed in cheap, thrift store frames.

"Look over there on the left wall," he commanded us. "Do you know who that is?"

We scrutinized a headshot of a toothy blonde woman, "We don't have a clue, Mr. Jessel."

"It's the 'Happy Hooker' herself, Xaviera Hollander," Jessel said, sounding a trifle let down.

In the 1960s, Hollander had been a $1,000-a-night call girl and the most notorious madam in New York City with a brothel called The Vertical Whorehouse. In the early '70s she wrote about all of it in her bestselling memoir, *The Happy Hooker*.

After the photos, came a trip down memory lane; a blow by blow description of his medals, militaria and various awards. Among the collection of oddities was an ivory-tipped cane given to him by Harry Truman, an honorary Oscar and numerous awards he received for his humanitarian work, much of it in support of Israel.

When the tour ended, Jessel recalled for us his memories of playing the Orpheum Vaudeville Circuit as part of the "Kid Kabaret" in 1911 when he was 13 years old. "I never danced in the act, but I did imitations of some of the stars who were famous in those days," he said. "Eddie Cantor used to imitate Al Jolson. Do you want to know an interesting fact? Jolson never saw a microphone until he was 68 years old."

We asked him what kind of parental care or protection he received when traversing the country at such a young age. "At first my mother took care of me. She also was the wardrobe master for the troupe. But later Cantor watched over me. He was much older than me."

Jessel remembered our hometown audience of St. Paul, Minnesota as being rather cold to performers. "And it had nothing to do with your climate," he quipped.

From vaudeville, Jessel went on to success on the Broadway stage. His biggest hit came when he played the title role in the theatrical version of *The Jazz Singer*. "I did 1,000 performances in that play," he said. "When it came time to make the film, Warner Bros. put out an option to buy it, but they didn't have enough scratch to buy a cheese sandwich. Jolson put up the money, made the film and saved the studio."

After eight Broadway shows, Jessel moved to Hollywood where he produced 20 mostly "B-movies" for famed studio head Darryl Zanuck at 20th Century–Fox. Jessel's career in his later years mainly consisted of delivering heartfelt panegyrics to dead show business friends, hosting dinners and fundraisers, writing a syndicated newspaper column and making occasional appearances on TV talk shows. He also filmed a cameo in the Warren Beatty film *Reds* where he talked with authority about the New York stage during the World War I–era. But most of Jessel's time back then was spent hitting the stump and speaking out against liberal causes and what he said was the growing moral decay of America.

"I've been banned from network television for nearly seven years. I made an attack on *The New York Times* and *The Washington Post*. I called them the *Pravda* of the West.

"Take television for instance," he ranted. "The curse of America is right in that box. It has captured America's mind. The worst thing about TV is its impact on politics. Moses stuttered. He would have been murdered on TV! I was a vice president at ABC for over a year. They had meetings every day with advertising companies. At these meetings the public is never mentioned. If he's got the money, he can buy the time and put your Aunt Minnie on. I don't think anyone should criticize any actor on television. When you finish a script, it goes to the advertising company and if they want to take out all of the jokes, they do. So you say the guy wasn't funny."

Although coherence might not have been Jessel's strong suit, no one could ever say he wasn't impassioned. "I'm responsible for the creation of a 90-minute new program in Israel. The county of Los Angeles has 10 million people—they have a newspaper and a half. New York City is down from 13 papers to three. There are 10 in Paris. I can go on and on."

That's something we never doubted. Since we seemed to have strayed off vaudeville and show business topics, we asked him for his thoughts on government funding for the arts, a hot topic at the time (as it still is). "What arts are there to control?" he asked. "The ballet? Don't make me laugh. I hate to be so pessimistic, but you have to face reality. I only hope Ronald Reagan can turn things around."

After leaving Jessel's house, we mused about the long arc his career had taken from a vaudeville and Broadway headliner to producing movies in Hollywood to anonymity in a shambling suburb of Los Angeles. We wondered what kept Jessel going (he seemed at times to visibly ossify in his chair during our visit). Was it distant memories of S.R.O.

audiences that he daily nursed and thereby kept intact and evergreen? Was it the talismans and tokens displayed on every wall, end-table and hutch that kept his eye from straying to a more prosaic reality—the kitchen wastebasket overflowing with TV dinner cardboard boxes?

When we got back to the car, we looked down at our notebook and found what might have been intended as a partial answer to our question. The Toastmaster General had scrawled something on the last page of our notes, probably while we were wandering from one piece of memorabilia to the next.

"Here's to the greats ... without a microphone," it read.

The encomium could have sufficed as Jessel's own eulogy, a summation of where he ranked himself in the show business firmament.

Definitely old school.

"How Do You Like Them Apples?"

Shirley Jones and *Rod Steiger*

During its glory years, Hollywood was considered to be a largely fraternal "company town" by many people who toiled in the major studios. We had heard that homey depiction more than once of Tinseltown being an inclusive place where everyone knew everyone else; and we heard it from stars that would have made strange bedfellows in any kind of imagining.

For instance, years ago during some desultory interview we had with Disney leading man Dean Jones about a film project now forgotten, he let slip that for years when he lived in Los Angeles he'd go dirt-biking on the weekends with Steve McQueen in the Mojave Desert. Jones told us that there probably wasn't a rock or cactus clump that he and Steve hadn't ridden over or been pitched into.

"We'd end the days drinking beer, nursing our abrasions and laughing about our near misses," he said.

We've always gotten a chuckle over that picture; the odd coupling of Walt Disney's perennial G-rated leading man (*The Love Bug*, *Herbie Goes to Monte Carlo*) laying a patch with one of filmdom's most iconoclastic anti-heroes and loners. The idea that two men as polar opposite from each other on the acting and charisma spectrum as you can get, burned rubber (and some jumping cholla) out in the barren hardpan north of L.A., is a tremendous kick and, if you ask us, it makes McQueen even cooler!

So it was with Shirley Jones and Rod Steiger. We interviewed them separately on the same day in 1995. They had starred together in the musical film version of *Oklahoma!* in 1955 with Jones making her film debut as winsome farm girl Laurey Williams opposite screen veteran Steiger, brooding and malevolent as hired hand Jud Fry who secretly lusts after Laurey.

We didn't know how close Shirley and Rod were in 1955 or if they had remained in touch over the intervening 40 years. Perhaps they crossed paths at a restaurant or,

Shirley in her living room

Hollywood being a company town, maybe a party or two over the years. We only knew for certain that we were the one degree of separation between them on that day and that we would be the point of intersection with a message to deliver from Shirley to Rod.

Shirley was in her early 60s when we met her in her home, a corner lot on one of the few unprepossessing streets in Beverly Hills. Dressed in a denim shirt, she looked lovely as she helped us navigate around piles of stuff in her living room to a couple of chairs. "I'm not a hoarder, really," she laughed apologetically, "We're just behind in putting things away."

Jones' name conjures up different images for different people. To a generation now in their "golden years," she was the fresh-faced young songstress in such musical films as *Oklahoma!*, *Carousel* and *The Music Man*. To baby boomers, she was Shirley Partridge, the matriarchal glue that kept TV's *Partridge Family* trilling in the early '70s. And to film buffs, she was an actress who found her dramatic footing as a hustling prostitute in *Elmer Gantry*, winning a Best Supporting Actress Academy Award for the role in 1960.

Making it big in show business has been likened to winning the lottery, and Jones was the first to admit that her meteoric rise to stardom was more an accident than a carefully charted career plan. Forty years after she burst onto the scene as Laurey in *Oklahoma!* Jones told us she attributed her success largely to happenstance.

"I never really set out to make anything happen," she said. "I was always able to sing—that was a God-given gift, but the pieces of my career just sort of fell into place."

That's when Shirley's husband, comedian Marty Ingels (of 1960s sitcom *I'm Dickens,*

He's Fenster fame) sprung from a chair that had been obscured by a giant cardboard box. "Did I hear you mention *Oklahoma!* he said. Ingels' eyes were as big as crop circles and registered a look—perpetually, it seemed—of having just been startled by a loud noise. Together with his beaky nose, squat build and Brooklyn street accent, he came across like a joke-telling koala just back from the Borscht Belt.

Although it was early afternoon, he was dressed in a bathrobe and he padded over to us in his slippers. "Wait, a sec," he said. "I have something to show you fellas."

Ingels disappeared into another room and we could hear boxes and junk being moved around. Shirley shot us a quizzical glance like she didn't know what to expect from her pugnacious husband, a world-class gadfly who had once been charged for making harassing phone calls to June Allyson and who had unsuccessfully sued radio personality Tom Leykis. Ingels was as loose cannon as they came.

"Found it," we heard him yell from the other room.

Ingels soon reappeared with a blown-up black and white photo (fully four-feet high) mounted on tagboard of Shirley dressed in her Laurey togs being spooned from behind in a burly bear hug by an ecstatic-looking Steiger on the set of *Oklahoma!*

"Rod was Jonesing for my wife," he quipped. "He had the hots for Shirley and could barely contain himself; he wanted to *shtup* her on the set of *Oklahoma!*"

We looked over at Shirley who had buried her head in her hands and was convulsed laughing. "That's true," she said. "I was young and kind of naïve about the ways of the world. But Rod's ardor cooled quickly which was kind of strange. Later I found out why."

"Odd coincidence," Dave said, "but we're interviewing Steiger later this afternoon."

"My God, you've got to get him to tell you the story of why he cooled down so quickly," Ingels implored. "Promise me, you'll ask him to tell you that story."

We promised.

A native of Smithton, Pennsylvania (population 800), Jones appeared in amateur theatrics, but really aspired to become a veterinarian. It was on a family trip to New York City where she met a pianist who insisted she sing for an agent friend of his. Within a matter of days after that chance meeting she was auditioning for Richard Rodgers and Oscar Hammerstein and was immediately cast in a chorus role in *South Pacific*. A part in another Rodgers and Hammerstein show, *Me and Juliet*, led to her being cast in the film version of *Oklahoma!*

During location filming in Arizona, the 21-year-old film novice was surrounded by screen veterans, including Gordon MacRae, Steiger, Eddie Albert, Gloria Grahame and director Fred Zinnemann (who also directed such classics as *High Noon* and *From Here to Eternity*).

"I was very lucky," Shirley said. "Fred was very patient, to the point where he was really Svengali. He asked me if I had ever performed before a camera. I said 'never,' to which he replied: 'You're an absolute natural.' I was really like a sponge and quite malleable. I had not done enough work on the stage to form any bad habits. I was very open to being directed and Fred loved that. I was also so naive, the camera didn't scare me."

After *Carousel* Jones starred in *The Music Man* which ranks to this day as one of the best big screen adaptations of a Broadway musical blockbuster. "It's an American classic," Shirley said, "like the great Westerns, and people love that show. I hear more about that movie than any other musical, especially throughout Middle America. I have eight and nine-year-old kids in my concert audiences calling me 'Marian the Librarian.'"

Jones said that Warner Bros. fought for Frank Sinatra to play the role of confidence man extraordinaire, "Harold Hill." "Meredith Willson had enough pull to insist on Robert Preston reprising his Broadway role which was great. Robert was so fresh all the time."

In between starring as the ingénue for Rodgers & Hammerstein and Meredith Willson, Jones also appeared in *Never Steal Anything Small*, a musical that flew under most people's radar but which co-starred a singing and dancing James Cagney.

"He was a good friend until the day he died," Shirley said. "We had a party once and Jimmy came over with his wife. He bonded with Jack Cassidy (Jones' husband at the time) and they became close friends because of the Irish blood. At one point, Jimmy pulled up the rug and tapped danced and it was great. He loved musicals more than anything."

But just as quickly as Jones' star had risen, the imminent death of the musical film by the late '50s almost counted her among its many casualties. "My movie career was over when musicals weren't being made anymore because I was typecast for those roles," she said. "I was forced to take television parts at a time when it was considered beneath a 'movie star' to do television."

It was Jones' Emmy-nominated performance opposite Red Skelton in a *Playhouse 90* production of *The Big Slide* that caught the attention of Burt Lancaster who was about to star in the film *Elmer Gantry*, based on Sinclair Lewis's satirical novel about a phony evangelist. After convincing director Richard Brooks that she was right for the part (he preferred Piper Laurie), she was cast in the role of the prostitute who blackmails the flim-flam preacher played by Lancaster.

Jones' first day on the set was particularly difficult as Brooks—still brooding from not casting Laurie—offered her no direction. "I went home that night in tears thinking he really hates me," she recalled. "The next day, Brooks took me aside and said, 'Shirley, I want to apologize to you. I left you alone because I wanted to see if you'd fall on your face. You didn't, and, as a matter of fact, I think you're going to win an Academy Award.'"

Although Brooks' prophesy came true, Jones herself didn't hold much hope for winning. "I really had no clue that I would win," she said. "Janet Leigh was taking home all the awards for *Psycho*. When they announced my name I was in shock."

"I would not have had a career if it wasn't for *Gantry*," she added. "That film and winning the Oscar gave me a chance to star in movies throughout the '60s."

With feature parts assured, Jones starred in a string of mostly romantic comedies opposite such stars as Marlon Brando, Glenn Ford, David Niven and Tony Curtis. By the end of the decade, she felt she needed a change. When an offer came along to star in a weekly television series about a single mother and her brood of aspiring pop singers, called *The Partridge Family*, Jones eagerly accepted it. But if *Elmer Gantry* saved her movie career, *The Partridge Family* effectively ended it.

"The show killed my movie career," she said. "Do I regret doing it? Absolutely not! I had traveled the world making movies and I needed a change. I had three young children to raise and my marriage was teetering. I needed to stay near home with as close to a nine-to-five job as possible. *The Partridge Family* gave me normalcy. It also paid me a lot of money."

During the five-year run of the show, Jones' co-star and real-life stepson, David Cassidy, became a teen idol. "The experience was really tough on David," she said. "He nearly had a nervous breakdown. After the show, he left the business for a year, went to Hawaii, sat in a field and played guitar. That kind of overwhelming adulation is tough on a young kid."

In light of the success a few years before we met her of *The Brady Bunch Movie*—a pastiche of another California "family" of the period, there had been talk of transferring the Partridge brood to the big screen.

"We've been approached about a sequel or some type of remake," she said. "But we never could get it together because David didn't want to get involved again. With the success of *The Brady Bunch Movie*, I wouldn't be surprised if somebody remade our show with a new cast. The adults of today grew up with our show and they're the ones going to movies today.

"I'm very choosy when it comes to the projects I select," she added. "I don't want to do something for the sake of being back on television or in a movie. I don't need the money and the roles are just not there for women in my age bracket."

As we were about to leave to drive over to Steiger's, Ingels reappeared still in his bathrobe and holding the tagboard photo. "Remember to ask Rod," he said.

On meeting Steiger, we quickly learned one salient fact about the man: he was a fighter who had been waging the same titanic battle ever since he left the mean streets of Newark, New Jersey at the age of 16 to join the Pacific Fleet during World War II. In those days, with the vicious murmurings of his classmates cutting into him like a razor, Steiger would be called out of school on a regular basis to pick up his inebriated mother from whatever neighborhood saloon she had just passed out in.

Steiger's struggle then, as it was when we met him in 1995, was for respect. It never changed or wavered. "I am convinced that my success and intensity in the movies comes from the fact that I have sworn somewhere to myself—deeply, psychologically—that I will succeed so spectacularly that the Steiger name will never be laughed at again."

During a long and rambling interview on the deck of his Spanish-style villa in the hills above Malibu, he said the anger and rage that didn't find an appropriate outlet a half century ago, makes money for him on the screen. "If I didn't fall into acting," he said, "I probably would've been a mean drunk who ended up with a knife in his ribs after a bar-room brawl."

Dressed in a flowing white-striped bathrobe (apparently it was *the* day for bathrobes), wearing sandals and with a token of a "little prince" hung on a chain around his neck, Steiger, with his bald pate gleaming in the late afternoon sun, conjured images of a groovy West Coast shaman about to impart to us the healing mysteries of the universe instead of acting anecdotes. Steiger did however confide that for years he suffered bouts of debilitating depression that waxed and waned without warning. He said that medication and the writings of Antoine de Saint-Exupéry were helpful in combating what fellow sufferer Winston Churchill called "the black dog on my back."

"I would recommend reading Saint-Exupéry's *The Little Prince* for anyone who has the blues. It's just magical," Steiger said. "After all it was Saint-Exupéry who said: 'It is only with the heart that one can see rightly; what is essential is invisible to the eye.'"

Steiger, who won a 1968 Best Actor Academy Award for his performance as a bigoted Southern sheriff in *In the Heat of the Night*, and was nominated for an Oscar in *On the Waterfront*, opposite Marlon Brando, had carved a career playing social misfits or outsiders on the fringe. They are roles (given Steiger's rough-and-tumble background) with which he had a certain empathy.

Indeed, his favorite starring role was as the misanthropic Jewish pawnshop owner tortured by memories of the Holocaust in *The Pawnbroker*. Although raised a Lutheran, Steiger, then a self-professed agnostic, grew up in a Jewish neighborhood and drew on his memories for the critically acclaimed and Oscar-nominated performance.

"As a boy, my best friend was Jewish and he invited me to his house one day for a steak dinner," Steiger remembered. "When I saw his mother put the meat into a frying pan with a ¼ inch of water, I nearly died. They were kosher, but what she did to the steak should never happen!"

In the mid–'90s, to get parts in films, Steiger told us he had ignominiously been reduced to doing something he never had to do before—sell himself. "Nowadays, I walk in to see studio heads who are about 34 years old and experts in marketing," he sneered. "Unfortunately, they know little about creating. One of them asked me if I could do a Southern accent. My first animal instinct was to hit him with a chair; then I told him I won an Oscar playing a sheriff of a small Southern town."

Moments like that convinced Steiger of the possibility that he might be a cipher to a whole generation of moviegoers, "My part as

Rod on the patio

the Cuban mob boss in the Stallone film *The Specialist* was a $40-million commercial to that generation that I exist," he said. The commercial paid off as Steiger subsequently booked no less than three films in 1998—*Incognito*, with Jason Patric; *Animals*, with Tim Roth; and *Modern Vampire*, a straight-to-cable fang flick.

An alumnus of the Actor's Studio in New York, Steiger hit Hollywood right on the cusp, when the old guard comprised of actors like Humphrey Bogart started to cede power to the avant-garde led by the protean talent of men like James Dean and Marlon Brando. Steiger worked with them all. We asked him to reflect on Brando, James Dean, Bogart and Gary Cooper. Steiger took the request literally and did something we had never experienced before during an interview. Before speaking about each actor, he told us to turn off our tape recorder. After an intense Zen-like period of contemplation that sometimes lasted almost a minute during which he'd close his eyes, he'd come out of his meditative trance and tell us to flip the recorder back on.

On Brando... In *On the Waterfront*, we didn't get to know each other at all. He always flew solo and I haven't seen him since the film. I do resent him saying he's just a hooker, and that actors are whores.

On Dean... Jimmy was a friend of mine and extremely talented. But he hadn't quite got his technique together. At the time of his death, he was working too much on instinct. He'd be brilliant in one scene and then blow the next.

On Bogart... In *The Harder They Fall*, Bogey and I got along very well. Unlike some other stars, when they had close-ups, you might have been relegated to a two-shot, or cut out altogether. Bogart didn't play those games. He was a professional and had tremendous authority. He'd come in exactly at 9 a.m. and leave at precisely 6 p.m.

I remember once walking to lunch in between takes and seeing Bogey on the lot. I shouldn't have because his work was finished for the day. I asked him why he was still on the lot, and he said, "They want to shoot some retakes of my close-ups because my eyes are too watery." A little while later, after the film, somebody came up to me with word of Bogey's death. Then it struck me. His eyes were watery because he was in pain with the cancer. I thought: "How dumb can you be Rodney!"

On Gary Cooper... I had great respect for him as a survivor. Acting had moved on a little bit from where Cooper was, and in the interim his career had gotten a little shaky. To publicize our movie, *The Court Martial of Billy Mitchell*, we did a live scene on *The Ed Sullivan Show*. He was as white as a piece of chalk; perspiration was dripping out of the cuff of his uniform. A couple of times during the scene he got lost a little bit, but he had the guts of a lion. Of course the other side of Cooper was every time we had a scene to shoot during the movie, I had to pound on Elizabeth Montgomery's dressing room door to get him out of there!

"We'd like to get your thoughts on one other star you've worked with," Tom said. "But this is more specific—it's about an incriminating photo that was taken on the set of *Oklahoma!* where you had Shirley Jones in a bear hug. We just came from her house and Marty Ingels told us to ask you about it."

Steiger didn't ask us to shut off the tape recorder. No contemplation was needed.

"It was Zinnemann, that bastard! He cock-blocked me! Shirley was so beautiful and I was gaga over her and would've made a big move, but Zinnemann noticed it. He called me over early in the filming and kind of took me confidentially aside and said: 'Rodney, you are the elder actor on this film and I'd like you to look out for Shirley and be her big brother. She's completely clueless about how attractive she is and that could be a problem. It was brilliant. In one fell swoop, Zinnemann neutralized me and by making me Shirley's bodyguard, he neutralized everybody else."

Steiger walked the walk. If you want respect, you've got to give it to get it and that's what he earned from Zinnemann by looking out for Shirley.

Seventy-two when we met him, Steiger was father to a five-year-old son. Although he wanted to continue to work in estimable projects in order to leave a legacy to his child, he faced a potentially debilitating handicap (although one decidedly less serious than the demons his mother faced).

"I'm a lazy lion," he said. "I sit around all day and read magazines, gaze at the ocean, have lunch and then dinner with my wife and child. But get me interested in a project, and I'm alive again." At that moment, Steiger drew a corollary to his mother. He told us that during the last 11 years of her life, she was sober and a regular attendee of Alcoholics Anonymous meetings. "I was so proud of her," he said. "She turned herself around. She came alive again."

The sun had set and Steiger, sitting some distance across the patio deck from us, had become indistinct. More to the point, he had become a visual effect: a disembodied voice that floated over to us from a pulsating white robe (like Claude Rains in *The Invisible Man*). And so it was the only interview in our career that *we* ended. Interview called on account of encroaching darkness. Steiger could've talked for hours. And we would have been willing listeners except for one nagging consideration; we were eager to snake back down curvy Zumirez Drive to the Pacific Coast Highway and get to a phone. We had a follow-up call to make.

"We just finished with Steiger," Dave said when Shirley picked up on the other end. "Rod told us how Zinnemann blackmailed him into being your on-set protector during *Oklahoma!*"

"'Jud Fry' … my hero … how do you like them apples?" Shirley giggled.

The Real McCoy

DeForest Kelley

Writer's Log, Stardate: 1982.6.

O.K., we'll admit it: we were "Trekkies." We grew up watching the original airings of *Star Trek*, Gene Roddenberry's innovative Sci-Fi morality teleplays that featured cheesy sets and a troupe of actors led by William Shatner's "James T. Kirk"; an overactor who chewed more scenery during the run of the show than "The Horta" consumed rock ("The Devil in the Dark," Ep. 25).

Nonetheless, scheduling an interview with DeForest Kelley, the actor who played the USS *Enterprise*'s Chief Medical Officer, Leonard "Bones" McCoy, was much easier than actually meeting him in the flesh.

In fact, getting a fix on the coordinates of our meeting place was almost as troubling as feeding Tribbles spiked amounts of the fictional high-yield grain Quadrotriticale ("The Trouble with Tribbles," Ep. 44). In our telephone arrangements, Kelley said we'd get together at a "Scandinavian" restaurant on Ventura Boulevard in the Los Angeles suburb of Encino. What he failed to tell us was that the restaurant was an IHOP (International House of Pancakes). Perhaps the A-frame architecture characteristic of the restaurant chain confused the good doctor into thinking that the pancake house had been beamed over to Southern California from Oslo's city center.

We had a prolonged "Where's Waldo?" moment as we drove back and forth past the restaurant three times before it finally dawned on us that Kelley might've meant the IHOP as where we were supposed to meet. *Uff da!*

At any rate, we finally connected with Kelley in the parking lot where he was lolling next to his vintage Thunderbird. He explained that the IHOP was a convenient meeting place because it was close to home and the nearby Vendome liquor store where he liked to stock up on libations which, we quickly surmised, might have contributed to all the confusion in the first place. Indeed, during our breakfast, Kelley, who was born in Toccoa, Georgia, spoke with a sonorous country drawl that was loopier than the Chattahoochee River on an August afternoon meander. Could he have been tippling on Saurian brandy like the Enterprise's Chief Engineer, Mr. Scott? ("By Any Other Name," Ep. 51.) We quickly nixed that possibility since the Vendome—at least back then—didn't traffic in intergalactic after-dinner cordials.

Over a stack of buttermilk flapjacks, Kelley told us that his role as the ship's doctor provided him a chance to break out of the mostly villainous roles he had been playing on the big and small screens. "It was not a big role at first, but I thought he (Dr. McCoy) had room to grow," he said. "I told Gene Roddenberry (the creator and producer of the show) that I'd love to do it if somewhere down the line they'd expand the character if he warrants it." Kelley's role did expand and by the show's second season, his name was listed in the opening credits alongside Shatner and Leonard Nimoy.

Kelley patterned the part after American journalist H.L. Mencken. McCoy, always the cynic, was a "simple country doctor" uncomfortable living in an era of molecule-scrambling transporter rooms, phasers and tricorders. His emotional outbursts, usually directed at the placidly logical Spock, made for some of the show's finest moments. "We were allowed a great deal of freedom to express ourselves on the show," he said. "In the beginning, all of our contributions were put in a pot and stirred up and it worked. We had a very rare organization on the original show. But I really was like McCoy. He has a lot of great traits."

During its run, the show revolutionized TV science fiction through its 79 teleplays, many of which addressed hot-button issues of that time (and are still relevant today) such as race and war.

"Bones" cracking up

"The writers were very cooperative when it came to changes, as long as we didn't change the meaning or the content," said Kelley. "A lot of times you find holes in scripts that are wide open and you have to say, 'Look, this just doesn't work.'"

In "The Empath" (Ep. 67), for example, two aliens try to teach a young woman to feel the pain of others in an attempt to save her planet from imminent destruction. The characters of McCoy and Captain Kirk are used as guinea pigs, nearly dying, before being saved by the Empath (actress Kathryn Hays looking like a very young Jane Wyatt). Filmed in a Dionysian setting that evoked ancient Greek tragedy, with a simple black stage and spot lighting, the episode still resonates as great television and was far ahead of its time when first aired.

"That episode was awesome television," Kelley admitted. "We worked awfully hard on that show. We were supposed to film episodes in six days. The studio, of course, would have loved to have us do them in five, which was impossible.

But mostly, we took seven or eight days. We had a lot of laughs because we were under constant pressure."

Although the series was canceled after three seasons, Kelley knew that his association with *Star Trek* was far from over. "The thing that took the show off the air was low ratings, but we broke every fan mail record at NBC," he said. "The Nielsens (ratings) just didn't add up to the amount of mail we received."

After cancellation, Kelley took parts that he said were unfulfilling but well paying. As a self-described lazy actor, he just stopped working when he found that he could make more money doing personal appearances than acting on television.

Kelley's first exposure to "Trekmania" came in the early '70s when he was invited to speak at a *Star Trek* convention in New York City. "They expected between 3,000 and 4,000 people," he said. "It turned out that there were 12,000. I walked out on stage and saw people hanging from the rafters and screaming and carrying on like you wouldn't believe. I thought, what the hell, we'd been off for a few years. I told them that something has to happen. I knew it wasn't over."

When the series ended its run, a worldwide group of avid fans kept the franchise alive until Paramount reunited the cast in 1979 for the big-budget, bloated and boring *Star Trek: The Motion Picture*. Under the direction of *Sound of Music* veteran Robert Wise, the film was successful only because of the pent-up audience demand to see the franchise resurrected.

"It's absolutely beyond me how they could arrive at a script like that on a comeback motion picture," Kelley said. "I felt that the relationships were not there. We fought, yelled and tried to tell them.

"*Star Trek* is very difficult to pull back into its original framework," he added. "When we did the film we were all asked what we would like to see done. I told Gene that I would like to see a simple science fiction story with a minimum of special effects used only when needed. I told him I thought it would be a breath of fresh air. I tried to tell them that, but I knew it would just be a special effects extravaganza with Paramount."

In 1982, the next incarnation, *Star Trek II: The Wrath of Kahn*, was a hit. The film franchise and the many TV series' that the original show spawned found an anchor point by bringing back one of Kirk's biggest nemeses, "Kahn Noonien Singh" (Ricardo Montalban), from the original series ("Space Seed," Ep. 22). That movie sequel successfully launched the nascent film franchise into space where "no movie studio had quite gone before."

And the original cast went along for a wild ride at warp speed that none of them could have predicted back in the 1960s. Although Nimoy, at one point in his career, tried to distance himself from his Spock character, Kelley, who died in 1999, always wholeheartedly embraced it.

"I feel that *Star Trek* is basically a winner and perhaps the biggest winner that has ever been presented on a television screen," he said. "Gee, I'm a pretty lucky guy when it comes right down to it. So I've tried to stop knocking it because I don't think it is right." Homespun advice from the good doctor, who still makes house calls wherever the series airs in syndication.

Breakfast over, we told Kelley we had to "beam out" of IHOP to a pre-scheduled interview in L.A. proper at another coffee shop but *sans* any discernible country-centric architectural embellishments that might confuse us.

For his part, Kelley told us he had a date with a bottle opener.

Passing Time

with *Gene Kelly*

Hollywood isn't cherished for its long memory. In fact, it's often derided as incestuous and infested with a particular brand of shark that gleefully devours those whose movies don't excel at the box office. However, even a town shot-through with *schadenfreude* and as insecure and unapologetically larcenous as Hollywood can sometimes reach a meaningful consensus about real art.

That happens to be the case concerning the legacy of song-and-dance man Gene Kelly. He was venerated everywhere in the film capital as a true original—no small achievement in a place with more than its fair share of poseurs and mere technicians. When Fred Astaire died in 1987, Kelly stood alone as the reigning elder of a joyous and uniquely American art form—the movie musical.

It was the summer of 1978 when we first met Kelly. As newly minted high school graduates, we had put in three hard months vending beer at Minnesota Twins baseball games to come up with the airfare to get us to Los Angeles. After nearly two years of persistent correspondence, Kelly, via his longtime secretary, Lois McClelland, had finally green-lighted a "brief visit" to his home at 725 N. Rodeo Drive in Beverly Hills.

To say we were fans of the Golden Age of Hollywood musicals, and in particular Kelly's huge contribution, would be a gross understatement. Our consuming passion for that era had inspired us to found a film society that brought the musicals of Kelly, Astaire, Garland and others to shut-ins at Twin City–area nursing homes. Full disclosure: under cover of that humanitarian guise, we were able to indulge our obsession by viewing obscure, forgotten musicals that didn't even make it on TV's late, late show.

On the appointed day, dressed in suits and ties, we walked through Beverly Hills (we weren't legal to drive in L.A.) enroute to Kelly's house. As we turned north on Rodeo Drive from Santa Monica Blvd., a police car cruised up to us and the officers inside called us over. "What are you guys doing?" one of them asked. "We're walking over to Gene Kelly's house, we have a meeting with him," Dave said. "Why do you ask?" The officer, a bit flustered, told us that they never saw anyone walking in Beverly Hills, much less dressed in business attire and that we looked suspicious. We assured them we weren't Jehovah's Witnesses hawking copies of *The Watchtower* door to door and we all had a good laugh.

For almost half a century Kelly had lived in the same French Colonial house with red window shutters on Rodeo Drive in the Beverly Hills flatlands just south of Sunset Boulevard. When we arrived, a bit footsore, an assistant answered the door and we were led into Kelly's expansive living room.

Any incidental knowledge we had that Kelly was a Francophile was underscored by just taking a 360-degree look around that room. The dark paneled walls were awash in paintings, many of them French Expressionist. The pictures were hung—just as in the galleries at the Louvre—side by side in a long row with the frames nearly touching each other. The cumulative effect was a continuous banner of riotous color.

On the opposite side of the room was a small bar with, just behind it, an oversized *Belle Epoque* dance hall poster ("Paris-Chicago Theatre de la Tour Eiffel") by French painter and lithographer Jules Cheret. Adjacent to the bar were sliding glass doors that looked out onto the backyard swimming pool.

Kelly appeared to us from his favorite room, the library, with an almost syncopated bounce in his step. We had seen it dozens of times before in his movies; whether gliding alone down a backlot "rue" at MGM as *An American in Paris*, or with two buddies in New York City out for a day *On the Town*. It was a jaunty, confident and athletic stride even at the age of 66.

He said that he had just been reading a bit about economics (he majored in the subject at the University of Pittsburgh). He then told us that he and his two children, Tim and Bridget, had been over at neighbor Harry Warren's house using the tennis court, as they often did, for a few quick sets. In 1950, Warren, a three-time Academy Award–winning songwriter, had written the score for *Summer Stock* starring Kelly and Judy Garland in their last film together. They made three including Kelly's debut film, *For Me and My Gal* in 1942.

"Wonderful, wonderful Judy, she was the greatest," Kelly said. For a moment, he seemed lost in a kind of reverie as he remembered. "She wasn't a trained dancer but she was such a hard worker. We did a number in *Summer Stock* in a barn called 'The Portland Fancy.' She was terrific, picked up the steps so quickly. And it wasn't an easy dance to do. Really, I never worked with a trained dancer who was so quick to learn steps as Judy was. You would run through a combination twice—and some were difficult—and she would have it down pat."

We took a seat on Kelly's couch underneath the skein of paintings. Right above our heads was a figure study done in dark brushstrokes that Tom thought he recognized as the work of Fauvist Georges Rouault.

"Is that a Rouault?" Tom rather timidly broached, pointing upward. "Yep," was Kelly's terse reply which signified to us that there would be no further discussion about the paintings which were everywhere.

We asked him about *Singin' in the Rain*, perhaps his most enduring film and a benchmark by which all other musicals are measured. It is a treasure trove of great numbers, but the "Moses Supposes" dance with Kelly and Donald O'Connor tapping out a rhythmic Morse Code like a couple of pneumatic drills, never fails to electrify audiences.

"Donald and I rehearsed that dance for days, but most critics dismiss it as a zany Marx Brothers romp," Kelly said. "They remember the clowning around with the vocal coach that precedes the number, but not the dance itself."

Kelly told us that he didn't own any prints of his movies. "MGM had a strict policy; they never gave out any films, even to the movies' stars," he said.

As he walked us to the door, Kelly gave us the thumbs-up signal, which he said he had also given to Barbra Streisand when he directed her in *Hello Dolly!* It was his message to her at the end of each camera take that she was on cue.

Every Christmas thereafter, without fail, we would receive a greeting card, some picturing the Kelly clan posed in their backyard along with whatever family pet was within grabbing distance when the shot was taken. For our part, we kept Gene supplied with copies of our various entertainment articles when they were published.

After 16 years of sending these missives to each other, we returned to Kelly's home on Oscar night, 1994. What a difference a decade and a half had made.

Season's Greetings from the Kelly clan

In the interim, the Rodeo Drive house had almost completely burned down in a December 1983 fire that started from faulty lighting on the family's Christmas tree. Kelly's 1951 Oscar awarded to him for brilliant achievements in the art of choreography on film, as well as an Emmy, dancing shoes and personal papers for a planned autobiography were lost.

The home itself had been completely rebuilt and seemed to us almost a carbon copy of the two-story colonial we had visited years before. But instead of those miles and miles of priceless paintings which had gone up in smoke, prints (Matisse limited editions and the like) that you see during closeout sales at middling art galleries, were hung here and there.

Dressed in chinos, a white Ralph Lauren polo shirt and wearing leather loafers, Kelly, then 83 years old, slowly made his way over to greet us. His steps were halting and measured due to "nursing a bum leg." Shortly after our visit he was hospitalized in San Francisco with cellulitis (a potentially dangerous infection) in his leg. In July 1994 and in early 1995 he was hospitalized again as a result of mild strokes.

For an instant it was hard to reconcile Kelly's enduring movie image of explosive athleticism (to say nothing of how he looked during our previous visit) with the reality before us—that of a slightly enfeebled octogenarian.

"Ah, the college kids," Kelly exclaimed. "Tom, you've changed; Dave, not so much." To this day, Kelly's quizzical statement has been an enduring "Rosebud" moment for us.

If the march of time had slowed Kelly's machine gun footwork to a slow shuffle, age had also sharpened his wit and deepened his memory.

"Historically speaking," Kelly said, "I'm one of the last ones left who can correct inaccuracies about MGM musicals in show biz books these days." As an example, he cited Hugh Fordin's *The World of Entertainment*, a book about producer Arthur Freed and his creative unit at MGM. "I, along with Vincente Minnelli, Judy Garland and dozens of others, was part of that unit in the 1940s and '50s," Kelly said. "You'd think that when the author was compiling facts, he'd have wanted to consult me. He didn't, and there are several mistakes as a result."

Kelly said history continued to be rewritten to the present day. The misinformation ranging from an erroneous birthdate in a popular biography of his life, to a German journalist who reported that MGM studio chief Louis B. Mayer "foisted" Debbie Reynolds on Kelly as his co-star in *Singin' in the Rain*.

"That is patently untrue," Kelly said. "Mayer wasn't even at the studio in 1952 when we shot the picture."

Sitting beside Kelly during our visit was his wife Patricia whom he had married in 1990. She had first met Kelly in 1985 at the Smithsonian in Washington, D.C., when he was the host/narrator and she the writer for a television special on the author of *Moby Dick*, Herman Melville. During our conversation, Patricia mostly sat silently as we discussed a meeting we had the day before with George Sidney who directed Kelly in *Anchors Aweigh* in 1945.

We mentioned that the widowed Sidney had recently married Corinne Entratter the former wife of legendary Las Vegas casino boss, Jack Entratter. "Is that right?" Kelly said. "I remember Corinne. She was a Copa showgirl and a real 'wow!'"

Attractive and reserved when we met, Patricia has, since Kelly's death, reinvented herself into a glamazon who barnstorms around the country as Creative Director and talking head of "Gene Kelly: The Legacy," a corporation established to commemorate Kelly's achievements and keep his memory alive.

The year before our meeting, *That's Entertainment! III*, another time capsule of classic MGM musical moments that began with the release in 1974 of the hugely successful *That's Entertainment!* had been released which starred Kelly, along with June Allyson, Cyd Charisse, Lena Horne and Mickey Rooney.

Kelly said that the best musical material from MGM's glory days had already been used in the two prior *That's Entertainment!* films. "But there are some historical oddities—like footage of vocal dubbing—that MGM would never have released to the public during its heyday," he said.

On the Town, which Kelly co-directed with Stanley Donen, was his all-time favorite musical, mainly because it was his directorial debut at MGM and the opening number, "New York, New York," and some establishing shots were filmed on location in New York City. "That was no small achievement back in 1949, especially when you consider the studio had a standing New York set that looked more authentic than parts of the real city," Kelly said.

In an issue of *The New Yorker* magazine (March 24, 1994) Pulitzer Prize–winning author John Updike, in a tribute to Kelly, cited *On the Town* as his favorite movie, too. However, he lamented the fact that Kelly rarely seemed to pair up with a female partner to good advantage, the way Fred Astaire did throughout his career.

"I thought Updike did a good job of summing me up," Kelly told us, "but he should know that the roles I was given were way different from Fred's. The mode of dance in the 1940s and '50s was no longer ballroom like it was with the Fred and Ginger pictures in the 1930s."

In spite of such comments, ample evidence exists to dispel the notion that Kelly's best dances were solo numbers. "My few quick turns with Rita Hayworth in *Cover Girl* to those beautiful strains of 'Long Ago and Far Away' were akin to the kind of dancing Astaire did," Kelly said.

Kelly admitted that, overall, movie musicals were largely icons of the past. Their decline was due perhaps to audiences that just can't bring themselves to suspend disbelief anymore when an off-camera orchestra begins to swell moments before a song number. However, others saw MTV, with its quick-cut camera work geared to short attention spans, as the modern-day spawn of old-time musical numbers. Kelly agreed with that premise.

"Film editors have become the choreographers today," he said. "Everything is 'bam!' a tight shot of a shoulder, a leg, half a pirouette, an ass. In my day, editors were simply called 'cutters'; now a whole musical can succeed or fail based on the editing."

Up until suffering the strokes, Kelly traveled the college lecture circuit discussing his old movies to sellout crowds. "If they can meet my price, I'll give 'em a spiel," he said. The year before our last visit, Kelly lectured in Atlantic City and was surprised when his old friend and "other" *Brigadoon* dancing partner, Van Johnson, showed up in the audience.

Future plans included finishing an autobiography and quashing the curious notion that he had departed the earth for more heavenly climes!

"The mix-up started with those GAP print ads, 'Gene Kelly Wore Khakis,'" he said. "Besides me, the first group of ads included Arthur Miller, Marilyn Monroe, Humphrey Bogart and a few others. Along with the phrase being in the past tense, all the other personalities were famously dead, except Arthur and me. People leapt to the natural conclusion. You wouldn't believe the number of phone calls I got from friends trying to figure out whether I was still here or not."

For two more years, Kelly was most definitely still *here*. He died in his sleep in 1996. But his musicals will always be around, emblematic as they are of a peculiar brand of sunny, "can-do" optimism that helped define the American Century.

The Last of the Great Anchormen

Ted Knight

One of the uproarious quirks of the "Ted Baxter" character on *The Mary Tyler Moore Show* (*MTM*) was his "gentleness with a buck." Ted's pathological stinginess was as reliable as WJM-TV's low ratings. After all, who but Ted Baxter would take his wife out on a dinner date to a restaurant with drive-up service? And who but Ted would consult a personal tax attorney not yet out of law school?

Ted Baxter brought literal meaning to "boob tube" or at least "boob" on the "tube." There have been few better in the history of TV sitcoms.

It was with mild surprise then, that we declined an offer of financial assistance when wc interviewed Ted Knight, who played Baxter so convincingly for seven years on MTM. At our meeting in 1981 during a lunch break while Ted was filming another hit sitcom at CBS in which he starred—*Too Close for Comfort*—we let slip that we were anticipating some lean cuisine in order to make ends meet during our three-week stay in Los Angeles to interview various movie and TV people for our college newspaper.

"Reporters don't become flush working for the *Minnesota Daily*, just tired," we told him.

"You be sure to come to me if you get strapped for funds," Knight said.

Our steadfast refusal to endorse one of Knight's blank checks (which he actually ripped out of his checkbook and gave to us) has haunted us to this day, because avaricious friends now consider us the worst kind of bubbleheads for not taking him up on his generous offer. One of the most unaffected celebrities we ever met, Knight (who died in 1986) had a carefree demeanor that might have been traced, ironically, to the type of television roles he played early in his career.

"I played five lead Nazi parts in the TV series *Combat!* And I got killed in all five episodes. If you spot me now in one of those old shows, you'll probably get a good laugh. I also played a KAOS agent on *Get Smart*, Knight said. "I think you'll find historically that many actors who play sinister roles have unusually happy home lives."

Why, we asked, was he typecast early on as a Hollywood heavy?

"When I came out here, the thinking that prevailed was a complete turnaround in terms of what criminals should look like," he said. "Instead of the pockmarked thugs with scowling faces, they wanted clean-shaven, all–American types. Since I have Aryan features, I fitted the bill perfectly. I had one speech memorized in German that I recited at every casting call. Translated in English it said that I had a terrific headache and wanted to go to bed. But I acted it with such venom and anger; I got cast in a lot of heavy roles."

In a career that began in the first grade, Knight worked as a ventriloquist, puppeteer and narrator of documentaries and commercials and—in a weird foreshadowing—as a broadcast journalist. "I fell off the couch playing Santa Claus in the first grade because I had forgotten my lines," he said. "I got such a big laugh, so I fell off the couch three more times and got bigger laughs and that's when I realized my future—the disease hit me. I'll probably wind up my career falling off couches as Santa Claus.

"Actually, it all started for me in 1947 in Hartford at the Randall School of Fine Arts … (Knight then morphed into the booming *basso profundo* Ted Baxter anchorman voice) … in a small 500-watt radio station in Hartford,

Ted talk

Connecticut. It wasn't easy in those days; you had to work hard and own a good suit with an unspeckled tie."

In case you're not an *MTM* trivia buff, that speech was Ted Baxter's opening statement at any banquet where he was fortunate enough to be nominated for an award—any award.

"The character of Ted Baxter is entrenched in the lexicon of American entertainment," Knight said. "Baxterisms in word and deed can be readily identified in many characters on television today. I loved doing him."

And Knight was *still* doing him! At that moment in our conversation, he joined in singing "Happy Birthday" to a crowd gathered at a nearby lunch table in the commissary, ending the song by rhythmically banging his soupspoon on the table. Knight then made an impossibly long lean over his salad bowl and stuck his beaming mug (with Pepsodent teeth so bright and blocky you'd think you were looking at a whitewashed house on the island of Crete) point-blank into the face of a pretty young starlet he thought was Deanna Lund (TV's *Land of the Giants*).

"Would you like to become a nun?" Knight said, leering and arching his bleached eyebrows like Groucho Marx, "because I'm feeling very priestly today. I want to hear your confession (And then to us) "My wife knows I'm a flirt but that's as far as it goes. You can't cut me off completely." The bemused starlet was speechless but her whole table roared.

The experience of performing on one of the few sitcoms (*MTM*) that is admired as a sterling example of near flawless writing and execution was not lost on Knight. "Comedy is one area I've learned an awful lot about," Knight said. "Seven seasons on *MTM* has helped and hindered me because I now have such high standards where TV comedy is concerned. I cringe more than I should. The *MTM* writers were very good, but in retrospect you tend to glorify or flatter more than is necessary. A moment I'll never forget is that emotionally charged last show when everyone in the newsroom was fired but me; that caterpillar crawl over to the Kleenex box on Mary's desk. It was our last scene together after seven years of performing.

"The tears, everything, it was all genuine. We were very close. It was a rare moment. We knew as actors, characters and human beings that were stepping out the door for the last time."

Too Close for Comfort a middling comedy series in the *Three's Company* mold, but, nonetheless the only new series that year from any of the three major networks that became a hit, was Knight's first bow as lead star.

"I have more responsibility as the top banana," he told us. "I enjoy it more. There is no sibling rivalry and I don't have the agony of fighting for more lines or being upset when someone else has more lines. All actors experience that whether they admit it or not. Actors' paranoia is more intense when you're a supporting player. Paranoia develops into another area when you're a STAR—if you let it, that is. The aging process kind of mellows you out after a while so that you don't give a rat's ass. I've got money. I've got enough to keep me happy and my family solvent for the rest of my days. The success has kind of worn thin all the attendant glamorous aspects that you envision when you're young. It has tendency to rust with time. It doesn't have the meaning it once had. It's all work, a job, a workplace, something I enjoy doing, the challenge of making something work that looks impossible.

"And I'll tell you another thing," Knight continued. "My costar on the show, Nancy

Dessault, is a brilliant comedienne who has yet to be discovered as such. She's got everything Lucille Ball ever had and she's a better singer. She's very inventive."

At the time, Knight told us that he felt the success of *Comfort* was due to a retrenchment of traditional values in the country (Ronald Reagan had been elected president that year), and not to the easy laughs stemming from clichéd predicaments that the writers dreamed up each week.

"The prevailing mood of the country is a swing to the conservative right," he said. "We try to exemplify the family cell structure in an accelerated society on our show. Mom and pop trying to make it with the kids—not literally, I mean! You know what I mean."

According to Knight, a capacity for hard work and a matter-of-fact receptivity to sudden change were the main ingredients for longevity on network television, and he should know. "You have to sweat blood to get a good product," Knight said. "If you go with the cheap shots, miss days, goof off, take dope, or just go with the original lines, then that will show. You have to have the integrity to really care about what you are doing." That goes for just about anything; would that it was so simple.

Clock Watching

with *Martin Landau*

It's never easy finding a parking space in the Beverly Hills flatlands. They are coveted almost as much as first look film deals. When you do find one, it's survival of the quickest as you test your parallel parking skills all the while hoping nobody disputes your claim which can result in an embarrassing, totally unproportional spat. Dare park in an unauthorized spot and the omniscient Beverly Hills police will have your car towed to the impound lot faster than you can say "Drop me off at Chanel on Rodeo Drive." And if you return to your ride a literal minute after the meter expires, you'll be greeted with the astronomical fee (also disproportional) of a parking ticket firmly tucked under your windshield wiper.

That was the vexing situation when we showed up for an interview with Martin Landau in 1995. We cut the appointment precariously close (thanks to typical Los Angeles gridlock), but were blessed to snag a meter and stuff it with the requisite coinage for the one-hour time limit. We then scurried up to his publicist's office just in time for our appointment.

Landau, who passed away in July 2017, ate, slept and breathed acting. He even dressed the part with a laughing mask of comedy signet ring prominently displayed on his finger. And when he wasn't up for a role, Landau could often be found teaching classes at the West Coast branch of the Actors Studio. At the instigation of his mentor, method coach Lee Strasberg, Landau—along with Sidney Pollack and Mark Rydell—opened the school a few years back. He had personally tutored Jack Nicholson (for three years), James Dean, Warren Oates and Anjelica Houston, among others.

"Acting is what I do for a living," he told us sitting at a conference table with his wary publicist on guard nearby, ever vigilant to the possibility we might ask a "wrong" question. "All I do is watch people's behavior. It doesn't matter what a person says, it's what he does that counts."

We thought we heard the publicist—perched like a predatory shrike—emit an audible squawk. But he might have been just clearing his throat due to a head cold. We'll never know for sure.

In any event, there was weight behind Landau's words. In a city referred to as a "company town," and populated by players who sincerely believe the infamous credo "You're only as good as your last movie," Landau had done the skeptics two better. In addition to his 1994 Best Supporting Actor Academy Award–winning performance as Bela Lugosi in *Ed Wood*, Landau earned Oscar nominations for indelible turns in two other films: *Tucker: The Man and His Dream* and *Crimes and Misdemeanors*.

For several years running, just like the mask on his ring, Landau was all smiles. But despite his successful ascent into the Hollywood firmament, Landau remembered some long dry spells when he felt compelled to take just about any role offered—usually one-dimensional villains in schlocky B-grade movies that were quickly relegated to the back shelves of video stores.

"There were a lot of years when I just wasn't being offered good roles," he said. "My whole motivation was to get a decent part so I could hit a homerun. All I wanted was a high, hard fastball to be pitched right over the plate. *Tucker* was that pitch."

According to Landau, Director Francis Ford Coppola initially thought the actor was too young looking and tall for the role of Abe Karatz, Tucker's unlikely partner. "I asked Francis if there were 10 days of rehearsal scheduled before shooting started," Landau said. "He said yes. I then told him not to worry about it, knowing full well he could fire me at any time. Each day of rehearsal I got a little closer and a little shorter. I even kept a log at the time. The first entry read, 'Here we go...' I knew this was my fastball."

At 67, Landau though gaunt and a bit hangdog, radiated the same intensity that he brought to a myriad of television and film roles, including his three-year stint as Rollin Hand on TV's *Mission Impossible*. It's that quiet spark that first brought him to the attention of Strasberg when, as a struggling New York actor in the 1950s, he and Steve McQueen were the only pupils from 2,000 applicants who Strasberg accepted into the Actors Studio.

"I guess you could say that I was Strasberg's protégé," Landau admitted. "He beat the crap out of me as a young actor because he expected a lot. It was hard to please him. Pretty girls pleased him more than ugly guys. I would do scenes in front of Kim Stanley, Maureen Stapleton, Elia Kazan and Marilyn Monroe—a lot of eyes. He would chew you up and spit you out saying, 'Perhaps next week you'll do better.'"

Tough as it was, Landau credited that early spadework with broadening his technique and opening a world of improvisational opportunities with each new role. A case in point is his characterization of "Leonard," James Mason's dutiful toady in Alfred Hitchcock's *North by Northwest*. "I played him as a homosexual," Landau said. "It was tricky, but there was no reason to be in the movie if I didn't portray him that way. Ernie Lehman, who wrote the script, picked up on what I was doing and added that pivotal line I deliver to Mason when I suspect that Eva Marie Saint is a double-agent: 'Call it my woman's intuition.' It pegged Leonard as gay."

At first, Landau said, Hitchcock expressed some misgivings, but he soon granted the actor permission to interpret Leonard any way he wished. Indeed it was Landau's ability to fully inhabit any role that led Hitchcock to cast him in the film in the first place. "Hitchcock told me in that inimitable cluck of his, 'Martin, you have a circus going on inside of you. Obviously, you can perform in this little trinket.'"

Landau had to call on all his actorly instincts to put over the part of Bela Lugosi in the biopic of the "world's worst director," Ed Wood. If the complexity of playing a "74-year-old morphine-addicted alcoholic with mood swings" wasn't challenge enough, Director Tim Burton upped the ante by telling Landau at their first meeting that he wouldn't do the movie if Landau refused to portray Lugosi.

"I did a screen test in full makeup," Landau said. "I learned two speeches from the script and we improvised with a hypodermic needle. Tim went to see the test and was excited. He said I 'nailed' the character 30 percent of the time. But at that moment my appetite was whetted. I knew I could pull it off."

According to Landau, the test was just the first step in a laborious and painstaking process. "I had to learn a whole new set of physical traits," he said. "My energy goes right to my fingertips. Lugosi's stopped in his palm, so he had a much softer hand. He used his hands much more than I do. I have a lot of teeth. You never saw Lugosi's teeth; his mouth was like a black hole. My eyes open wide; his were squinty."

In a scene from the movie, Landau, as Dracula, delivers a famous non sequitur, "Pull the string!" The serio-comic moment underscores the depths to which Lugosi's career had sunk at that time. It also helped Landau clinch his first Oscar statuette.

At this point in the interview, Dave took a furtive peek at his wristwatch, checking the time against the nearly expired parking meter. Always traveling on a shoestring budget, we could ill afford the ruinous expense of a fine on our rental car.

Although Landau appeared to be in no apparent rush, the momentary glance at the watch seemed to perturb him. "Do you have someplace better to go?" he admonished us. Dave, turning crimson, explained to a baleful Landau our parking situation. But since we had not gotten around to asking about his latest film project, Landau was not entirely interested in cutting off the interview. "I'm an actor—you see!—it's my business to notice everything, even subtleties," he said almost triumphantly as if we had just been caught with our hands in the cookie jar.

At this juncture, Landau's publicist started to wildly flap his wings or maybe he gestured with his arms. We'll never know for sure. So, we continued.

The film in question—the one Landau wanted to talk about—was one where he literally "pulled the strings" as master puppeteer "Gepetto" in New Line Cinema's animated/live action production of *Pinocchio*.

"I went to Prague specifically to learn about European marionette techniques," he said, always the consummate craftsman. "You could hang the animated cells from the film up in your home as artwork—they are so beautiful."

As we departed making no pretense about our overweening desire to replug the meter, we asked Landau if he ever wore the frowning mask of tragedy as a companion to his other ring. Landau shot us an inscrutable smile that seemed straight out of an Actors Studio master class.

"Tragedy tomorrow, comedy tonight," he said, grinning.

The Art of Perfect Timing

Burton Lane

Call it happenstance, harmonic convergence, or maybe just perfect timing, but Burton Lane was certainly at the right place at the right time throughout his long, rich career as a songwriter of Hollywood and Broadway musicals.

Case in point: In 1933, he wrote a little ditty called "Heigh-Ho, the Gang's All Here" for *Dancing Lady*, an MGM film starring Joan Crawford and Clark Gable. That song introduced movie audiences to a lithe Broadway hoofer named Fred Astaire who had just ankled the Great White Way for a shot at motion pictures and who would soon be on the verge of a harmonic convergence all his own.

Thirty-five years later, Lane, coincidentally, helped Astaire ring down the curtain on his legendary dancing career when the elder statesman of movie musicals starred in the film adaptation of Lane's and lyricist E.Y. Harburg's landmark Broadway show, *Finian's Rainbow*. The show had several song hits, including the popular "Old Devil Moon."

In fact, it was pretty much by chance that Lane (83 when we met him in 1994) embarked on a career as a songwriter at all. "I had a very aggressive father and whenever he saw a piano, he'd say, 'Burt—play!'" Lane said looking dapper in on open-collared striped shirt. He was seated at the piano in his apartment overlooking New York City's Central Park. An Al Hirschfeld sketch of the composer and his frequent collaborator Alan Jay Lerner overlooked him from the wall.

"One time over the Christmas holidays, we were staying down in Atlantic City at a little inn off the boardwalk. At the coaxing of my father, I was playing some tunes for the guests at an upright piano in the parlor. Suddenly, a woman came over to dad and announced that she was George Gershwin's mother. She said: "When I heard your boy play, he sounded like my Georgie, and when I looked up, he looked like my Georgie from the back.'"

The upshot of that chance meeting was Lane being invited to the Gershwin home on the Upper West Side to meet George. A fast friendship developed and Gershwin soon became a mentor to the teenaged Lane. "For my money, George Gershwin is still the greatest songwriter ever," Lane said, pointing to an autographed photo of George on the wall next to the Hirschfeld lithograph. "Truthfully, until I met him and his brother Ira, I didn't know there was a career in songwriting for me. I didn't know if I would fit in anyplace."

Lane, like Gershwin before him, landed a job for $17 a week writing songs for Remicks, a large music publisher of the day. "I was still going to high school then," he said. "However, I want to point out that I did earn $3 more a week than George did when he worked at Remicks!"

After writing songs for several shows staged by the Schubert brothers in New York City and environs, a partner of Irving Berlin's in the music publishing business encouraged Lane and his lyric-writing partner, Harold Adamson, to "Go Hollywood."

"We got the nod to contribute to *Dancing Lady*, and I was in the screening room at MGM watching Fred Astaire's screen test (the one that spawned the infamous studio evaluation: 'Can't act. Can't sing. Slightly bald. Can dance a little') when a couple of studio

Lane and his Hirschfeld doppelganger

executives came in and sat down," Lane said. "I remember one guy said to the other, 'I can walk down the hall and get dancers like this for $75 a week.' I was absolutely incredulous. Those guys didn't have a clue of what they had in Fred."

Lane collaborated with several lyricists throughout his career, including Frank Loesser, Alan Jay Lerner and E.Y. "Yip" Harburg. With Lerner, Lane wrote the score for *Royal Wedding*, a 1951 musical starring Astaire and Jane Powell. One number, "How Could You Believe Me When I Said I Loved You When You Know I've Been a Liar All My Life!" was, for many years, the longest song title on record.

"We know that song," we declared. "The lyrics are a mouthful." Lane smiled and sat down at his piano and played and sang the tune. It's the only time we ever had the temerity to join in singing a composer's tune to the composer as the composer played it. Happily, we managed to stay mostly on key but suffice to say there weren't any A&R men waiting to sign us up for a recording deal at the finish. For his part, Lane just seemed pleased that two guys knew a novelty song that had long been resigned to obscurity and had been written a decade before each of them was born. That was enough for him.

"Alan was staying at the Bel-Air Hotel when we were writing the score for *Royal Wedding*," Lane said. "I picked him up in my car to drive to the studio, and before he got in he told me that Astaire wanted to do a low-down vaudeville number in the film. He then hit me with the 'How Could You Believe Me' lyric. I told him I thought it was great and should be sung to a tune something like this. I then repeated the lyric humming a tune made up on the spot. All this occurred in the span of about five seconds; Alan still hadn't stepped foot in the car. Alan replied, 'Not something like that—*that!*' He got into the car and on the 15-minute drive to the studio, we wrote the rest of the song."

According to Lane, at the film's preview, the number literally stopped the show. "The screenplay to that movie was dull, ridden with clichés," Lane said. "But writing for Fred, that was the spark. He was a great deliverer of songs."

Royal Wedding contains one of Astaire's greatest solo numbers; the justly famous duet he performs with a wooden hat rack as his partner in the gym of a ship during an

Atlantic crossing. During his career, Astaire's appalling perfectionism created many such screen classics in which he was able to make inanimate props spring to life and obey his commands. In that magical way, Astaire was an inspiration for not only song and dance men but also, more improbably, the witty physicality of Jackie Chan. Chan has even gone on record that certain set pieces in his action movies were informed by the choreography of Astaire, Gene Kelly and even the great silent film comedians.

Lane told us that the tune to Astaire's hat rack dance was called "The Sunday Jumps" and originally had a lyric by Lerner. "But when Fred was laying out the number, he jettisoned the lyrics and just danced to the tune I wrote," Lane said. "The lyrics were about a guy that had the 'jumps' after being out all night drinking" and just didn't fit the situation of a dance in a gymnasium."

Another great singer that Lane personally helped "deliver" to the world was Judy Garland. Lane happened to hear little Frances Gumm (Judy) perform with her sisters on the stage of New York's Paramount theater in 1934.

"I introduced Judy to the folks at MGM where she sang for the top studio brass for hours. In the crush and confusion of that memorable day, no one thanked me, including Judy," he said. "Flash forward seven years later and I was assigned to write the score for *Babes on Broadway*, co-starring Mickey Rooney and Judy. I was told by producer Arthur Freed to walk over to the soundstage and help the kids go through some of the songs. As we neared the rehearsal area, a little girl came running up and threw her arms around me. It was Judy. She apologized for not thanking me that day. 'I was so confused by all the attention,' she said. 'I can't thank you enough for what you did for me.'"

Like Judy, Barbra Streisand's voice has often been touted as being without peer. Lane, who wrote the score for *On a Clear Day You Can See Forever* starring Streisand, readily attested to the "greatness" of Streisand's "vocal instrument." However, he said that in his estimation she often "sings to herself and forgets what she is singing about."

Lane attended Streisand's Madison Square Garden concert the year before our visit in which she sang the title tune from *On a Clear Day*. He said he enjoyed himself immensely.

One rendition of a song that Lane enthusiastically endorsed without qualification is a Barbara Cook/Barry Manilow duet recording of "Look to the Rainbow" from *Finian's Rainbow*. The song is featured on Manilow's *Showstoppers* album released in 1991 on the Arista label. "I've kept it on top of my stereo for about two years now," Lane said. "I just love playing it so much I can't put it away."

Manilow got it right: Burton Lane—Showstopper.

Janet and Tony
and the Art of Crowd Control
Janet Leigh and *Tony Curtis*

Once upon a time in Hollywood (the early 1950s to be exact), there lived a beautiful princess named Janet Leigh and her crown prince, Tony Curtis. As a married couple, their union in 1951 had been properly sanctified by an ordained minister and by God. Beyond that, it earned the beneficence of another—perhaps higher power—Metro-Gold-wyn-Mayer Studios.

You see, the star-crossed couple generated considerable box office heat in those days; with the hegemony of television making Pepto-Bismol the aperitif of choice for most movie executives, the king of studios responded ravenously to balance sheets in the black. And Leigh and Curtis with charisma galore certainly delivered the requisite numbers along with a large and soothing dose of old-style Tinseltown brio.

Generally, life was simpler back then—or perhaps just simply repressed. In any case, even media-generated hype and spin had an innocent hue and took longer to build than the egg-timer industry average of today. However, in the case of Leigh and Curtis, as the rpm of their individual careers increased, their combined celebrity became a veritable juggernaut drawing unruly crowds that literally buckled seaside piers during personal appearance tours.

According to Leigh, the big difference between her and, say, today's crop of young media-concocted icons (we talked to her in 1996) is that she was schooled by the studio to court publicity and, if not the adulation that sometimes came with it, at least learn how to take it in stride. Howard Strickling, head of publicity at MGM, taught her a valuable lesson in the 1950s, one she said that held her in good stead; it was the fine art of crowd control.

"The surge comes because the crowd thinks you are going to run away from them," she explained. "So if you remain calm, they settle down because they think you're extending yourself. It really works, but you've got to keep moving—never stop. If you stop, they'll corner you."

Leigh's explanation wasn't disdainful—far from it—it was a thoughtful, if somewhat dispassionate, deconstruction of crowd dynamics. For us, it conjured certain advice Midwestern farmers used to dole

Psyched-out

out when working around livestock. "...Move slowly, deliberately, no jerky movements and always keep a watchful eye on the bull."

Cattle calls, we surmised, must be the same all over, be they of the four-hoof or two-legged variety.

We interviewed Leigh and Curtis—separate visits two years apart—at their houses, each perched on the spine of the Santa Monica Mountains but at opposite ends of that low, crusty range of hills.

Leigh greeted us in the early spring of 1996 at the 10-foot-high driveway gate of her home just off Summitridge Drive in Beverly Hills, the same street that Big Band leader Artie Shaw had lived on in the early 1940s and for which he named one of his catchiest swing tunes. The gate effectively screened the house from any "Peeping Toms" who ventured into those oxygen-thin reaches of upper Beverly Hills to gawk at the immortal star of *Psycho*. Our first glimpse of her was when she gave the most furtive of peeks around the partition which she had opened just a sliver in order to ascertain we were who we claimed to be.

For just an instant, it felt to us like a distaff real-life role reversal of when Anthony Perkins as Norman Bates played the creepy voyeur looking through a peephole into Leigh's motel room in that film.

"I've been stalked," Leigh said matter-of-factly. "Jamie (her daughter with Tony, Jamie Lee Curtis) has had several stalkers, so she's nervous. You just have to take precautions."

All in all, the apple doesn't fall very far from the tree in the Leigh household. Jamie Lee Curtis, started in the movie business starring in horror films such as *Halloween*, *Terror Train*, *Prom Night*, and *Friday the 13th*. To a generation of spooked teenagers, she earned the endearing appellation, "The Scream Queen." Back in '96 Leigh was playing a part made to order in the latest in the latest installment of her daughter's *Halloween* franchise—*Halloween H20: 20 Years Later* as, what else, Jamie Lee's mom!

Separately or in tandem, with Janet Leigh and Jamie Lee, blood—along with a little bloodletting—does tell!

The house itself which Leigh shared with her husband, Los Angeles businessman, Bob Brandt, seemed like a continuation of the steep mountainside incline on which it was built—all angular rooms and vaulted ceiling; Westside modern meets Babylonian ziggurat.

"Here is where I draw the line between my public persona and my private life," she said.

Looking svelte from a regimen of regular tennis matches with friends like fellow MGM star, Jane Powell, Leigh, 71, plopped on a sofa and told us that contrary to F. Scott Fitzgerald's famous prescient pronouncement about his own trajectory, some American lives do have second acts.

"I've become a writer during these last several years," she announced proudly. To that date, Leigh had written an autobiography entitled, *There Really Was a Hollywood*, as well as a well-received book on the making of *Psycho* which was published in 1995 to coincide with the 35th anniversary of the film. That same year she also published her first novel, *House of Destiny*.

"The first time I saw my name printed on the dust jacket of my first book, it was every bit as thrilling as seeing my face up on a movie screen for the first time in 1947 in *The Romance of Rosy Ridge*," she said. "As an actress, you are such a small part of the overall movie, just a cog in the machine. But writing a book is introspective, personal and you go at it 100 percent alone."

According to Leigh, writing and performing were definitely aligned. "You prepare for a role the way you prepare a character for the written page," she said. "For example, when I played 'Marion Crane' in *Psycho*, I constructed her whole life. I knew what she was like in school; her tastes, frailties, strengths. I knew what kind of sister she was, and what kind of daughter."

Just as Leigh faced a blank sheet of paper alone, she also flew solo developing her character in Hitchcock's most disturbing suspense thriller. "Hitch had a hands-off policy unless you really were blocked," Leigh said. "He was the consummate shot-maker and he trusted his actors to come up with their own motivations. I do remember that he didn't feel there was enough passion between John Gavin and I in the opening hotel room scene, even with me just dressed in a slip and brassiere, so he told us to turn up the heat, which we did."

It's no shocker that Leigh remained unimpressed with the quartet of *Psycho* clones that had been lensed in the intervening years—although she saw them all. When pressed to choose the least objectionable entry in the series, she picked the 1990 made-for-cable prequel version. "In that one you saw what a loon Norman's mother was, so you figured out why he went bats," she laughed. Leigh added she had no intention of appearing in the big screen (unsuccessful) remake of the film that was subsequently made with Vince Vaughn and Anne Heche, a pallid substitute for Leigh as "Marion Crane."

"The thing about Hitch, and this has been well-documented," Leigh said, "was that everything was storyboarded, everything was down. He knew exactly where the actors were to stand in a scene, what lens was on the camera for a particular shot—everything. As an actor, what you have to do is bring what you want to bring to your character, but you had to move when he wanted you to move. That's where the crossed swords came with many actors, because they felt that he was curtailing their creativity or their freedom of expression. You could take it that way."

Leigh took it another way entirely, as creative latitude. "I took it in a way which I felt was healthier, since that was the way it was going to be, regardless." she said. "I took Hitch's direction like he was saying: 'Look, you're an actress. I've hired you. I believe you can do Marion and you can do with her pretty well what you want. Bring to her what you kind of have in your mind unless it interferes with what my whole concept is. If it doesn't, I'm not going to bother you at all.' I took his confidence in me as a supreme compliment."

Leigh said that she was the only actor in the movie that was sent the novel *Psycho* by Robert Bloch with a letter from Hitchcock asking her to consider playing the role of Marion Crane. "I would have done the movie without even reading the book because of Hitchcock," she said. "I mean, I would've been the biggest dumbass of all time if I said no."

With her second career as a memoirist burgeoning, Leigh found herself in a nostalgic mood about Old Hollywood and what it was like when she started in the business. "Oh, God, it was fantastic," she said. "I was a part of something that I'd watched since I was born. I used to go to the movies all the time. To be a part of that; but then I really wanted to learn what it was all about. It was an opportunity. It was like going to college. I loved it."

She also remembered her first day of work as a contract player at MGM as if it had happened the day before. "I walked in that gate twice," she said. "The first time was when my agent took me from MCA and I walked through the pedestrian entrance of the big MGM gates and Jose Iturbi opened the door for me and I just about died. I mean, I'd just seen him in *Holiday in Mexico*.

"Then the next time was when I went back. I signed a contract that day," she continued. "I got the appointment with Lillian Burns (the head dramatic coach at the studio) that day. I went back to MCA, signed all the papers, which I loved doing. Then the next time I walked through there, I walked through as a part of it. I walked through that gate that I had seen in pictures since I was able to go to movies, and I was a part of it. I belonged there. My name was there. The guard said, 'Oh, yes … you're on the payroll.' I was a part of this fantastic organization."

* * *

Two years later during our visit with Tony Curtis, he wryly admitted that he broke into movies the same way a thief enters the second story window of a mansion he's going to rob—surreptitiously, almost undetected. It was the antithesis of Leigh's dreamlike contract signing full of magic and stardust.

"People didn't know who I was—I just snuck in," Curtis said, laughing the same incredulous laugh he did in 1948 when Universal first put him, a largely unknown acting quantity, under the standard studio contract. "I was like a weed that grew out of a crack in the cement only that crack happened to be located on a studio lot."

Thanks to an irresistible combination of darkly Semitic matinee-idol looks and an engaging grin that illuminated the screen, Curtis's stealthy break-in to the business soon became a four-alarm fire. Separately, and with his equally photogenic wife, Leigh, Curtis became a monolithic sex symbol long before hype and marketing spin made such phenomena easier to construct.

"Janet and I ended up being a movie couple, but without intending to be," he said. Curtis met Leigh at a cocktail party, but the studio balked when they became a regular item. "They didn't like the idea that maybe I would even marry her. And that got me so pissed off that I did," he said. "It gives you an idea how clumsy the times were. We fell in love and the next thing we knew all the magazines went 'ga-ga' over it. Eddie Fisher and Debbie Reynolds could have been our maids in comparison… Elizabeth Taylor and Richard Burton could have been the couple who lived in our gatehouse and looked after the garden. That's how big the buzz around us was in those days."

To hear Curtis retell it, his impact in films was unprecedented. "When I hit, in 1948, I really hit big," he said, "and no one knows why. The movie guys up to that point had been in the service. The men were coming out and they were 35 and 40 years of age. There were no young leading men. It was Burt Lancaster, Kirk Douglas—who started after the war—but they were in their 30s already. But the young teenagers didn't have an idol out of that maelstrom. It was Robert Wagner, me and Marlon Brando who came out of the service about the same time. John Derek was at Columbia and Marshall Thompson was over at MGM. There was a half-dozen. But nobody punched it out like I did. I didn't have to kiss anybody, kiss anything."

Half a century later, the march of time—not the ravages of it—had tempered Curtis's good looks into a formidable, but not vestigial presence. The rippling chest of yore, barrel-shaped in '98, still emanated powerful strength. And he still could high-beam that glistening smile at will, which he did unstintingly. In fact, for Curtis, it had all become about living life in the affirmative.

Then 73, Curtis lived in a gated community in the hills of Bel-Air about a Henry Moore stone head's throw across the 405 freeway from the Getty Center art museum. It was a propitious location for Curtis since acting in movies had largely, though not completely, given way to his second career as a painter. He told us that at last count he had perhaps 1,500 canvases and 2,000 drawings stacked in a studio he kept in Woodland Hills and which one of his sons managed. Looking around the living room of his hacienda-style house, much of the overflow seemed to recline against all available upright surfaces. Matisse-like still lifes were propped next to framed animation cells of Tony as "Stony Curtis" from *The Flintstones*, cartoon show, and blow-up photos of he and Jack Lemmon dressed in drag and reclining on a divan on the set of *Some Like It Hot*.

But apart from the multicolored neck ribbon of Curtis's *Légion d'Honneur* (bestowed by the French Government for meritorious cultural achievement) which peeked at us from its half-opened box, very little chronicling Curtis's show business career was visible.

"You wouldn't know to look around here that this is the home of a movie actor. You'd think a painter lives here, and that's the way I like it," he said in that familiar low-clipped tone that conjured images of a street urchin boyhood in New York City.

Back to that medal. An impression many people had of Curtis the preceding last few years, largely through his appearances in the media, was of a loose cannon. Flouncing into gallery and nightclub openings with the *Légion d'Honneur* hung prominently around his neck like the "flair" on a Denny's waitress smock, Curtis brought to mind a younger version of Georgie Jessel in all his overblown military regalia. It would've been easy to dismiss Curtis's eccentricity, like it was Jessel's, as a joke, a publicity ploy, but that would be wrong. Curtis, you see, made it abundantly clear that he didn't give a shit! To wit; he had seen and done almost everything, and, good or bad, he had come out alive on this end wiser for the wear. To Curtis's way of thinking, that clarity also provided the liberating freedom of not having to buckle to peer pressure—or pretty much any pressure. Curtis had, in effect, achieved a Zen-like state of placidity the last few years.

"My dear friends, every minute of the day it can't get better than it is right now," he recited, mantra-like, in the ritualistic cadence of a twelve-step program brochure (Curtis told us he was a program adherent after liberally abusing cocaine and heroin in the 1970s). "And that minute will give way to the next 'best' minute. I'm not jerking myself off here. I've never been busier. I've never looked better in my life. Everywhere I go people love me. I get tables anywhere in the world. And I love it all!"

An ego successfully rehabilitated? Almost. Curtis did confess to a kind of wistful *ennui* about receiving recognition from his Hollywood peers for what he considered to be about 20–25 great films out of 110 movies in which he starred. "That's part of the uniqueness of my situation," he said. "I've done some excellent films, like my favorite, *The Boston Strangler*, but I guess I'll have to leave any affirmation in the hands of the Gods."

But really, affirmation of sorts came almost daily for Curtis. There used to be a mural of him in a white T-shirt (taken from an early Curtis role in *City Across the River* in 1949), painted by a graffiti artist on an overpass that spanned the Hollywood Freeway, and it could almost stop traffic. More famously, Curtis was depicted on the cover of The Beatles' *Sgt. Peppers* album and, of course, there's "Stony Curtis." Not bad for the former Bernie Schwartz from "Da Bronx."

However, in the end, Curtis exhibited a repeated penchant for green-glassing any lingering sentiment about his career. "My dear friends, I don't give a shit," he said. "It's not that important, it never was and it never will be; it's a profession, a career that I chose. And during the period of time when movies were made before television, that was when a lot of my movies were made, there was no such thing as, 'Well, next year it'll end up on a network or a program on TCM.'"

"Those tiny little pop-culture affirmations prove that I made my mark during a period of time," he said. "They make me feel good but that's all."

What didn't make Curtis feel good when he was at his apex was working with Marilyn Monroe during *Some Like It Hot*, one of the very best comedies ever filmed. "She made it tough for everybody," Curtis said. "If you're in a chain gang and you're tied to someone else, who's also tied to someone else, and so on … and the fifth guy down the line is screwing around and not paying attention, it will delay everyone else. That was the case with Marilyn. You're being paid good dough to work and you're doing 10–12 hour days. You don't want to have to baby someone unless the script calls for babying.

"She would play Jack Lemmon off against me or me against him and Billy Wilder against both of us," Curtis continued. "We had to slow down for Marilyn because she couldn't memorize lines at that time. She was quite awkward in her behavior with everybody. Marilyn was getting even with every guy who ever fucked her—anybody—any man that made her put those kneepads on! That's my read on her. But I never said kissing her was like kissing Hitler! I don't know where that came from."

A full frontal barrage with Curtis telling it like it was—with no particular axe to grind or anything to purge. He told us he began to tell the unabridged truth years ago. "There's nothing for me to be upset about," he said. "There isn't anyone alive who wouldn't want to be a major player in Hollywood. Walk down the street and point to anybody. You get everything you ever wanted."

Through the years, various actor friends and artists shared with Curtis pearls of wisdom that he filed away and learned from. One was from his acting idol, Cary Grant. "Cary once told me the way to judge a fine bottle of white wine was that after chilling, it should taste like a cool glass of water," Curtis remembered. 'It's so artful that it's artless,' Cary said. Curtis instantly related Grant's sommelier advice to his own profession

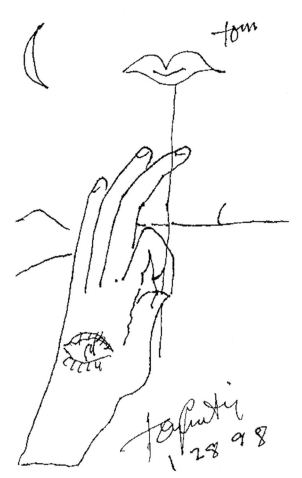

Sketch by Tony for Tom Johnson

and considered it one of the best acting tips he ever received; that less is more. Indeed, underplaying scenes may have helped ensure the long run Curtis enjoyed in movies.

"I don't want my work ever to look as if, when you see me in a scene and the subtitle comes underneath: 'Watch Tony get mad now!' You could do that with a lot of actors," he said. "I know a lot of actors that telegraph what's coming; Jack Lemmon does, George C. Scott does. I could name a whole slew of actors who are constantly telegraphing what they're about to do, but that's their style of working in a movie. There's no one style to movies. Movies aren't a profession like brain surgery where you've got to make certain cuts a certain way. Some people star in movies because of their tits; some because of their hair; some because of their size or their sex. One thousand years from now the films I made will probably still be around in some form," he said. "If you look at it that way, they have their own kind of perpetuity."

During the interview, Curtis had been intermittently doodling with a pencil on a small sketchpad. As he got out of his chair, he handed us the sketch he had been working on of a hand pulling a cord dangling from a floating cloud that was rendered in the shape of a smile.

It was Curtis depicting for us the equilibrium he had come to feel—that life was good; weightless, in fact. And who could ask for better affirmation than that.

Mum's the Word

Mervyn LeRoy

It was an oppressively hot summer day in Los Angeles and we were straitjacketed into cheap-ass wool and polyester blend suits that seemed to dampen with every footfall. Mervyn LeRoy, a man storied for producing *The Wizard of Oz* and for having once had Lana Turner under "personal contract" was expecting us for an interview and we weren't really in the mood.

As we rode the elevator up to his suite on the top floor of an office building in West Hollywood just over the meridian from Beverly Hills on the Sunset Strip, one shared thought kept running insistently through our minds. It was Dorothy Gale's epiphany near the end of *Oz*.

"If I ever go looking for my heart's desire again, I won't look any further than my own backyard," she had squeaked to good witch Glinda about lessons learned during her trek down the yellow brick road. "Because if it isn't there, I never really lost it to begin with!"

"Good thinking there," Tom muttered as beads of perspiration from his forehead streaked down the inside lenses of his glasses, bisecting his field of vision like some sort of crazy bug. Could we have been under duress in sunny Southern California, a place where "laidback" isn't a pejorative but a lifestyle?

Perish the thought.

It was just that we were late for the interview, 2000 miles from home in an enclave that at times could give Munchkinland a run for its money. All both of us really wanted to do was follow Dorothy's lead and retreat poolside to our motel where we could take the Nestea Plunge.

At the seventh floor the elevator door opened for Ronnie Schell, better known as "Duke Slater," Jim Nabors' barracks chum in the *Gomer Pyle, U.S.M.C.* TV series. Ronnie glided onto the elevator with the quiet confidence that surely must have come from knowing his face is familiar to handfuls of people. Sadly, Ronnie's entrance was marred when his left arm got caught in the closing elevator door. His wristwatch was hammered along with any sense of decorum he might previously have used in public spaces. From the seventh to the 20th floor we were witness to a cascade of invective that would have kept him on KP duty peeling spuds through three seasons of TV bootcamp.

When we opened the door to LeRoy's suite, we were barraged again—this time by 130 (LeRoy's count) framed and autographed glossies that wallpapered his outer office. Stills from such classics as *Little Caesar*, *I Am a Fugitive from a Chain Gang*, *Mister Roberts*, *Madame Curie* and *Gypsy* attested to a successful directing career that began in 1928 and lasted for decades.

"A remarkable roll of the dice," mused LeRoy's clerical assistant, a silver-haired man impeccably dressed in a Lord & Taylor pinstripe suit. "Mr. LeRoy is a survivor and that's a breed apart in this town," he said. "Please make yourselves comfortable while I ring him up. Meantime, can I mix you a drink or pour a cup of coffee or tea?"

It struck both of us as slightly incongruous that a man as solicitous and tactful as LeRoy's secretary would be working in Hollywood as a coffee gofer. He belonged in an English drawing room serving crumpets under the primping stare of an oil painting by Gainsborough, not seated in an outer office underneath a studio still of Edward G. Robinson as a wounded gangster bleeding out. We concluded that he was probably a character actor (butler roles a specialty) sent over from central casting for the afternoon.

"May I present Mr. LeRoy," the secretary announced.

Like many slightly-built men, LeRoy had a disproportionately large head with a few folds of neck wattle that seemed to swell out the top of his dress shirt like he had just been garroted by his own necktie. Dave said later that he couldn't help thinking of "Cecil Turtle" from *Looney Tunes*.

"Glad to meetcha," LeRoy said, his slang a nice contrast to the secretary's posh play-acting. It was an introduction made even more memorable since LeRoy's salutation was practically the only thing he was able to articulate during our visit. Although well-meaning and as endearing as "Elmer Fudd," LeRoy was about as loquacious as Helen Keller before her water pump epiphany. It didn't help that during the course of our interview he busily chewed on a cigar that aided little in our comprehending him.

In her wonderful book, *The Making of the Wizard of Oz*, Aljean Harmetz wrote, "People always used to wonder how Mervyn was ever able to direct a picture. He'd say: 'Put a little more into it, baby.' But he somehow got his emotions over to his actors. They understood him in some way."

When we asked him about a collegiate musical he directed early in his career called *Harold Teen*, starring eccentric dance sensation Hal LeRoy (no relation), Mervyn gave us carte blanche to invent any quote we thought might make an appropriate answer.

"I can't think of one of my own," he said.

The Heart of New York, a 1932 comedy starring Smith & Dale of "Sunshine Boys" vaudeville fame was LeRoy's favorite movie of all the ones he directed. We asked what the experience was like.

Mervyn speechless

"Did you direct them?" LeRoy said.

"No, you did, Mr. LeRoy," Dave replied. "Remember … in *The Heart of New York* … your favorite film?"

"I made that," he declared.

Slowly it dawned on us why LeRoy had decorated his office walls with so many celebrity stills. If a picture paints a thousand words, then LeRoy could be contentedly mute for the rest of his days. When words failed (as they invariably did), LeRoy calmly strolled over to his big metal filing cabinet and produced a picture of James Cagney from *Mister Roberts*. It was instant 8 × 10 vindication of former glory and better articulation.

At LeRoy's request we read so many "sincere testaments" and "heartfelt inscriptions" that the office began to give Tom palpitations. After winsomely directing our attention to a few more glossies, LeRoy did manage to conjure up a reminiscence of *The Wizard of Oz*. In a startling burst of eloquence, LeRoy took full credit for the legendary film.

"Arthur Freed is sometimes given credit for producing that movie. He's full of shit! Now that he's dead, I don't want to say anything about him. It's all the same to me but I was the boss of all my pictures. I'm not saying that for ego or anything. And Ray Bolger (who played the scarecrow), he's a real mean man. He thinks he's a genius. He's a real person. And those Munchkin bastards, what a time I had with them. All they did was screw each other. To settle them down on the set, I'd threaten not to pay their salaries."

Turning the tables on us, LeRoy asked who else we'd like to see in L.A. that we hadn't already booked. We mentioned we had tried to interview Jimmy Stewart a couple of times but were never able to close the deal.

He startled us with: "Hold on, I'll get him on the phone." We watched as LeRoy dialed and then held the line. "Busy signal," he said and hung up. It was probably just as well. We had trouble imagining how LeRoy would be able to intelligibly convey to Stewart that he had two kids in his office that wanted to have a sit-down.

In 1945 LeRoy won an Academy Award for a short subject that preached tolerance (*The House I Live In*), and in 1975 he was given the Irving G. Thalberg Memorial Award for his body of work as a producer. But his proudest achievement and perhaps most enduring legacy is *The Wizard of Oz*.

"The play's the thing. Shakespeare agrees with me," he said. "*Oz* will live forever in the hearts of children."

At the end of the film there is a scene where the Cowardly Lion is given the Medal of Honor for courage in "liquidating" the Wicked Witch of the West. "Shucks folks, I'm speechless," he says. It's more than just a sweet line from a monumental Mervyn LeRoy production. For the producer-director, the phrase had become doctrine.

Jerry-Rigged

Jerry Lewis

Presenting Jerry Lewis; the self-styled Emmett Kelly of spasm.

To some stalwart admirers, he is a Nobel Peace Prize–nominated crusader who annually raised millions of dollars for the Muscular Dystrophy Association until being unceremoniously dumped as the organization's long-time national chairman in 2011. To others, he is a rubber-legged (and faced) comedian who successfully contorted his body into megalithic nightclub and movie contracts long before he ever heard the acronym, MDA. For the overwhelming rest of us, he remains a mixed blessing; Dean Martin's man-child sidekick; a knock-kneed *nebbish* you either love or hate whose sonic falsetto makes fingernails raked across a chalkboard seem like an aural tonic and whose hair oozes an annual oil reserve that could bust a cartel.

"I'm very unique. You have to understand that," Lewis said to us during an interview a few weeks before Thanksgiving in 1984. He was in Bloomington, Minnesota to perform his nightclub act at the Carlton Celebrity Room (long-since defunct). "There aren't many comedians who are SuperJews... Hello..."

Oy vey!

Perhaps more than any other American entertainer, Lewis exists on a dichotomous level that has kept him in the vortex of heated debate long after his movies waned at the box office in this country. In France, critics call him the *grandiose cinéaste*—the master filmmaker. Lewis has been awarded the *La Légion d'honneur* as the "French people's favorite clown," and his name was (and sometimes still is) routinely uttered in the same reverential tone usually reserved for *auteurs* like Orson Welles and Federico Fellini.

In America, critics think of him (when they do at all) as little more than a mega-lomaniacal brat with a bilious temper who irreparably maimed his career in a vain attempt to be a writer, producer, director, star and thus heir to the mantle of Charlie Chaplin.

"You have to know that France is on the smallest scale compared to Italy, Germany, Spain, the Netherlands and Belgium," Lewis told us. "Lewis mania is four times stronger in Germany and Italy and it's all related to filmmaking. In those countries they have a deep respect for the director and they know what it takes to get a picture up on the screen. That's why the director is always billed before the star and the title of the film. The respect has nothing to do with audience reaction or acceptance.

"In America they go to the movies and just watch what's on the screen," he continued. "They don't care who did it or how it got there. When I made films as an actor for Hal Wallis, there was no reaction in Italy at all except that I was acknowledged as a popular star. The fanaticism didn't start until I became a director."

Lewis bristled when we suggested that he was journalism's favorite clay pigeon. He claimed that "the bullshit" about his running battle with the press was "all horseshit" and that the occasional screaming headline of him pulling up stakes and moving to France was just a pathetic attempt (at that time) to sell tabloids to housewives on runs to the grocery store.

"It all started when someone read it in the *National Enquirer*," Lewis said, his gorge rising. "Anybody who reads the *Enquirer* would drink their own bathwater. Anybody who reads the *Enquirer* would eat their young. So anytime you read something about me in there they either have me moving to France or getting a hysterectomy. I have property in France and it was made a matter of public information and all of a sudden people have me moving there. I'm not giving up my country. Are you nuts? You can't get a fuckin' egg cream in France and you're not gonna find any India nuts there; are you crazy? I'm not sure I can get one in Minneapolis."

Although the consensus of opinion has calcified to polar opposites concerning Lewis—you love him, you hate him, in all probability you change the channel when a comedy of his airs on TCM or some other retro cable channel. But what remains undeniable is that his movie career, while almost barren of verbal wit, contains sight gags that are evergreen; slap*schtick* tinged with genius.

Lewis's best moments were comic visual effects—Jerryatrics—choreographed to some kind of syncopation. His role as a buck-toothed nutty professor herking and jerking to the downbeat of a college dance band; pantomiming all the instruments to Count Basie's "Cute" over the radio in *Cinderfella*; mouthing the commands of a studio boss to Basie's "Blues in Hoss Flat" in *The Errand Boy*; or furiously working the keys of a non-existent typewriter in *Who's Minding the Store?* Those numbers (and there are many more) are stuck in moviegoers minds as firmly as the Jujyfruits they once plastered under their theater seats. For the record, Lewis told us his own favorite moment from his films is a sight-gag from *The Bellboy* where he takes a flashbulb picture of Miami at night that illuminates the whole city like the blinding flash from a nuclear detonation.

"You're seeing too much cerebral comedy today," Lewis said. "I think young comics haven't had vaudeville to look at and they also don't have places to be bad. Besides Atlantic City and Vegas, all you have are comedy rooms and they're begging for cerebral comics. There's nothing wrong with Woody Allen because he's cerebral as well as being visual. He's one of the most brilliant comics we have working today. But the young guys I see standing up for 40 minutes in one spot are doing what I call visual hi-fi. You can buy a record and stay home without putting on a tie. When I get on stage, I don't make a very good target because I'm moving all the time. Dick Brooks—who's a writer—he doesn't write the stuff I write, he writes heavier stuff, once said to me that he couldn't remember one line from *Gunga Din* but he remembered what Din looked liked when they killed him in the movie."

After a pregnant pause and to vindicate his nascent theory that the younger generation is clueless about the classics, Lewis dared us to remember two lines from *Gone with the Wind*.

"Frankly my dear, I don't give a damn," Tom said trying to affect a Rhett Butler baritone.

Like he was banking on a seven come eleven dice throw at a Sands crap table, Lewis upped the ante: "One more and I'll give you a $100," he said in a slightly tremulous voice that sounded like audible flop sweat to us.

"I can't think about that today; I'll think about that tomorrow," Tom squeaked trying to affect a coquettish Scarlett O'Hara delivery but coming off more like Lewis' "Homer Flagg" character in *Living It Up*.

"But please, Mr. Lewis, don't ask me to tell you what they looked like when they spoke those lines," Tom said.

(Silence.)

"Don't you want my mailing address?" Tom asked

"Nope," Lewis said, "but I'll get you later, though."

During one four-year span at Paramount Studios, Lewis said that he wrote, directed, produced and starred in *The Errand Boy*, *The Patsy*, *The Nutty Professor*, and *The Family Jewels*. Increasingly, scenes of pathos would be crow-barred into these movies, with Lewis positioned as the down-trodden *Schlemiel* bravely persevering against adversity (like Chaplin's "Little Tramp"). It is in those moments of blatant pandering to the tear-ducts of a movie-going public weaned on melodrama that Lewis mortally sinned against audiences in America.

Lewis' juxtaposition of funny and sad sequences was rarely handled with the kind of finesse needed to effectively bring them off. In *The Disorderly Orderly* scenes of a suicidal patient spilling her guts to a psychiatrist were intercut with shots of Lewis' slapstick antics out on the hospital grounds (although Lewis' character who is afflicted with "neurotic identification empathy" and suffers the same symptoms of other patients predates Woody Allen's neurotic, shape-shifting "Zelig" by decades). A mere suspension of disbelief won't make those scenes any easier to swallow. Nothing short of cryogenic deep-freeze can keep people in front of their TV sets when Lewis decides to get "serious." It's moments like those that critics cited when they branded Lewis as certifiably pathos-illogical.

"The point is that the bottom line underneath the comic is tragedy," Lewis told us. "All you have to do is bring it to the foreground every once in a while because you have a specific audience that it will touch. But you have to be careful to correct it, weigh it, and adjust it in the cutting room. You have to lean on it or it will become maudlin and heavy. A comic is always close to the fine line between love and hate and laughter and sorrow."

Nobody outside a Wallenda has walked that high-wire for so long. And Lewis was still doing it in 2016 when we caught up with him—virtually—in between doing publicity for his latest and last film (*Max Rose*) and appearances on TCM cruises. He was 90 years old and too tuckered he said to do a face to face sit-down, so we emailed him a few questions.

* * *

Fantle & Johnson: *When did you first get hooked on Charlie Chaplin and why do you think his work is still important today?*

Lewis: I was a kid when my dad first showed me Charlie's work. I just got a DVD of Charlie's early films which are almost 100 years old ... and they still hold up. Physical comedy done well will always work. We all learned from Charlie. I got to go to his home in Switzerland and spend time with him and his family. It's one of the highlights of 85 years in show business. *City Lights* (which Charlie gave me a print of in exchange for a print of *The Bellboy*) and *Limelight* with Claire Bloom who played my wife in *Max Rose*, are classics. *Great Dictator* ... you can't go wrong with Charlie Chaplin.

What is the sagest piece of showbiz wisdom you ever remember getting from someone?

My dad said always put the audience first!

What did Hal Wallis mean to you in terms of your film career and please tell us about him as a man and as a producer?

Hal produced dramatic classics like *Casablanca*. Comedy didn't come naturally to him, so we didn't necessarily see eye to eye professionally. Personally, I liked him a lot. He did a lot for Dean and me in Hollywood—and for Elvis Presley. I returned the favor when I took him to see Shirley MacLaine in *Pajama Game* when Shirley (the understudy) went on for Carol Haney.

Is there any comedian performing today that really makes you laugh; that you think stands apart from the crowd?

There are a lot. It's tough to start naming names because I'll feel guilty if I forgot someone who should be on the list. There are some really good people out there today making us all laugh.

Who was someone that broke you up back in the 1940s–50s that might've remained largely unheralded or unsung as a laugh-getter (this could be a character actor, a former vaudeville star or someone not necessarily a comedian); someone who really got to you?

My dad Danny Lewis was an incredible singer and entertainer. Al Jolson was a big star and someone I admired. Take a look at the character actors and actresses in my films. I only used the best!

What was the special chemistry that made you and Dean such a legendary team? Is it explainable or quantifiable at all?

Can you explain lightening in a bottle? We genuinely loved each other and were having as much fun as the audience which had a lot to do with it.

Do you think it takes more artistic talent to create a comedy film that doesn't use profanity?

It's a cheap laugh. Certain comedians can make it work and its funny, but there has to be something there to back it up. The shock value today is working clean.

* * *

The interview concluded with neither new bets made or old debts paid. (We bid a final *adieu* to the c-note Lewis owed us.)

Like Mount Rushmore or the world's biggest ball of twine (you choose), Lewis endured until his death at 91 in 2017. In 2009, he received a much-deserved Jean Hersholt Humanitarian Award at the 81st Academy Awards. (It had been 50 years since Lewis last appeared on an Oscar telecast.) But whatever the final tally becomes on his haphazard legacy, we know what Jerry would probably have said: 50 million Frenchmen can't be wrong!

Right?

"Great Songs, Drudge Assignments, It Never Mattered"

Jay Livingston and *Ray Evans*

Residing on Jay Livingston's grand piano in his Bel Air, California home were three Best Song Oscars, awarded to him and his partner Ray Evans for "Buttons and Bows," "Mona Lisa" and "Que Sera, Sera (Whatever Will Be, Will Be)" Ironically, their biggest hit of all, "Silver Bells," written in 1951, never took home a statuette.

"No regrets," said Livingston matter-of-factly. "It has sold more than 140 million copies. It's our annuity."

Chatting with them in Livingston's mid-century modern home on Tortuoso Way, words like "collaboration" and "compromise" took on added weight. You could see it in the way career recollections lateraled seamlessly between them, in a kind of pianissimo with a rest thrown in only every bar or two.

Livingston and Evans were both 84 when we met them in late March 1994 on the 60th anniversary of when they first got together and began to collaborate at the University of Pennsylvania. Together, they formed the longest running partnership in the songwriting business. They met while students in 1934 when both were members of a now defunct fraternity, Beta Sigma Rho. Playing music at fraternity "rushes" led to Livingston and Evans working in bands for Holland America Cruises—a great way to see the world during the depths of the Depression.

"We were in Russia in 1937," Evans said. "Nobody got to Russia in 1937. In those days, the cruise lines would book Eastern college bands to play dance music. With that 'in,' we could write our own ticket and we took advantage of it completely. We cruised every country in South America, a million trips to the West Indies, the Caribbean—we were living like millionaires on a poor guy's salary."

Livingston played piano and Evans who admitted to having a "tin ear" ("I could read well but couldn't improvise. No ear and a bad sense of rhythm") was first saxophone in the band. It was during a river cruise in 1937 that Evans suggested they stay in New York and take a whack at writing original songs. "Ray always said he wanted to write lyrics," Livingston said, "so that's how we started."

After a few fruitless years, song publishers' doors began to creak open slightly by

Music on demand: Evans (at left) and Livingston

way of a jazz instrumental Livingston wrote called "Swing Sonata." But according to Livingston, the duo's first published song had a more ignoble genesis. "Jack Mills the music publisher sent word he wanted to see us. He said: 'I understand you boys do cruises.' We still did occasional cruises. He asked if we ever went to Curacao. I told him as a matter of fact we were going in two weeks. He told us about a bottle of mouthwash there that he wanted us to bring back and that if we brought back a half-dozen bottles, he'd publish a song of ours. The song was 'Monday Mourning on Saturday Night.' Unless you read it, you couldn't understand the pun. It wasn't bad but it wasn't recorded. Nothing ever happened to it and it just played once on the air."

"The kicker," Evans chuckled, "was that we brought back the wrong mouthwash but it was too late. Mills had already published the song."

Pearl Harbor stopped Livingston and Evans' career cold after a couple of minor successes. Livingston enlisted for the duration while Evans (4F because of a bad "football knee") got a job at an aircraft plant on Long Island. "Right after the war, life was pretty grim," Evans said. "We migrated West with Olsen and Johnson (a popular comedy team of the era). Olsen said that if we could make it as far as Chicago, we could hitch a ride with his secretary and spell her on the drive to California. He even said we could stay at his house until we found our own digs."

"The only place we could get breakfast was a drugstore about a mile from Olsen's house in Brentwood and we had to use our ration coupons," Livingston said. "We walked there everyday. Eventually they got us a small office at Universal Studios even though we weren't working there. It gave us a little lift. We could tell people to call us at Universal if you can find us."

Their big break finally came when Martha Tilton sang a few of the team's songs in a B movie musical called *Swing Hostess* for Producers Releasing Corporation. "Martha was a Capitol recording star and Johnny Mercer was founder and president of Capitol so he had to listen to the songs Martha sang," Evans said.

"About a week later, Johnny's secretary calls us and says that he wants to do one of our songs ("The Highway Polka") on his radio show," Livingston said. "That was our opening. And then we wrote a song especially for him, 'The Cat and the Canary' which had a lot of Mercer-style rhymes. (Livingston said that he and Evans often 'practiced' writing songs for specific artists like Bing Crosby and Betty Hutton.) Mercer sang it on the air right away and then we were rolling. We next wrote a song called "Band Baby" about the girls that hung around orchestras—groupies. Johnny was a mentor, the biggest man in town. He was generous. So many people in this business will tell you, 'I owe my success to Johnny Mercer.' And we certainly do."

Evans said after another dry period in which he was down to his last $50, the pair got a "magic phone call" from Paramount Studios to contribute songs ("I'm Just a Square in a Social Circle") to a Betty Hutton picture called *The Stork Club*. Again, the recommendation came from Mercer. That year, 1945, the two men began a 10-year tenure as studio songwriters at Paramount where they wrote some of their biggest hits, including the holiday perennial "Silver Bells" for the Bob Hope film, *The Lemon Drop Kid*. The song came about almost by accident (the familiar refrain of so many immortal hits).

"We were told to write a Christmas song for Hope's film," said Livingston. "We both thought that a Christmas song was doomed to fail, but the studio brass was intractable. They always play the same ones every year. New ones never make it." Fortunately, sitting on Evans' desk at the time was a small silver bell (given to them by character actor William Demarest) that provided inspiration for the song. "Ray and I stared at the bell and wrote a song we titled 'Tinkle Bell,'" Livingston said. "We thought we'd insert it into the film and never hear it played again."

If they had kept that title, their prophecy might have come true. But Livingston's wife questioned the choice of the title. "She thought we were crazy titling a song 'Tinkle Bell,'" he said. "She pointed out the fact that tinkle has a bathroom connotation. It was a revelation to us!"

Evans continued, "The next day Jay came into the office and said we have to change the title. Our eyes finally focused on the silver bell on my desk and we changed the title. We never changed a word of the song, except that 'Tinkle Bell' became 'Silver Bells.'"

More than creating a lasting legacy, Livingston said composing a timeless Christmas song "assures a hit record every year. Not many songwriters can lay claim to that."

About the day to day mechanics of their collaboration, Evans said he'd usually arrive at the studio around 9 a.m. because he worked better in the morning with Livingston coming in around 11 a.m. "We had two desks facing each other," Livingston said, "and a beat-up typewriter and a piano that had a cigarette burn in one of the keys and holes in the carpet. We were told Rodgers and Hart had worked on the piano and that Ralph Rainger had written 'Thanks for the Memory' on it."

The team won their first Oscar for "Buttons and Bows," from another Bob Hope comedy, *The Paleface*. "I was so nervous the night of the Oscar ceremony," Livingston said. "I drank half a pint of whisky on the drive over there. I did it every time we had a nominated song. After we won, Paramount raised our salary, painted our office and put a new carpet in."

According to Evans, a song's real immortality, however, hinges on how it touches the "average Joe."

"I once heard a guy singing 'Que Sera, Sera' as he washed the windows of a castle in Salzburg, Austria," said Evans. "That's more thrilling, any day, than hearing it played on the radio." According to Livingston, the song's title came to him when he saw the movie *The Barefoot Contessa* starring Rossano Brazzi and Ava Gardner. "The words were cut in marble in Brazzi's home in Italy," Livingston remembered. "Ava asks him what the phrase means and he answers with 'What will be, will be.' I wrote it down in the dark of the theater. It was the first time we wrote a song not on assignment. Two weeks later we got a call from Alfred Hitchcock who needed a song for *The Man Who Knew Too Much*. He told us Doris Day was in the picture and needed a song. 'I don't know what kind of a song it should be,' he said. 'It should have a foreign title and be sung to a child, a boy.' We waited two weeks and didn't do anything. Then I sang the song to Hitchcock and he said, 'Gentlemen, that's the kind of song I want.'"

On the flip side of made-to-order songs that garner rave reviews, Livingston and Evans characterized Country singer Conway Twitty's vocal of "Mona Lisa" to be nothing short of excruciating. "He sang it not even close to the melody," Livingston said. "But once the song's a hit, you can't be hurt too bad."

Evans said that one of the "biggest insults" they ever had to endure was when Johnny Cash wrote his own words to their classic TV theme for *Bonanza*. "We could have sued him for that but he didn't take any royalties," Evans said. "That was ego depressing but by the same token, you don't make waves about a Johnny Cash record so we rolled with the punches."

Two songs that typify the solid underpinnings of Livingston and Evans' lifelong collaboration—from the sublime to the ridiculous—are "Mona Lisa" and the television theme song to the raucous sitcom *Mr. Ed*.

"We chased Nat King Cole around for a year before he recorded 'Mona Lisa,'" Evans said. "He had never done a song quite like it before, and he was a bit squeamish."

"Paramount pulled some strings and we saw him at his house," Livingston added. "I was trying to sing him the song. All the while this little girl is running around the room bugging the hell out of me—that was (daughter) Natalie. We couldn't have known then that the song would have a wonderful rebirth on her *Unforgettable* album a quarter century later."

The song had a perilous life after Cole recorded it. "Capitol Records was never going to release it," Evans said. "They didn't like it and thought it wasn't right for Nat and it went on the shelf for cancelled projects." Evans said that the next Cole singles release ("The Greatest Inventor of Them All") was billed as his pinnacle. "That's when some underling reached in the file and put 'Mona Lisa' on the other side of the album," Evans said. "It wasn't even mentioned in the ads and the A&R guy at the time was out of town. He said if he had been there it wouldn't have happened. The deejays played 'Mona Lisa' instead of the other featured track and the rest is history. Boy, were we lucky!"

"Mona Lisa" remained Evans' favorite of all the songs the team wrote together. For Livingston, it was "Never Let Me Go." Nat King Cole recorded definitive versions of both songs.

As freelancers in the 1960s, Livingston and Evans could've written a survival guide on how they rolled with the knockout punch that rock music delivered to the traditional songwriting business. "We wrote to spec, whatever anyone wanted," said Livingston.

Although the *Mr. Ed* theme was just another assignment designed to put groceries on the table during lean times, the song has lived on in parody as one of the many disposable pop-culture anthems viewed fondly by a generation of baby boomers raised on corny sitcoms.

The irony wasn't lost on Livingston and Evans. "Of the more than 200 songs in our trunk, that goofy novelty song is probably the only one most young people today can sing," said Evans. "We became known as the title song writers (*To Each His Own*, *Golden Earrings*, *Bonanza*, *Vertigo*)."

"Great songs, drudge assignments, it never mattered," Livingston said, summing up their peripatetic partnership. "We've had serious arguments, but no real separation. We argue our way through a song, really. When you have a winning team, you don't break it up," Evans added. "Jay writes the music, but since both of us work on the lyrics, we've learned the art of compromise. After all, two heads are better than one."

We could relate to that.

Nice and Easy Does It Every Time

Karl Malden

That famous schnozz—like a small mass of unshaped modeling clay—reaches your eyes first. It dominates the face of Karl Malden, and, taken together with his other features, seems to telegraph in an instant several verities about the man: his ordinariness, good cheer and natural candor. In fact, talking to Malden back in 1998 about his recently published autobiography, winning an Oscar, or working with Marlon Brando, was like chatting up your neighbor over the back fence during a break raking the fall leaves. It was easy and informative.

Although consigned by his looks to supporting roles as best friend, father confessor or the occasional heavy, Malden, over the span of 50 years, had shown the world how indelibly he could etch those characters. *A Streetcar Named Desire*, for which he won a Best Supporting Actor Academy Award in 1951, *On the Waterfront*, *Baby Doll* and *Patton* as G.I. General Omar Bradley are just a few movies that wouldn't be nearly as good without Malden lurking in support, to say nothing of his role as Lt. Mike Stone during five seasons of *The Streets of San Francisco* on television.

"Nonsense!" Malden said with genuine self-effacement over coffee and Danish at a small hotel off Sunset Blvd. just down the slope from the Getty Center that hulked over the landscape for miles like a giant white colossus. "Honest, upright and honorable is the way I've been described. Just watch me screw up right now."

Perhaps it was the face allied to the distinctive baritone; maybe it was the long track record of memorable movies or Malden's 21 years of "…don't leave home without it"

American Express Card commercials, but a flicker of recognition slowly came into the eyes of our busboy, a young Mexican kid to whom ESL classes were obviously what he could pick up from diners between setting out the ice water and clearing the dessert dishes. He was beaming as he approached us for a coffee refill.

To us, that meta-moment served as an effective reminder of the true measure of fame that American pop culture provides—the kind that pervades (more now than then) everyday life and every ethnicity. Malden knew that as he furtively smiled one of those unspoken "I-know-you-know-I'm-somebody" acknowledgments.

"*Una tajeta* American Express, *no salga sin ella.*"

Everything was understood without a word, English or otherwise, being spoken.

It was disconcerting then, to hear that Malden received only three calls for movie work the year before we met with him. One of them, *The Long Kiss Goodnight* starring Geena Davis, Malden termed: "Terrible!"

"I don't belong in the movies they're making today," Malden said. He was dressed that day in a blue windbreaker and Tommy Hilfiger shirt with its wreathy coat-of-arms shield. "They've kind of passed me by, but I don't care. I used to do two or three films a year and then the five years on *Streets of San Francisco*. But, as Ecclesiastes says: 'To everything there is a season.' That's it, my friends, either enjoy it or die miserable. I'm not going to die miserable."

Far from it. Along with his daughter, Carla, Malden took advantage of his enforced hiatus and wrote an autobiography, *When Do I Start?* which Simon and Schuster published the year we met him. "When I found that suddenly I had nothing to do, it was untenable. My dad used to ask me at the dinner table, 'What did you do today, son?' Sometimes I would say nothing and he'd say: 'Well, that's one day shot to hell, isn't it?'"

Working every day for three or four hours over the previous two years, Malden and his daughter shaped the richly anecdotal book. "To write a book with a family member is amazing," he said. "They laugh and cry right along with you—and they learn."

What Carla learned, if she didn't already know, was all about the underpinnings that made Malden such a staunch everyman in many of his movies. In his best work, Malden seemed to be shot through with the same kind of steel he helped pour in the mills around Gary, Indiana where he grew up. "I learned a lot about life there," he said. "Richard Widmark says we're all ditch diggers, all actors go out there and dig a ditch. Sometimes it's deep and sometimes it's shallow, but we keep digging that ditch. I think the best that can be said about me is that I never shirked my duty whether it was in a steel mill or in a movie. I think I came ready to work. That's it."

Although Malden cut his teeth theatrically with the Group Theater in New York (*Golden Boy* was his Broadway debut), audiences rarely saw the Method behind the acting. It seemed as effortless and natural as breathing. "During that time I began to hear phrases like, 'What's the beat of the scene? Where's the spine?' I didn't know what the hell anybody was talking about, but gradually I came to understand."

Malden came to understand so well that one day director Elia Kazan approached and asked him to read for a part in a gothic southern drama just completed by Tennessee Williams called *A Streetcar Named Desire*.

"When Kazan gave me the play to read, my wife and I were living in New York in a one-room apartment. I read the play while she ironed some clothes. I then asked her to read it. We both felt it was the greatest play either of us had ever read—and I've read a lot of plays. It was pure poetry."

Malden worked with both Jessica Tandy who originated the role of "Blanche DuBois" on Broadway and Vivien Leigh who portrayed her in the 1951 film version. "Vivien, sadly, had many of the tragic qualities of Blanche," Malden said softly. "Jessica was a sensational actress; one of the most beautiful human beings I've ever met in the theater. Marlon and I have talked about this. Everyone says Vivien was the greatest Blanche, but Kazan could control the film by cutting it and putting the emphasis where he wanted it—on Blanche—if he wanted. It's an unfair comparison.

"Besides," he continued, "no one noticed anything else when Marlon came on stage, I don't care who was in the scene. He changed the style of acting in American with his role as 'Stanley Kowalski.'"

According to Malden, Brando's untapped abilities as a director were every bit as prodigious as his acting gifts. In his single directorial effort, Brando directed the 1961 Western *One-Eyed Jacks*, co-starring Malden as a corrupt sheriff.

"The industry lost a great director when they didn't give him another movie to do," Malden lamented. "Marlon had something that I didn't have as a director. (Malden directed the film *Time Limit* (1957), and when Delmer Daves fell ill during the shooting of *The Hanging Tree*, he took over direction of that film for two weeks.) He couldn't be pushed. Producers would say: 'Hurry up, you're two days behind schedule, pick up the pace! Faster, faster!' On the other end, as a director, he had to motivate the actors. Marlon was a sergeant caught in the middle trying to do a good job. He did it on his own time. He couldn't be pushed and I respect that and I wish I had that quality."

As an addendum, Malden did say that he "didn't respect" when Brando intermittently went on record with reporters calling actors "whores."

Tom remarked that as a kid, the first movie he ever saw in a theater was the revenge Western *Nevada Smith* starring Steve McQueen and featuring Malden as a cold-blooded killer who had murdered McQueen's parents.

"I'll never forget your last lines, in fact the final lines of the movie, after McQueen shot off your kneecaps and you were leeching crimson into that creek up in the Inyo National Forest," Tom said. "McQueen finally got a conscience and wouldn't finish you off and you screamed at him…"

Before Tom could recite the line himself, Malden beat him to the punch: "You're yella, you haven't got the guts!" he thundered so loudly that other diners stopped eating and looked our way. It had been 32 years since filming had wrapped on *Nevada Smith* but Malden could still project like he was hitting the third balcony at the Ethel Barrymore Theater in *Streetcar*.

Life as a film/TV actor-cum-diarist seemed to suit Malden. He said it gave him more time to spend with his wife of 58 years, two children who lived close by and assorted grandchildren. For a man who approached acting throughout his career by the book, he had become interested only in what's in the book—his own.

"After you buy it, don't leave home without it," he quipped, smiling that smile and waiting for the chuckle he knew was imminent.

The Karl Malden Method—foolproof.

The "Toy King"

Louis Marx

Decades before George Lucas became the canniest billionaire around by not re-negotiating a higher writing and directing fee for *Star Wars* in favor of Lucasfilm retaining ownership and merchandising rights for the prodigious array of toys that would be spun-off the film franchise, a man named Louis Marx reigned supreme as the "Toy King" in the United States. In fact, that's what *TIME* magazine dubbed him when they put him on the cover in 1955.

Marx, like a few others before him, saw there was a potential gold mine in licensing and merchandising comic character toys which, in the 1930s and '40s, typically took the form of wind-up, tinplate toys with colorful lithography. Although, truth be told, years before Marx entered the business, in 1898, Richard F. Outcault's "The Yellow Kid" (from the comic strip "Hogan's Alley") had been exploited in such merchandise as cigarettes, chewing gum, cookies, soap and even mustard, and later a line of toys.

The mechanism of the Marx toys, often wound with a key, was simple, the "action" almost always comical: Dagwood Bumstead's oversized head sticking out of an airplane cockpit, Popeye and Olive Oyl dancing a jig on the roof of a house riotously litho'd with scenes from the comic strip, Superman rolling over a fighter plane, Amos & Andy rollicking in their "Fresh Air Taxi" or Milton Berle in his "Crazy Car" popping a wheelie.

For generations of Americans, Marx toys, readily identifiable on store shelves by the circular logo with a giant "X" behind "MAR" on the box, were a treasured link to childhood. Unlike Lucas who concentrates on producing and marketing toys related to his own films, Marx was a savvy businessman who saw the toy industry writ large.

The man himself was balding, thickset and squat like a hydrant. But he loved the gleam in children's eyes when he presented them with a toy. When out in public, in a surefire grassroots branding approach, Marx often filled his pockets with compact treasures that he could readily hand kids when he encountered them.

Louis Marx started out as a toy salesman at Ferdinand Strauss Toy Company of New York, and in 1919 launched his own company with his brother, David. The big secret to Marx's success was mass-producing high-quality toys and offering them at low prices (most well under $1). Competitors and critics mocked Marx toys as "cheap," but they were just inexpensive. The toys generally had uncomplicated designs, but were under-pinned with sturdy, durable construction that lasted for years.

In 1921, Louis Marx rented factory space in Erie, Pennsylvania, and bought two dies from Strauss for an Alabama minstrel dancer and another for Zippo the climbing monkey. By the following year, these two tinplate toys had sold eight million units apiece, making the Marx brothers millionaires.

One key to Marx' marketing was getting the low-cost toys in front of the public, through the Sears, Roebuck, & Co. and Montgomery Ward catalogs, and via distribution at chain stores like Woolworths. In the 1930s Marx began to create toys based on popular comic-strip and radio-show characters like Popeye, Amos & Andy and Charlie McCarthy and sales picked up even more with catchphrases on the boxes that encouraged kids to "collect 'em all."

Our friend Carl Lobel, a Vermont-based collector/dealer who for decades has helped people build toy collections and who has written extensively about comic character toys, sheds light on a little known area of Marx lore—the great warehouse finds of the early 1970s—discoveries that really ushered in a golden age of comic character toy collecting. "One of the things that causes a field of collecting to have explosive growth is the sudden availability of supply," Lobel said. "Without a lot of toys around, you don't attract a lot of new collectors because they aren't getting to see very much stuff."

According to Lobel, Louis Marx had a couple of warehouses in West Virginia and Erie, Pennsylvania where his toy factories had once been located. "They were custodial warehouses and a big secret," Lobel said. "Marx was no longer selling comic character toys; they were just in storage in these nondescript brick buildings in the center of town. The Marx warehouses weren't like an Amazon fulfillment center. It was just one guy, like a night watchman, on duty with nothing to do."

Smart toy collectors started to canvass neighborhoods in Erie, and surrounding towns. They asked homeowners about the possible existence of the warehouses and were told exactly where they were. A couple of collectors that Lobel knew managed to gain entry and it was like entering a time capsule from childhood; storerooms with pallets stacked to the ceiling with mint-in-the-box, uncirculated toys—many of them comic character toys from the 1930s and beyond.

"My understanding is that possible bribes were made to the caretakers or watchmen to let these collectors in," Lobel said. "They would take a few toys and then pay for them."

Lobel told of an auction he attended in the 1970s soon after the warehouse leak had become a flood. After buying a few toys which he surmised were from the warehouse finds, Lobel was approached by Bill Yatsko, a mythic figure in the toy business and one of the anointed few who had gained entry into the Marx warehouse in Erie. "This guy (Yatsko) comes up to me and introduces himself and says: 'This auction stuff is sh-t! I got the really good stuff.' He gives me his card, says he lives in Long Island and I should leave the auction and follow him back to his house and buy the really good stuff."

According to Stephanie Sadagursky in her book, *The Road to Happy Days: A Memoir of Life on the Road as an Antique Toy Dealer*, Yatsko was a

Uncle Wiggily Crazy Car and Popeye and Olive Oyl Jiggers, circa 1935 (author's collection)

world-class curmudgeon who was reputed to have tried to gain free entrance into toy shows dressed in a Nazi uniform. In other instances, when customers refused to buy toys he offered them for sale, in a rage, he would destroy them. What is indisputable: Yatsko had amazing vintage toys stacked to the rafters in his home and garage.

"He had Donald Duck Duet toys floor to ceiling along with Milton Berle Crazy Cars," Lobel said. "And he hinted that there were even better toys but that he had only one or two of those. I asked how much he wanted for the Donald Duets. He said, 'They're not for sale, but if you spend $5,000, I'll let you buy one.'"

Yatsko remained irascible and contrarian to the end, at one point surviving a home invasion in which he and his wife were bound and gagged and their inventory of toys liquidated in what Yatsko claimed was an "inside job" perpetrated by a disgruntled client.

Eventually what Marx warehouse toys hadn't already been pillaged by roving collectors were later sold in several Sotheby's auctions in New York City. The auctions generated huge news and created that uptick in public awareness and collecting that exists even today for Marx toys.

In later years, Marx playsets became popular, many based on hit TV shows like *The Untouchables*, *Dragnet* and *Gunsmoke*. But what had once been the largest toy company in the world in the 1950s, by the early 1970s had been surpassed by other more visionary toy companies. Louis Marx sold out to Quaker Oats in 1972 for $54 million. He died nine years later at the age of 85.

However, a legacy of sorts has lived on. After all, nostalgia for the idealized innocence of one's youth is damned hard to extinguish, and generations after his death Marx keeps toying with our affections.

Steve McQueen was a longtime collector of tin windups by Marx (and others) when he gave his avocation some screen time in his last movie, *The Hunter*. In an early scene, McQueen returns home from his latest bail bondsman job with a Buck Rogers Rocket Patrol windup (in pristine condition) that he presents as a gift to his girlfriend (Kathryn Harrold). "It's original and very rare," he tells a somewhat crestfallen Harrold who perhaps was expecting something a bit more on the order of a Gucci bag.

Other celebrity toy collectors who preferred vintage windups to, say, plastic lightsabers, include Bette Midler, Michael Jackson Robert Blake, Jane Withers and the late madcap comedian Jonathan Winters who for many years was a fixture roaming the packed aisles of the annual All-American Collector's Show in Glendale, California.

Still, according to a recent survey by the National Retail Federation, *Star Wars* toys rank second only to Lego in the hearts and minds of young boys. And now hybridization is occurring as Lego teams with Lucasfilm to bring out a line of action toy/Lego blocks built around the lucrative film franchise. As far as toy revenue is concerned, the "force" has definitely been with Lucas these last decades.

And that is sure to make the execs at Fox a trifle wistful. For years, the studio assiduously protected ancillary rights of toys, t-shirts, novelizations, essentially anything connected to movies released by the studio. But when its 1967 film, *Doctor Dolittle*, did little at the box-office or in toy stores, Fox became skeptical about potential profits to be made in any areas outside revenue generated from the movies themselves.

If only the Fox brain-trust remembered the long, successful parlay of Louis Marx and his line of comic character novelties, they too might have become "Toycoons" instead of ceding that moniker to Lucas.

Frankly Speaking
Billy May

Sometimes timing is everything. For trumpeter, bandleader and veteran arranger Billy May, it was the happenstance of having an empty study period to fill in high school that led him to the tuba and contemplation of a career in jazz. In a more cosmic sense, he also had the good fortune to come of age during the brief Renaissance in the late 1930s and early 1940s when Big Bands ruled the roost.

"Coming up in the 1930s in Pittsburgh when the big swing bands were flourishing, everything just worked for me," May told us while relaxing on the couch of his condominium in Burbank, California in 1996. (May died in 2004 at the age of 87.) "I've had a wonderful life when I look back. I mean how many people can say that at the age of 14 or 15 they discovered what they wanted to do for the rest of their life and did it?"

Indeed, at age 79, May exuded contentment. With a face and manner that at times suggested a gray, slightly impish cherub, he was—in a word—becalmed. May brought to mind the whole community of jazz artists of that period—men who were the epitome of cool and who carried their provenance in their instrument cases. As a breed, they were hip in a way that most movie stars could only envy.

In 1928, May wrote some arrangements on spec for Charlie Barnet who headed a hot, swinging band. A few months later, Barnet invited May to become the band's arranger at $70 a week—big money in that Great Depression era. Before long, May was also blowing trumpet for Barnet.

"New York was a blast in those days," May said. "Barnet's band played on 52nd Street at The Famous Door. It was a cellar in a brownstone tenement building. The ceiling was about 4½ feet off the floor and it was made of metal. We had six brasses in the band and when we hit a combined note, the sound would reverberate off the tin ceiling. The sounds we made are probably still ringing! People would be packed in there like sardines, smoking. They loved it."

May recalled when he and Barnet trudged home late after a club date. "Charlie came from money and had a three-room suite at the Park Central Hotel," May said. "In fact, I think his mother owned a piece of the hotel. I bunked there and so did another guy named Herb Reese. He was a song plugger and a good friend of Charlie's. Well, we came in the room that night and Chick Webb's whole swing band was there, including Ella Fitzgerald, who was just a young kid starting out as a singer with them. The party lasted till dawn." Two decades later, May, as arranger and conductor, would collaborate with Ella on the *Ella Fitzgerald Sings the Harold Arlen Songbooks*—seminal entries in Fitzgerald's landmark American songbook series of recordings.

After touring with Barnet for a couple of years, May got a call from Glenn Miller offering him a spot playing trumpet for $150 a week. "I didn't particularly like the band, but the money was good and playing with Glenn was considered a prestige gig," May said. "Miller's band was number one in the country."

Relaxin' with Billy

According to May, Miller's band was tight and regimented in a way that would have been alien in Barnet's band. "Band members had to always be exactly on time for rehearsals, and we even had to smoke Chesterfield cigarettes because they sponsored Glenn's radio show."

At the height of Miller's popularity, May appeared with the rest of the band in two movies—*Sun Valley Serenade* and *Orchestra Wives*. And that was when May says that Miller became obsessed with seeing action in World War II. "He once told me, 'Billy, this war is going to be a big thing and I'm going to come out of it some kind of a hero.' He didn't realize that it would be as a posthumous hero."

After the war, with Big Bands quickly going the way of the dinosaurs, May relocated to Los Angeles and found work writing musical bridges on *The Adventures of Ozzie and Harriet* radio show. He also arranged for Bing Crosby, the Andrew Sisters and Harry James, among others. In addition to fronting his own orchestra, May reached his arranging zenith with his work on a series of Capitol and Reprise recordings with Frank Sinatra, one of which, *Come Fly with Me*, remains Sinatra's most popular album from his most fruitful era, the late–'50s.

"Writers like to harp on all the trouble Frank caused everybody because it apparently sells books," May said. "But I always got along very well with him. We did the *Come Fly with Me* album in about four days. Frank was best on the first take or two. If the band got it right, he'd say, 'Let's move on.' The musicians really dug that attitude too. Frank could always tell if the band was on. He was a good musician."

In all, the Sinatra-May tandem formed the basis of three best-selling Capitol albums: *Come Fly with Me* (1958), *Come Dance with Me!* (1959), and *Come Swing with Me!* (1961), as well as several later albums recorded on Sinatra's own label, Reprise. Their collaboration and friendship lasted until Sinatra's death in 1998 with May serving as an honorary pallbearer at the funeral.

Here is May's extended riff on working with "Ol' Blue Eyes."

* * *

Fantle & Johnson: *When did you meet Sinatra?*

May: It was in the late 1930s when he was singing with Harry James and I was with Charlie Barnet. We just ran into each other at some saloon in New York. All the musicians used to live in three or four hotels between 45th and 50th streets. It was real common for us to hang around at various bars at night after work.

When did you actually first work with him?

The first actual arranging I did was in the mid–'40s when he was working on the *Lucky Strike Hit Parade* radio program. Axel Stordahl, who was Frank's arranger and a good friend of mine, was overburdened with work and asked me if I would "ghost" a few arrangements for him. My first arrangement for Frank was Cole Porter's "Don't Fence Me In," which he sang on the show.

After that, you didn't arrange for Sinatra until 1958.

Frank started working with Nelson Riddle full time, and it was a very successful collaboration. Nelson was a great arranger and a good buddy of mine. In 1958, Frank called me to do *Come Fly with Me*. And how that came to be, I don't rightly know. He called me one day and said: "Do you want to do an album with me. You'd be good for the kind of things we're going to do." So I did it. It's considered one of his best Capitol recordings, but the ones he did with Nelson (*Swing Easy! In the Wee Small Hours, A Swingin' Affair!*" etc.) were really sensational, too.

Since you arranged for Sinatra in the 1940s and '50s, can you compare his vocal abilities and how they might've changed from one decade to the next?

It's quite apparent to anyone who knows Frank that his voice matured. That's the best thing I can say about it. He approached his repertoire with a more mature outlook.

Wasn't his phrasing improving and his baritone richer?

Whether the phrasing was something he consciously thought about or it just happened, I wouldn't venture an opinion. He was a remarkably talented man. A much better musician than he let on.

It's funny you use the word "musician" since he couldn't read music.

Right, but he knew what the hell was happening in the band. He was very fond of musicians because these were the guys he came up with during the big-band era.

When you cut an album like Come Fly with Me, *how many days did you spend in the studio recording the tracks?*

We did the 12 songs in, I believe, three three-hour sessions, so we would complete the album in a week. I wrote the arrangements ahead of time and would meet with Frank and his piano player, Bill Miller, and we would pick the keys. We would go through the arrangements and select the final cut of songs we would record. I would occasionally call Frank and ask if he would feel more comfortable if I brought a song up a half note higher, or something like that, and then we would make adjustments.

Is it true that when it came time to record, Sinatra was more comfortable singing before a small group of his friends?

We'd call this group his entourage. Toward the end of his association with Capitol, he'd always show up with a couple of attorneys. He always had a couple of ladies in tow, and since his kids were older, he sometimes brought them.

Is there one experience that stands out for you from these recording sessions?

Yes. A production assistant inadvertently scheduled a *Come Swing with Me!* recording session on December 12, Frank's birthday. Frank came in that night and started fronting the tunes down, and I saw that he wasn't making it. I asked him if he was having trouble with the lead sheet or something, and he said: "I can't even see the son-of-a-bitch." He told me he had just come from a restaurant where they were doing some early birthday celebrating. Finally he just hollered out to the band, "Come on guys, the hell with this! Let's go up to my house." So we did and went up to Frank's house for a party. He was a good cat.

In films, Frank was said to do his best work in the first take. Was that also true of the recordings?

It was at his funeral that the two words he hated most were "take two." I can vouch for that.

Did you ever have disagreements on a take where you wanted to do it again but Sinatra didn't?

We never got to that point. A couple of times we discussed things like that and resolved it. Sometimes he'd say: "Yeah, maybe we can do it a little better." But that was rare. We had a very positive collaboration; I knew he could be a pretty tough guy. I've seen him chew out people, too. He could be very vitriolic when he wanted to be. I was never subjected to that. We got along very well. It was a very happy, pleasant association and I'm very sorry that he's gone.

Would you characterize Sinatra as a jazz singer?

He never was as stylized as Sarah Vaughn. And Ella was more of an all-around jazz singer. I think Frank could improvise, but he seldom had occasion to. He was a little more conservative. But I know that he appreciated the other jazz vocalists.

Sinatra would always record before a full orchestra. That's different from the way sessions are handled today. What's changed?

We did them all live—none of that dubbing. He wouldn't allow it because he thought it was a cheat on a performance, and it is. When they lay the vocal track down after the instrumental track like they do today, it's not really a true performance; it's a manufactured song. Frank approached a recording session the way he would a live concert.

Your last collaboration with Frank came in 1979 with the Trilogy: Past Present Future *album. How did that come about?*

The producers planned for Nelson to do the arrangements, but I got asked in after the two had a tiff. I think this was unfortunate for both Frank and Nelson. Until the end of Nelson's life, they never spoke to each other again, and that was too bad because I think they both respected each other very much.

By the late 1970s, did you consider Sinatra's vocal powers to be diminishing?

They seemed to get better as far as I'm concerned. I think on *Trilogy*, he sang the hell out of it. The *Duets* album, I think, was a mistake. That's my opinion. But somebody made a lot of money on it.

From your perspective, what made Sinatra so unique?

I think he was a better singer and he knew how to "sell" a song better than any of those other guys. He was the last really good voice to push good music. The music today is so cheap and has no body to it. Everybody listens to the lyrics, and the music today is crap! Frank appreciated the material and that came through in every song he sang.

Baked Alaska

Virginia Mayo

The afternoon built slowly, inexorably to a punch line that was as campy as it was unexpected.

At a chic restaurant called Boccaccio in the Los Angeles suburb of Westlake Village, 1940s screen star Virginia Mayo had just received her flaming Baked Alaska from a waiter (a bit of a flamer himself) who, as if auditioning for a part, served it up with pomp and circumstance that would have suited a three-star cafe straight out of the Michelin "Red Guide." In retrospect, it was a dessert as overpriced and overproduced as any Busby Berkeley production number from Hollywood's gilded age—and we were paying for it.

That's when Mayo, not to be topped by the third course of any *haute* meal, said it. After a masterful pause as the flambéed confection was placed before her, and as diners at other tables paused to take in the theatrics; with appropriate parrot-like vocal inflection, she aped the iconic line delivered by her co-star James Cagney in the classic 1949 film *White Heat*, just before he blew himself to smithereens in the exploding oil refinery finale.

"Made it ma, top of the world," Mayo said.

We cracked up. The whole restaurant cracked up. And the waiter minced back to the kitchen with a surefire anecdote he doubtlessly unloaded at cocktail parties for years. Nonplussed, Mayo just sat back, waited silently for the blaze to abate, then ate her fill.

When we picked up Mayo at the modest Thousand Oaks home she shared with her daughter, son-in-law and three grandsons who Mayo said were being homeschooled, the actress had fallen completely off the grid. In fact, that week, during other interviews, we often mentioned that we were going to visit Mayo. Invariably we were met with startled looks ("She's still alive?") that melted into softer, nostalgic expressions. "She was a real looker in her day," Gene Kelly told us as if we hadn't seen her curvaceous, leggy turns in such films as *The Best Years of Our Lives*, and *The Princess and the Pirate*.

To say that the afternoon built to a punch line is true, but that priceless capper was preceded by several bumbles (on our part) that left us—if not Mayo—convulsed. At her home, Mayo, who had really dressed up for the lunch (like she was anticipating a night at Ciro's), showed us a painting she had done of her husband.

Dave, in utter seriousness, said he hadn't realized she had been married to the comic character actor with the donkey-bray voice, Andy Devine.

Mayo said curtly that the painting was of Michael O'Shea who was the titular star of her debut 1943 film, *Jack London.*

It's a toss-up over which was more egregious, Dave's embarrassing myopia or the fact that Mayo wasn't exactly Mary Cassatt in the painting department.

Born Virginia Clara Jones in 1920 in St. Louis, Missouri, Mayo said it was not her mother, but an aunt who nurtured her early ambition to become a performer when at age six she enrolled in her aunt's School of Dramatic Expression. "My aunt was very famous in St. Louis," Mayo recalled. "In fact, Thomas Eagleton, you know, the guy that ran for vice president with George McGovern, took elocution lessons from her. In addition to diction, we learned movement and how to be comfortable performing before an audience."

Ironically, Mayo said her aunt—a real "stage aunt"—was a taskmaster who never offered her much encouragement. "She didn't think I had any talent," Mayo said. "I was kind of ugly and awkward. She tried to help me as much as she could but she had other pupils who she felt could sing, dance and act better than me."

With a steely determination that seemed to compensate for any artistic shortcomings, Mayo landed a prestigious role in the St. Louis Municipal Opera Company, where she performed in the popular musicals of the day. (MGM singer Kathryn Grayson—a contemporary of Mayo's—was also a native of St. Louis and, as a young girl, would climb over the fence of the St. Louis Municipal Opera to watch performances.)

At age 17, Mayo left St. Louis, changed her name and toured the United States in the musical comedy act, "Pansy the Horse." After four years with the act, Mayo moved to New York City and joined legendary nightclub impresario Billy Rose's new revue at his famed Diamond Horseshoe. It was while appearing at the Horseshoe that Mayo caught the eye of two Hollywood studio moguls, David O. Selznick and Samuel Goldwyn.

After making a screen test, Selznick took a pass proclaiming that Mayo was in need of more "dramatic experience." However, Goldwyn, who also tested Mayo, detected something in the erstwhile performer that apparently eluded Selznick, and signed her to a long-term contract.

Goldwyn, more than anyone else, said Mayo, was responsible for making her a star. In fact, he took almost an obsessive interest in his new charge, inviting her into his office almost daily to review the previous day's film footage and to critique her performance He also invited her to his home, which was a launching pad for some famous Hollywood parties.

"Mr. Goldwyn was very much a gentleman and only interested in high-class movies," she said. "He never put junk on the screen and I admire him for that. I remember while shooting *The Princess and the Pirate*, he was always coming on the set and glaring at me when the cameras were rolling. During one scene, I was supposed to act frightened because of this pirate attack. Mr. Goldwyn said to Bob Hope, 'Look at her, she's so nervous.' And Bob replied, 'Leave her alone Sam, she's supposed to act nervous. She's great.' Bob was always playing golf on the set. He'd have his writers insert gags which added a lot of comedy to the picture. I loved making it, it was so relaxing with Bob."

The crowning achievement for Goldwyn was his 1946 "prestige picture," the postwar drama, *The Best Years of Our Lives*, directed by William Wyler and starring Fredric March, Myrna Loy, real-life double-amputee Harold Russell, Dana Andrews and Mayo.

The film swept the Oscars winning nine, including Best Picture. As "Marie Derry," Mayo played the slatternly wife of Andrews in a convincingly unsympathetic manner. Mayo told us she had no inkling of the classic status the film would almost instantly attain.

Another memorable role was that of "Verna Jarrett," James Cagney's tough gun moll wife in the last great Warner Brothers gangster film, *White Heat*. Mayo credited Cagney with adding "little touches" such as the cluster headaches that made the film more than just another B-grade, run-of-the-mill mobster movie.

"Jimmy wasn't enamored of Hollywood," Mayo said. "He was plain Jimmy Cagney. He never really socialized on the set and neither did I. I was in my dressing room studying my part. I will say that the director of *White Heat*, Raoul Walsh, was a character and very different from Wyler. Walsh's direction to me in a heated, hurried scene where I had to hustle was: 'You're going to run around here and get around that corner. You've heard they're serving free beer around the corner!' He was so funny."

When the studio system died out by the late 1950s, so did Mayo's screen career, although she continued to appear on stage in musicals and comedies and on television in episodes of *Remington Steele*, *Murder She Wrote* and *The Love Boat*.

"I have a girl come in to answer fan mail for me. I pay her," Mayo said. "I got a letter the other day from a girl who saw *Best Years of Our Lives* and said that it inspired her to become a stripper! Can you believe it?"

When we squired Mayo to lunch in 1997 (eight years before she died), her appetite for work (if not combustible desserts) was a thing of the past. That year she had appeared in a minor role in what would be her last film; a tiny, independent production called *The Man Next Door*. In the movie, a young woman tries to escape from a psychopathic killer. Fifty years before, *White Heat* took a similar tack, only she was the quarry and Cagney was the unbalanced murderer.

It's funny sometimes how life can come around full circle.

Tops in Taps

Ann Miller

Tap dancer Ann Miller was, perhaps, the quintessential female MGM musical star of the late 1940s and early 1950s. Whirling like a dervish around prehistoric bones in a natural history museum (*On the Town*), the disembodied arms and instruments of a hot swing band (*Small Town Girl*), or kicking out a staccato rhythm on a coffee table (*Kiss Me Kate*), Miller was tops in taps for a studio famed for its musicals and knee-deep in terpsichorean prowess.

Miller's movies were pure confection: cookie-cutter, candyfloss escapism spun from a studio system geared to helping audiences forget their troubles and, well, just get happy. And it didn't hurt that when she wasn't riffing out taps like a Tommy Gun gone bonkers, Ann (or Annie, as we learned her friends called her) had an ingratiating Texas twang that lightly insinuated itself into her singing voice and gave it a jaunty lilt that complemented the pizzazz of her dancing and seemed to sum up the whole optimistic post-war period in America.

As Frank Sinatra, another alumnus of MGM's Golden Era recounted in the 1974 compilation film *That's Entertainment!*: "Musicals were fantasy trips for audiences of their day—boy meets girl, boy loses girl, boy sings a song and gets girl. The plots were that simple."

More important was the certainty that at least three times during a 100-minute musical, Miller could be counted on to beat out a spunky tattoo with her feet that rivaled any jackhammer on a Manhattan street corner.

At 79, when we met her, Ann still claimed she could click out 500 taps a minute. "I still know how to lay down the iron," she proudly exclaimed.

The thing about tap dancing, Miller said, "is that it's very electric. No matter what you're doing—reading the paper, washing the dishes—when a big tap number comes on, you just sit up because the 'click, click, click' gets your attention. It's like drumming. I just love it. My mother wanted me to be a ballerina; I've got a little Indian blood in me so when I heard those drums, I just took off."

On the day of our visit back in the spring of 1998, Miller was late for a hair appointment that, unfortunately, cut our interview short too. "I get my hair done once a week if it needs it or not," she told us in her Texas drawl that had the strange, sentient effect of drawing us in and making us instant confidants. From our angle, as she descended the curved staircase from the second floor of her Beverly Hills home on Alta Drive, Miller didn't need a coiffure. Her jet-black bouffant was piled skyward like a three-tiered chocolate layer cake that not even the fiercest Santa Ana wind could topple.

With her makeup impeccably in place (she looked a bit like a paraffin model that had just exited Madame Tussaud's waxwork museum), Miller was as well turned out as her pet Airedales that flanked her every move in the house. In fact, the troika reminded us of her haughty "Nadine" character and the two Russian Wolfhounds she took strolling down Fifth Avenue in *Easter Parade*—a 1948 hit that costarred Fred Astaire and Judy Garland. Of all the MGM leading ladies we interviewed, Miller's everyday demeanor might have paralleled the closest to her film portrayals; a brassy simulacrum where acting wasn't much of a stretch, just an extension of what came naturally.

"It was the culmination of a dream dancing with Fred Astaire," she told us. "But I was really too tall for him. I had to wear ballet slippers and when the dress flares out during our number, 'It Only Happens When I Dance with You,' you can see them. Now I've shrunk an inch and a half and would be the perfect height for either Fred or Gene Kelly. Cyd Charisse was the same height I was and so was Rita Hayworth. Cyd sort of crouched down in more of a ballet knees-bent thing so you didn't notice the disparity as much."

Miller said the she and Astaire got along fine during the filming of *Easter Parade* because both were perfectionists. "I will tell you one thing, though," Miller said. "Fred didn't want to do *Broadway Melody of 1940* with Eleanor Powell. He didn't want to tap dance with anyone who could dance as well as him, and, of course, she was marvelous. I was pretty damn good, too, so he kind of shied away from that. I was the heir to Eleanor; I came after her."

"Ginger was perfect for him though," Miller continued in a kind of fusillade of memories. "There was nobody like Ginger, she was ideal—the height, everything. They were just like coffee and cream somehow. Ginger was my dear friend up until the day she died.

I was a Texan and she was a Texan and she used to call me 'stringbean' because I was so skinny. She called me 'stringbean' in *Stage Door* and it stuck. I was 'stringbean' until the day she died."

Miller's home was decorated in what could be best described as French Rococo-meets-the-MGM-prop-warehouse, as if a few gilded furnishings from the Palace of Versailles (or an approximation of it on the back lot) had errantly plopped down on the Westside of Los Angeles. After entering the expansive foyer of Miller's house, we were immediately confronted by a full-length painting of Miller in all her glamour that was fully 10 ft. tall. It hung suspended in the stairwell between the second floor and first floor landing and was *Ancien Regime* all the way; more Jacques-Louis David than, say, John Singer Sargent.

A couple of cement lions stood guard at her front door and brought to mind not French (or even Beverly Hills) despotism, but the roaring trademark of Miller's MGM alma mater, king of the Hollywood dream factories that once boasted of having "more stars than there are in the heavens."

Although the day of studios with dozens of stars under exclusive contract is a historical footnote, Miller took pains to maintain a vibrant connection with her MGM contemporaries. As she pointed out, although the U.S. Senate is considered the most exclusive club in America, the fraternal order of MGM leading ladies had an even more rarified pedigree. "Politicians abound and Congress is always in session, but they're not making any more of us," she laughed.

Point taken.

"I hosted a luncheon not long ago with Debbie Reynolds; just a little get-together at a Chinese restaurant off of Wilshire Blvd. for some of us who used to work together at the studio," she said. "MGM was like our finishing school because many of us never went to college—we were working. Esther Williams came and so did Ann Rutherford, Janet Leigh, Cyd and Margaret O'Brien. June Allyson even flew in. We had a ball. It started at half past noon and we didn't get out of there until 5 p.m. All the dishing that went on—thank God we didn't invite the press."

Wistfully expounding on the "class reunion" of MGM acolytes, Miller spoke for the group when she told us she missed the studio system era with its meticulous machinery that assured that stars under contract would want for nothing.

"Gosh, we were so protected," she said. "If you went on a trip, you had a publicity man; they got the tickets. They helped with the luggage. If you were in a foreign country, they got you through customs. You were babied. It's like being a fish out of water for me now. We were petted and groomed and combed like French Poodles. Everybody fussed over us. We had our own hairdressers and makeup people. The costumes were gorgeous and there were over 100 people in the press department. All they did morning, noon and night was publicize and dream-up stories about the stars and starlets. If you wanted to go to a premiere, they loaned you a beautiful dress or fur coat or jewelry; if you needed a limo, they gave you one; if you need an escort, they got you one."

Miller's favorite film is a toss-up between *Easter Parade* and *Kiss Me Kate*, but *Parade* does contain her favorite number, "Shakin' the Blues Away." "Maybe it's because I'm out there on stage all alone and the tune by Irving Berlin is so good," she said.

At that moment Miller got a phone call. She picked up the receiver from a side table near her chair and chatted amiably for a few minutes. After she hung up, she told us that her caller—Robyn Astaire (Fred Astaire's widow)—had just invited her to dinner (Chinese food) later that week. "Robyn's a sweet girl," Miller said. "She loves her planes and she just bought a jet and a helicopter. You know the whole flap about her partnering with the Dust Devil vacuum cleaner people and using Fred's image superimposed dancing with the vacuum is really nothing. She needed the money to help finance an air cargo business she runs. She's a pilot, you know."

We remembered that particular television commercial. It involved a clip of Astaire taken from when he danced with a wooden coat rack in the 1951 film *Royal Wedding*. The commercial, the subject of more than a few editorial condemnations, caused a negative stir especially among film purists who thought the idea of substituting a vacuum cleaner for the coat rack and thus relegating Astaire to a corporate shill doing housework was an unforgiveable blasphemy.

"Don't know how Fred would have reacted, but we could take a guess," we said. Miller just shrugged. "Fred's daughter Ava is a darling," Miller said, changing the subject. "She's really a sweet and classy woman. I think she and Robyn never got along. They don't even really know each other. It's a shame."

During the late 1940s Miller was lady-in-waiting to the reigning tap dance queen on the MGM lot, Eleanor Powell. Although at age 12, Miller had studied ballet alongside Tula Finklea (who was 14 at the time) at the studio of Nico Charisse, the man Tula would eventually marry at age 17 (changing her name to Cyd Charisse in the process); Miller said she herself never took a tap lesson.

"There was a Capezio shoe shop across the street from the dance studio on Sunset Boulevard where we practiced," she said. "I would go over there and the owner, a man named Morgan, would let me practice on the tap mat at the back of the shop. He made me a pair of tap shoes that had little jingles in the toe taps. That's where I developed my high-speed tapping. It all came from the man upstairs. I don't mean Mr. Morgan, I mean the other Guy!"

Movie musicals flourished with the advent of sound and began to wane as staple entertainment in the late '50s. Miller lamented that audiences are hard-pressed to suspend disbelief long enough to let film musicals thrive, especially in light of the fact that they, along with jazz, are America's only true indigenous art form—our gift to the world.

"You have to have a good story now," Miller said. "The great thing about the old musicals was that they were so innocent and sweet. You left the theater with a lift and there is nothing wrong with that. But today's audiences—even the children—have become so sophisticated. Musicals can't compete against the special effects movies now. They'd be going up against aliens and rubber toys that talk … there's a thought! Maybe a porno-graphic musical or one with an animatronic dinosaur doing a big tap number would work!"

Sidestepping the nauseous thought of a chorus line of gyrating purple Barney's (or possibly Velociraptors), we reminded Miller that tap dancing had achieved new currency (back in 1998) with the popularity of the Riverdance troupe of Celtic highsteppers. "Michael Flatley, the lead dancer, stole two of my steps," she said. "And they're the two best steps that he does; always get big applause. I even bought the video to revisit the steps again."

The legendary hoofer Bill Robinson once remarked that if you could copyright a step, nobody could lift a foot. "Bojangles" knew that the true art of Terpsichore lay not in individual steps, but in how thrilling tap combinations were strung together to create a memorable cohesion—the signature Morse Code of American musical theater.

We knew she could have expounded on all this but Miller just smiled the all-knowing smile of someone who had traversed that territory countless times before ankle-strapped into her own flying pumps.

Besides, it was time for her hair appointment and we could see that Miller's Lincoln Town Car had pulled up out front right next to the cement lions.

MGM's Amazing Technicolor Dreamcoat

Vincente Minnelli

Sometimes life imitates art.

In the sad case of director Vincente Minnelli's gutted and abandoned home on North Crescent Drive in Beverly Hills, it's an instance of his former manse imitating silent screen siren Norma Desmond's decaying brickpile from Billy Wilder's *Sunset Boulevard*.

In August 1981, we interviewed Minnelli in the house where he lived with his socialite wife Lee. Situated on a pie wedge-shaped lot just across the street from the Beverly Hills Hotel, back then, the Regency-styled home and grounds were beautiful; meticulously cared for by the usual phalanx of Latino housekeepers and gardeners that the rich of Beverly Hills hire by the gross.

In the ensuing years, the house became the subject of a tug-of-war between Lee and Vincente Minnelli's daughter with Judy Garland, Liza Minnelli. After Lee died, the house languished in legalistic limbo and it wasn't long before squatters took claim and made the derelict home uninhabitable.

The circular driveway we drove up more than 30 years ago is now overgrown with opportunistic weeds that have sprung up from cracks in the cement and the exterior is devoid of color, blanched white by the sun. Another irony, considering that the man who died there in 1986 trailblazed a string of movie musicals in the '40s and '50s that were noted for their luminous palette and honed visual sophistication.

Minnelli wasn't just concerned with the workaday mechanics of filmmaking; he was an artist (more than most directors) who painted in a palate of Technicolor and was capable of creating movies that shimmered like the brushstrokes of Monet painting a canvas of his garden at Giverny.

With such films as *An American in Paris*, *Meet Me in St. Louis*, *The Band Wagon* and *Gigi*, Minnelli more than any other director fulfilled the standing MGM commandment: "Do it big, do it right and give it class."

Dressed in a white linen short sleeve shirt and with a cigarette always wedged between his index and middle fingers, Minnelli ushered us upstairs to the library/office located on the second floor. A slight man with large eyes and sensuous lips but given to small, decorous gestures when emphasis was needed to underscore a particular point, Minnelli seemed to us an aesthete through and through. It was frustrating then (probably more for Minnelli than us), that he was maddeningly inarticulate in conversation. For a

Vincente in his atelier

director so brilliantly skilled in marshaling the tricky cohesion (on so many complicated fronts) needed to make a film successful, Minnelli just couldn't connect the dots verbally—without a whole lot of patience and prompting—and more than a little sign language. Then again, Minnelli's stunning adroitness with the visual composition of his movies might have been a direct result of his lack of verbal acuity—compensation in one area for the lack in another.

"I guess I set the standard for color in those musicals," Minnelli said. "I knew what I wanted to achieve from my previous experience as an art director doing Broadway shows for the Shuberts. I knew it was possible."

To literally illustrate his point, Minnelli pulled out from a cabinet in his library a voluminous bound scrapbook of clippings he had gleaned from newspapers and magazines over the years. In its tremendous girth, it resembled a fantastical prop; something that the half-giant Hagrid might tuck under his arm in the *Harry Potter* series. As such, it took a dedicated effort by Minnelli to hoist it onto a desk. Yellow and brittle from age and use, the bulging clipbook chronicled various vogues of interior design and clothing for more than 40 years.

"I got into the habit of making use of the clip room at the Los Angeles Public Library," Minnelli explained. "By referring to these cutouts, I was able to bring some measure of authenticity to each of my movies—whether they were costumers or more modern stories."

Minnelli began his directorial career in Chicago, dazzling State Street sidewalk shoppers with his arrangement of the window displays in the Marshall Field's department store. Not long after that, he went to New York City and became, at 29, the youngest set and stage director in the history of Radio City Music Hall, a certifiable "wunderkind."

"I was there 3½ years. I did the stage lighting, designed the costumes and conceived the sets. I also did five shows with Beatrice Lillie," Minnelli said. "Arthur Freed (MGM's legendary producer of musicals) saw my work and brought me out to Hollywood in 1941 as a sort of protégé and troubleshooter. I pitched in on any film that needed doctoring. I'm afraid the art department at MGM didn't like me much. They considered me a young upstart from Broadway with fresh ideas. But when I got my own films to direct, they left me alone."

Minnelli's *An American in Paris* and *Gigi* won Oscars for Best Picture of 1951 and 1958. But he felt that to make any real impression on the throngs who cast their Academy Awards votes (or anyone else), a musical must be exceptional. "Most musicals are light-hearted entertainment with no other pretensions," he said. "I do believe a film should do more than just entertain. *Cabaret* (starring Minnelli's daughter, Liza) is a marvelous example of a deeply disturbing, ominous, yet entertaining musical drama."

Lust for Life, the film version starring Kirk Douglas of Irving Stone's biography of the life of Vincent Van Gogh, ranks as Minnelli's favorite film. It is truly homage from one artist to another with Minnelli doing vibrant justice to the genius of the Dutchman. "We shot the movie entirely in Europe. I used locations in Paris and Belgium. I even shot scenes at St. Rémy, the mental institution where Van Gogh had himself committed toward the end of his life," Minnelli said. "One problem we had to resolve was Vincent's suicide scene in the wheatfield at Arles. I shot it on a cold fall morning. We had to fly in some mature wheat and treat it chemically so it would stay alive while Vincent painted his famous last canvas of the black crows flying over the field; all for the sake of accuracy."

The distraction of keeping wheatfields alive in mid-frost would be enough to drive any director to his own padded cell at St. Rémy, but Minnelli had his own sanity-saving methods. "I would disassociate myself completely at night," he said. "To take my mind off the job, I'd read detective stories."

Among the many stars with whom Minnelli worked was Judy Garland who he described as the consummate performer. "I tried to direct her as little as possible," he said. "She would be powdering her nose with a disinterested gaze and I wouldn't be sure I was getting through to her. But when the camera rolled, every inflection and nuance was in place—sheer perfection. Gene Kelly was the same way. I'd tell him to make a scene jauntier. Gene would look at me quizzically. He was, of course, the definition of the word jaunty."

A pivotal point the in the careers of both Minnelli and Garland was the film—an enduring classic of Americana—during which they fell in love, *Meet Me in St. Louis.*

"Judy didn't want to make that film back in 1944; she wanted to do more sophisticated parts. She thought the teenage role of Esther Smith would set her career back 20 years," Minnelli said. "She asked MGM studio chief Louis B. Mayer and the film's producer Arthur Freed to intercede for her but she couldn't get anywhere, so she came to the set the first day of rehearsal secure in the knowledge that she would at least make life miserable for 'this squirt director Minnelli from New York.' I've been lucky to have great success with things that at first glance didn't seem so good."

In 1945, Minnelli directed the cinema's two greatest dancers, Fred Astaire and Gene Kelly, in their only routine together, "The Babbitt and the Bromide" from *Ziegfeld Follies.* It stands as a unique historical pairing of two legendary hoofers with vastly different styles who were in their artistic prime—a curio forever captured in the time capsule of film.

"The rehearsals were maddening," Minnelli explained. "Astaire would demonstrate an idea for a step and ask Kelly what he thought of it. Kelly would say, 'fine, great, swell.' They tried to convince each other and be so polite. That dance took three weeks to rehearse, but it turned out well. Fred Astaire is lighter than air you know and Gene is earthier. Both are perfectionists to the nth degree. It was a fascinating thing to witness."

Thirty-five years ago we asked Minnelli what he thought of the infrequent occurrence of new film musicals, *The Wiz* in particular. He told us he saw a screening of the film which starred Diana Ross in the role of Dorothy and Michael Jackson as the Scarecrow and was an all-black version of a hit Broadway musical that was, in turn, based on the 1939 movie starring that "consummate performer," Judy Garland.

"I decided then and there not to see any more new film musicals," he said.

For the nonverbal Minnelli, it was a mouthful. Some things, you see, just can't be improved on.

TV's Funniest Shrink

Bob Newhart

The Hotel Bel-Air in Los Angeles is a five-star boutique hideaway that's been favored by such dignitaries as Princesses Astrid of Norway and Margaretha of Sweden, H.S.H. Grace de Monaco ... and Bob Newhart.

In an undeniably Tinseltown-style statement predicated on a movie mania only Southern Californians would have the temerity to take credit for, the Bel-Air management prominently displays in the lobby signed glossies of everyone of significance who stayed there from international royalty to those with merely a Hollywood pedigree.

So much for anonymity.

Back in 1981, in the dark recesses of the hotel's café, we met Newhart for breakfast (he favored corned beef hash straight out of the Hormel can). That quiet spot was his choice and it seemed to be in keeping with the proper manner we had always associated with his character on *The Bob Newhart Show*. Considering the often outlandish tenor of sitcom's back then—and even more so, now—memories of Newhart's droll approach to laugh-getting and his unruffled demeanor should be treasured.

"One of the keys to the success of my character was that I let the ensemble on my show grab a healthy share of the laughs," Newhart said. "It worked for Jack Benny on radio and television, and it worked for me."

Newhart's oblique entry into show business was the result not of any particular burning ambition on his part, but rather due to his ineptitude as an accountant. That day at the Bel-Air he even looked like one on a casual Friday dressed in a v-neck sweater right off the rack from Robinsons-May, a cotton shirt, slacks and wearing black loafers with those ornamental brass gizmos attached to the tongues—the only frippery (visible

or verbal) detectible during the interview.

"I used to balance the petty cash box
where I worked with money out of my
own pocket," he said. "If it was a dollar
under, I'd take it out of my pocket. If it
was a dollar over, I'd put it into my
pocket. My boss kept telling me to balance it correctly, but I said 'You're paying
me $3 an hour to find 50 cents. It just
doesn't make sense!' I guess that's when
I knew I wasn't cut out to be an accountant."

Newhart said there aren't words in
the English language to describe how
nervous he was before taking the stage
for his first standup comedy gig in 1960
at the Tidelands Motor Inn and Nightclub in Houston, Texas. "The first three
years I was on stage I just stared straight
ahead," he said. "Hecklers used to bother
me but they don't anymore. Sometimes
they actually make for a better show; you

Bob's full accounting

can have a lot of fun with them. There was a guy in Vegas when I was performing there
who was sound asleep with his head resting on the stage. He slept all the way through
the first act. I kept referring to him but he never stirred. For awhile, I thought he might
be dead. But just as I was finishing and the band was playing my exit music, he lifted his
head and looked as if he wasn't sure where he was."

Regardless of his professional seasoning, Newhart said he still got "butterflies" before
heading out on stage. "Hey, it's the most natural thing in the world to saunter out in front
of 1,000 people with the clear-cut understanding that you're going to make them laugh,"
he said. "I don't know anybody *that* fearless."

As far as his material went, Newhart said, just like in earlier vaudeville days, set
routines could last for months, even years, with topicality customized in when the need
arose. "I used to do 'The Driving Instructor' and 'The Submarine Commander' night
after night," he said. "When I did college concerts, I never really dealt with the audience;
they were just a black void out there in the middle distance. But in a nightclub, you have
to deal with the audience."

Newhart said that after about six years of performing in Vegas, he developed the
habit of peeking through the curtain before going on to see if the front row had drunks
or malcontents that could spell potential trouble. But a watershed moment occurred for
him at the Sands Hotel when he got involved in a conversation with a manager and forgot
to check the house. "My entrance music came on and I realized I didn't have to check
the audience," Newhart said. "I could handle them. It was a professional turning point
for me."

Soon after, nightclub comedy gigs gelled into riotous monologues on comedy albums
such as *The Button-Down Mind of Bob Newhart*, in which his routines "The Driving

Instructor" and "The Submarine Commander" gained Newhart national fame. "I know albums tend to use a comic's material faster than he can replenish it, but for me it worked in reverse. The album was the only reason for me gaining prominence at all," Newhart said. "People came wanting to hear those routines. Comedy constantly changes and you have to be aware of it and anticipate it. I think that era ended with *Laugh-In* and its quick blackouts. You couldn't do seven- or eight-minute monologues; you had to do three- and four-minute skits."

And as far as hiring a legion of writers á la Bob Hope to keep his comedy topical, that never worked out well for Newhart who felt that exclusively performing other writers material would make him little more than a corporation. "I think I've bought only one routine in the last 22 years," he said. "I'd have to find a young writer and lock him in a room somewhere and not let him know the world exists out there. I actually enjoy writing my own material; it's the ultimate satisfaction—when it works.

It was while performing in Las Vegas that Newhart first developed a friendship with another comedian that has stood the test of time—many decades of trading each other insults. "Don Rickles was playing a hotel lounge in Vegas. His wife knew my wife, so we all arranged to meet for dinner before Don had to go back and do his third show," Newhart said. "During the meal, he asked my wife questions about how old our kids were and I thought: 'What a lovely man!' As you probably can guess, Rickles' act differed from what our conversation was based on that day. Well, we went to see his act and he came out from the wings and promptly called me a stammering idiot and my wife a former hooker from Bayonne, New Jersey. We've been friends ever since."

The Bob Newhart Show came about because Newhart said he had high regard for the quality and professionalism of Mary Tyler Moore Enterprises (the production company behind *The Mary Tyler Moore Show*).

"Lorenzo Music, who wrote for *The Smothers Brothers* program and who played Carleton the Doorman on *Rhoda*, and Dave Davis were a writing team. They came up with the concept that I should play a psychologist. It was a great idea but my only reservation was that it was a potentially dangerous area. I didn't want to portray really sick people like schizophrenics. As it turned out, I did have the distinction of being on television six years and never curing a patient. Mr. Carlin was probably worse off at the end of the show than at the beginning."

The pilot for Newhart's series lacked many of the show's now familiar faces. Marcia Wallace (Carol the receptionist) and Bill Daley (Bob's ditzy neighbor, Howard Borden) weren't featured, and the whole show had to be reshot because the network, for unknown reasons, objected to the script's use of the word "condominium." Go figure! According to Newhart, Wallace was discovered by none other than the head of CBS, William Paley who recommended her to the producers. "And nobody tells Paley to buzz off," Newhart said.

If they were halcyon days for Newhart, the nights were closer to Halcion. "One director we had had absolutely no sense of humor," Newhart recalled, bemused. "We rehearsed with him for five days when I finally told our producer, Michael Zinberg, that I thought one of the essential ingredients a comedy director should possess is the ability to laugh. It's like a team having a ball player with poor eye/hand coordination. After that, we hired Dick Martin to direct. God bless him! He sat in the director's booth for three months watching us block and rehearse, in order to acquaint himself with the show."

The show's six-year run provided high points that to this day still manage to conjure up what Woody Allen would call "legitimate laughs" during re-runs in syndication. "Bill Daley is responsible for many of the biggest laughs in the show," Newhart said. "His part of Howard was so nonsensical that he seldom had anything to do with an episode's particular storyline. In one show he had just returned from the Fiji Islands and he came in and said: 'Bob, do you think I'm getting shorter? … Because I think I'm engaged to a Fijian princess and if I don't marry her, the chief said I will be cursed. To seal the ceremony, they gave us two cows. Do you think the state of Illinois will recognize the marriage?' I said, 'I'm sure they will. You'll be the couple with the two cows.' Stuff like that, totally off the wall; the writers loved it."

Newhart also credited Daley with the biggest laugh line in the show's history. "I was working with a prison group and Emily (Suzanne Pleshette) and I both had our hands against the wall. Howard came running in and he thought we were holding up the wall. When we walked away, he said: 'Hey, aren't you going to help me? I can't hold this up all by myself.' The audience howled."

At about the time of our interview, almost 35 years ago, Newhart hinted that another TV series might be in the offing. (Newhart's phenomenally successful follow-up to *The Bob Newhart Show*, *Newhart*, began an eight-season run the next year.)

One of the keys to the success of Newhart's character (besides his impeccable timing and milquetoast delivery) was that he often stepped aside and let the ensemble grab a healthy share of the laughs. "It's been the key in radio and television," he said. "Even in nightclubs, I've found that the stronger the opening act is, the better it is for me. The crowd is already primed to yell and scream. You can't give ultimatums like an emperor. You can't be (Jackie) Gleason and storm out of a room. You're working with creative people who take pride in what they are doing."

Telling words from the taciturn, button-down mind of Bob Newhart.

The Great American Flyers

The Nicholas Brothers

Nobody ever got "air" like the dancing Nicholas Brothers, not even Michael Jordan in mid-leap during a monster jam. Fayard and his younger brother Harold were, by almost unanimous consent, the greatest airborne flash act in show business history. Their specialty was somersaults into mindboggling leg splits from which they rose almost in slow motion, and rapid-fire tap dancing that sounded like short bursts from an angry Gatling gun.

For the record, the Nicholas Brothers were running up walls and doing backflips (into splits) long before Donald O'Connor's justifiably famous "wallies" in his "Make 'Em Laugh" routine in *Singin' in the Rain*.

The brothers were a legendary act at Harlem's Cotton Club during the 1930s where they spun and flipped to the swingin' bands of Cab Calloway, Chick Webb and Duke Ellington. (The original club, located on Lenox Ave., shuttered its doors in 1935—more

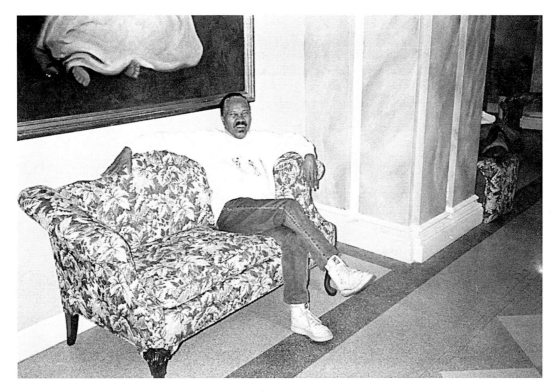

An earthbound Harold Nicholas

than 80 years ago.) Later on, their specialty numbers in such movies as *Stormy Weather*, *Orchestra Wives*, *Down Argentine Way* and *Sun Valley Serenade* generated wild applause in movie houses coast to coast.

Harold and Fayard began their show business careers as a child act in their hometown of Philadelphia in 1930 where their mother played piano and their father played drums in an orchestra called the Nicholas Collegiates. It was Fayard who caught the dancing bug first, lingering after his parents' stage performances to watch other acts on the bill.

"I liked what I saw," he told us during an interview we had with the brothers in 1999. "They were singing, dancing and telling jokes … having fun up there. So, just by watching, I taught myself how to perform."

When we met, Fayard was garrulous about the Nicholas Brothers and their legacy. He was dressed in a blue leisure suit and sported a Planet Hollywood baseball cap. Harold, more taciturn, wore thready sweatpants and a gray sweater and had his gray hair tied back into a nubby ponytail. His inscrutability seemed even more so, accented as it was with a wispy Fu Manchu goatee.

The Nicholas Brothers started out as pint-sized performers and remained lithe, super-charged and hobbit-sized throughout their careers. There must be a physics postulate somewhere about minimal body mass and lightning-fast propulsion leading to spectacular aerial dynamics. Just don't make the mistake of calling Fayard and Harold a flash act!

* * *

Harold: We weren't a flash act. We did tap and acrobatics.

Fayard: Yes, "flash" is a bad word. When you say, "flash," you think flashy. Be we did classical tap. In our routines you'd see a little bit of ballet, eccentric dancing and you see acrobatics and classical tapping. We can do a routine without any splits, just tap dancing.

Fantle & Johnson: *We read in Marshall Stearns' wonderful book,* Jazz Dance: The Story of American Vernacular Dance, *that the film choreographer Nick Castle said your hands (Fayard's) were as beautiful as Fred Astaire's.*

Fayard: Actually, he said that my hands were the best in show business. I love Fred Astaire. He was a perfectionist and he did all those wonderful things. He used his hands like I do; I just did more of it. I went to a rehearsal hall in Philly and rented a room with mirrors so I could see myself. I figured I was going to do more with my hands, and work with my whole body—to give this a Nicholas Brothers style! That's what I taught Harold.

Do you have a favorite routine from all your movies?

Harold: I thought the thing we did in *Stormy Weather* was great—the one where we slide down the gutters in a split for our big finish. We did that number in one take. You know Astaire said that was the best number he ever saw in a movie.

Fayard: I like all our routines because I could see progress in all of them.

You worked with Gene Kelly in The Pirate *in 1948.*

Harold: It was the first time we did straight dancing … no tricks or tumbling or anything. But it was interesting because the three of us synchronized our moves. Gene had seen us in New York and told us that some of the stuff we were doing was what he'd like to do.

Fayard: Producer Arthur Freed at MGM called Gene into his office one day and said: "Gene, I've got the story that you can do with the Nicholas Brothers" It was the script for *The Pirate*, but Freed warned Gene that any number he might do with us could be cut out when the picture played theaters in the south. Gene said: "I don't give a damn! It'll play the same all over the world, so why do we have to just think about the south? The movie played in the south and they never cut us.

Who was the greatest dancer you ever saw?

Harold: "Baby Laurence" Jackson was fantastic. Guys today are dancing like Laurence danced back in the 1940s and '50s. Savion Glover … he's thinking Baby Laurence even though he may have never met him. I know that's the kind of rhythm he's doing.

Fayard: We danced with about every dancing star there was. Outside of my brother, I would name Eleanor Powell. She could do ballet, tap, ballroom, splits, acrobatics … everything. And she could do it all well. Some say she was the world's greatest female dancer, but I say she's the world's greatest dancer. She's better than everybody.

Sadly, Eleanor Powell had a relatively short film career.

Fayard: Yeah, but when she was on screen, you paid attention. I remember one of her friends threw a birthday party for her and they transformed her garage into a theater. We watched all her movies and then they played the Nicholas Brothers movies over and over. And she sat next to me and held my hand and would say: "Did you see that?" And she kept squeezing my hand, never taking her eyes off the screen and saying: "Watch this," like I had never seen the routine before. Then, after she blew out the candles on her birthday cake, I said: "Eleanor, I don't count when I dance." And she said she didn't either, and I said: "Well, we do have something in common." I then said: "Eleanor, I pick up a lot of steps that I don't have names for." And she said: "Me, too!" Then I said: "Wow, we really have something in common."

Fred Astaire's Silent Partner

Hermes Pan

Of all the stars manufactured in the great Hollywood dream factory, no one, with the possible exception of Charlie Chaplin, has given more sheer joy to more people than Fred Astaire. In particular, the movies he made with Ginger Rogers remain as testaments to a golden era of filmmaking, a time in our history when movies could be innocent, witty, elegant, exuberant and fun—and still attract a mass audience.

Even today, the nine landmark musicals that Astaire and Ginger Rogers made at RKO Pictures retain a freshness and vivacity that are astonishing. During the Great Depression, they helped people escape the harsh realities of unemployment and breadlines. Today, they still have the power to transport us out of our own time. The Astaire-Rogers movies didn't just break old, shopworn molds of how to portray dance on film; they became a measuring rod of excellence by which all other dance films were—and still are—compared.

What many moviegoers may not realize is that the Astaire-Rogers duo owes a large measure of its success to Fred's silent partner—Hermes Pan, a man as courtly and soft-spoken as Fred himself. With Astaire, Pan choreographed all of the Astaire-Rogers pictures from *Flying Down to Rio* in 1933 to *The Story of Vernon and Irene Castle* in 1939. In 1988 (two years before he died at the age of 80), we interviewed Pan about his career and how he helped Fred Astaire become legendary.

Pan was born in Memphis, Tennessee in 1910 and a couple of years later moved with his family to Nashville, where his father was employed as Greek Consul to the southern states. On the side, he also operated a restaurant that Pan remembers as of the best in the entire state. In Nashville, Pan was exposed for the first time to jazz dance, rhythms and riffs.

"Sam Clark was a black kid who was our houseboy and drove for us," Pan said. "He was a little older than I was and he used to teach me all kinds of shuffles, the Black Bottom and the Charleston. From those beginnings, I got my show business start, dancing in speakeasies in the 1920s at the age of 16."

Young Hermes also squired his sister in a dance act that landed the team specialty spots in a few Broadway shows. "My sister's name is Vasso. It was taken from our hometown of Vassiliki in the Peloponnesos," Pan said. When he wasn't gigging with his sister, Pan danced in the chorus of *Animal Crackers*, starring the Marx Brothers.

"Groucho was sarcastic, I never did like him," Pan said. "Chico was alright, but he was always skirt-chasing. Harpo was the nicest." Zeppo Marx, the brother whose presence amounted to a bit part in most of their shows and movies, became Pan's agent in Hollywood.

"He never did a damn thing for me," Pan recalled. "Everything I ever did I got on my own." That included getting up the gumption to motor west for a shot at the movies.

"I drove out to Los Angeles in 1930 with my mother and sister," Pan remembered. "Busby Berkeley was doing things along with such dance directors as LeRoy Prinz and Seymour Felix. I had worked for Felix back on Broadway in *Top Speed* and I thought it would be a cinch to land a job."

Unfortunately for Pan, in the early '30s the camera covered more ground than most chorus lines did. "I never got picked once," Pan said. "I remember Berkeley would line all the boys up and say: 'You, you, you and you … the rest of you can go home.' Half the time the selectees didn't even have to audition. In those days choreographers weren't dancers. Busby Berkeley couldn't dance a step; he was an idea man. They let the camera move for them. They'd have 500 pianos floating around or girls with violins in geometric configurations. It wasn't dancing at all."

In 1933, Pan got his big break as dance assistant to Dave Gould on *Flying Down to Rio*, a picture featuring a fresh young dance sensation from back east—Fred Astaire. Pan himself had just "happened" back into town after an abortive road trip with a traveling dance troupe.

"We had played one-night stands up and down the California coast," Pan said. "We were stranded every other week. In fact, one time we were stranded in Modesto and we had a booking in Antioch for three days. We told the hotel management that we would come back and pay the bill, but they wouldn't budge. I had to leave my mother for security. Years later, when I won my Academy Award for dance direction on *A Damsel in Distress*, one of the kids came up to me and said: 'Don't forget, I remember when you had to hock your mother.'"

Fortunately for Pan, he was able to pay the bill, retrieve his mother and follow a tip that led to Dave Gould's office at RKO. "I had gotten together with my sister and worked out about a chorus worth of steps to 'The Carioca,' a tune from the movie. I showed the routine to Dave and he liked it and I was in."

On his first day of work, Pan was told to, "Go over to stage eight and see if Fred Astaire needs any assistance." A daunting proposal to anyone, the idea terrified Pan. "It scared the life out of me because Fred was already an international star," Pan said. "I introduced myself by saying my name is Pan. Fred called me by my last name from that moment on. He had been working on a solo tap dance which he hadn't quite finished. He was stuck for a little break step and asked me if I had any ideas. At that moment something clicked in my mind and I remembered a break that Sam Clark had taught me back in Tennessee. I showed it to Fred and he loved it. After that he always called for me, never for Dave Gould, who had two left feet. Fred would yell: 'Pan, Pan, where is Pan?'"

Astaire once said that dancing for the screen was approximately 80 percent brain-work; that only 20 percent of the strain was on the feet. According to Pan, that 20 percent part of the equation seemed to yield a disproportionate share of calluses, shin splints and bruises. "We'd knock ourselves out," Pan told us. "We would come in, usually at 10 a.m. and work until 1 p.m. After an hour's break, we would come back and rehearse until we got too tired—around 5–6 p.m. It was almost constant dancing."

The brain trust of Astaire and Pan extended beyond just mentally mapping out the five or six necessary dance routines for each film. When it came time to actually do the dance, Fred always rehearsed the duet numbers with Pan before Ginger ever appeared on the sound stage. "A lot of times Ginger would be working on another picture," Pan said. "Also, we liked to work without her because in the initial stages we weren't always sure what we were going to do. I would do Ginger's part and then Ginger would come in and I'd teach her the steps."

Pan also dubbed in the taps for Ginger's routines, drudgery she was glad to avoid. "We would shoot the numbers to pre-recorded music and then post-record the taps days or even weeks later."

That kind of perseverance paid off when Fred cited Pan as his "best dance partner"—a subject not open to critical debate since the Astaire-Rogers films were always shot on closed sets. Pan, on the other hand, felt that in Astaire's career of over 35 musical films, Ginger Rogers holds the coveted position as his best partner. "Ginger wasn't the greatest dancer, but to my mind she was Fred's best partner. There was a quality when Fred danced with Ginger that didn't occur with any of his other partners. I worked with Cyd Charisse and Vera-Ellen when they teamed with Fred. They were better dancers than Ginger, but the same magic wasn't there."

Astaire wrote in his 1959 autobiography *Steps in Time* that Pan had an uncanny knack for coming up with great trick dance ideas. The golf dance in *Carefree* and the title number from *Top Hat* solidified Astaire's renown as a "solo" performer and Pan's reputation as a surefire "idea man" in his own right. But it is the "Bojangles of Harlem" number from *Swing Time* that contains a perfect balance of screen gimmickry and fancy footwork. The number, an acknowledged screen classic, has Astaire dancing in and out of syncopation with three huge shadows of himself projected on a wall behind him.

"The idea for that dance came one morning when I was sitting with Hal Borne, our rehearsal pianist, waiting for Fred to arrive," Pan said. "Hal started playing and I was dancing around the stage when someone flipped on some overhead lights up in the rafters. They shone down on the dark stage and I could see three shadows of myself. I commented to Hal on what a great effect it made and said I was going to tell Fred about it when he came in. Well, Fred arrived and I said: 'I think I've got a great idea.' He replied: 'It better be good!' Anyhow, I told him and then we went to the special effects department and they said it would be no problem."

Pan was also capable of choreographing more intimate solo numbers for Astaire. One of his best came in an unheralded 1950 Paramount Studios film called *Let's Dance*. It was during those years; when Astaire was "Gingerless," that he would often rely on knockout solo numbers to maintain the momentum not only of the film, but also his career. The solo, called "The Piano Dance," was considered a tour-de-force of versatility by no less an authority than ballet superstar Rudolf Nureyev.

"Fred didn't originally want to do that number," Pan remembered. "I had layed it out so that at one point he would be hanging over the top of the baby grand with one leg dangling in the air. Fred was adamant that he just couldn't do that. I showed him, he tried it, and then said: 'My God, that was easy!' At the end of the number he has to exit the club while dancing over some chairs. He was also skeptical about that. He said he might break a leg. I told him, 'Look, hold my hand, step on the seat of the chair, put your foot on the top, balance, push with your right foot and push back with your left and you can go over as slowly as you want to."

During the 40-year span of his movie career, Pan choreographed pictures that starred Rita Hayworth, Marge and Gower Champion, Bob Fosse and Shirley MacLaine. He even worked in *Sun Valley Serenade* with the greatest flash-dance act the movies have ever known—The Nicholas Brothers. "Those guys had so many backflips, splits, riffs and steps, and they did them all at the speed of light," Pan said. "I gave their numbers for that film some cohesion, but I can't do a backflip into a split, so I mostly just let them go."

In 1968, 35 years after Pan made his fateful visit to stage eight on the RKO lot to see if he could "help" Fred Astaire, both men were reunited to work on *Finian's Rainbow*. The film proved to be their musical swansong.

Although Pan and Astaire are long gone, the dances they created will, as the lyric of an old Irving Berlin tune says, "linger on," providing joy and inspiration for generations of movie-lovers to come.

And to us, that is the perfect finish step.

Of Mockingbirds and Maniacs

Gregory Peck

In the same way that Charlton Heston was lauded for his commitment to conservative politics and for not shying away from discussing them in any venue, including during our visit with him, on the opposite end of the political spectrum, Gregory Peck was always front and center adding Hollywood heft and erudition to progressive platforms; a polemical balefire for others to rally around.

In 1981, when we met him, Peck had been out stumping for "unpopular" liberal causes long before then Screen Actors Guild president Ed Asner became vocal about rebels in El Salvador. But unlike his contemporaries Ronald Reagan and Senator George Murphy, Peck, although a firm adherent to the pieties of liberal Hollywood, never used his elected positions in the entertainment business as a springboard into the national political arena; a curiously popular enticement for movie and television stars—especially these days!

"I've been called the Hollywood equivalent of John F. Kennedy because of my devotion to liberal politics," Peck told us at his Bel-Air home. "Naturally, I am flattered, but I'm afraid the comparison ends more or less where it began. You have to be very careful with your good deeds that you don't do more harm than good."

After handshakes, we mentioned to Peck that we had just come to him from interviewing songwriter Sammy Cahn ("Three Coins in the Fountain," "All the Way," "Call Me Irresponsible").

"Did he sing for you?" Peck asked. "There's no earthly way you can stop Sammy from singing."

"We got about three questions in and then he was off to the races. We couldn't get a word in edgewise after that," Dave said.

"He's very entertaining," Peck laughed. "He'll do his whole show for you, which lasts about two hours."

Dressed in khaki shorts and an old dress shirt with the sleeves rolled up to his elbows, Peck, ever the courtly host, asked if we'd like something to drink. Momentarily, a houseboy appeared with a tray of flavored teas and coffees from which to choose. The late afternoon sun was beginning to slant so we moved out to an upstairs terrace and watched as Peck's son, Tony, tossed a football back and forth to a friend. From our bird's-eye view vantage point (tantamount to the owner's box at Anaheim Stadium, probably), Tony looked to have the bionic arm of Joe Namath bulleting 50-yard perfect spirals to Don Maynard.

"He's putting together a rock band right now," Peck said with the bemused detachment of a parent used to his children's fevered—and ever-changing—enthusiasms. "We'll see. What I suggested to him, and he accepted my advice, was to get stage training and experience in the theater—voice, body, stretching your imagination, learning self-control, acquiring poise in front of an audience—and then gradually learning ways to reach out."

At the time of the writing of this book, 36 years had passed since we had

Positively Peck

tea with Peck. In 2017, President Trump, in his first federal budget plan, proposed eliminating the National Endowment for the Arts (NEA), an organization with which Peck had been involved early on. For eight years, from 1966–68 and 1970–76, Peck served on the embryonic National Endowment for the Arts Commission with such luminaries as John Steinbeck, Agnes DeMille, Isaac Stern and Leonard Bernstein. Following the passage of the Arts and Humanities Act of 1965, the NEA was afforded a whopping $4 million annually in scholarship and grant subsidies. The money was intended to blanket the cultural needs of the entire United States.

"We would meet six times a year and quarrel for hours over which writer, regional theater, or ballet company best deserved a $2,000 grant," Peck said. "I think we got pretty good results, but I do remember a certain politician from Iowa who used to eternally wail to his colleagues on the floor of Congress, 'Tax money for toe-dancers over my dead body!'"

The confounded reality that in 1966, a city the size of Hamburg, Germany, gave $7 million to their local opera company alone while the entire U.S. muddled through with a mere $4 million in cultural subsidies made Peck's social consciousness crawl.

"The total amount has grown now to $160 million in the United States, which is still not much," he said. "Most of the performing arts don't pay their way back at the box office with the cost of production and other expenses. I know it's hard for many people to accept. They feel that cultural groups should pay their own way, but if we want our young people to expand their horizons and personalities and to reach their highest aspirations, then the arts must be nationally subsidized. The private corporate sector has already taken up most of the slack."

An argument as implacable and tenacious in 1966 as it was in 1981 or 2017.

On the Beach, *Gentleman's Agreement*, and *To Kill a Mockingbird*, for which Peck won an Oscar in 1962, were films that crusaded for topical social issues—the threat of thermo-nuclear destruction, anti–Semitism and racism, respectively. They were Peck's dream movies and remained dear to his heart because they had a duality, enlightening audiences as they entertained them.

"*Gentleman's Agreement* was a cause celebre around Hollywood because it was the first movie to deal directly with anti–Semitism," Peck said. "When Darryl Zanuck decided to do it, people advised him not to rock the boat. 'Business is great,' they said. 'Why deal with such a controversial subject?' Zanuck replied that it was a very good dramatic story that also made observations about racial prejudice. We all felt we were pioneering in a small way. Nowadays it would be nothing, but in 1948, it was something."

We wondered if the screenwriter, Moss Hart (a Broadway juggernaut who had written classic comedies like *Once in a Lifetime* and *You Can't Take It with You* with frequent collaborator George S. Kaufman in the 1930s) had ever mentioned to Peck what he thought of his performance in the film.

"He was a little too smooth and diplomatic to offer any critiques," Peck said. "That wasn't his job. Critics are critics and writers are writers. I would never criticize another actor's performance, certainly not publicly. We all have to make a living and we all do the best we can. Some people do it better than others; some people bring different qualities, personal characteristics to it. Denigrate another actor's work is something I would automatically not do."

The era of movie producers like Zanuck, who were passionately interested in every line in the scripts of their movies, had by the time we met Peck given way to a generation of soulless conglomerates that couldn't squint past the stockholder equity column on their balance sheets.

"I don't know any studio heads today and I don't want to know them, because they probably won't be here next year," Peck said. "They all seem to be a page in Gulf and Western's portfolio. That fellow in the tall building at Columbus Circle in New York, Charles Bluhdorn, he turns the pages, and if a company like Paramount didn't do well last year, he'll throw the rascals out and get some new rascals in. They are essentially crapshooters. Zanuck was a walking computer. You could call him from the set if you had trouble with a line and he'd rewrite the line with you right there on the telephone. If you call one of those fellows today, chances are they won't know what the hell you're talking about. The same was true to a varying degree with Jack Warner, Harry Cohn and Louis B. Mayer. The passion was there. Today, it's passionless. It's dollars and cents."

In 1962, Peck portrayed Atticus Finch, the morally upstanding, courageous lawyer who defended a black man accused of rape in *To Kill a Mockingbird*. The character is strongly reminiscent of the quiet determination of Frank Capra's everyman idealist of the 1930s and '40s. It is Peck's favorite role, and was one of the most challenging of his career.

"I think one of the hardest things to do as an actor is to make a good man interesting, because they can be awfully dull. If a man is predictably nice, he can put audiences to sleep," Peck said. "Atticus was a good man if anybody anywhere was ever good. We managed to make him compelling. Today when I'm with my wife and we walk down Fifth Avenue in New York, people will come up to me and say how much *To Kill a Mockingbird* meant to them. One young man even said that his decision to become a lawyer was formulated at the age of 14 after he saw the film."

Peck told us at the time that if Harper Lee wrote another book as good as *To Kill a Mockingbird*, and there was a part for him in the film version, he would consider doing it. Thirty-four years later, in 2015 and 12 years after Peck's death, Random House published Lee's controversial sequel to *Mockingbird*, entitled *Go Set a Watchman*. We can only speculate on what Peck might have thought of the surprising turn the character of Atticus takes, becoming hardened in his racial views. According to Peck's son Stephen, the actor considered Lee a friend and would have welcomed the discussion generated by the book. (Lee gifted Peck a pocket watch that had belonged to her father—the model for Atticus—and he wore it the night he won the Oscar for his performance in the role.) But, Stephen Peck has said that his father also probably would have cautioned against publishing the sequel as it could have potentially tainted the character of Atticus and in doing so also *Mockingbird*.

The Boys from Brazil (1978) in which Peck played the part of Dr. Mengele, the diabolical Nazi death-camp experimenter, was the diametric opposite of Atticus Finch. No subtle character shading was necessary; as such, the acting muscles that required flexing were minimal. "To play Mengele, a raving lunatic, was not difficult," Peck said. "I got down the German accent, blackened my hair, shaved the hair-line back a couple of inches, and affected a kind of laboratory pallor. It has been said that the greatest role an actor could play would be a dipsomaniac dope fiend being dragged to the electric chair. You can climb the walls and claim its great acting."

Peck was dogmatic in more than just a political sense. He was chewed to pieces by salivating canines in the finales of two of his films, *The Omen* and *The Boys from Brazil*. But he held no grudge. "I don't want to make a career as dog food," he said. "The only thing my German Shepherd, Roger, has a fondness for teething on is old Hawaiian Tropic Suntan Oil bottles." (The dog was busily engaged perforating one during the course of our interview.) Still, it was a bit disquieting discussing his role as the infamous Dr. Mengele with a Shepherd sharpening his incisors just a few feet away. "Mealtime's in about an hour, Rog," Peck said, cuffing his ears.

One of the "old guard" Hollywood directors Peck remembered fondly is William Wyler, a master of many genres, from historical epics (*Ben-Hur*) to dramatic "message pictures" (*The Best Years of Our Lives*) to musical biopics (*Funny Girl*), and one whose economical direction would give any Stanislavskian pause to rethink his method.

"Wyler's direction was considered to be death on wheels to method actors," Peck said. "When I was working on *Roman Holiday* with Audrey (Hepburn), he'd say, 'Audrey, get mad; you have to cry in this scene.' She had to produce tears without analysis. On the contrary, method actors might say, 'Grandma hurt my feelings when I was five, and if I can recall that, I can cry for you.' It's kind of like dry fly fishing. You drop the fly in the water and when the trout grabs it, you set the hook. There are directors who wouldn't recognize a valuable nuance if you hit them in the face with it. But Wyler was omniscient. He'd wait until a scene was right if it took three days."

According to Peck, Wyler also knew a surefire extemporaneous gag when he was presented with one as in the scene with Peck and Hepburn at the *Bocca della Verita*

(Mouth of Truth). "That wasn't in the script," Peck said. "I thought of it right before we were going to shoot it—the old shtick where you stick your hand in the mouth of the monument and if you're telling the truth, you can withdraw your hand intact. But if you're lying, it will bite your hand off. I told Willie (Wyler) that there was an old gag I'd seen Red Skelton do where you come up with your hand inside your sleeve and you shake hands with an empty sleeve. I said: 'Willie, how 'bout if I do that with the mouth and come out with an empty sleeve?' He said, 'Great, but don't tell her.' We didn't and when Audrey screamed, it was real."

As for his remarkable longevity in the film business, Peck referred to the old saw of actors loving acting so much that they'd do it for nothing if forced to. "I'm like that," he said. "To me, going to work in the morning and putting in a full day of play-acting is invigorating. It just seems to suit me. Maybe the audience reads into that, that I'm trying to give them their money's worth; trying to do the best I can for them. I do feel responsible to the audience when I'm in front of a camera, even though a lot of technicians are going to have a crack at it—slice it and snip it and shape it and eventually put it in cans and ship it around the world."

Peck cited Burt Lancaster and Kirk Douglas as his contemporaries when he began in the movie business in the mid–1940s and said, like them, he "never looked back and just took what came." But he did betray to us a bit of yearning for an earlier, more glamorous era in Tinseltown that he missed by about a decade.

"Glamour is a byproduct of interesting personalities," he said. "I was watching *Dinner at Eight* and *Grand Hotel* the other night on TV. Those were glamorous pictures because the stars in them were so individualistic, so unique. There is no other Garbo, no other John Barrymore, not even another Wallace Beery. They were, as the saying goes: 'bigger than life.' Things weren't so marginalized back then as they are now. And there were a lot of them around: Cagney, Lombard, Gable, Cooper, Bogart, Rosalind Russell. When these people burst forth on the scene with their energy, ambition and personality, they couldn't be denied. They had that charismatic intangible called 'It.' They were, well, just naturals."

Modest man that he was, we knew Peck wasn't in the slightest being self-referential, but he could just as easily have been talking about himself.

Maledictions in a Minor Chord

André Previn

Not everyone we ever interviewed who worked in Hollywood during the Golden Age had golden memories about that era; some recollections were closer to dross. One of those with a fractious view backward was composer André Previn who had been a "boy wonder" at MGM in the late 1940s and early '50s where (at the age of 19) he started orchestrating scores and conducting.

"All that is ancient history, why even bring it up?" he groused over the phone during an early attempt to set an interview date and time.

Fans of movie and TV stars often tend to deify their idols swathing them with unconditional love that provides a protective carapace to even the rankest heresy. For years, Previn saw the famous and talented up close and personal, warts and all, and silently took his measure of them. There were few illusions to shatter because he didn't harbor any to begin with. And in the final analysis, as he told us, he just had better things to do.

It took two solid years to convince Previn to sit down with us for just a few minutes to get his unexpurgated take on working in Hollywood. That happened in 2016 in New York City at Previn's Upper East Side apartment when he was 87. In the intervening decades since he had ankled Tinseltown in the mid–1960s, Previn carved out a prestigious career as a composer, conductor and pianist; a gifted interpreter in both classical and jazz idioms. We never got the impression that Previn's jaundiced comments (when he made them) were in

The maestro in repose

any way gratuitous, contrarian or that he had a particular ax to grind, but he was dismissive about that time in the cavalier way someone might be when talking about a years old and therefore inconsequential traffic ticket.

Arthritic and housebound when we called, Previn beckoned us in without getting out of his chair. From a small room—his library—he immediately apologized for the clutter of LPs, books and assorted *tchotchkes* (to us, the apartment was homey). Previn's four Oscars had "house seats" on the windowsill with a pigeon's-eye view of 65th Street below.

A child prodigy, Previn with his family escaped Nazi Germany in 1939 for Los Angeles and in 1946, while still in high school, he started working part-time at MGM, Hollywood's most exalted dream factory. By the time he was 35, Previn had collected a mindboggling 14 Academy Award nominations, winning four Oscars, his last coming in 1964 for scoring *My Fair Lady*.

"I loved it," he said about his first day working at MGM. "There was something about walking into that gate, and for an 18-year-old, it was like a kid in a candy store. But I got over that after a while and it became a job. It was a factory in which they did very artistic work, but they didn't write factory-style music. It was an awful place to grow up musically, except I learned how to write arrangements and how to orchestrate very quickly and under adverse conditions."

In 1948, Previn became part of the Arthur Freed Unit, the prestigious assemblage of artists most responsible for the glorious MGM musicals (*Meet Me in St. Louis, An*

American in Paris, Singin' in the Rain). His first Freed screen credit came (Previn worked on eight Freed films) with *Kismet*, a film he called "dreadful." Nonetheless, he soon became a foursquare and indefatigable member of the Unit.

"Arthur took no bullshit from anybody," Previn said. "He may have been—not illiterate—but non-verbal, but he ran his own unit and nobody could get near it. I got along with him very well. Arthur was a complicated man. He was an orchid fancier. He didn't want problems that he couldn't handle. We had some confusion on what to record first in the movie *Invitation to the Dance*, so I went up to his office and explained the situation to him. He said, 'Just a minute' and he got up and left the office. After about 10 minutes I thought, 'What is this?' and I went out and there was his secretary, Helen. I asked: 'Where's Mr. Freed?' and she said he went home. That was his way of saying, 'You handle it. I don't want to worry about that.' His great trick was getting the right people to do the right thing.

"I never liked musical films to tell you the truth," he continued, "but I liked Freed's films because they usually started out with a very classy idea and if they didn't work, they didn't work, like *Kismet* which was ghastly.' I saw *Summer Holiday* and I thought it was wonderful. I loved it and I give Freed points for pushing the envelope."

Previn allowed that he admired Freed for his other ambitious failures as well, including the film, *The Pirate* starring Gene Kelly and Judy Garland and for which Previn did some uncredited work. "I loved it," he said. "But audiences at the time didn't get the joke. I didn't like Gene in that movie. He was over-the-top. I loved the way Judy sang, but I have to say that when she read dialogue, especially when I look at it now, I always think she sounds like she's on the absolute knife's edge of hysteria. Even if she said, 'Could I have breakfast?' it made me very nervous."

A rising star in his own right at MGM, Previn said he became friends with Garland, one of the studio's biggest and most bankable assets. "She was a funny lady, very funny and she was great company," he said. "But you always knew that at any second she could go up in smoke. I took her out once. We went to see Chaplin's *City Lights* before it was in general re-release at a little theater on La Brea Avenue. She wanted to see it, so we went. Halfway through it she said, 'Get me out of here! Get me out of here!' She was sweating and frightened and who knows why? I don't know about all of those stories about how they mistreated her at the studio—probably."

At the opposite end of the singing spectrum at MGM was the studio's reigning coloratura soprano, Kathryn Grayson. Suffice to say, there was no date night in the offing for Previn with Grayson. "She was the most untalented musical star I've ever heard," he said. "Something you ought to watch next time you see a Kathryn Grayson film, no matter what the song is, whether it's Mozart or *Show Boat*, (the 1951 musical in which she starred) focus your attention on the last note where she goes 'whee' reaching for a high note an octave above where it was written—only because she thinks that's showbiz. God, she was so unmusical. Johnny Green (the film's arranger) did the song 'Bill' with her. There were 103 intercuts within that one song. She could never do it."

In 1955, Freed produced what in hindsight is now considered an overlooked gem, one of the last of the original Hollywood musicals, *It's Always Fair Weather*. The film reunited *Singin' in the Rain* writers Betty Comden and Adolph Green with the film's directors, Stanley Donen and Gene Kelly. Previn was tapped for the first time to compose a score of original songs. "It was a milestone for me," he said. "It meant I was the conductor, the arranger and the songwriter. There wasn't any aspect of the music in the film that I was not responsible for. It was great fun. It was Comden and Green and Stanley and we all misbehaved so terribly."

When the film was being cast, efforts were made to reunite Kelly with his *On the Town* co-star Frank Sinatra, but a couple of years earlier Sinatra had won a Best Supporting Actor Oscar as "Maggio" in *From Here to Eternity* and he had no interest in reuniting for another musical sashay down memory lane. So, dancer Dan Daily and choreographer Michael Kidd (in his acting debut) starred with Kelly. It was to be the last film Kelly and Donen co-directed. Their partnership had become acrimonious with tension running high on the set.

"I liked Gene very much, but he wasn't as pleasant to be with as Stanley," said Previn. "As long as things went his (Kelly's) way, he was fine. But you had to do it his way. With Stanley you could argue and discuss it. There was a dance with garbage can lids and I wrote, at least for that time, some pretty wild music and Gene said, 'Jesus, Andrew, I don't like that.' And Stanley said, 'Leave him alone, it's perfect for that number,' and he talked him into it, otherwise Gene would have thrown it out like he did Michael Kidd's big solo number, 'Jack and the Beanstalk.'"

When we said we had read that Kidd's number was cut because it was determined that it interrupted the flow of the film, Previn didn't mince words. "Bullshit! Michael really stole that part of the picture and Gene said very calmly, 'No, not in my movie.'"

At the 1959 Academy Award ceremonies, Freed's production of *Gigi* (released in 1958) took home a record-shattering nine Oscars, including Best Picture and Best Score for Previn. It was one of the few productions with which he was involved that Previn remembered without a sour note attached.

"I remember sitting in a Paris restaurant and the only reason I drop names is that there would be no point to the story without it," he said. "I was with Alan Jay Lerner and Frederick Loewe, Vincente Minnelli, Louis Jourdan, about 10 of us in all, and Hermione Gingold said, 'I've never worked for Arthur Freed before and he doesn't seem to be doing much. What does he do that's so terrific?' And Alan said, 'Well, look around the table, we're all here.' And that sums it up. He was amazing."

According to Previn, the French were aghast at how much money was spent by Minnelli and others to produce the film but the final result was worth every franc. "It's a good story, an intelligent, adult picture," Previn said. "I saw it about six months ago and it's still pretty good. I was proud of *Gigi*. I still think to this day that it's the best musical I have ever seen. Vincente could make the most beautiful looking movies in the world. That was one Oscar I really wanted to win."

But with every pinnacle reached comes a trench that must be endured and that happened the very next year when Previn found himself working with director Otto Preminger on the film adaptation of George Gershwin's *Porgy and Bess*. "Oh my God, that was rough," Previn said. "Preminger was a tyrant and he was so cruel to people. At one point, Sidney Poitier said, 'You do that once more and I'm going to paste you all over the wall!' Preminger was yelling at Dorothy Dandridge and said to her with that German accent, 'Are you aware that everyone on this set hates you?' You just can't do that to an actor."

In 1964, Previn moved to Warner Brothers for *My Fair Lady* where he won his fourth Oscar for adapting the Lerner and Loewe score to the screen. The show had been a monster hit on Broadway catapulting a young Julie Andrews to stardom. However, it was Audrey Hepburn, an established movie star and thus considered more bankable, who played the iconic "Eliza Doolittle" in the screen version. Previn said that working with Hepburn was a joy in equal measure but in an inverse ratio to the misery caused by Rex Harrison who played "Professor Higgins" and Oscar-winning costumer Cecil Beaton.

"I liked both ladies very much," he said. "I'm still a good friend of Julie's. But it was hard not to be in love with Audrey Hepburn. She was just wonderful. She was also—what's the word I want to say—pretty sassy. I was standing on the set and Mrs. Alan Jay Lerner, Micheline, the French lawyer—my God, how can any guy marry a French lawyer? Anyway, she came to talk to us and I thought that she wore the most awful dress. When she left, suddenly Audrey grinned at me like a little school girl and said, 'Dior makes that look so long.'"

The studio brass made the heavily disputed decision that Hepburn's singing voice was not up to the Cockney accent requirements for the role and that her vocals would be dubbed. "Her voice was better than serviceable," Previn said. "It fit her, but the studio wouldn't have it and Marni Nixon came in to do the vocals. When Alan Lerner corrected Marni for the 100th time on something, Marni said, 'Are you aware that I dubbed for Audrey, Leslie Caron and for everybody?' Alan shot back at her: 'That's true, but are you aware that they all dubbed for your face!'"

Rex Harrison had earned a reputation as being a fire-eater and colossal jerk to fellow actors, directors, even stagehands who slavered anonymously in the theater and in films. Before the movie was filmed, Previn experienced that contentious ego firsthand.

"Before we started, Harrison said to Alan Lerner and Jack Warner, 'I don't want André Previn, I want Franz Allers who did the Broadway show.' That was impossible since they already hired me. Harrison said, 'I don't care, I'm used to Franz and he was sensational. That's who I want.' Lerner had a wonderful idea. He said to Rex, 'I'll tell you what, why don't you make one big recording with André, 'Why Can't the English.' So he did it with me. We finished the recording in record time and Alan said that he had just hung up the phone with Rex and said that he thought the recording was wonderful. Alan asked him, 'did you get along with André' and he said, 'Yes, and he's a lot better than that Germanic son-of-a-bitch we had in New York.' It was a complete turnaround.

"But Harrison was a terror," Previn continued. "In many ways he was the worst man I ever met. There are things that he did that I won't spread, but he really was an awful man. He was mean to people and belittled them. He had enormous charm when he wanted to, but I couldn't stand him."

Previn also had little use for Cecil Beaton. "He was terrible to Audrey. After the first rehearsal at Ascot, he came in and in front of the whole crew he took the hat that she was wearing and with a swish he twisted it on her head and said, 'This way you dumb bitch.' You just don't do that. It's like listening to Trump!"

By the mid–'60s Previn's days in Hollywood were numbered (gratifyingly to him). One of the last films he worked on was scoring Billy Wilder's *The Fortune Cookie* in 1966.

"That was the last time I set foot in a studio and I loved Billy, so that was all right," he said. "After all, that's 53 years ago and my interest has not kept up. Sometimes people are kind and have long memories and will ask me to do a movie, but it would have to be something extraordinary—not because I'm special, but it just doesn't interest me. When you spend any kind of time there, which I did, it's always easier and funnier to remember the charlatans than the talented people. A lot of studios made very interesting movies back then. You can say that they took risks, certain ones. But for every one that took a risk, there were 10 that didn't."

For many people, rosy retrospection (the tendency to recollect events more favorably than when they first occurred) is a cognitive bias that may aid the psyche in creating a buffer from bad memories. To us, there was little that was discernibly "rosy" about the vestigial angst Previn largely felt toward his years working in the studios. Each good memory seemed to have a countervailing negative one so that it all jumbled into something bittersweet.

Still, we oddly believed that how Previn felt and what he chose to recollect about those years amounted to a work-still-in-progress about Hollywood's Golden Age; that despite his incuriousness, he hadn't exited so very far from Tinseltown after all.

Unsinkable

Debbie Reynolds

Debbie Reynolds' screen career flowered during the last decade of Hollywood's Golden Age, the 1950s. As studios buckled under the encroaching pressure of television and began to shed their rosters of stars, Reynolds became a survivor. Her likable "girl-next-door" quality still provided her home studio, MGM, with a good ROI and Debbie's fresh-scrubbed, pert innocence was a perfect tonic for audiences in the post-war era. Topping it all off, Reynolds had an endearing trait that evinced itself in scores of interviews and countless chance meetings with fans; she was legitimately humbled to be part of show business and nobody was a bigger fan of the movies.

And Reynolds remained just that—a fan and a survivor—until December 28, 2016, when the crushing grief of her daughter Carrie Fisher's untimely death just a day before at age 60 became too much for her to bear and she succumbed at age 84. "My mother has had bad relationships; so have I," Carrie told us in a 1997 interview. "She talks a lot and is friendly and upbeat, so am I. She's a survivor, so am I. The show must go on. It's her life. It's a relationship that is real, not a Hallmark Card."

Born in El Paso, Texas, Reynolds along with her brother and parents moved to Burbank, California when she was eight years old. Even living in the shadow of Warner Brothers Studios, she said she harbored no ambitions of ever seeing her name on a theater marquee. "I went to the movies as a fan, but I had no dreams of a show business career," she said. "I wanted to be a gym teacher. Making pictures was really accidental."

The "accident" occurred when at age 16 Reynolds entered a local beauty contest to win a bathing suit. Her lip-synching impersonation of Betty Hutton won Reynolds the title of "Miss Burbank." As fate would have it, two of the pageant judges were talent scouts at Warners and MGM. With a toss of a coin, the Warners' scout got dibs on Reynolds, filmed a screen test and signed her to a contract. At the insistence of studio head Jack Warner, Mary Frances Reynolds became Debbie.

Unlike many stars who fought tooth and nail against the hierarchy of the studio system and bitched incessantly about the "indentured servitude" that was sometimes emblematic of studio contracts, Reynolds said she never felt hampered by a creative noose. "It didn't bother me because I never had lofty ambitions," she told us during a 1994 interview. "I wasn't a Gene Kelly who was a great director, a brilliant dancer, a person driven to succeed. Gene wanted to be a star. I was happy with a steady salary and free acting, singing and dancing lessons all day. Kelly knew how to put all the elements together. I learned that now, but in those days I was just a little girl."

It's become Hollywood lore that in 1951, not long before he was ousted from the studio, MGM Chief Louis B. Mayer, despite objections from Kelly, wanted Reynolds to co-star with him in *Singin' in the Rain*. Kelly denied the story, but Reynolds begged to differ.

"His memory and mine are different," she said. "But that's what happens when you get older. My memory is probably as incorrect as his. I recall that first meeting when Mr. Kelly said, 'do you dance?' and I said, no. 'Can you do a time step?' and I said, yes and did a time step. 'Can you do a Maxie Ford?' and I said, is that a car? He wasn't thrilled."

Long before Madonna, Princess Di, "Brangelina" and the Kardashians monopolized tabloid headlines, there was Reynolds. In fact, her life has served as some of the juiciest media fodder of the past 60 years, including stealing the headlines for a last time with her untimely passing.

Reynolds' on-screen persona stood in stark contrast to the real-life soap opera she played out under the unsparing klieg lights of the world press. A stormy four-year marriage to crooner Eddie Fisher ended in 1959 when he jilted her for Elizabeth Taylor who was Reynolds' close friend at the time. The heartache Reynolds experienced added an edge and maturity to future film roles, including *How the West Was Won* (1961) and her Oscar-nominated performance in *The Unsinkable Molly Brown* (1963).

But Reynolds proved especially buoyant when her second husband, shoe tycoon Harry Karl, spent the '60s squandering his personal fortune of $15 million and Reynolds' show business earnings of $10 million. Bankrupt, divorced and distraught, Reynolds rose again and scored personal triumphs in the Broadway musical revivals of *Irene* (1973) and *Woman of the Year* (1983). Reynolds as a survivor was a little bit like the Eveready Battery bunny that "keeps going and going and going."

"It's an artificial life, but it's also very seductive," Carrie said about the siren call of celebrity. "It was difficult to go down the street with my mother. It was hard to feel that she was just my mother. I had to share her with the world. I got the leftovers. It has its liabilities, but it also has a lot of privilege attached to it. I knew she was an extraordinary looking woman; other mothers didn't look like her."

Reynolds' encompassing love of Golden Age Hollywood led her on a 40-year quest to preserve its history via the acquisition of hundreds of pieces of classic movie memorabilia, including iconic costumes worn by Audrey Hepburn and Marilyn Monroe; Charlie Chaplin's bowler hat, Laurel and Hardy's wheezing Model T; and most representative of all, a vaunted pair of ruby slippers worn by Judy Garland in *The Wizard of Oz*.

It all started in 1970 when Reynolds spent about $600,000 at MGM's multi-day auction that liquidated the studio of most of its artifacts. For studio owner, Kirk Kerkorian it was a way to generate revenue before bulldozing the historic backlots, selling the land off to developers and then investing in Las Vegas hotel properties.

"The MGM auction absolutely broke my heart," Reynolds said. "That's why I went to the bank, borrowed money and attended the auction every day. I think it's our fault

Unsinkable

that we don't protect our own culture," she said. "We're sort of materialistic in the sense that it's all about the almighty dollar. I don't believe that and I don't work that way. I'm very emotional in my attachments. So I've spent millions on my collection. I hope people will loan these collectables to museums and we will use the proceeds to help older stars who are in financial problems and have not been taken care of through residuals."

And about those ruby slippers that Reynolds added to her collection: "I didn't buy them at the MGM auction because they weren't really hers," she said. "Judy wore a 4½ shoe. And I had tried those shoes on that went up for auction. They were big, like a 7½. So some man bought those for $11,000, but he bought Judy's stand-in's shoes."

When we interviewed Reynolds in 1994, she was gambling her name, reputation and assets on what she described as the biggest challenge of her life—Las Vegas hotel owner. In the game of high stakes hotel and casino management, Reynolds was a small-time player. The Debbie Reynolds Hotel, Casino, and Hollywood Movie Museum was located just off the Las Vegas Strip on Convention Center Drive. Formerly it had been the Paddlewheel Hotel & Casino. Reynolds purchased the 200-room property at an auction in 1992. After an extensive renovation, including decorating the hotel in a Hollywood motif and building a new 500-seat showroom, Reynolds reopened the hotel under her name in 1993.

"I'm not in competition with the big players on the Strip," she told us then. "They're huge conglomerates. I run a real 'ma and pa' hotel. I'm here all the time. I don't think you'll see Mr. Wynn (Steve Wynn, chairman of several Las Vegas mega-properties) signing autographs or singing songs. In fact, Mr. Kerkorian comes here to relax. My place is small. You can bring your girlfriend and sit in a quiet corner."

Reynolds might just as well have added a codicil to that statement: bring your girl-friend and if you're early, get an AARP discount. Seated at a ringside table with our wives, we were the youngest fans at Reynolds' show by half, adrift in a sea of blue hair and Chanel No. 5. As she went through her paces, singing, dancing and introducing film clips of her performances in a raft of vintage musicals, Reynolds eyed us warily, as if we were guerrilla-style usurpers planted there as a practical joke by a provocateur like Howard Stern.

Before long, Reynolds (who was 62 then) started integrating us into her show, saying to her audience: "Look at these youngsters, they don't know me from a hole in the head, but I bet they're familiar with my daughter Carrie … (then in a stage whisper aimed directly at us) … that's Princess Leia to you." Drawing first blood, Reynolds became the provocateur. She needn't have bothered.

Grainy film clips and grainier comedy shtick aside, after the show, we witnessed something remarkable. Reynolds came out from the wings, walked down the center aisle and positioned herself at the back of the theater where she patiently signed showbills, old albums and glossy photographs for any fan that came forward (and there were dozens). "I don't forget my fans," Reynolds remarked as she wielded a Sharpie marker over a black-and-white still of her as Kathy Selden from *Singin' in the Rain*. "Once you commit that treason, it's over." She stayed signing and gabbing until the last fan had wandered off.

Her energy boundless (Reynolds told us that unlike her father, mother or brother, she was always "ahead of the train"), she took time after her main stage performance to visit in the hotel's Hollywood Palm Cafe, a 24-hour full-service restaurant that played host on weekends to a "Jazz & Jokes" marathon (from 10 p.m. until 2 a.m.) and featured Reynolds, the comic slapstick of Rip Taylor, a trio of local musicians and a steady stream of "drop in" guests.

"Initially, I just wanted a museum to house my collection of movie memorabilia," she said. "This place happened to be a hotel I could fix. The museum is the only one of its kind in America. What I want to do is preserve the history. I didn't have in mind what I was going to do with all this. I just kept buying and buying."

Reynolds foray into the hotel business and finding a home for her precious collection (estimated at the time to be worth $30 million) was not to be. Mired in financial problems the casino closed in 1996 and Reynolds was forced to file for bankruptcy protection the following year. The property sold for auction in 1998.

But for her it was just another hurdle to overcome. For years Reynolds tried to find a permanent home for her collection, including making frequent overtures to the Academy of Motion Picture Arts and Sciences that they acquire her collection en bloc. Finally, in a series of auctions starting in 2011, her collection was auctioned off piecemeal over several days.

Before we left her hotel and after Reynolds gave us a tour of the part of her collection that was on display, she told us wistfully that she was the last contract player, "Me, Leslie Caron and Pier Angeli," she said. "But no matter what happens here (with the hotel and her collection), I hope I'm always foremost an entertainer."

Coda

Less than four months after Reynolds died (and more than two decades since our visit with her in Las Vegas), the 8th Annual TCM Classic Film Festival was held in

Hollywood. The Festival was dedicated, via tributes, to several stars and Reynolds was one of them.

"Club TCM" (a room in the Roosevelt Hotel dedicated to the Festival) was the locus for many special events and was draped with vintage movie posters from the Golden Age. Along one wall, away from the almost continuous traffic of attendees coming from or enroute to screenings, was a glass display case that held the costume Reynolds wore in the "Good Morning" number from *Singin' in the Rain*—the one where she danced all over the living room furniture flanked by Kelly and O'Connor.

On the Festival's closing night, *Singin' in the Rain* was screened at the TCL Grauman's Chinese Theater. It was the perfect venue since Grauman's appears at the beginning of the movie as the theater hosting the premiere of silent screen heartthrob Don Lockwood's "The Royal Rascal."

Reynolds' son, Todd Fisher and her longtime friend, actress Ruta Lee were on hand that night to share a few anecdotes, but the event really didn't need their benediction. Sitting in the darkened theater with all its ersatz chinoiserie decoration marvelously preserved, and Reynolds' hand- and footprints enshrined out front in the theater's forecourt, just seeing the film was invocation enough.

As *Singin' in the Rain*'s opening credits scrolled onscreen to the lush melodies of Arthur Freed and Nacio Herb Brown, the packed audience began to stir. From the front row to the back row, the old movie palace was filled with fans; what Reynolds always called "my people." And when she made her first appearance on screen after Kelly jumps from the top of a trolley into the front seat of her jalopy, for a moment the movie seemed to freeze-frame as if lost in time and, for the audience, Reynolds was once again that beaming ingénue, forever 17, at the beginning of a storied career and before failed marriages, bankruptcies, setbacks and comebacks had tempered her. And that's the way we'll remember her: singing and dancing, irrepressible and unsinkable.

The Merchant of Venom, Defanged

Don Rickles

Don Rickles was a study in contrasts. The man who made a career out of sarcasm and insults and who has been variously tagged with the monikers "The Merchant of Venom" and "Mr. Warmth," couldn't have been a nicer guy … offstage. But onstage, it was a different matter altogether.

During Rickles' show (he did about 20 a year, give or take before he died in 2017); a sort of blood fever took hold as his furious ad-libs zinged their intended targets. The applause and laughter (which was always thunderous) spurred him to such improbable feats as attempting a James Cagney impersonation from *Yankee Doodle Dandy* complete with the tap dancing. At that moment, Rickles had the stout, compact body of the Merrill Lynch bull; two a-rhythmical legs that were born *not* to dance; and a perspiring head that looks like a snub-nosed .38 caliber cartridge.

He literally sweated bullets. It was all heady stuff even for a guy who'd been traversing that comic ground for more than 68 years (Rickles was 90 when he died).

It's odd then that Rickles' stage persona vanished as quickly as the final curtain on his stage show. It was a complete sea change; the calm after the storm. In reality, Rickles offstage was unfailingly polite and rather stiffly decorous; almost formal. It was as if after such verbal bloodletting, a weird catharsis took place and there was nothing left to do but be placid.

"In the beginning, when I was just starting out, there were people who resented me," Rickles told us during an interview back in 1999. "But that's the price you pay when you try to do something different. And being different has allowed me to be a headliner in all the major gambling cities across the country. Not a bad tradeoff."

Rickles graduated from the American Academy of Dramatic Arts in New York City with dreams of becoming a serious actor. But when he found out there were no takers, he let his natural sarcastic bombast bubble up into a career.

"It's always been my personality since I was a kid in school and in the [military] service," he said. "I was always a sarcastic guy. I could never tell a joke, per se. I was never a jokester as you could see if you watched my performance. My current attitude developed over many years of doing bad impersonations and telling lousy jokes. I started to talk to the audience and talk about things around me. That become a performance and I found that they responded great to that. In the rough days when I worked in the low-life 'jernts,' you did anything to get the audience's attention."

There was an almost ritualistic aspect to being on the receiving end of a Don Rickles putdown. Audience members in pricey front row seats seemed to court it like they would a visit from the Publishers Sweepstakes minivan. And that's probably the single biggest reason why Rickles didn't really prickle anymore. It had become politically correct—a red badge of courage—to merit one of his insults. (In 1980, Princess Margaret invited Rickles to join her at her table after being mocked at a fundraising gala.) This from a man whose gags should have, on the face of it, made most PC practitioners, well, gag.

Yours truly (Tom) was on the receiving end of one of Rickles' diatribes at the Desert Inn in Las Vegas one night. I was in a front row seat which is ground zero for Rickles. I was wearing a double-breasted suit with my shoes buffed to a high sheen. Further sartorial splendor included a Brioni tie and pocket square. Rickles saw me, sized me up in a millisecond and then strafed me like he was a Messerschmitt 109 and I was a stalled milk truck on the autobahn. 'Look at you, he snarled, contempt oozing out of him like a viscous substance, 'you gotta be Italian—nothing matches.' The audience (most of which couldn't see me) roared. And what made his line even funnier to me was that I'm about as Italian as lutefisk and my whole ensemble that night perfectly matched.

A couple of years ago we caught up with Rickles again in his dressing room renamed the "Mr. Warmth Room" for the duration of his gig at the Potawatomi Hotel & Casino in Milwaukee. A bottle of Grey Goose vodka was visible on a nearby counter ready to provide Rickles with his pre-show relaxer. He was still performing his usual shtick, this time liberally imbued with clips of his appearance at Ronald Reagan's 1984 inaugural gala and featuring TV segments of many *Tonight Show* and Dean Martin roast appearances often skewering his favorite target, Frank Sinatra. It struck us as faintly melancholy as we watched Rickles, with stage lights dimmed, crane his head to watch as his departed friends and show business cronies appeared on the screen. Dressed in his usual tux, Rickles sat for the entire 60-minute performance with a cane at his side.

His grumpy salutation upon seeing us was: "I'm sitting here in this cellar and I have to do this Mickey Mouse conversation? I just think how much longer I have to live, but I'm very proud that I'm still working at 90 and it helps the wife with the jewelry and her expenses."

We reminded him that George Burns, if and when he turned 100, had gigs prescheduled in London and Las Vegas.

"My plan is if I'm around, I'll call you," he said.

After years in circulation, Rickles' cauterizing abuse may have lost some of its mortal sting but none of its sense of fun. In fact, he's won a legion of younger fans to add to the brigades of middle-aged men and women who have been following him since his caustic appearances on the old *Dean Martin Show*.

Younger audiences seemed to like the "retrofit" of a club comedian who tells Phyllis Diller jokes as if she's still a force to be reckoned with in the entertainment industry. And they respected Rickles who stayed

Rickles before the kill

the course for decades and raised low humor to high art. Rickles might not have been your cup of Earl Grey, but like him or not, he (like the late Joan Rivers) was unique.

Perhaps not since the salad days of Groucho Marx had anyone co-opted so utterly completely the genre of "dishing out the dish." "I'm an equal opportunity insult artist—definitely!" Rickles told us. "Anytime a comedian takes the stage, there'll be people who won't like him. Not everybody comes out of the theater and says, 'I love Don Rickles.' If they did, it would be a miracle."

Did he ever fear the day when the comeback won't come and he would be staring into the smirking face of a casino drunk who's just bested him in a verbal duel? "With 70 years in the business under my belt handling every kind of impromptu situation, if I start to worry about that, I got a problem," he said. "It's like a fighter with a good right-hand punch. You know it's there and you don't think about it. The day someone gets the upper hand on me and I just stare at them with nothing coming out of my mouth is the day I interview you!"

The same goes for retirement. "As long as the promoters still want me and people show up, I'll be there."

Rickles pointed to three men as the biggest influences on his career. Dean Martin's hugely popular 1960s TV show provided a national prime-time platform for Rickles' humor. And during innumerable appearances on Johnny Carson's *Tonight Show*, Rickles solidified has fan base. But it was Frank Sinatra's "Midas Touch" that ordained Rickles as the "in"-sult comic Hollywood celebrities should watch. It was in 1957, at Slate Brothers, a tiny Hollywood nightclub, that Sinatra walked directly into the unknown Rickles' gunsights.

"I just saw your movie, *The Pride and the Passion* and I want to tell you the cannon was great," Rickles said. "Make yourself at home Frank, hit somebody." Sinatra doubled up laughing and a beautiful friendship was formed that lasted until Ol' Blue Eyes shuffled off this mortal coil in 1998.

Another long run for Rickles was his 51-year union with his wife Barbara, a first marriage for both. "I got married late in life," he told us. "The whole secret is that my wife never looked for the limelight. She was a secretary for a guy involved in motion pictures when I met her, so she knows the business. But she never wanted to be a part of it. She's not a crowd pleaser. She's low-key. I'm the crowd pleaser and kidder."

On the subject of enduring friendships, Rickles and comedian Bob Newhart were such fast friends that, along with their wives, they often vacationed together. "Barbara and I still go on the occasional cruise," he explained, "but I constantly get accosted by passengers who don't think I'm a paying customer. They think I'm there to perform. Many of them come up to me and say: 'What time is the show tonight?' I say: 'No, no, I'm a paying customer like you are.' And they say: 'O.K., call my brother a moron and my cousin a jerk. We'll be sitting in the front row.' Then they sit there and wait until the ship docks…!"

Zing!

Behind the Tinsel

Mickey Rooney

An interview with Mickey Rooney is as close as we've ever come to spending time with a live-action cartoon. He didn't just enter the lobby of the Hyatt Hotel in Westlake Village, California, near where he lived; he trundled in like a miniature Sherman Tank and waved us down with such theatrical exaggeration, we thought he was in the finish step of a Busby Berkeley dance fantasia at MGM.

"My car ran out of gas down the street and I had to get a refill can from the filling station," he implored, wheezy, red-faced and dripping in his own nervous flop sweat. "I'm almost never late and I hate when other people are."

Understood.

When we met him in December 1998 at age 77, Rooney's energy was inexhaustible.

We got winded just witnessing him verbally scuttle from one topic to the next with the same manic energy he employed in jumping over fence posts with Judy Garland in those lovable, ridiculous *Andy Hardy* show-in-the-barn epics.

Fifty years, eight marriages and about three career incarnations later, Rooney had

Slipping us a Mickey

become a world-class gnome with barrelhouse arms and legs that seem to spring akimbo out of the solid mass of his torso. His face, with oval eyes, was round as a pie plate and the full-figure effect was as if someone had precariously balanced a dove's egg atop the larger hen's egg of his body. Oddly, Rooney brought to mind those old Victorian children's book drawings of a perfectly symmetrical "Humpty-Dumpty" perched on the wall before his great fall.

For sure, Rooney certainly had as many ups and downs—and even some egg on his face—in his long, honored and erratic career.

"I'll tell you anything you want to hear, including how bald I am," he huffed, as we sat on a couch in the reception area of the hotel lobby as guests checked in and checked out all around us. It was an odd, too-public site in which to conduct an interview, but Rooney, at that moment after his long jog, seemed emptier than his gas tank—a state of affairs that didn't last very long.

He also had some free advice for a middle-aged autograph-seeker that had been circling our couch like a raptor honing in on a field mouse. We could tell she was biding her time while trying to positively fix in her own mind Rooney's identity. The instant she did, she swooped.

"Mickey… I think you're just great… I just want to—"

Rooney cut her off in mid-sentence with: "Dear, I'm doing an interview right now and it's rude of you to interrupt like that." He waved her off like a potentate dismissing a vassal at court. It was really quite funny, although we did feel some sympathy for the lady who reacted with a confused grimace as if she had just stubbed her big toe. At least Rooney cured her of any future career as a celebrity stalker.

In solidarity with the LAPD (and to cover his barren pate), Rooney wore one of the department's baseball caps along with a striped Izod sport shirt. With pride he showed us a giant silver ring bearing his real name (Joe Yule) that his wife had made for his last birthday.

"I've done more pictures than anyone in the business—300," he blurted. "Twenty-seven of them alone were *Andy Hardy* movies." His latest (at that time), the sequel to *Babe*, called *Babe: Pig in the City*, had been released the previous month. Rooney spoke mostly in short declarative sentences and keeping him on topic was fruitless, unless, of course, it was a topic he could make a short declarative sentence about.

The interview soon took a bizarre turn where, as journalists, we became comically impotent and seemed to have out-of-body experiences in which spied ourselves on the couch sitting limply by while Rooney held forth grandly.

We'd been slipped a Mickey!

"At MGM all the contract players had a home," he mused. "And nobody was coddled, despite what a lot of the leading ladies at MGM have said. We were considered part of the family. We had a place to hang our hat, a place to sleep. We had a job when a lot of people around the country were on the breadlines."

For three consecutive years during the 1930s—including the pivotal blockbuster year of 1939—movie exhibitors voted Rooney the number one box office star in the country. In today's terms it's like Leonardo DiCaprio having a solid three-year run of super-stardom complete with the unearthly adulation he received after the release of *Titanic*. Weird thing: Rooney was dismissive about his own achievement.

"It was nothing, really," he said sounding like he meant it. "There was no difference in my life. The great kick about it was that I was opposite the best of the best at the time; men like Cagney, Gable, Tracy and Bogart. Being a nice person was more important to me because with being number one, someday inevitably you'll be number 15. And now I'm not even on the chart.

"I've had a 76-year career in the movies," Rooney continued, summing up. "I was in pictures when I was one year old. I'm a writer, director, painter and pilot. I play golf and tennis. That's the secret of remaining forever young and getting through the tough times in life. And believe me, I've had a few. You need to be enthusiastic."

The contagion of Mickey's irrepressibility led him and some of his limited partners to investigate such schemes as "Mickey Rooney's Feel-Great Insurance Company" ($50,000 life/health policies for $25 a month); "Movie Moguls" (a Hollywood board game that resembles Monopoly); and "Complete: for the man who wants to be" (a spray-on hair tonic for baldness).

"It does away with toupees," Rooney said. "You shake it up and it frizzes out like cotton candy and then you just rub it in."

And so the interview ended—abruptly—much like how Rooney arrived on the scene in Hollywood when he portrayed a series of fresh-faced hustlers wrapped in a kind of innocent Americana that might have struck a false realistic note, but that was MGM's stock-in-trade nonetheless. "I hate the word seniors," Rooney said, off topic for the last time. "I like to think of us as experienced people, that way it isn't such a brand. Just remember; our lives are in front of us, not behind us. We all have new vistas to conquer."

It was a valuable perspective that had kept Rooney grounded during a career with more ups and downs than, as he said, the roller coaster on the Santa Monica pier. It was also a pronouncement that would come back to haunt him because the healthiest perspective in the world is scant protection when the infirmities of great age separate you from being able to make decisions that govern your own life. That's what happened to Mickey in his final years (he died at 93).

In his last years, Rooney was habitually abused and financially depleted by some of his closest, most trusted family members. By the end of his life, the singer, dancer, actor, impressionist and drummer—in essence "the *white* Sammy Davis, Jr."—a man who had made many millions on stage and screen, had a reputed $18,000 left in his bank account.

In the months before Rooney died, we exchanged emails with his daughter-in-law Charlene Rooney, who along with her husband, Mark, had taken the nonagenarian into their care in their Studio City, California, home. By then Rooney's independence had become interdependence. In his lifetime, Rooney had transmogrified from the king of the box office to a tragic figure reduced to pauperism, squeezed out of his last pennies by avaricious kin who saw the faded star as nothing more than a payday. When the curtain was pulled back from Rooney's celebrity by the tabloids, the world saw for the first time the sad reality that lay behind the glitz.

It would be cold comfort to think that Rooney's riches-to-rags story is uncommon in Hollywood. But we all know it isn't. After all, that's why it's called Tinseltown.

The Also-Ran

Benny Rubin

Waiter … taxi driver … man at bar … roulette croupier … janitor.

Comedian Benny Rubin's career after performing in vaudeville on the Orpheum Circuit was a litany of bit parts in movies and on television that could be clocked with an egg timer. Although Los Angeles after the advent of talking pictures was chock-full of former two-a-day headliners who couldn't scare up a gig, Rubin was a special case— one of Hollywood's first victims of reverse discrimination.

With dark, saucer-shaped eyes and a pronounced proboscis, Rubin had what casting agents considered, a *Yiddishe Punim*. Ironically, in a town largely founded and run by Jewish movie moguls sometimes just a generation removed from the *shtetls* of Eastern Europe, looking or sounding too Semitic was a drawback. After all, these powerbrokers had a fervent desire to weave themselves into the American tapestry; they were also dream merchants selling their idealization of America to an overwhelmingly gentile audience. And so, the prejudice and repudiation.

However, trouper that he was, Rubin shouldered the bias and soldiered on, appearing in movies during the 1930s, as a semi-regular on Jack Benny's television show in 1950 and in slurry of other TV shows from *Perry Mason* and *Adam-12* to *Gunsmoke* throughout the 1960s and '70s.

But that was much later.

A self-described "Boston original," Rubin got his start in vaudeville before the 1920s really began to roar, and was shocked when playing the Midwestern theaters of the

Orpheum Circuit for the first time in 1922, that he didn't see "cowboys and Indians in the streets."

Audiences in St. Paul, Minnesota (Rubin was making $62.50 a week then, he remembered exactly) weren't as "fast" as audiences in the big eastern cities like New York, he said. "It's not that the people in Minneapolis or wherever weren't as smart … it's just that … if you were living in New York, it was a tough hustle to make a buck. It's tough when you get into trouble and rough to stay out of it, so your mind works faster. In places like St. Paul, your stomach would go into waltz tempo. They are nice, neighborly people there; they know each other. It's like: 'Hey, Charlie, how 'ya doin?' kind of thing. So if you made a flip remark and the audience didn't get it, some acts would say that they were dumb. But they weren't. They just moved in waltz tempo."

We asked him about performing on a vaudeville bill with George Jessel, but almost before we got the question out, Rubin pre-empted us with: "Cut! Who next? I don't want any bad talk. I hate a lot of people, and if you mention them, I'll say, 'Cut!'"

The rest of the interview was like negotiating a booby-trapped killing field connected to a laugh track; we never knew what names might trigger Rubin's wrath. It actually became a kind of game with us throwing out names and Rubin punching back remembrances like he was rushing the net at Wimbledon.

* * *

Taps for Benny

Fantle & Johnson: *What about Jack Benny?*

Rubin: The closest friend I ever had. I was with him in 1926 when he changed his name from Kubelsky to Benny.

Jackie Gleason?

I'm a teetotaler and you'd see a guy like Gleason and he couldn't wait to get on a bill with Pat Rooney so they could get drunk together.

The comedy team of Wheeler and Woolsey?

Didn't like Woolsey much because he lived off Wheeler. Woolsey was a bad straight man who, nonetheless, called himself a comic. If it weren't for Bert Wheeler, he'd have been parking Model-T's.

Milton Berle?

He was a dirty bastard … still is. His mother would go see other acts while Milton performed. Then she'd go backstage and give all the best jokes to Milton. But then when Milton found out what was going on, he stole them himself!

* * *

In the parlance of the day, Rubin performed his act (mostly) as a single (no need for unfunny straight men slowing things up) in an act that used his gift for mimicry and dialects. In fact, during the 1930s, Rubin was considered among the greatest show business dialecticians around and even worked for a time as a vocal coach. "Like I said before, being a Jew kid in Boston was tough. The Irish kids—and later the Wops—used to punch us around. That's where I began to perfect different dialects. That's also the time I took boxing lessons. I had a helluva record: 30 fights and I never won one of them!"

Although Rubin saw Bill "Bojangles" Robinson perform his legendary stair dance, Jack Benny play the violin and Burns & Allen trade barbs with each other on stage, he reserved his greatest praise for a staple of vaudeville, it's veritable backbone: the animal acts. "There was a guy with a dog named 'Louie,' and that mutt wouldn't do a damn thing on stage, which I thought was brilliant," Rubin said. "No matter what he said, the dog wouldn't budge. You can use whips or treats to teach animals stage tricks, but to teach a dog to do absolutely nothing—that's great!"

When we met Rubin, he lived in a rather shabby apartment building on a stretch of Hollywood Boulevard that we surmised might've become fairly dicey around dusk. In fact, our interview almost never came about. We had to pass a kind of half-assed quiz to prove that we were really two journalists who, as we told him, came from Minnesota.

At his apartment building speaker box, after we rang his number, Rubin's voice came on asking us what the meaning was of "Ma-Han-Khaato."

We were flummoxed and that egg-timer was apparently ticking. "Ma-Han-Khaato?" We told him we didn't know what he was talking about.

"Oh, no … you're not getting in. Get the hell out of here!" he said.

It didn't help that Rubin had an epic head cold and his phlegmy pronunciation of "Ma-Han-Khaato" was channeled through an ancient apartment squawkbox that, in turn, emitted a high-pitched hiss that made passing dogs yowl. Suddenly, it occurred to us that he might have meant "Mankato," a small farm town in southern Minnesota. Either that or he was fluent in another dialect—Ojibway. As we suspected, it was the town not the tribe and he buzzed us in.

Rubin told us he was semi-retired but that if his agent called, he'd work at "the drop of a hat."

During our visit (after giving us a look at the wooden clogs he used when dancing in vaudeville) he showed us a miniature silver star embedded in faux marble and framed in a shadow box. He said that since the entertainment community had never honored him with a star on Hollywood Boulevard's "Walk of Fame," family members had come up with their own commemoration.

To us, the makeshift token seemed defiant and a bit sad at the same time, but Rubin was long past holding grudges (excluding any venom expressly reserved for George Jessel). Suffused by the encompassing love of his family and with memories indestructibly intact of a long career in the business he loved, Rubin seemed to practically glide across the room to replace the plaque in its prominent place on a credenza.

It had taken him nearly half a century (with a full life's worth of triumphs and tragedies wedged in between), but it seemed to us that Rubin had finally learned to move in waltz tempo.

A Delicate Balance

Eva Marie Saint

Success is defined many ways in Hollywood. It can be living in the tony 90210 ZIP Code or signing a contract to make $20 million for one film. Others benchmark success by how many Academy Award nominations/wins they rack up over the course of a career or the number of "A-pictures" in which they star. For Eva Marie Saint, a Best Supporting Actress Oscar winner herself for her 1954 film debut *On the Waterfront*, fame, fortune and choice parts were all well and good but they never supplanted—even for an instant— her devotion to family matters.

For more than half a century, Saint has oscillated between her life and career to achieve a delicate balance, which like her best films, is a work of art in itself. Against the capricious backdrop of a "company town," where real-life relationships are often more ephemeral than the ones portrayed on celluloid, two statistics attest to the success of Saint's balancing act—a marriage that ran 65 years to director Jeffrey Hayden, and a son and daughter miraculously scot-free of the crippling neuroses that often plague celebrity offspring.

"It really wasn't that hard balancing everything because I made it my plan to never do more than one film a year," she said. "When I made *Exodus*, it was in the summer and I took my kids, husband, mother, father and mother-in-law. Along the way there were many things I turned down—like a role in *Quo Vadis*. I just wanted to be a working actress with a home life that worked."

After raising their two children in a house they owned for 22 years in the Mandeville Canyon section of West Los Angeles, "It's always in the news because the canyon is always on fire," Saint said, she and her husband "simplified," relocating to a luxurious high-rise apartment on Wilshire Boulevard near UCLA.

When we met with her in 1996, Saint, 72, greeted us at the door with the same perkiness she showed neighborhood kids trick-or-treating each Halloween. After ushering us into the living area, she excused herself and was back before we could blink with a couple of glasses of her favorite fruit juice, Tropicana pineapple-orange.

"I have a life and it is not lived on the set," she said. "I felt that way when I was raising my kids and I feel that way now. I don't want make-believe children. When Donna Reed, the perfect American mother to millions of TV viewers in the 1950s, ended her show, her kids were teenagers. She said to me, 'Now I'm going to get to know my kids.' I thought that was so very sad.

"My kids never had the feeling that we were both in show business," Saint continued. "I remember our son came home from a school field trip and said, rather excitedly, 'Mom, I saw Gregory Peck's chair with his name on it.' I said, 'Honey, I think you met Mr. Peck when you visited me on the set of *Stalking Moon*.'"

Saint gave birth to her boy, Darrell, just two days after she received the Oscar for *Waterfront*. We didn't need a crystal ball to guess which event overshadowed the other. "Once you get an Oscar, it becomes an appendage that you carry around the rest of your life," Saint said. "…Announcing Eva Marie Saint… Oscar winner! But working with Marlon Brando and Elia Kazan was worth it."

According to Saint, *Waterfront* producer Sam Spiegel and director Kazan "scouted" her on Broadway where she was appearing with her lifelong mentor, Lillian Gish, in *The Trip to Bountiful*. "They asked me to come over to the Actors Studio to audition for the role of 'the blonde,' Saint remembered. "I was to improvise a scene with Marlon Brando, who I was in awe of from my time as a student there.

"Just before I went on stage, Kazan set the scene for me," she continued. "I was a very religious girl who went to Catholic school. Marlon was coming to see my sister who was out of the house, and it was my mission to keep him from worming his way into the house. Now I don't know what instructions 'Gadge' (short for "gadget," Saint's—and others'—affectionate nickname for Kazan) gave Marlon, but during the scene he charmed his way in. He then swept me off my feet and asked me to dance. I was sort of crying just a wee bit, but then, as we danced, I became more attracted to him. Gadge could see there was chemistry between us. I guess that's what the improvisation was supposed to show, or not show in the first place."

During shooting, Saint remembered Brando to be a princely, cordial man who would often loan her his overcoat to wear between scenes on the chilly set. "It was cold in Hoboken on the waterfront where we shot the film," she said. "I would wear red flannel underwear for warmth, and every so often would lift up my skirt—red bloomers aflutter—and do an impromptu Can-Can dance for the cast and crew just for a laugh. You know the simple act of laughing would warm us up."

While Saint showered nothing but accolades on Brando, her other co-star, Rod Steiger, was more measured about the experience of playing Brando's older brother, once telling us that he found Brando distant. Saint speculated that any possible bad blood that existed between the two could be traced to the pivotal scene they played together in the back of a car.

"It was rather amusing, but apparently (I wasn't there when they did the scene in the car) when they had closeups of Rod, Brando wasn't there because he had in his contract that he was in some type of analysis and he had to leave at a certain time," she recalled. "I don't know who gave him his lines whether it was Kazan or somebody else, but every time Rod would see me—because we would run into each other at different places through the years—he would come up to me and say: 'That was so unfair of Kazan to do that and not have Marlon there.' I listened to him the first time, the second time, the third time, the fourth time. By the seventh time I said, 'Rod if that's what you're going to talk about, I don't want to talk with you. You must get over it and he never ever did. He would see me and the light would go on; he just associated me forevermore with that terrible experience he had. It was a brilliant scene. The first time he confronted me, I told him it was a brilliant scene: 'Rod, you were wonderful,' I said. 'I don't care who was giving you lines. You were wonderful. And then by the 10th time I said, 'I don't even want to talk about it. He was obsessed. He was truly obsessed."

After *Waterfront*, Saint as an independent contractor not tethered to any studio, starred in a series of major motion pictures including *Exodus*, *Grand Prix*, *The Sandpiper* and, perhaps most memorably, as another enigmatic blonde, Eve Kendall, in Alfred Hitchcock's *North by Northwest*.

"I was very impressed that Hitchcock had his bacon flown in from Denmark," Saint said. "In the auction scene I was decked out in a very expensive red dress, and during a lull I went and wandered off to get a cup of coffee which I proceeded to drink from a Styrofoam cup. Well, Hitchcock stopped me dead in my tracks. He said, 'Eva Marie, you don't get your coffee, we have someone get it for you. And you drink from a porcelain cup and saucer. You are wearing a $3,000 dress and I don't want the extras to see you quaffing from a Styrofoam cup.'"

From that moment on Saint added, "Every set I was on, while I don't drink coffee, I drink hot chocolate, you will never spot me with a Styrofoam cup." She added that Hitchcock's gentle remonstration amounted to a mouthful from him. "Hitchcock didn't talk about the lines and what they meant," she said. "He cast people based on how they could and would work a certain way and there wasn't much direction as far as motivation and relationships. He left that all to us."

Saint's *North by Northwest* co-star, Cary Grant, 20 years her senior, lived up to his larger-than-life screen image. "He was such a gentleman. When we first met me on the set, he said, 'Eva Marie, you don't have to cry in this film (referring to *On the Waterfront*), we're just going to have fun.' And oh-my-God, yes we did."

Saint told us a story about the generosity of Grant that she wasn't sure she had ever publicly shared. "I have blue eyes and if something is really bright, I'll squint. Like at night when I drive, if those oncoming lights are really harsh, I'll squint. In one scene, Cary saw me squinting a little for a close-up—from the lights. He stopped the scene and said to the first assistant, 'Those lights are just a little too strong for me.' Cary had something in his contract pertaining to the brightness of the lights, how strong they should be and they were just a little too bright so they angled them down, and of course I didn't squint anymore. I just thought to myself, 'Oh, what a gentleman,' he did it for me, but he didn't say, 'Miss Saint, she's squinting.' No, he just said, 'It's a little strong for me,' What a gentleman, right?"

Although Saint admitted that assessing the relative merits of Hitchcock and Kazan was like comparing apples to oranges, she was unstinting in her praise and affection for her mentor, Lillian Gish, who starred in silent movies before Kazan was wearing long pants. Saint appeared with Gish in the original stage production of Horton Foote's *The Trip to Bountiful*. Decades later, Geraldine Page won an Oscar reprising Gish's role in the film version of the play.

"Lillian had that odd mixture of strength and vulnerability which I feel I have at times," Saint said. "She was the first one at rehearsal and the last one to leave at night. And she was at all times, unfailingly honest. I remember years after our *Bountiful* experience, I was starring in a television adaptation of a George Kelly play, *The Fatal Weakness*. I wore bangs in the part because I thought it was right for the character. Anyway, at a party in Malibu that was being held for Lillian, I arrived and was told by the host that Lillian wanted to see me—alone. 'You should never wear bangs,' she scolded me. 'You have a nice forehead, why do you want to hide it!' The funny thing was that my husband never liked me in bangs, but it took Lillian's scolding for me to cut them."

In *Exodus* (1960), Saint worked with director Otto Preminger, known for his autocratic style on the set. "It was an enormous project with so many cast and crew," she remembered. "We were on that ship and somebody who had been on the original *Exodus* said—as the hot sun was beating down on us, 'Time on the real *Exodus* was easier than time on this *Exodus*.' That pretty much sums up that experience!"

Five years later, in *The Sandpiper*, Saint co-starred with Richard Burton and Elizabeth Taylor, who had married shortly before filming commenced. Saint said the chemistry between the two could not be ignored. "They were in love and I thought that was a beautiful thing," she said. "I'd never met him, Richard Burton, before filming, but I knew Liz from *Raintree County* and adored her. Every time we ran into each other it was hugs and kisses. She was a very dear, giving person. I know many, many things she did for people. She was a kind lady. I just really adored her. I was very happy for her and for him at the time."

In the spring of 2017, we had an opportunity to catch up with Saint, then 92, and widowed from her husband who died the previous December at age 90. Saint said she was thrilled when her friend and mentor Kazan received an honorary Academy Award in 1999 (he was 89 at that time), despite protests from some in Hollywood citing the director's 1952 testimony in front of the House Un-American Activities Committee that was working at that time to snuff out communists from the entertainment industry. On the night that Kazan received his Oscar, he was met by protestors outside the Dorothy Chandler Pavilion, but inside he received a warm, if not overly enthusiastic reception. Saint did not condone the protesters' behavior.

"I was so happy for him that I wrote a letter when I heard about it and I was so upset with—I don't know the actor's name and I don't care—the people who didn't applaud in the audience when he won it," she said. "First of all, I thought it was impolite. Second, I thought it was just naughty. How were those people brought up? I shouldn't use naughty, but I just thought it was such an insult to such a talented, wonderful man. I felt if they didn't want him to get that and they knew that he was getting it they shouldn't have been in the audience."

A couple of years after winning her Oscar, Saint co-starred with Bob Hope in the comedy, *That Certain Feeling* (1956). At the mere mention of the film, Saint broke into singing the eponymous title number. After singing a verse and the chorus, she recalled for us what it was like working with "Old Ski Nose." Saint also appeared with Hope in the 1972 clunker, *Cancel My Reservation*.

"I don't even want to talk about that one," she said. "When I have bad memories of something, I don't even want talk about it, I don't even remember. I do remember someone gave me a little dog. I had a little dog in my dressing room. I remember I wore hot pants. Hot pants were in style at that time. I enjoy working and I had a good time, but the film just didn't come off.

That Certain Feeling was a different story, she said. "It was interesting because I had just come off *Waterfront*. This was obviously just a totally different experience. Bob was so kind and so dear, so giving, but the first time on the set—don't forget I'm from the Actors Studio and you maintain a quiet set so people can think and prepare, etc. Well, we were about to do a scene and I saw about 15 women beautifully dressed with all very funny, but stylish hats so you know how long ago that was. They just strolled in and then they were watching and I thought, 'Oh my God, I thought is it going to be a quiet kind of set, I'm not used to this?' On my previous movie, the set was very quiet and I had done many years of live television, everything was quiet when you worked. I just went with it and I remembered something that Strasberg (Lee Strasberg, the renowned Method Acting coach) had said to me, 'You are the instrument, the director is the conductor and you just have to play your instrument.' The image at that moment was perfect for me and before I started acting, I just smiled at the ladies and they smiled back and they were very quiet and I decided, I'm doing a play and they're the audience."

All things considered, playing comedy was a welcome respite for Saint. "I love the scene when we're in our Chinese pajamas and playing the ukulele, he's playing—it was crazy. I remember I was going across the table for something during rehearsal and it was bad—they had used polish and I slipped and fell right on the floor, on the back of my head and knocked me out a little bit. I found myself saying, 'No photos. Please no photos.' But Bob was wonderful to work with. He had to stop at 5 o'clock. I, of course, was younger than Bob and when I had most of my close-ups, he'd left for the day."

Despite the flurry of activity that continues to fill her days and the loss of her husband of 65 years, Saint never regretted opting for family before career. In the 21 years between our two interviews with her, we had often ruminated about what exactly impressed us most when we first met Saint. We both agreed that she possessed that indefinable balm called "star quality," however Saint didn't exude the "oomph" that many of the MGM contract ladies we had interviewed seemed to pulsate by the kilowatt. (Truthfully, it's hard to have much "pizzazz" when you insist on pouring Tropicana fruit juice to a couple of thirsty reporters.) But that's just the thing; for us, it came down to this: despite a career playing coolly sophisticated women who mostly nabbed their leading men, Saint is the most gloriously ordinary of any actress we've ever met. Happily unadorned; shorn of most of the trappings of Hollywood and completely at ease with herself and her place in the world, Saint is as real as it gets in a town famed for refracting relative truth through a prism of make-believe.

"I think the fact that I came from a loving family, my mother and father, my sister there was a lot of love, a lot of care there," she said. "My mom even made everything we wore. My dad was on the road a lot with BF Goodrich Tires, a rubber company. My dad would call every day at five and we'd all get on the phone. I mean, he was home, but he was traveling a lot. My mom had been a teacher and she gave us so much of her time and love. That's the kind of mom she was and that's the kind of dad he was, so I think we're so influenced by those early years and watching our parents.

"I tell you it pays off," she continued. "I'm without my Jeff now and my daughter lives not far in West L.A. My son is up in San Francisco and he comes down with his wife. My grandchildren call and they visit. I don't know how you would get through something like this without a family, but every one of them is dear. That's something that you'll have if you're a mother who's there and a father who's there. Jeffrey and I worked it out. There were things that I did turn down and I had an agent once who said, 'Eva Marie, if you keep turning these down, these roles, you're not going to be a superstar.' I said, well, I guess I don't want to be a superstar, and I walked out of the office and never looked back. I even got a new agent!"

Truer words were never spoken—on balance.

The Pen Is Mightier Than the Clarinet

Artie Shaw

During the big band era of the late 1930s and '40s, Artie Shaw wielded the hottest licorice stick this side of the *Down Beat* Readers Poll or, at least, Benny Goodman. When his orchestra struck gold in 1938 with their hit recording of Cole Porter's lush ballad, "Begin the Beguine," an odyssey of one-night stands quickly led to Hollywood and a brief fling in B-movies.

Shaw, a legendary lothario with more notches on his bedpost than tone holes in his clarinet, readily embraced the eat, drink and debauch credo of the film colony and became a stern-faced, controlling guru to a bevy of infatuated starlets including Judy Garland and Elizabeth Taylor. Like bowling pins, actresses Lana Turner, Ava Gardner and Evelyn Keyes, in turn, fell for Shaw's alpha male charms and took their places as his wives (he had eight) in marriages that could be clocked by the second hand of a stopwatch.

In the case of "Sweater Girl" Turner, after adding some tempo to a 1939 Metro-Goldwyn-Mayer Studios trifle called *The Dancing Co-ed* in which she starred, Shaw married the platinum blonde bombshell. A scant four months later they were divorced to banner headlines and the ecstatic delight of tabloids and Tinseltown fanzines.

We met Shaw in 1983. By then he had become a self-styled expatriate from the garish excesses of Beverly Hills and its environs. His letter hinted at the kind of visit we could expect:

> "My phone number (I live just over the line in Ventura County, since I can't stand Hollywood and its general mentality!) is xxx-xxx-xxxx; and you can try me shortly before or after you arrive. If I'm able to do so at that time, I'll be happy to set up some time for an interview. I must prepare you, though, by stating that I really haven't much use for showbiz values, attitudes, criteria, etc.; so you may not get the kind of views from me that you might expect.
>
> In any event, if you want to try … well, that's entirely up to you."
>
> Best wishes, either way.

He lived in Newbury Park (a suburb of Los Angeles in the western reaches of the San Fernando Valley), drove a moped (which he showed us parked in his garage) on grocery store runs and was vitally concerned about global overpopulation, water shortages and energy conservation.

"When I putter up to a red light and see some blue-haired old lady fiercely idling in her Cadillac enroute to buy makeup, it makes me sick," Shaw said. Despite a few errant

Artie on the downbeat

strands of hair working hard to cover his bald pate, some belly paunch and a gold neck chain so wide it looked like it could keep a surly pit-bull tethered to a yard stake, Shaw still cut a handsome figure. And for us, it somehow felt reassuring to know that he had not lost any of the pugnacity that had made him a difficult customer to deal with on set and in the *boudoir*.

Shaw's two-story Italian villa–style tract

home was undistinguished from the outside and had the cookie-cutter look of many of the homes in the area but it was cluttered with mementos from his life on the road, including a Japanese battle flag captured on Guadalcanal and autographed by Admiral Halsey. (Shaw served in the U.S. Navy during World War II, leading a morale-boosting band in the South Pacific.) Scattered haphazardly on walls and tables was all manner of art, including a painting by German artist George Grosz and a small Dadaist sculpture that could be dissembled and put back together.

What wasn't visible was any sign of his clarinet. "Contrary to rumors, I didn't make it into a lamp," Shaw huffed. "I still have three of them around here somewhere. I was playing to make a living then I got caught up in the art form of music. I had to formulate for myself the difference between an artist and an entertainer."

Shaw told us that he ankled moviedom after experiencing an epiphany of sorts. "One day I awoke and realized that the whole Rodeo Drive scene was cosmetic bullshit. Socrates wrote that 'the unexamined life is not worth living.' I've always been introspective. From the age of 20 I knew I wanted to be a writer. Playing jazz was my method of financing a writing career. I really thought band-leading was a dead-end."

It had been more than 25 years since Shaw last blew a note, but the trade-off of clarinet for typewriter had reaped a few dividends (if not dividend checks). In the interim, Shaw wrote a valedictory of the swing era and its musicians called *The Trouble with Cinderella*. He also authored a volume of short stories entitled *The Best of Intentions*. When we visited, he was working on a gargantuan autobiographical account of his life entitled "The Education of Albie Snow" which remained unfinished and unpublished at his death in 2004.

"I've got 90 chapters so far and I've done about 20 drafts of each chapter," he said, pulling out a manila folder from a portable fireproof safe. "I wouldn't care if the whole house burned down as long as the manuscript is safe, but I fear I'll be old as a Sequoia when I finish." Shaw couldn't possibly have known the prescience of his remark: he was 94 when he died and had, by that time, probably used up a giant redwood's worth of pulp on rewrites.

"Writing is a measured and thoughtful approach to expression. That's what I crave. Jazz can never be that," Shaw said. "It's a spontaneous bag of tricks that you play as fast as you can. You are never where you would ideally like to be. An attraction of writing is that it can make even a stupid person seem halfway intelligent. If only the person will write the same thought repeatedly, improving it a little bit each time. It's like inflating a blimp with a bicycle pump, anybody can do it, it just takes a lot of hot air."

One of the slapdash films that Shaw and his orchestra appeared in during his brief sojourn in Hollywood was a middling musical called *Second Chorus* starring Fred Astaire. In a rare position of scrutiny, Shaw saw past the happy-go-lucky elegance of Astaire's public persona and into the appalling discipline of a dancer who rehearsed seven days a week, 12 hours a day.

"Astaire was a sweater. He toiled. He was a humorless, Teutonic man; the opposite of his debonair image with a high hat singing 'April in Paris,'" Shaw said in a pointed, reductive analysis. "I liked him because he was an entertainer and an artist. There's an important distinction between the two terms. An artist is concerned only with what is acceptable to himself, where an entertainer strives to please the public. Astaire did both. Louis Armstrong was another one; he always had an eye on the public but he did what he had to do to please himself."

The artist vs. entertainer distinction had the effect of a wakeup call for Shaw. In fact, it's the reason he retired from making music. Shaw told us that not long after "Begin the Beguine" became a signature tune, his orchestra became a commodity. "It soon became evident that no matter how badly we played on a certain night—and there were nights when we couldn't find our groove and nothing jelled—the audience still whooped and hollered. They were oblivious. Our fame had preceded us; outdistanced us."

To Shaw, a fan was a "heedless person admiring celebrity," and it didn't take a soothsayer to understand that that was anathema to everything he stood for. "I had to get out because I saw the end of my life foretold," he said. "When you become a professional you reach a level of excellence below which you cannot fall. Pretty soon the audience can't distinguish the difference between superlative and mediocre playing, but the artist can discern it if he remains true to himself and doesn't succumb to his own favorable publicity.

"You can easily fall into a plush-lined rut where a form of death occurs," he continued. "I see creative people who ended their lives 40 years ago and are still walking around. When that happens, you'd better get out of the business or resolve yourself to becoming Lawrence Welk. He's a happy man but if he could hear with my ears what he is doing, he would commit hara-kiri on his baton."

Shaw admitted that he never regretted giving up jazz because performing at an exceptional level is "just too hard."

"It's like asking Muhammad Ali if he does road work for his own amusement," Shaw said. "When I hear something played on the clarinet I suffer because I can feel the intensity of effort. I might remember a bad reed or the trouble I had with the second trumpet player or God knows what. The quintessential question that people ask me is why I don't play even for fun anymore. I've inured myself to that kind of examination. I just tune them out like a bad television commercial."

Only Shaw's last two CD recordings (*The Last Recordings—Rare & Unreleased*, Music Masters, 1992 and *More Last Recordings—The Final Sessions* Music Masters, 1993) measure up to his supreme critical gaze. In what amounted to an authoritative statement, he said: "If I could erase all the rest of my work, I'd be happy."

Stepping out of the performing limelight in 1954 didn't mean passing up television talk show guest spots, the ideal forum to plug his books. Shaw was a participant on Johnny Carson's second *Tonight Show* and appeared on every star roster from Dick Cavett to Merv. But even guest shots went the way of the clarinet after a while.

"You can't really talk on television. No one wants to hear you," Shaw said. "Dick Cavett is a bloody bore. If you want to be a philosopher then get the hell off TV. It's the wrong medium. Truthfully, I'm not your ideal TV guest. On the *Merv Griffin Show*, which is all things to all people, I likened the crowds at Woodstock to a bunch of muddy pigs. I was booed off the stage. By and large, TV is blight. So everyone knows the latest Henny Youngman joke … big deal!"

If that sounds like the phlegmatic raving of an embittered misanthrope, Shaw would've been the first to admit (albeit in a bellicose manner) that he never lost his maverick streak and that to him celebrity was a "total dislocation of character."

"You come to a point where loneliness doesn't exist and solitude is a valuable thing," he said. "I guess you could say I don't have much patience with pointless people. Some of my most heated run-ins were with interviewers. One guy desperately wanted me to write a Hollywood exposé. I said that I would do it only if he agreed to the title 'The

Platinum Vagina.' He asked why and I replied that platinum is expensive, hard, cold and potentially harmful. I get tired of reporters who only seem interested in the color of Lana Turner's bedspread or what was under her sweater."

Straight, no chaser. That was Artie Shaw.

By George!
George Sidney

The lion's mighty roar has been tempered to a barely audible meow. Metro-Goldwyn-Mayer's Culver City, California, dream factory is owned by another studio and what remains is a film production and distribution company that, except for the lucrative James Bond film franchise, lives primarily off its glorious history.

Formed in May 1924, MGM was a marriage between Metro Pictures, the Goldwyn Company (named for Samuel Goldwyn, although he had no involvement in the merged companies), and pioneering producer Louis B. Mayer. The studio was organized as a subsidiary of the giant New York–based theater chain, Loews, Inc. While some studios could boast of making the finest gangster movies or the best horror films, MGM carved out its own special niche from the 1930s through the 1950s with a long string of lavish musical productions.

At the directorial helm of many of the studio's most successful musicals was George Sidney who worked at MGM for nearly 20 years and was responsible for such pictures as *Anchors Aweigh*, *The Three Musketeers*, *The Harvey Girls*, *Show Boat*, *Kiss Me Kate*, *Annie Get Your Gun*, and *Viva Las Vegas*, with Elvis Presley. Away from MGM, Sidney directed *The Eddy Duchin Story*, *Pal Joey*, with Frank Sinatra and *Bye Bye Birdie*, starring Ann-Margret.

"The first thing you have to understand is that you're talking to an insane man," Sidney warned us as he launched into an epic screed about his dog Rover. "This dog belongs to every museum in the world," he said. "When I took out my membership in the Museum of Modern Art in New York, they asked me if I had any children. I said yes, I have Rover. And they asked me what his age was. I didn't know so I put down 10 years old. Later the president of the museum sent me back a letter that read, 'Unfortunately, your son is too young for a junior membership, but anytime he's in the city, he'll have the run of the museum.'"

Born in 1916 in Jamaica, Long Island, Sidney (who died in 2002 at age 85) grew up in a show business family. His mother started performing when she was four years old as one of the three Mooney Sisters at the Winter Garden Theater in New York. His father held just about every job in show business, ultimately becoming a top executive at MGM's parent company, Loews, Inc.

"When my parents got married there was a thing coming along called movies," Sidney said. "They got a little bit of money together and opened a shoe store, rented some chairs and then put them down in the shop. The aisle was all cockeyed and crazy. They got a projector and some films and charged 10-cents and showed the 'flickers' on a bed sheet. That's how they started."

Before the ripe old age of six, Sidney himself was a veteran performer. He played the smallest cowboy in the Tom Mix westerns and starred in the silent version of *Little Lord Fauntleroy*, complete with long blonde curls.

Whether meeting Sidney in his Beverly Hills office as we did for the first time in 1980 (we walked in on him to big band swing tunes blasting from a reel-to-reel tape recorder mounted in his wall as he fiddled around with about 50 troy ounces of gold bullion and assorted Krugerrands on his desk), during subsequent visits over lunch at "his club" (Hillcrest Country Club) or at his Beverly Hills home on North Rexford Drive, Sidney was, to us, the embodiment of the old studio system—"Mr. MGM Musical." He was the quintessential raconteur—the personification (in precociousness if not in lack of compunction) of author Budd Schulberg's antihero "Sammy Glick" from *What Makes Sammy Run?*, still the greatest novel ever written about Hollywood's chancrous underbelly.

Talking to Sidney over the years, we also sometimes wondered if he wasn't the oldest living example of attention deficit disorder. It's not that he couldn't stay on topic; it was just that no matter what issue we brought up in conversation, Sidney would find some personal nexus with it, like water finding its own level, but in his case, instantly.

It could be an innocent noun like Polaroid, an obscure restaurant in New York only we thought we knew about, or a museum in Minneapolis (or Turkistan), Sidney would have a connection to it that he felt compelled to share. Sometimes it seemed like we were conversing with a cross between the *Encyclopedia Britannica* and a panelist on *Information Please*. But the saving grace about the anecdote that would inevitably follow is that Sidney never seemed boastful or even needy about imparting it. That's what made his frequent soliloquies palatable—that and the fact that they were usually real corkers.

"By the time I was six-years-old I knew I didn't want to be an actor. I decided to become a director," Sidney proclaimed. "During the interim I did odd jobs around Broadway. At the same time I was studying music. I play four instruments. When I was 14, I came out to California and got a job as a messenger boy at MGM."

Through hard work, pluck and the conscious decision not to cash in on his well-placed family connection, Sidney gradually worked his way up through the ranks at MGM where he spent 18 hours a day learning everything there was to learn about filmmaking. Hollywood studios have been compared to factories and to prove that analogy Sidney would often swap places on the MGM "assembly line" with other tradesman, just to learn a new facet of the business.

"The unions weren't so stringent then," he said. "You could trade jobs. I was in the sound department at one time and wanted to be in the cutting department. The other guy (in the cutting department) wanted to be down on the set, so we just switched punch cards."

Following his apprenticeship, Sidney directed *Our Gang* comedies—a chore he recalled with disdain. "It was impossible working with those kids," he said. "I'd have to listen to the high frequency of their voices all day, and then I'd go into a projection room and turn off the sound. I finally went to the studio brass and said, 'Listen, if I make two of these films in one week, do I get two weeks off?' And they said, 'Sure.' So we would write a script with the same sets and costumes and make two shorts at once. I got the supreme luxury of two weeks off before I had to face them again."

Desk jockey

After winning Oscars for his direction of two specialty shorts, MGM studio chief Louis B. Mayer promoted Sidney to feature film director. He then went on to direct 27 films beginning with *Free and Easy* in 1941 and ending with the British musical, *Half a Sixpence* in 1966. "Something strange happened when we did *Sixpence*," Sidney said. "A thing called 'Beatlemania' happened. It was a different beat."

Perhaps Sidney' most famous musical number of the dozens he directed is Gene Kelly's adagio with Jerry the cartoon mouse in the 1945 film, *Anchors Aweigh*. Upon completion of the filming, Kelly joined the Navy. It was only then that Sidney realized there was a problem. "We put it all together and ran the number," he recalled. "It looked great, but there was one thing missing. Kelly's reflection appeared on the floor. The mouse was a cell layed onto the film, so there was no reflection. For continuity's sake, we had to go back and make 20,000 mouse drawing reflections. While we were doing that sequence the mouse became so real. We talked to him and panned the camera around to accommodate him. That's why nobody thought about Jerry throwing a shadow."

Sidney described his approach to filmmaking by explaining the shooting of the Academy Award–winning song "On the Atchison, Topeka, and the Santa Fe" from his 1946 film, *The Harvey Girls*. "In that number Judy Garland does the entire nine-minute song in one shot. But it took us a week to lay the whole scene out. It's easier to make a lot of setups, but then you're going to get chop suey and you're not going to get a seamless flow. When Judy gets off that bloody train and goes into the song, we just swing along with her. The camera should have a fluidity that goes along with her."

To Sidney's mind, such directorial gestures helped to define the American musical film as something unique. "The American musical is indigenous to the U.S. and no place else in this world," he said. "It belongs to the people. It's amazing when someone will make a musical and it's not the way people think it should be; the way they tear into you! And they are harder to make than any other kind of film. It's two films in one, because you make a musical film and a book film. If you're lucky, you blend the two together."

Kiss Me Kate, Sidney's 1953 film with Cole Porter songs and featuring a very young Bob Fosse was the only musical shot in 3-D, a short-lived fad (back then, anyway) that was an attempt by the industry in the early '50s to combat the encroaching hegemony of television.

"The utmost care was taken making that film," he said. "We really made it twice— in 3-D, and in flat. We'd shoot a scene in 3-D, then we'd pull the cameras back and I would restage it. Now when you look at the film you don't know whether you're watching the 3-D print or the flat one."

Sidney probably filmed more Broadway musicals than any other person, but he preferred directing original screen musicals over proven Broadway successes. "It's more of a challenge. In so many Broadway musicals, the first act is really the finish of the musical. The second act will be all musical numbers. And you have to make a film that the audience thinks is exactly the way they saw it in the theater. When you get a critic who says, 'Oh, he did nothing, he just photographed the stage play,' you've had it. For example, we made *Anchors Aweigh* as we went along. And that's a very exciting way to get up in the morning."

Two other Broadway blockbusters that Sidney adapted for the screen were *Show Boat* starring Kathryn Grayson and Howard Keel and *Annie Get Your Gun* with music by Irving Berlin. "Movies have always used the Sacramento River as a stand-in for the Mississippi," Sidney said. "I went up and down the Sacramento and said, 'Wait a minute, this doesn't look like it.' Outrageously, we flew to the Mississippi and actually photographed the Mississippi—10 days of shooting outside Natchez, Mississippi."

As far as *Annie Get Your Gun* was concerned, Sidney had big shoes (or actually little ones, size 5½) to fill when star Judy Garland's MGM contract was terminated. "I thought Betty Hutton would be great in the 'Annie' role," Sidney said. "People at the studio cautioned that she was a wild one—insane. I sent for her, got her in the office and told her, 'First, you have to understand no one wants you. This is my idea. You start acting up with me and I'll kill you—I'll actually kill you with my hands.' Well, Betty and I had the ball of all time!"

As rock 'n' roll swept over the traditional musical film genre like a cultural tsunami, changing forever how musicals were made and consumed by the public, in 1966, Sidney decided the time was ripe to abandon filmmaking and pursue other interests, including the study of law, paleontology, medicine and art history. To that end he received an honorary doctorate in the '60s from Hahnemann Medical College in Philadelphia for his film on cardiovascular research.

Away from the camera, Sidney married three show business heavy-hitters. His first wife, Lillian Burns, was a famed drama coach at MGM and the person Louis B. Mayer once said was the only woman qualified to run a major studio. His second wife, Jane, was widowed from actor Edward G. Robinson (she died in 1991). His last wife, the former

Corinne Entratter, was married to the late Las Vegas Sand's Hotel impresario Jack Entratter who headlined friend Frank Sinatra and the "Rat Pack" at his hotel in the 1960s. In
1958, under the pseudonym Lari Laine, Corinne had been *Playboy*'s "Playmate of the
Month" for May.

"Every film has a life of its own; it's a circular thing that happens to a group of people
and it's an experience," he said, in full pontification mode during that first visit in his
office. "It starts out and you have an emotional or a sexual or whatever reaction, a whole
association with people. Sometimes it can be a lot warmer than other times. And when
it's all over, you can never recapture that emotion."

With Sidney at Hillcrest Country Club …
a Couple of Years Later

Hillcrest Country Club in Beverly Hills was founded with vengeance as a motive.
In the 1920s, about the only place to play a game of golf in West Lost Angeles was on one
of the Los Angeles Country Club's two sprawling 18-hole-courses. Douglas Fairbanks
and Joe Schenck, a man who gave definition to the term "movie mogul," were barred
from entering the grounds on the grounds that they were "movie people," an unpardon-
able sin to the highly-stratified society of the day that was ruled by the WASP elite.

In response to that ostracism, Fairbanks and Schenck founded the Hillcrest Country
Club, which was semitically inclusive and nearby.

"My wife and I are seldom in Beverly Hills for any length of time anymore," Sidney
said from a lunch table in the men's grill. "I'm an Anglophile so we live in London much
of the time. I also try to get back to Hong Kong at least twice annually, and then there
are always the cruise tours on the Royal Viking Line. Ostensibly I'm retired from the
movie business, but we can negotiate free passage anywhere, in the lap of absolute luxury,
if I bring along a couple of my films to screen and give a movie lecture to the passengers.
You might call it a career dividend."

To the septuagenarians who fill the Viking Line's cabins and staterooms, Sidney's
Eddy Duchin Story was a perennial favorite. For a couple of hours viewers could nix the
deck chairs and shuffleboard and transport themselves back to their era of vitality, when
swing music was "Solid Jackson."

"When I was filming that movie we had a bit player under contract at the studio
who I felt would be perfect casting for the love interest," Sidney said. "Her name was Kim
Novak. We were sitting on a couch discussing the film and I was telling her about my
idea of tagging Duchin's arrival in New York City to Lindbergh's transatlantic flight. Kim
gave me the big eye all through my talk and after pondering for a moment said, 'That's
a wonderful story you made up about that guy who flew across the ocean.' I couldn't
believe my ears. I said, 'But Kim, Lindbergh's flight is a historical fact—it really happened!'
She just replied, 'I suppose it doesn't matter, I wasn't born then anyway.' Statements like
that can quickly reduce your esteem of humankind."

In a hectic world where attention spans could be measured in milli-seconds, Sidney
remained a modern-day Renaissance man devoted to the painstaking acquisition of
knowledge. Case-in-point: at the age of 50, he enrolled at the University of Southern
California.

"Bored people should use the power of their intellect to fill up their days," Sidney said digging into a dish of stewed prunes. "I get depressed when I think that I'm about 400 years behind on the information spectrum and I'll never catch up on all the things I'd like to know about. One of my interests is paleontology. I was in Africa where Dr. Leakey uncovered the remains of earliest man. I then went down to Pretoria and held the skullcap of "Missy," a relic thousands of years old. People say to me in awe, 'Gosh, you directed Lana Turner.' All I can say to that is, 'Who cares? I held in my hand the skull of Missy.'"

During our chat, the men's grill filled up to lunchtime capacity and Sidney began to point out "Jewish movie people" with the intense glee of a child selecting a chocolate babka from the Canters Deli bakery case. In five minutes time he introduced us to Pandro Berman, producer of the Astaire-Rogers musicals; Izzy Freedman, former clarinetist with Paul Whiteman; Irving Brecher, screenwriter for the Marx Brothers movies *Go West* and *At the Circus*; Herman Citron, Hollywood powerbroker; and last (and least), Monty *Let's Make a Deal* Hall.

We had read our share of unauthorized movie biographies and definitive tell-all tomes, but it was different to see people "in the industry" in their element—table-hopping and kibitzing—about points, percentages and million-dollar deals. We felt a kind of nervous excitement, as if we might suddenly appear in the pages of a Sidney Sheldon novel.

"I've been a club member since 1932, but I don't come here to make deals or bullshit about the pictures I'm going to make," Sidney said, dousing our reverie. "The dues are $35,000 a year and I don't play tennis, golf, or cards. As far as I'm concerned, they toss a great Cobb Salad."

We noticed that one large table was conspicuously crowd-free, George Burns being the only person seated there. Sidney leaned over to us and whispered almost reverently, "What you're witnessing is the end of an era. That used to be the Hollywood version of the famous Algonquin New York roundtable. Burns, Jack Benny, George Jessel, Eddie Cantor, and the Marx Brothers all used to have lunch there regularly. You took your life in your hands if you sat down with them uninvited. Their combined wit could slay you alive. Burns is the last one.

"You just can't live in the past, it's no good," Sidney continued, already moving on as we starred transfixed at the hunched-over image of Burns nursing his soup. "Take it from me—a paleontologist who's been around."

The Untouchable

Robert Stack

To us, judging from his flinty portrayals in movies and on television, it always seemed that Robert Stack fully lived up to his appellation as one of the "untouchables." As Eliot Ness in the late '50s TV crime drama, granite-jawed Stack squared off weekly for four seasons against Al Capone in Prohibition-era Chicago and rarely cracked a smile, his icy reserve as impermeable as a Kevlar vest. That stoicism (and monotone delivery) continued

30 years later when he hosted *Unsolved Mysteries*, the viewer call-in show that fingered fugitives from justice. In 1980, Stack's limestone facade was even spoofed in his portrayal as no nonsense Capt. Rex Kramer in *Airplane!*

So, when we scheduled an interview with Stack in 1994, we expected our preconceived notion of him as a walking, talking calcified stalagmite to be borne out in reality. We were wrong. The idea that in real life Stack was dour bordering on sour was entirely our own construct; an illusion. Face to face, he was almost preternaturally cheerful and very expansive.

Initially we planned the interview to take place at the house Stack (78 then) shared with his wife Rosemarie in Bel-Air, but the day of our meeting he called and said he had to fly out of town on some urgent business and then attend the Dinah Shore golf tournament later that week out in Rancho Mirage. Shore had died the month before and this would be the first tournament without her presence on the links. Could we, he asked, meet at Jan's Restaurant (just down the street from the dive we were staying at on Beverly Boulevard)? He would swing by our motel on his way to LAX, pick us up, and we could have a cup of coffee (hyped as the best in L.A. at the time) before he continued on to the airport.

Trouble was, that scenario presented us with a paradox of our own. We were a bit embarrassed by the cut-rate motel in which we stayed (the Beverly Wilshire it was not!). But since we always met our interview subjects in their homes or at restaurants, it never was a problem. Now—for us—it had become one.

Stack insisted that he pick us up in his limousine. Seeing no graceful solution to our dilemma, we agreed and gave him our address. We did, however, tell him to phone us when he pulled up and we'd come right down, perhaps mitigating the embarrassment somewhat. About a half-hour later, to our horror, Dave looked out the window (which looked down into the rectangular inner plaza of the motel) and saw a Lincoln Town Car parked. The jig was up.

To make things worse, the plaza, if you could call it that, was about as wide as a soccer goal and the limo driver, to our bafflement, had managed to wedge the car in sideways. With walls and right angles jutting everywhere, and one way in and out, the geometry of exiting the place would've stumped Euclid.

We entered the car as the driver, Bill, was in the middle of cranking the wheel so hard to the left we thought the steering shaft might explode from the tension. "Fellas, thanks for being OK with the last-minute change of plans. Dinah was a dear friend, an angel," Stack said. "She's one of the goodies. I, along with Peter Falk and Wayne Rogers have been supportive of the LPGA since it began. The pro women golfers couldn't get arrested or make any money. It's interesting (the tournament) in a town so difficult to behave in with so many jealousies, that it's scandal-free and very philanthropic."

At this point we had settled back but were wincing as Bill maneuvered the limo backwards out the plaza entrance just missing the iron fence that surrounded the pool and which looked like it had been scraped more than once by drivers not as skilled as Stack's.

"Let me tell you something about fame," Stack said. "I was playing golf one day with David Janssen (another legendary phlegmatic leading man). *The Untouchables* was just ending its run and David was just beginning to hit in *The Fugitive*. A bunch of girls started running toward us. I was used to the fact that David was a big draw with the ladies. I was out there already with a big smile in front of David. They ran right past me right to David. You wait long enough, and it's the next guy."

Robert Stack over easy

About two minutes later we arrived at the restaurant. Stack asked Bill if he wanted to join us. Bill said yes and that he'd park the car. Our waitress at Jan's was a woman named Ingrid. "You're Ingrid and I used to be Robert Stack," Stack said. "You have a sexy voice," Ingrid said. "Thank you, you made my day," Stack beamed.

By the early 1990s, Stack had certainly made a life of crime really pay off. As host of *Unsolved Mysteries*, he said it was a nice change to positively affect the outcomes of many real-life dramas. "*Unsolved Mysteries*, has helped police apprehend more than 40 percent of the fugitives profiled on the series since it premiered in 1987," he told us. And as one of television's first interactive series, the show had picked up six Emmy nominations as Best Informational Series.

"I came in as a replacement for Karl Malden," Stack said. "You learn to base your decision-making on who's invited to the party. The audience adopts you and allows you into their house. If they push that button, you're gone. It's fulfilling for me to go out, play a tennis tournament and have people yell that they love the show. That's what it's all about."

Stack had "walked the beat" in four other major television series' that dealt, in one way or another, with the criminal element. Starting in 1959 with his Emmy award-winning role as Ness in *The Untouchables*, Stack went on to portray the editor of *Crime* magazine in *The Name of the Game*, followed by roles on the police action shows *Most Wanted* and *Strike Force*.

"It's truly a heady thing when you realize that millions of people tune in each week to get what amounts to the latest police blotter report," Stack said, referring to *Unsolved*

Mysteries. "But the show really isn't about acting; it's about making the little moments work on a special level." Making those little moments work had been Stack's stock-in-trade since he began his show business career in the 1942 Jack Benny comedy, *To Be or Not to Be.*

"I approached the acting profession in a totally different way than most actors— almost offhandedly," he said, his voice shifting to a lower register. "You see, I had already succeeded in other areas of my life. I was one of the five best skeet shooters in the world. I was never one of the five best actors in the world." We thought Stack's modesty was charming, particularly when his youthful exploits would've made prime fodder for a TV movie-of-the-week. At age 16, he was a national skeet-shooting champion and in college at USC he rode polo ponies, that is, when he wasn't racing speedboats. But then, more often than not, we seemed to detect a correlation between the sunny calm of people like Stack who were firmly rooted with family ties and a sense of place vis-à-vis the quiet desperation evinced by others in Los Angeles who had come there for a fresh start to reinvent themselves.

You see, Stack was a fifth-generation Californian whose ancestors were among the first U.S. families to settle in the dusty little pueblo that became Los Angeles. Stack's great grandfather was a prominent figure in the early Los Angeles social scene and owned the area's first opera house. "The oldest standing frame house in Los Angeles, in Heritage Square, was my great grandfather's," Stack said. "It was built in 1876 at the end of the horse car line in Boyle Heights." But the illustrious lineage didn't stop there. Stack's father was an advertising executive who worked on the Schlitz beer account and coined the slogan, "The Beer That Made Milwaukee Famous."

"My father considered the advertising business like show business," he said. "That's why he made my brother and I promise that we would never go into acting. It was only after he passed away and some bills came due that I decided to defy my father's wishes and become an actor.

"I took a different approach to this profession because of my upbringing and exposure to theatrical people," Stack added. "We had stars at our house all the time, but I just knew these guys as people I could beat at athletics." Despite growing up with Clark Gable as "practically a surrogate father," Stack said he never planned a career in front of the cameras until financial necessity made it a viable option.

Stack's first professional acting job was in the 1939 film, *First Love*, opposite screen sweetheart Deanna Durbin. "I was only with her on screen … unfortunately," Stack said.

After serving in the Navy during World War II as an aerial gunnery instructor, Stack returned to Hollywood to star in a clutch of popular movies, including *Fighter Squadron*, *The Bullfighter and the Lady*, *The High and the Mighty* and *House of Bamboo*. His film career reached its apogee in 1957 when he picked up a Best Supporting Actor Academy Award nomination playing a playboy millionaire in the classic melodrama *Written on the Wind.*

"I never got another part like that," Stack said. "As for not winning the Oscar, Jimmy Stewart once said, 'You never win the one you should. I should have won for *Mr. Smith Goes to Washington*. But I won it for something else.' I remember what the great acting teacher Stella Adler once said, 'I feel sorry for my gifted ones who were never given the chance to show their gift.' I've never felt that. I've always felt that I was an all-American."

Throughout his life Stack was blessed by good fortune, and that lucky aura may have explained his insouciant attitude toward his craft. "Acting is like kindergarten recess time," he summed up, "it is fun when it's done right." (Our interview was peppered with his aphorisms and similes: "An actor has to be crazy to be an actor or being an actor *makes* you crazy," "Man proposes, God disposes.") But the acting as kindergarten image had real validity since it set the tone of Stack's work in the hit comedy spoof, *Airplane!* "The film's producers, the Zucker brothers, were gifted but certifiably insane," he said. "During the course of the movie they managed to insult every minority group and no one got mad—God bless them!"

Religious and racial epithets notwithstanding, the movie introduced Stack to an audience that wasn't even born when he was busting the rackets as Eliot Ness. "I came off a golf hole once and ran into a goofy, semi-drunk bunch of college guys who recognized me and then began to spout my lines from the movie—weird! And I'll tell you something about Leslie (Leslie Nielsen, the star of *Airplane!*), he was possibly my best friend and I was the only actor to show up when Les got his star on the Walk of Fame. We were there cheering because he was one of us—he made it from being a character actor into a big star."

For Stack (another character actor who made good) it was just the reverse. It was as Ness, special agent of the F.B.I., that he really hit his stride as a television actor. Although the show ran for four seasons on ABC, it originally started out as a two-part special. "I had a lot of friends tell me, don't do a television series, you're a film actor. It will kill you. After a sleepless night, I went to the producer Desi Arnaz, and asked him, 'What are you going to do with this show because I'm scared?' Desi replied, 'We're going to make the best damn series on television.' I was scared to death about making the transition from film into a weekly series."

Stack's fears proved to be unfounded. His portrayal of the crusty agent who nailed Al Capone, even won the seal of approval from Ness's widow. "I got a letter from Mrs. Ness when the series aired that I've never published," Stack said. "It went like this: 'Dear Mr. Stack, I was afraid of a television series about my husband. I loved him very much and am very protective of him. But I'm happy to say the show is decent and good. In particular, I was worried about your interpretation of my husband. I don't know how you did it, maybe by osmosis, but you have picked up several of his characteristics that are quite striking. You are very much like him in attitude.'

"The only value an actor has in terms of power is irreplaceability," Stack continued. "The machinery on how the actor got the role doesn't matter. Whoever thinks that someone is right for the part doesn't matter because, usually, the producers are wrong."

Stack said that he based his character on the fact that Ness was brave and "put his money where his mouth was." In fact, his inspiration for the character was based on two men; legendary Hollywood stuntman Carey Loftin and Audie Murphy—the most decorated American soldier of World War II. "When the movie version of *The Untouchables* came out in 1987 with Kevin Costner, Paramount wanted Kevin and me to pose for pictures, but I refused," Stack said. "I felt it was Kevin's movie ... my TV series."

It was about then that a burly guy who had been eavesdropping on our conversation from a nearby booth timidly approached our table. He said he was a truck driver and liked to come to Jan's for a quick bite. He asked Stack for his autograph and then held out a napkin smudged with maple syrup and egg yolk.

"Looks like you're going to get the short stack again, right now," Tom said to the trucker. Stack laughed when the pun sailed high and wide. Then Stack handed the soiled doily, now with his signature Sharpied on it, back to the trucker who walked over to the cashier to pay his bill.

Stack dropped us off at our motel, but this time Bill didn't attempt to navigate into the plaza area, he wisely parked at the curb. "Rosemarie and I will have to have you guys out to the house soon," Stack said cheerily before closing the door and driving off. We had an idea that he felt kind of sorry for us on account of where we were billeted. We never made it over to his house but we've always appreciated Stack's *noblesse oblige* (although that characterization would probably have made him cringe). Only on TV was he an untouchable tough guy. In person, Stack was anything but; from reel to real, a delightfully winning paradox.

A Long Meander with RJ

Robert Wagner

The word "terrific" pops up frequently when talking to Robert Wagner.

At first we thought it was just a maxim he tossed off liberally, without thinking—kind of like Bob Hope's meaningless placeholder "…but I wanna tell ya," which the comedian habitually tacked on after his punch-lines.

But then we remembered the word as a signature descriptor Wagner seemed to voice once each episode in one of our very favorite late '60s TV series, *It Takes a Thief*. As Al Mundy, the groovy and urbane super-thief dragooned into U.S. government espionage work that utilized his faultless precision and unique skills, Wagner would recite it inflected with dripping irony (in a life or death situation) or suavely (when at episode's end he was about to bed his gorgeous guest star). In that regard, Mundy got luckier on a weekly basis than the horndogging Capt. Kirk did with a galaxy of compliant aliens.

We met Wagner who also starred in *Hart to Hart* and *Switch* on TV as well as in such movies as *The Longest Day*, *Midway* and most memorably as the hyper-amiable boyfriend in *Harper*, in the office of Rogers & Cowan, a venerable Hollywood PR and marketing shop that dates back to 1950 and that at one time or another has represented most of the town's old guard celebrities. Their office was located in the "Center Green Building" on the campus of The Pacific Design Center, a 1.2 million-square-foot labyrinth of a facility located in West Hollywood off Melrose Avenue.

Wagner's publicist led us into one of the agency's interview spaces that looked like an interrogation room you might see at Guantanamo Bay—a couple of scuffed, hard-working chairs, a small sofa and a side table with a phone. No art prints on the stark white walls; nothing to distract. The place had great Wi-Fi, though. "Hi fellas, call me RJ," Wagner said as he entered the room. That was something else we learned. Wagner is RJ to his friends and that includes almost everyone he spends more than a half-minute with after first being introduced. He had just finished filming scenes the night before for the TV series *NCIS* in which he has a recurring role.

We had a deep sheaf of questions to ask but about two minutes into the interview we somehow knew that our visit with RJ was not going to be the rote back and forth of a standard Q&A. Instead, we jettisoned the playbook and embarked on a sometimes provocative but always interesting three-hour ramble, like the kind you might have with an inquisitive stranger you just met sitting on a park bench who becomes ever more engrossing as the minutes tick by.

* * *

RJ: I had a scholarship to go to college but I wanted to go into the movies. I started working as an extra and I knocked around and we used to go around to all the studios and do readings. Paramount had what they called 'the fishbowl' which was a window of plate glass and you'd play a scene in front of it and on the other side were producers. You could see them smoking their cigarettes. Finally, I got to Fox and this terrific woman, Helena Sorell took a liking to me and she guided me and I did a scene on film and got signed to a three-month contract to Twentieth Century–Fox, then it was extended to six. I got her into the Actor's

Emphatically RJ

Home out in Woodland Hills and she died a few years ago at 105.

Fantle & Johnson: It Takes a Thief *lasted three seasons on TV and we loved it.*

RJ: What a character for television. It was based on the movie *To Catch a Thief* with Cary Grant and Grace Kelly—the Hitchcock movie. I had the good fortune of knowing Cary. So I went to him and asked him to give me some ideas about playing the part. I happen to love Cary Grant. I liked him so much; he was such a terrific person and such a courageous actor. Good God, look at the stuff that he did. So versatile and his "takes" and looks were so marvelous. He was really—to me—*the man*. So, Cary said: "You know, RJ, don't try to do a character. Take the material to yourself and do you." That basically is what all really good actors do, they make it become them and, in a sense, they get their own personalities out of the way.

On some elemental level, after seeing you in various movies and things, we thought that character was kind of you ... without ever really knowing for sure, of course.

I was living in Europe, in Rome, and came back to the U.S. My representative made an arrangement with Universal where I was under contract to them as a motion picture actor. Lew Wasserman called me into his office one day and he said, "I've got this script and I think its right for you. It's television." I said, "Lew, I'm not really interested in doing TV." He said, "I think you should consider it." He pulled opened a drawer and pulled out a *TV Guide* and said he'd like to see me on the cover of it. He said he thought I could make the transfer from movies to TV. He told me that if I agreed to make the pilot for the TV series, and if it didn't sell, he would make a movie out of it for me. Lew had been my agent before he became head of Universal.

I made the pilot. Eddie Dmytryk with whom I'd done a couple of films with Spencer Tracy, directed it. They showed it to ABC and ABC didn't buy it. So now I'm going to make the movie, right? Lew puts everybody in it that you can imagine—from heavyweight boxing champ Joe Louis to every guest star you can imagine. We go up to Canada, to the Expo in Montreal, and we get Senta Berger and he makes the movie. ABC sees it and says they gotta have it! So then I'm down in Brazil directing a documentary on the music festival in Rio. I had Quincy Jones down there, Andy Williams, and I'm putting together this documentary. It was when the bossa nova hit big. I wanted to make a documentary about it about how it came off the beach and the rhythms. I get a cable to come back. We're gonna start making *It Takes a Thief*.

You had the Fifth Dimension guest on one of the episodes.

Wasn't that great with Marilyn McCoo. I had a love scene with her but ABC wouldn't let us kiss. And then they cut Marilyn out when it aired on TV stations in the south. Can you imagine that?

And Fred Astaire played your father in three episodes.

I had a life-sized cutout of FA in my garage. I'd drive right up to him everyday in my garage. He was such a great person. I went to school with his son, Peter, this military school called Hollywood Military Academy. I was a boarder. My family sent me out from Michigan to board at this school because my father was going to move from Detroit to Los Angeles, which he did. I was six or seven years old and being a boarder, a lot of the kids would ask if I wanted to come to their house for the weekend.

Scott Eyman and I open our book (*I Loved Her in the Movies: Memories of Hollywood's Legendary Actresses*) talking about my treasure chest for keepsakes, old matchbooks, that kind of thing. Irving Thalberg Jr. was in the school and I went to his house and I met his mother, Norma Shearer. I remember it so well; we were taken upstairs. She lived at the beach. She was doing *Marie Antoinette* at the time (1938). She gave me a picture and inscribed it: "To Wagner, a friend of my son Irving. Love always, Norma Shearer." I kept that picture in my treasure chest and I still have it. The thing is; I didn't know who Norma Shearer was or who Marie Antoinette was. I was just a wide-eyed kid. Well, they showed *Marie Antoinette* at the school and I remember thinking to myself: "I don't remember seeing those guys at her house—all those guys with the wigs. That's not her house!"

Fred came to the school in his yellow Packard convertible to get Peter. And I remember him picking me up and putting me in the car. I didn't know who he was, but that's how far I go back with Fred. When it came around to him possibly playing my father in *It Takes a Thief*, you can imagine how excited I was. I remember asking Universal not to 'handle' Fred but to give him whatever he wanted. I didn't want to let the pencil-pushers deal with him, they've ruined our business, really. I was just so thrilled at the opportunity of working with him. We played a lot of golf together and I played a lot of pool with him. He gave me a wonderful pool stick. He brought me back a beautiful belt from Ireland which I gave to my daughter. He'd come to our house for dinner. He was so wonderful to me, so encouraging. I was so thrilled to have him playing Alistair Mundy and we had such plans for that show. It could still be airing today!

My son came up for an idea for a remake of the show where I have a daughter. A beautiful European actress—someone like Claudia Cardinale or Catherine Deneuve—calls me and says she wants to see me. I, as Al Mundy, am living in Las Vegas and run a club called Mundy's. So, this woman flies in on a private airplane and tells me that when she and I were together, she had a child, my child. Anyway, she says the kid has grown up to be a foreign correspondent in Iraq and—get this—she's just been captured and it's up to me to get her out. So I go in, working for the government again and find her but she doesn't know I'm her father. Complications ensue.

What do you miss most about the Golden Age in Hollywood? You were on the cusp of the great change when the studio system gave way to actors becoming free agents.

It seems like in society, not just the movie business, ethics are gone. Corporate influence has become so overpowering. I think in my case having been in this profession for such a long time, when I started, people had a vested interest in the business; they had their name on it. Now, everything is a committee decision that takes the individuality out of the equation. I'm not talking about the top directors like Spielberg who can write their own ticket.

What do you think of the whole "gotcha" aspect of entertainment reporting where entities like TMZ seem to be calling the shots?

They can do anything they want to now to anybody, you know. The individuality of the movie business is gone now—where stars were special. Now somebody's on fire for two seconds and then they're gone. And I think that infects them too.

Karl Malden, I started with him. The first picture I was ever in, *Halls of Montezuma* with Richard Widmark. And I just gave a poster to my daughter because the only woman in the picture was Marion Marshall who played a nurse. Marion and I were married and had Katie together.

You guys interviewed Virginia Mayo. She was great in *White Heat* with Cagney.

When we met her she was kind of shut away from it all. She lived in a little tract house in the western part of the San Fernando Valley.

That must have really been shocking for you.

We had interviewed Artie Shaw out there in the West Valley, too. He was offbeat.

But a very, very intelligent man.

Yes. He hated Hollywood with a passion.

But an interesting guy. He was involved with some very beautiful ladies. He cut a swath, as did Mickey Rooney. You know the great story about Mickey Rooney with Norma Shearer don't you? He had an affair with her. Apparently, she was very loyal to Irving Thalberg (*Norma's husband and head of production at MGM during the studio's glory years*), but she was a player and Mickey was going down on her in her dressing room when he said: "How do you like that, Andy Hardy going down on Marie Antoinette!" You know Mickey; he'd say anything to anybody.

There was never any filter with Mickey.

He was totally certifiable. I've had a lot of experiences with Mickey and he was crazy. He'd grab me a few times and cry right into my face (*Wagner blubbers like a baby*). But he had more talent in his little finger than most.

He was the white Sammy Davis Jr.

But now, Virginia Mayo, she's gone isn't she?

Yes. She died a while ago.

How did it happen? Did she have a bad third act?

Age-related stuff.

Can you imagine me dying in Jimmy Cagney's arms and I'm just starting in the movie business! (*Wagner's referring to* What Price Glory *in 1952*) And John Ford (the director) is giving me so much shit you can't believe it. I was the kid in the barrel with him.

He always had to pick someone out to terrorize during his shoots.

And he picked me. I was in a trench; it was a World War I story. He had Danny Borzage (*younger brother of director Frank Borzage*) playing the accordion and he's playing some French song and I'm in this trench and Ford looks over and says: "What are you doin' there, boob?" He called me boob. Then Ford asked where the music was coming from. I said, it was coming from over there and I pointed to Danny. Ford shot back: "Don't talk back to me! Just do what I tell you to do. Don't look over at where the music's coming from." Danny starts to play again, and I kind of looked over and I could see Ford pick up a rock. He was going to throw a rock at me. So I went after him, and Cagney was there. And he caught me and said, "Just take it easy." And the amazing thing—Ford died in my sister's former house in the desert. Cagney was an amazing guy. I used to jog his horses. He owned horses.

There used to be a wonderful restaurant here called La Scala. I went in there around 4 p.m. Natalie was going to meet me there. Through the backdoor from the alley came Jimmy in his baseball cap. He was shuffling along. This was after he'd had a stroke when he was old. He sat down in a booth. Nobody's there. I get up and walk over to him and say, "It's RJ Wagner." He says, "Ohhh, yeah, RJ. How are you?" I said, "More importantly, Jimmy, how are you?" He said, "These things happen." What a line. It broke my heart. (*Wagner tears up*). But he kept going. The interesting story about him is that woman who took care of him.

Marge Zimmerman, we went through her to get the interview with Jimmy.

You know how she got involved with him don't you? He had a farm, "Verney Farm," in upstate New York (*Stanfordville, NY*). Jimmy was unbelievable. He had horses, a boat down in Newport. He created the Screen Actor's Guild. I do a big piece in my book on Joan Blondell who Jimmy worked with. Anyway, that woman, Marge, was working at a gas station/country store up in Dutchess County there. She was working the counter selling crackers and fruit and candies and whatnot. And Jimmy and his wife would stop in there to fill the car up with gas. She asked Jimmy if he'd like sandwiches sent up to his house. And that led to her staying in the house as a kind of caretaker. I don't think the kids wound up with any money; I think they got a little bit. She worked her way in just like a snake. That happens to a lot of people.

That happened with Fred Astaire. We don't know and have never met his widow, Robyn.

Oh, Robyn's a fucking pain in the ass! I went after her and they printed it. She was going to sue me and I said: "Go ahead, sue me!" She's still got some of Ava's stuff there (*Ava Astaire-McKenzie, Fred's daughter*) at Fred's old house on San Ysidro Drive. When Fred built the house in the 1950s, I was there. He took me up there for a tour of what he was going to do. I played a lot of pool there with Willie Mosconi and him. His mother lived with him up there, and Fred would say: "Good night, mother." And you'd hear her faint reply from another room, "Good night." She was a lovely person and Ava lived there, too, as you know.

Fred had kept quite a bit of Phyliss's furniture (*Fred's wife of 21 years until her death in 1954*), her good things. She came from a very fine family, an old New York family, so she inherited a lot of really fine pieces. When FA passed on, she cut everybody out. Telephone numbers were changed eventually. Greg (Gregory Peck) and Veronique (*Peck's wife*), and myself and Jill (*Jill St. John, Wagner's wife*)—all of his really close friends; they were out. Jill would cook dinner for Fred when he'd come to the house. She stopped Fred from racing and she's a jockey! The door just shut. And then when he died, nobody was invited to the funeral out in Chatsworth where he had a ranch. Bill Self (*TV producer of such series as* Batman, M*A*S*H, Lost in Space, Daniel Boone, *and many others*) who was very close to him found out and went to the funeral and was standing behind a tree watching. He told me.

When there was a tribute to Fred in London at the Palladium, Robyn wouldn't allow any film clips of Fred to be used. Ava put that together. So, Ava can't get the furniture, the things she's entitled to from her.

Can you give us some composites of working with Barbara Stanwyck, Bette Davis and Spencer Tracy?

You know I've been sitting here and trying to figure out who you look like (*Tom*) and it's Art Carney—when he was young.

(Tom) Thanks for at least saying I don't resemble Carney in Harry & Tonto.

(*Laughs*) Natasha, my middle daughter, has just created a fragrance in her mother's name called "Natalie." Natalie did a film with Barbara Stanwyck called *The Bride Wore Boots* (1946). Barbara told me this story. Natalie loved the "Jungle Gardenia" perfume that Barbara wore in the movie, so she gave her a bottle and Natalie wore it all of her life.

Working with Barbara was thrilling (*Wagner and Stanwyck starred in* Titanic *together in 1953*). We fell in love with each other and what an experience for me, a young man, to have the good fortune to be in love with an older woman. I didn't realize it at the time so much, but she was fabulous to me. She was a giving and loving and caring person. I've really been blessed.

After Natalie died, if I didn't have my children, I wouldn't be here. It was such a devastating, horrible time. Then Jill came into my life. If anybody had ever told me that I would have been involved with Jill, I wouldn't have believed them. It was so fortunate that she came into my life and she held me up, was holding my elbow up. I was so raw.

Stefanie Powers was a great contributor to the success of *Hart to Hart*. Nobody wanted her; the network didn't want her. Only Tom Mankiewicz (*director and creative consultant on the series*) and myself said she had to be the one. They finally said, "Don't talk to us anymore about Stefanie Powers, who we want is Natalie Wood." I told them that would never work because nobody would be home for our kids. We would never have had a life. Then they wanted Lindsay Wagner because it would be great to have Wagner/Wagner. I said the girl to play opposite me is Stefanie Powers. We had worked together before and she also had worked with Tom. We kept rejecting people and the shoot date kept getting closer. I just thought she was great and we had chemistry. And that can make up for a lot of things because you can't get the great scripts all the time. It's like one big snowball behind you. But we had fun making the show.

Is it true that you were approached to play James Bond?

Cubby Broccoli (*Albert R. Broccoli, produced many of the Bond films*) was a friend of mine. I gave the eulogy at his funeral and also for his wife, Dana. Cubby was the first agent I ever had. I was thrown out of MGM with him. Cubby took me to MGM with him and we were thrown out because he had a client that Louis B. Mayer was trying to have an affair with and one of the agents was balling her and that went down the line and we were thrown out. I thought it might be the end of my career. He said, "Don't worry." So, yeah, he talked to me about it. I said, "Cubby, James Bond is an Englishman and I'm too much of an American. You got him right here, Roger Moore. He's perfect."

Stanley Donen told us he, like you, admired Cary Grant.

Stanley's not a man I want to talk about. He's the most terrible person I ever met in my life. I raised his two sons. Marion was married to him. Katie's mother, who I married, Marion Marshall, was married to Stanley Donen. He had two sons—Josh and Peter. He absolutely wrote them off. And I raised them. Josh is very, very close to me. Peter died. When Stanley came out here to the funeral, they had a reception. He stayed about 15 minutes and left.

We had a combative interview with him years ago when he lived in Bel Air. The visit kind of went awry.

Stanley used to sleep on Gene Kelly's couch in Gene's house. Gene is responsible for Stanley Donen's career and Stanley pissed on him. All our kids were raised together. And Gene was so wonderful to me when Natalie died. He was at my house right away holding me in his arms. When Gene lost his wife Jeannie Coyne, she was a "dance-in" for Natalie on some of Natalie's movies, we were the only ones at the funeral, Natalie and myself and Jack and Sheila Baker. He didn't open up the funeral to everybody.

Stanley was married to Yvette Mimieux when we interviewed him in the 1980s. She came into the den nude from the shower; didn't know we were there, apparently, and all hell broke loose.

She was nude? Oh my! I would like to have seen that! I worked with her. I couldn't make a move on her because she was going with a guy who was a friend of all of ours and I was also involved with Jill. Yvette is a beautiful woman. I was watching her the other day in an old movie on TCM about Picasso (Picasso Summer *co-starring Albert Finney*). If you get a chance, see it. It's a wonderful movie from 1969. I've had some fun with Albert Finney. We'd had some laughs. We were in Vegas together and in London, knocking around with him and Peter O'Toole. Lots of drinking. Yvette looks so fucking great in that movie; she must've looked great in the nude; it must've knocked you out!

How did you like Milton (Berle)?

Came into the Friar's Club for the interview in a raincoat and an old grey Trilby Fedora. He looked like he could have been selling encyclopedias in 1952.

(*laughs*) How about Debbie Reynolds?

We were the only people in the audience under 70 when we saw her show at her casino in Vegas, which had been the old Paddlewheel.

I got her involved with Steve Wynn up there because she was going to sell the gambling license and if you don't have gambling, you can't make it in Vegas. You got to have gambling. We all sat down and saw her show and at the end of it, she asked his advice. And Steve told her not to sell it. Well, she sold it. And the location was very bad for that hotel/casino—too far off the Strip. Best food in America is in Vegas.

(Publicist enters asking if everything is OK. The interview had lasted a couple of hours by then.)

(*Wagner, in a stentorian, actorly baritone*) This is absolutely the worst interview I've ever been subjected to.

* * *

What did we ourselves think of the longest, dishiest interview we ever conducted; one entirely about the "Old Hollywood" we cherished every bit as much as Wagner did; a give-and-take that never seemed to stay on point (but was immersive nonetheless) and instead eddied unpredictably along like the lazy loops and channels of an ancient river?

In a word, *terrific!*

Benchwarmer

Eli Wallach

In 2014, two decades after we met him, Eli Wallach, one of the most venerable character actors that ever ping-ponged between Broadway and Hollywood, passed away at the age of 98. Although he studied at the Actors Studio in New York City and won a Tony Award in 1951 (in his Broadway debut, no less) in Tennessee Williams' *The Rose Tattoo*, Wallach will probably be best remembered for scintillating performances in a clutch of movies, including *The Misfits* with Marilyn Monroe, *Baby Doll*, *The Magnificent Seven* and the iconic spaghetti western *The Good, the Bad and the Ugly* opposite Clint Eastwood.

"You know," he told us, "when I played Mexicans in those westerns, I wore gold teeth which I clipped onto my real teeth. I'd smile and the light would hit them and I'd upstage Clint every time!"

Wallach said that he learned to ride horses while attending college in Texas and it probably contributed to why he was cast so often as a bandit in movies. As for being cast so many times as a *Mexican* bandit, "I'm a Jew from Red Hook, Brooklyn, so go figure," he laughed. "I lived in a sea of Catholics. I was the only Jew in the area. When I did my first western, *The Magnificent Seven*, I said, 'You hear about bandits robbing banks and holding up trains but you never see what they do with the money.' So I figured I'd wear a red silk shirt and put two teeth in gold caps, have a beautiful saddle and a great horse and everyone will say, 'Jesus, that's a rich bandit!' So that's the way I did it and I carried it over into *The Good, the Bad and the Ugly*."

Our encounter with Wallach was—in its own way—as quintessentially New York as he was. He insisted that we meet at a favorite park bench off Riverside Drive near where he lived so he could look west over the Hudson River to New Jersey and contemplate (like Jack Kerouac did at the end of *On the Road*) the great bulge of America that lay beyond it.

Real New Yorkers don't look like the well-dressed Jean-Paul Gaultier mannequins you see in movies like *Wall Street*. In fact, they usually come across slightly disheveled as if they just spent the morning rolling around on the grass of the Sheep's Meadow in Central Park with their pet Malamute. Wallach, with a cane to steady himself and wearing a ratty old raincoat and dirty sneakers, instantly betrayed his provenance. In fact, sitting with him was like playing a scene from Edward Albee's *Zoo Story*, but without all the bloodletting.

"I feel like we're away from being wiretapped and all that shit," Wallach said, easing himself down onto the wooden slats of the bench which was positioned on the long, narrow shoulder of greenery that abuts the Drive and stretches from 72nd Street to the George Washington Bridge on Manhattan's Upper West Side. "I've had a wonderful career," he said, "but I'm proudest of the work I've done with my wife, Anne (Wallach was married to actress Anne Jackson for 66 years). "In fact, that's why I picked this spot; it's within sight of our apartment and my wife can keep an eye on me." We all chuckled at another real New Yorker tell: eternal vigilance in any situation.

The night before, we had seen Wallach perform in what turned out to be his last Broadway play, *The Flowering Peach*, a revival of a Clifford Odets drama which itself was a modern take on the Biblical Noah's Ark story. Wallach played Noah and Jackson played Noah's wife, Esther.

It struck us as that in the play, at age 78, Wallach moved with a kind of balletic delicacy that we also remembered from some of his films (arm out-stretched with fingers splayed like he was ready to stiff-arm a tackler—but gracefully) and which seemed slightly incongruous given his rodential face and small build. Tom even pinpointed a scene in a movie that reminded him of that; near the end of *The Good, the Bad and the Ugly* when Wallach—arm gingerly outstretched—runs in circles around the graveyard tombstones with the camera fixed on him in a dizzying 360-degree pan that can cause seizures.

"I studied with Martha Graham," Wallach said, putting the mystery to rest. "I use a Graham movement at one place in the play and no one knows where it is. I put it in as a tribute to her."

Wallach said that he also embedded into his performance a "salute" to his father (a teacup against the side of his head). "A lot of the character is based on his rigidity, stiffness and anger—it's all there," he said. But for Wallach, such characterization is all part of a larger piece. "The biggest challenge for an actor is to get a role and work on it," he said. "To fix it, to play it. Play it nightly. Each audience is different. That's what a magician does. He knows the trick and to bond with an audience of 4,500 people each night is a wonderful thing. You make a movie and two years later actors are edited and you have to churn up your reaction and say: 'Oh yes, I remember that, but it's different.'"

According to Wallach, movies are a difficult medium but mechanical, and that's the rub. "If you yawn in one place, they can take it and put it somewhere else so it has little to do with the actor. It's like doing a crossword puzzle in your head. You spend two days coming in a door saying: 'Hello, Jack!'" (Wallach repeated the phrase rapidly about six times, all with different inflections, in what amounted to a keen display of his Method Acting acuity.)

Wallach played a Sicilian cotton gin operator named Silva Vacarro in first movie, *Baby Doll* (1956) but realized there was a hefty penalty to be paid by actors that become too associated with a role—especially in television. "Look at Peter Falk and *Columbo*," Wallach said. "You become very wealthy, but you pay a penalty. I like the actor who can change colors. I was a jewel thief for Disney. I was a half-breed in Cambodia. I've played Mexican bandits and Mafia godfathers. But movies today … every word is fuck, fuck, fuck and humping. In my day, if a man was in bed with a woman, one leg had to be on the floor, and that takes a bit of acrobatics."

Despite Wallach's cautionary tale about aligning oneself too heavily with a single role, he was wistful about a particular part he played just once on TV. "Guess which role I get the most fan mail of anything I've ever done?" he asked.

"Haven't a clue," we said.

"It was for 'Mr. Freeze' on the old *Batman* TV series," Wallach said. "I got $350, I think, for a half-hour show 35 years ago. Schwarzenegger signed to do the same character and got $22 million. My wife said I should start lifting weights."

By his own count, and apart from his wife, Wallach played opposite some "great ladies," among them, Jeanne Moreau, Audrey Hepburn, Whoopi Goldberg, Carole Baker and Marilyn Monroe in her last movie, *The Misfits* (1961). "Marilyn was wonderful in the movie but her marriage to Arthur Miller was breaking up and it was difficult," Wallach said. "I love John Huston (the director). He was a remarkable man with X-ray eyes. He knew all the defenses a person builds up around himself, the cocoon they put themselves into, and he could see it. The day after we finished shooting, Clark Gable had a heart attack. President Eisenhower who had suffered a heart attack called Gable and said: 'Don't worry about it.' Ten days later Gable had another one and he went out. Marilyn was just devastated by his death and she tried one more movie after that (*Something's Got to Give*)."

At the time of our sit-down, Wallach said he was putting together notes for a memoir of sorts. "Mine wouldn't be an autobiography," he said. "David Niven wrote a book called *The Moon's a Balloon* which was full of anecdotes about the movies. I could do two chapters on my experiences with horses and doing Italian movies which are funny and touching and irritating."

A Method Actor from the ground up, Wallach said that he wasn't interested in penning a tell-all because those kinds of distinctions hardly mattered to him—it was, he said, always about the work. "That's the way the book will be," he said, "rather than who I slept with or where I traveled. I'm interested in the craft and joy of creating characters." In 2006, Wallach published the book that he envisioned, entitled: *The Good, the Bad, and Me: In My Anecdotage*.

As we gazed across the Hudson at the sparse river traffic (a couple of small luxury craft and a Circle Line sightseeing boat packed with tourists) Wallach mused about Frank Sinatra who had passed away recently. In 1953, Wallach had accepted the role of Angelo Maggio in *From Here to Eternity* but then turned it down because he had agreed to appear in Elia Kazan's Broadway production of *Camino Real*. Sinatra, whose acting career had tanked, got the part (for a reputed salary of $20,000) and won the Best Supporting Actor Oscar for his performance adding luster to his legendary comeback story.

"We were born five days apart, two miles apart—right across this river from each other," Wallach said. "Frank took an actor's adjustment to the lyrics he sang. A singer sings things, but an actor does something to it. When he sang: 'Its quarter to three,' he's not only singing, he's sitting in a bar thinking, 'What did I do wrong? Where the hell is she?' Barbra Streisand's another one. I knew her when she was 17. She sang 'Happy Days are Here Again' as though her mother just died."

Wallach then craned his head 90 degrees, looked over his shoulder at the apartment building and said: "I gotta go."

"Got to rest up before tonight's performance, huh?" Tom asked.

"Not that," Wallach said. "My wife's giving me the *malocchio*. I can see it from here." With that, he sprang to his feet in a seamless move that would've startled Martha Graham and left.

We quickly scanned the apartment windows that looked down on the bench but couldn't make out anyone, much less Anne Jackson. We thought maybe Wallach learned that Italian phrase—"evil eye"—from Sinatra or as a boy during his Brooklyn days awash in the "sea of Catholics," but maybe not. At any rate, it was a nifty exit line.

A Friend of Dorothy

Charles Walters

In describing the film work of director Charles Walters, *Village Voice* film critic, Andrew Sarris, wrote, "If the word 'nice' could be defined with any precision, it would apply to most of his films." That statement, as unadorned as it is straightforward, is deceptively insightful; for Walters directed some of the most entertaining musical and light comedy films Hollywood ever produced. And yet, perhaps because Walters never had a signature style like Vincente Minnelli, he's never been on anyone's short list of the most influential or even memorable directors.

Walters, who passed away from mesothelioma in 1982, was a native Californian born in Pasadena in 1911. Fresh out of high school and with no formal dance training, he journeyed to New York City in quest of stardom. During the 1930s and early '40s Walters enjoyed great success on the musical comedy stage as both a performer and choreographer. He appeared in such shows as *Jubilee*, in which he introduced the Cole Porter standard, "Begin the Beguine," and *Du Barry Was a Lady*, in which he starred with Betty Grable.

But Walters' most closely-held ambition was to someday return home to California and replace George Murphy, whom he considered to be a poor dancer, in film roles. That goal was partially realized in 1943 when Walters was asked to choreograph a number for the film version of *Du Barry*. Although he never replaced Murphy, Walters did land a long-term contract at MGM and for the next 22 years would mainly work under the auspices of producer Arthur Freed. The Freed Unit, as it came to be known, consisted of the finest musical talent in the world.

After performing choreographic chores, most notably for *Meet Me in St. Louis*, and occasional on screen dancing roles with Judy Garland, Walters graduated to full directorial status in 1947 when he helmed *Good News*. For the next 18 years Walters maintained a remarkably high standard directing such musicals as *Easter Parade, Summer Stock, The Barkleys of Broadway, Lili, The Tender Trap, High Society, Jumbo* and *The Unsinkable Molly Brown*.

Although not a gifted colorist like Minnelli, Walters' did have a strong suit when it came to directing musicals. As a dancer/choreographer himself, Walters innately knew how to frame a number—especially a dance—for maximum impact and fluidity. For example, in "Dig-Dig-Dig for Your Dinner" from *Summer Stock*, Walters' camera tracks Gene Kelly and Phil Silvers around a long dining table as they sing the song. When Kelly continues on alone, gyrating around the table a second time, the camera shadows his every spin providing an ideal POV whenever Kelly makes a choreographic flourish. At one point, Kelly, sitting on Silvers' lap, is bucked off and lurches in a full body extension to a wall on an emphatic beat in the music and to a quick and faultless camera cut. But instead of being jarring, the moment is seamless. Before the number has even begun in earnest, the audience has been primed by the buildup for Kelly's explosive tap dance that follows.

The wonder is; Walters achieved that intricate effect routinely in dozens of numbers in different films over many years. Nice, indeed!

The '60s sounded the death knell for original Hollywood musicals and Walters suffered the same fate of many of his MGM colleagues. Projects seemed to evaporate over time and then came to an abrupt halt, except for scattered directorial chores on a few television shows.

We interviewed Walters in 1980 in his Malibu condominium. At that time, he was teaching students at the University of Southern California a course called "Film Style Analysis—The Work of Director Charles Walters." Walters seemed to epitomize the laid-back, California beach lifestyle, greeting us at his door wearing a bathrobe, tinted shades and flip-flop sandals. A Marlboro was never far from Walters's reach and between drags he quaffed a prodigious amount of decaffeinated coffee from an apparently bottomless pot. Walters introduced us to his partner Joe, a young guy with similarly tinted sunglasses and a square-shaped handlebar mustache that drooped down the sides of his chin like a bristly lawn wicket. "Chuck's choreographing an act for me that I hope to take to Vegas," he volunteered.

Walters told us that he was in the process of adopting Joe (they had been together for more than a decade), a legal gambit that many gay couples used then to circumvent estate inheritance laws that denied tax-free assets being passed along to a surviving spouse who wasn't part of a heterosexual union.

Our discussion with Walters covered his career, from Broadway up to the present with a special emphasis on his professional and personal relationship with Judy Garland that began when Walters worked on the Garland film, *Girl Crazy*, in 1943. In that sense, "Chuck," as he insisted on being called, was, both literally and figuratively, "a friend of Dorothy."

* * *

Fantle & Johnson: *It has often been said that to crack the entertainment industry you have to be at the right place at the right time. Was that true in your case?*

Walters: It couldn't be truer. Being at the right place at the right time and having what is needed at the time. As for instance, the greatest dancer in New York at my time was Paul Draper, a classical tap dancer. My dance partner and I were appearing in a Theater Guild musical called *Parade*. The scuttlebutt around town at that time was that Sam Harris, Cole Porter and Moss Hart (the biggest names in New York) were on a Caribbean cruise writing a new show to be called *Jubilee*. People were guessing, of course, that Paul Draper would get one of the lead roles. I don't know whether you know this, but the chorus kids get *all* the dirt. All of a sudden, while I was in *Parade*, rumors started that Sam Harris, Monty Woolley, Cole Porter and Moss Hart were out front to see me. Finally, when I leave the stage door there'd be agents and they'd say, "Chuck, sign with me. I think I can get you an audition for *Jubilee*." Forget it. To me, who could compete with the elegance of Paul Draper? Well to make a long story short, they found out that Draper stuttered. Now that was a real left fielder for them. Now they've got to look around for a juvenile. I had never sung and I had never acted. Now I'm called in to read for Monty Woolley. If you remember Monty Woolley in pictures, he had a beard and was very pompous and ominous. So into a back office we go and I read for him. He came out and said, "All right." That's how I got *Jubilee*. But I told them I couldn't break with my partner, we were doing very well. So they said, "We'll give her a part in the second act, but we can't pay any more." So I split my salary with her.

Your first job at MGM and first association with the Freed Unit was in Du Barry Was a Lady?

Du Barry was the last show I was in as a performer and my first Freed film. Again, it's being in the right place at the right time. My manager-agent-best friend and I were living together in my house and he also handled Gene Kelly. Kelly had just done *For Me and my Gal*. He called our agent and said, "Is Bob Alton (a choreographer) available? I cannot stand Seymour Felix (another choreographer). I just can't work with this guy again. And he's scheduled to do my next picture, *Du Barry,* with Lucille Ball." Well, my agent told Kelly that he just signed Felix for *Ziegfeld Follies*. And Kelly said, "Geez, is Charlie Walters around?" Gene's the only person in the world who ever called me Charlie. So Kelly asked me to do this number for him and I was signed up for four weeks. I'll show you my contract; it's on an inter-office communication. Well, Kelly liked the number I did so they took another number away from Felix, gave me that; took another number away, and I ended up doing the picture. They liked the picture so they put me under long-term contract. I was there 22 years, 52 weeks a year.

The number you were originally signed to choreograph was to the Cole Porter song, Do I Love You?

That was the number I was signed to stage. For some strange reason I asked for a script. "What do you need a script for, you're just going to do solo staging for Kelly?" they asked. I might have been curious, having been in the Broadway show. I might have been curious what they did with it and if Kelly was playing my part or another part … that might have been it! I never thought of that.

Anyway, it happened that Kelly had a scene in Lucy's dressing room before the number, and then he left the dressing room and jumped on stage. I thought, gee, wouldn't it be nice if we could start the number in her room with a look of encouragement from her and continue the number out of the dressing room and up on stage. Now he's got a motivation to be up and gay and bright. So I told the producer—Arthur Freed—my idea and he just looked at me. I thought, oh Jesus, I really bombed! Well, he said, "Chuck, that's the way directors think. That's very good. I like it."

Arthur was the kind of man who never forgot. The seed was planted in his mind that someday I would be a director.

How did you land your first directorial assignment, the 1920s college campus musical, Good News?

I was very big in dramatics, if you can imagine, at Anaheim High School. The senior class play was to be of my choice. We've never done a musical and *Good News* was very popular at the time. So I said, let's do *Good News*. We got the high school orchestra and then we found out that we couldn't afford the rights. So we used the same storyline, but different popular music.

Later on, at MGM, we were running dailies of "Madame Crematon" (a number Walters staged for *Ziegfeld Follies*), and Arthur Freed, who was always very non sequitur, said nothing. I looked at him to see what he thought and he said, 'I bought a new property today, *Good News*.' It was like somebody had put a firecracker under me. He said, 'Chuck, that might be a good first picture for you."

*You brought your first three pictures (*Good News, Easter Parade *and* The Barkleys of Broadway*) in under budget. How did you accomplish it and what kind of impression did it make on the studio brass?*

I had been a dance director for four years and it was only the last year that I was able to cut and shoot my own numbers. Before that time, I would stage a number, and the director would take it and shoot it his way. When I finally got to shoot my own numbers, I would film them so they couldn't be chopped. I found that I was automatically staging for cutting. Then, when I got into directing, I would shoot only what I wanted, so all the cutter could do was cut off the leader and glue them together. I wanted to protect what I visualized.

What was it like working with Judy Garland and Vincente Minnelli (who directed) on Meet Me in St. Louis?

Oh, that was a lovely experience. The only funny thing about that was I thought Ralph Blane and Hugh Martin had written an original score. I thought, what the hell is this "Skip to My Lou?" I couldn't get any handle on how to stage it. One evening I had my parents over for dinner, and I told them there was one number in the picture I didn't know what the hell to do with. Well they pounced on it and started singing "Skip to My Lou." That song was around when they were kids. So my square, untheatrical parents helped me choreograph the number.

Vincente Minnelli is given directorial credit for Gigi, *but didn't you do much of the filming?*

How did you know I did things on *Gigi*? I never said anything. I never let the cat out of the bag. Wow! I did all the retakes and shot a lot of the numbers like "The Night They Invented Champagne" and Louis Jourdan doing "Gigi." As a matter of fact, I redid the scene where he comes in to propose to her. I also reshot "She's Not Thinking of Me." I couldn't think of how to tag it, how to get Louis Jourdan so annoyed at Eva Gabor without her having done anything to him. That's why I had him pour champagne down her front in frustration which was a big laugh. *Gigi* was one of the toughest things I've ever done because I had to blend the studio footage into the Paris backgrounds. Lerner and

Loewe (the composers) wanted to send me a flowered horseshoe, but they were afraid it would get back to Vincente, which wouldn't be very nice.

Your choreographic style seemed to have, for lack of a better term, a kind of elan or sophistication. How would you appraise your style?
      Pure bastard.

You directed Astaire and Rogers in their last film together, The Barkleys of Broadway. *What was your reaction when you were given this assignment, they were childhood idols of yours, we're guessing?*
      Once I found out that Astaire was going to be in it, my knees got weak because he was my hero. So when you say sophistication—I loved the way he danced, the way he walked, his entire style. I never copied a step, but just his whole attitude was wonderful. I think a lot of that rubbed off on me.

Was Ginger Rogers a good dancer?
      No. She could do the steps, but she was such a good actress you didn't care.

How about Judy Garland?
      Good faker.

You always seemed to bring out the best in Judy's dancing.
      The interesting thing about Judy was that she was so insecure, except to get up and sing. For instance, we were doing a number that she was scared to death of. I don't know how I thought of it, but one day I said, "Judy who's your favorite dancer?" And she said, Renee DeMarco, who was part of a famous dance team. I told her, "From now on, whenever we rehearse, you're Renee DeMarco." From then on she was just perfect. Now if you remember "Get Happy" (from *Summer Stock*), I told her to be Lena Horne. This got Judy away from "me dancing" and she felt Lena. It worked beautifully.

We've read that you and Gene Kelly literally carried Judy through Summer Stock, *which was her last picture at MGM before the studio cancelled her contract and let her go.*
      That's true. The bets around the studio lot were that we wouldn't finish it. So that's an encouraging note on which to go to work every morning. I would look at the dailies and say, "How dare this look like we're having fun!" How dare it when we were just sweating blood. I can't stand watching *Summer Stock*. I was on nothing but coffee and cigarettes during the filming. I ended up getting an ulcer on the film.

What was your role in Judy's New York stage triumphs in the early '50s?
      I staged both of Judy's Palace shows. It was my idea to give them more than just a personal appearance, like: "Here I am, little Judy Garland." We had a wealth of musical material to draw upon and Judy loved the idea of having production numbers.

What do you think of the Garland cultists, which are legion out there?
      Well, she couldn't figure it out, so I don't know how the hell I can. I'll tell you one interesting story about her opening night at the Palace. The impact of opening night hadn't hit us yet. We were at the Plaza before the opening having a steak sandwich and martinis; the martinis came first. We were both a little uptight so we just picked at the steak. And I had to go on that night and do the tramp number with Judy ("A Couple of Swells" which Judy had performed with Fred Astaire in *Easter Parade*). I thought this was very unfair. I hadn't been on the stage for 10 years and the Palace meant something

to me. So that was an excuse for another martini. Anyway, we got a cab and when we got to the little pie-wedge traffic island at Broadway and Seventh Avenue—all we saw were people jammed on the pie. The cabby said, "I don't know if we can get any farther, they have the fuckin' street blocked off." I asked him what was happening. "Garland's opening at the Palace tonight." It was like somebody punched us in the gut. Anyway, the show was absolutely fantastic. After the show she was getting dressed in a lovely evening gown to go to a big party, which incidentally was for me. Somebody mentioned to us that the people were still standing out in the pie. Judy said, "I don't believe it. What do they want?" "They just want to see you," somebody said. "Well shit," said Judy. "I'm going out the front door instead of the stage exit. If they want to see me, they're going to see me." Well, the lobby was filled, as was the pie. As we walked through this sea of humanity—not a word! She's getting into the limousine and says, "What the hell is this, nobody's saying a goddamn word?" A silent tribute… I can't tell that without choking up.

What in your opinion caused the demise of the Hollywood musical?

Money; that's my guess. It just got too expensive. In those days at MGM we had a stock company of dancers and other musical talents.

What do you think of today's films and filmmakers?

I think that's why I'm not working today. Most of them (the films) I don't understand after I've seen them, let alone read a script and say, I'll do it.

Do you have a favorite and least favorite among the 21 films you directed?

I decided the other day that I think *Jumbo* is my favorite because I had done so many intimate and small comedies and musicals. To get a chance at a "biggie" was a thrill. My least favorite was *The Belle of New York* (a 1952 musical that starred Fred Astaire and Vera-Ellen). I hate it. I just hate it. It was like putting a gun to your head every day. I couldn't stand Vera-Ellen. I would talk to her about a scene and she'd be doing pliés. That's the kind of concentration you got.

What do you tell your students at USC about the art of musical film direction?

When I started there was no such thing as a school or a book. It had to be on a gut level. For openers I tell the kids, learn all you can, then throw the book over your shoulder and go from your guts. It's the same with you and writing. There is only so much you can learn, then it's up to you—your blood and guts.

Lullabies and Nightmares

Harry Warren

If compelled to pick the most underrated composer of film musicals, a strong case could be made for Tin Pan Alley tunesmith Harry Warren. He was 87, retired and living in a mansion just off Sunset Boulevard with what could have been the longest driveway in Beverly Hills when we met him in August 1980. At the time, Warren was enjoying something of a late-era career resurgence thanks to a few ditties he composed nearly half a century before.

Unfortunately, the newfound popularity of his songs, perhaps, had come too little and too late to counterbalance a cantankerous personality that was the result of professional resentments nurtured over many years. Harry Warren, you see, was a world-class curmudgeon.

"I guess I wasn't newsworthy," he told us leaning heavily on his cane. "In the first place, the average person that you see advertised a lot wants to have his name known. He's got what they call *chutzpah*, which I've never had. I'm very shy. I don't like to play piano in front of a fellow that plays well. It gives me an inferiority complex."

In 1933, along with lyricist Al Dubin, Warren wrote the score for the film that would revolutionize the Hollywood musical, *42nd Street*. In 1980, producer David Merrick and director-choreographer Gower Champion combined forces to recreate the simplistic backstage plot for the Broadway stage which subsequently enjoyed unparalleled success at the Winter Garden Theater. The show's popularity was due in large part to such Warren standards as "Lullaby of Broadway," "Shuffle Off to Buffalo," "We're in the Money," and, of course, the title song.

"You know that show is amazing," Warren said. "My wife went to New York to see it; I couldn't go. She said as soon as the play started, the audience jumped up at every number. It's fantastic. But you'd be surprised; I get more fan mail from England than I do from the U.S. I can go to London, make a personal appearance and be a big shot."

Dressed in slacks hitched up to his mid-section with a white belt, white dress shirt, and wearing loafers, Warren looked like he might have just come from a gin-rummy tournament at a Sun City recreation center. His beak nose and piercing eyes (what we could see of them from behind his tinted sunglasses) gave Warren the countenance of a barn owl scrutinizing a field mouse, only Warren's head wasn't on a

No wrong notes

swivel. On the other hand, it was all we could do to keep our own heads from rotating a complete 360 degrees at some of the *infamnia* he occasionally spouted or what we heard later from his friends.

We followed him past a tennis court that Warren said Gene Kelly (then 68) "borrowed" from time to time to a detached bungalow located at the back of his estate. It was in this sunny aerie that Warren listened to music, watched TV and played the piano. His three Best Song Oscars sat on a window ledge, rays glinting off the heads and shoulders of the statues and radiating miniature sundogs on the walls opposite. Warren was nominated for the Academy Award for Best Song 11 times during his career and won for "Lullaby of Broadway," "You'll Never Know" and "On the Atchison, Topeka and the Santa Fe." Stacked on bookshelves were videocassettes of all Warren's movies. The bungalow, we had learned, also acted as a kind of refuge for Warren. According to Nick Perito, a close friend of Warrens who served as Perry Como's longtime conductor/arranger, it was the only place Warren could escape the "Teutonic" henpecking of his wife Josephine whom he had married in 1917.

"She could never identify with Harry's Italian ethnicity and it bothered him," Perito told us. "He really preferred the company of boys such as myself and other composers like Gene DePaul and Johnny Mercer."

Perito also revealed that the octogenarian Warren used his bungalow hideaway as a place to view adult entertainment recalling for us a time when he brought his boss, Como, over for a surprise visit that soon devolved into a mini-stag party. "Harry was overjoyed to see Perry and quickly sat him down to view a video," Perito said. "It was the first time Perry had ever seen an adult video and he was intrigued enough to watch. All of a sudden, Harry's wife and some other woman walked into the bungalow—they had somehow heard that Perry was there. Without missing a beat, Harry flicked the VCR off and *Howdy Doody* appeared on the TV screen. As soon as he ushered the ladies out, the video resumed. That was cantankerous Harry."

But Warren's "loner" penchant for privacy also had a downside and may be the prime militating factor that has consigned him to the second tier of artists who composed the Great American Songbook. "Harry was a very low-key individual and I don't know why he's so obscure in the public's mind," singer Alice Faye told us from Rancho Mirage, California, when we phoned for her assessment of the songwriter. Faye was a prime interpreter of Warren's tunes. In 1943, she introduced the Oscar-winning standard "You'll Never Know" from the musical *Hello, Frisco, Hello*. It became her signature song and the sheet music alone sold over one million copies. "I was fortunate to be at the right studio (Twentieth Century–Fox) to sing his music. I'll always remember him and I can't say that about all the people with whom I've worked."

Warren had the distinction from 1935–1950 of having had more top-ten songs on the radio program *Your Hit Parade* than any other composer, including Irving Berlin, Cole Porter and Richard Rodgers. His list of hits is endless; everything from sultry Academy Award–winning ballads ("You'll Never Know"), to up-tempo dance numbers ("I Only Have Eyes for You," "Chattanooga Choo Choo") to goofy novelty songs ("Jeepers Creepers"). Other hits include "September in the Rain," "Serenade in Blue," "On the Atchison, Topeka and the Santa Fe" and Dean Martin's signature Neapolitan crowd-pleaser, "That's Amore," to name just a few.

And Warren's contribution to the Hollywood musical goes much further than *42nd Street*. His music can be heard in over 60 films that were made between 1933 and 1961.

As the first major American songwriter to write primarily for the movies, Warren has been given the encomium: "Mr. Hollywood Musical," and rightfully so. He was the only composer who conquered all four major Hollywood studios—Warner Brothers, Twentieth Century–Fox, Metro-Goldwyn-Mayer and Paramount. Indeed, Warren's music (if not the man himself) has become part of the American pop cultural fabric and stands as a historical link to major events of the 20th century, notably the Great Depression and World War II.

"I never took part in any Hollywood nightlife in those days, I was too busy working," Warren said. "My wife used to ball me out all the time because we couldn't go anyplace. I don't know any other songwriter that worked as much as I did. I worked for something like 24 years in the studios."

"Harry Warren was an absolute giant," singer Mel Tormé told us from New York. "He's one of the great songwriter gods to me. I'd lump him with (Jerome) Kern, Rodgers and (Lorenz) Hart, Gershwin, Porter and Berlin. Warren stands head and shoulders with each of them." Torme compared Warren to Ira Gershwin, whose fame was eclipsed by his older, more celebrated brother George. "Warren was the alter ego of Ira, who stayed in the background," he said. "There was a colorless aspect to Harry that transcended him getting the kind of due he deserves."

Born Salvatore Antonio Guaragna on Christmas Eve, 1893, in Brooklyn, Warren (the youngest of 11 children) recollected starting to play the piano around age 10 but said he never had a single lesson and he took pains to discount his rare, untutored gift. "I think you're just endowed that way, born that way. I think it's a God-given gift. That's the only excuse I can give you," he told us. To hear Warren tell it, before he achieved success with his first published song "Rose of the Rio Grande" in 1922, he did just about everything including playing the snare drum in a band, acting in silent films and even working in a circus.

Warren's first real musical triumphs came at Warner Brothers, where he and Al Dubin wrote most of the music for the Busby Berkeley extravaganzas. Warren recalled for us one of the more humorous days at Warners. "One time we were doing a number for Berkeley and he told the entire set that he was waiting for me. I was holding him up. And there was a Mexican number called 'Muchacha' which had guys on horseback riding on a treadmill. Anyhow, they called me at nine in the morning. In those days I used to get up at noon. So I got dressed and rushed over there.

"I had a piano player who was sort of a musical secretary," Warren continued. "I said to him, 'I'm going to fake something. Try to remember what I'm going to play.' So there's Jack Warner and everybody, about 100 girls and a piano. And they asked me, 'Where's the rest of the number?' So I sat down at the piano and faked it. And they thought it was great."

Of the four studios in which he toiled, Warren said Warner Brothers provided the worst working atmosphere. "The studio executives knew nothing about musicals. How could they? They didn't have any experience in music. Some people are still around attempting to make musicals but know nothing about it."

A career pinnacle was achieved in 1944 when Warren signed a long-term contract with MGM—the acknowledged masters of movie musicals. "My favorite musicals—best work—were all at Metro but it never showed," he said. "I didn't like the other pictures at all. I didn't like the scripts. There was nothing to them. I like a story script where you can write something to it. At Metro, nobody bothered you. When I worked for Arthur Freed, you didn't even know you were working."

But there is a bittersweet coda to Warren's songwriting career at MGM. Two of his best musical scores at Metro—*The Barkleys of Broadway* noted for Fred Astaire and Ginger Rogers' last screen pairing and *Summer Stock* which co-starred Gene Kelly and Judy Garland in her last film for MGM—were sullied by the interpolation of other composers' music into Warren's complete scores, something that is anathema to any songwriter. It was a wound Warren was still smarting from 30 years later.

"Arthur Freed, the producer of *Barkleys*, played a dirty trick on me on that picture," Warren said. "He inserted George and Ira Gershwin's 'They Can't Take That Away from Me' for Fred and Ginger's reunion dance when they should have reprised my 'You'd be Hard to Replace.' I was so mad at him I couldn't see straight. The same thing happened on *Summer Stock*. Producer Joe Pasternak who was nothing more than a singing waiter, added 'Get Happy' by Arlen and Koehler for Judy. After I write a whole picture, they inject someone else's song; it's not fair. But, hey, they don't give a damn."

In an effort to ameliorate the situation and lessen the sting of Warren's still palpable disappointment, we mentioned that *Barkleys* contained to our mind one of the best tap duets Astaire ever danced, with Ginger, to Warren's tune, "Bouncin' the Blues."

"Funny, I wrote a tune and took it over to Fred and he rehearsed with it," Warren said. "He had a huge mirror and a piano player; that was all. I brought the tune over and Fred said it sounded pretty good. The next day he called me up—Fred was so apologetic all the time, not like Gene—and asked, 'Do you think you can write me another tune? This one doesn't seem to work out so well.' I said, 'Sure, Fred.' And that's how I came up with 'Bouncin' the Blues.'"

Warren deferred telling us which one of his films contained his favorite score. But he did imply that it was the seldom seen and much neglected 1948 MGM film *Summer Holiday*—the musical version of Eugene O'Neill's play, *Ah, Wilderness!* "I was very fond of that film. I think it's the best thing I ever did at Metro. The script to *Ah, Wilderness!* lent itself so nicely to music. It just flowed. You could write music to every word. I think it will be rediscovered," Warren said. "As for a favorite tune, I can't answer that right now. It's like asking a guy which of his 10 kids he prefers most. They are all my kids."

During his years in Hollywood, Warren wrote music for many of the film industry's biggest musical stars. We asked for descriptions of some of his contemporaries and Warren, succinctly, ticked down our roster:

Dick Powell: "He was a wonderful guy. I never had any trouble with Dick. You know, sometimes you have trouble with singers in a picture who don't like what you write for them. I never had trouble with any actors."

Al Jolson: "He was a little troublesome. He was somewhat of an egotist, but he was the greatest entertainer of his era—a superstar."

Ruby Keeler: "She was a nice gal."

Carmen Miranda: "After I wrote the 'The Lady in the Tutti Frutti Hat' for her, she wanted to know how I could write Brazilian tunes. I told her they weren't Brazilian tunes, only the beat was Brazilian."

Busby Berkeley: "Another egotistical guy. Some guys are crazy or semi-crazy; we have musicians like that, they are overactive on everything. You see, a choreographer can't do anything until he gets the material—the songs. He can't stage a number without a song; you have to write a song for him first. But Berkeley thought he was doing the whole thing by himself."

Jerome Kern: Well, I loved Jerome Kern. Richard Rodgers on the other hand was a great composer but he wasn't a nice fellow.

Glenn Miller: Oh, wonderful Glenn. Of course I knew him before he had a band.

Fred Astaire: "I would say that he really wasn't a vocal singer, but he could put a song over without any effort. He had great style. There was something very gracious about the way he sang. You know another thing about Fred, I wrote 'I Wanna Be a Dancin' Man' for him for the film *The Belle of New York*, but he never performed that song outside of the film. Fred had a TV show at one time and never performed the song. Maybe he thought people would think he was calling too much attention to himself. I don't know."

Gene Kelly: "Gene was a little different than Fred. The difference between them was night and day. Gene's voice was a bit brassier."

Judy Garland: "Judy was just fine. We never had any trouble with her."

Bing Crosby: "I like Bing, but he was kind of a distant guy. The only picture I ever did with him was called *Just for You*. I think Leo Robin and I wrote about 10 or 12 songs for that picture. He came into a little rehearsal room we had—a piano room. We played him the songs; he said 'fine' and walked out."

Jerry Lewis: "I wasn't happy working with Jerry Lewis. I watch his telethon just to see if he's still as crass as he used to be. He was a pain in the ass!"

Although Warren never gained a large measure of personal fame (like Irving Berlin) from his songs, the awards he won (three coveted Oscars) didn't impress him; in fact, he seemed to have unjustified contempt for them. "I only went to receive the first one for 'Lullaby of Broadway.' Now I use them as doorstops. I'm not proud of them," he sniffed. "I was in Palm Springs when I won my third and I told Harold Arlen 'You're two Oscars behind me.' I quit the Academy."

By the end of the '50s film musicals were on the wane, as were requests for Warren's services. "They retired me. I never got a call from a studio anymore," Warren said. "They said I made too much money. They never even asked me how much I wanted. Well, nobody is making musicals anymore. If they do it's because they know they can make their money back on album sales. I don't know why people buy these albums. I wouldn't be caught with one of them."

Warren once opined that he thought they bombed the wrong Berlin in WWII—he meant Irving, but he reserved his greatest rancor for contemporary music. When we mentioned that the Beatles, Elvis, and the advent of rock 'n' roll were partially responsible for the demise of musical films, Warren launched into a sermonette that seemed to rise with his gorge. "I can't figure out why the Beatles were such a sensation. Nobody has ever been able to explain that to me. They started all that ragged clothes look, too. My wife just came back from New York and told me that people are walking around in the worst looking clothes. Everybody looks like a tramp comedian. They don't dress for the theater anymore."

Although he died at the age of 87, the year after we visited him, Warren lived long enough to enjoy the dubious honor of seeing "Chattanooga Choo Choo" go disco. "What can you do?" he asked. "If they buy it you can make some money on it. You see we have funny laws in this country. Copyright laws are supposed to give you a monopoly on your own material. But once a company makes a record you have to let every other company make a record. So naturally it's no monopoly at all. I've heard records of my songs that I thought were horrible, but you can't stop them."

Harry Warren assiduously avoided the show business limelight, preferring to occasionally tinker at the keyboard if a melody came to mind. He said his greatest pleasure came from listening to the symphonic music of Puccini, Verdi, Rachmaninoff and Tchaikovsky. "I'm getting so I don't want to go out to eat anymore," Warren said as we made ready to leave. "For my age I look pretty good, but I'm old. I should be dead, really."

When he did pass away, several notes were etched on Warren's tombstone from a song he wrote and they are as ironic an epitaph as you're ever likely to see from a man who's been called the greatest forgotten songwriter that ever lived. The notes are from "You'll Never Know."

Despite the fact that he is responsible for some of the catchiest, most insistent earworms in American music, true appreciation of Warren's songs may not be fully realized for years to come, if ever. Fortunately for Warren's psyche if for no other reason, back in 1980, it was a waiting game that held little interest for him. Call it an occupational hazard of what can happen when, over time, lullabies turn into bad dreams.

A Short Take on The Three Stooges

Jules White

MOE: "Remind me to murder you later!"
CURLY: "I'll make a note of it."

Such dialogue is usually followed by a combination of two-fingered eye pokes, face slaps and hair pulls to the sound effects of a plucked violin and whip-crack.

Ladies and germs: introducing The Three Stooges!

Jules White, Hungarian expatriate, head of Columbia Studios short subject department and the Three Stooges' producer-director in dozens of films in the 1930s and '40s, summated for us when we interviewed him in the 1980s what made Moe (Howard), Larry (Fine) and Curly (Howard) comically tick. "My theory is that those pictures were so fast and furious the Stooges didn't give time for audiences to think, so people didn't feel guilty about letting out a laugh," White said.

Full disclosure—like the thread of a plot from one of his comedy shorts, White, a testy fellow, initially did all he passive-aggressively could to discourage having us interview him. "I'm headed to the High Sierra on a dove hunt," he blurted. Although at age 84, he would've needed the power of the Palomar Hale Telescope on his shotgun to sight a bird. We stood fast.

"The interview will be quick, like one of your shorts," Tom said a bit too cheerily.

· ·*(Silence)*

"O.K., but then you gotta get out," he replied in a voice thick as goulash. "I'll be loading my gun … just a warning."

The universality of outrageous sight gags which rarely date over time (unlike verbal comedy which tends to be more trend-driven and topical) has continued to keep the Stooges' in the comedy equation long after their deaths. Just a few years ago, an epony-mous feature film directed by a couple of other brothers—the Farrellys—introduced a new generation to the slapstick mayhem of the Stooges. And then there is always that best-selling t-shirt "Just Say Moe!" emblazoned with Moe Howard's stern face and sig-nature soupbowl haircut.

In fact, in 2014, the Warner Archive Collection made available for order *Classic Shorts from the Dream Factory, Volume 3 featuring Howard, Fine and Howard*. The col-lection showcases six of the Stooges' short subjects from the 1930s.

As the head of the short subject film department at Columbia Studios, White directed over 500 comedy films starring Buster Keaton, Lucille Ball, Betty Grable, Charley Chase, Chester Conklin and The Three Stooges, among others. Harry Cohn, boss of Columbia, saw one of White's films (a *Pete Smith Specialty*) at Grauman's Chinese Theater. "He just happened to be sitting with my agent and I was hired," White told us. "Cohn and I had a good rapport which he didn't have with everyone. I cried when he died; I was one of the few who did."

The secrets of White's prolific success in an industry not particularly known for career longevity can be attributed to economy and resourcefulness. "I knew how to chisel dollars. That's why I stayed around longer than anyone else (White was producing comedy compilation films in the 1970s). I also knew how to deal with adversity. In 1946, when Curly had a stroke on the set of *Half-Wit's Holiday*, I was shocked. I had just come back from lunch and we had six hours of filming left to do. Luckily I found a double to stand in for him and we weathered the storm."

Nobody's stooge

What made the short list of White's favorite short subjects? "All of them are wonderful in one way or another," he said. "Like a loaf of fresh bread, each slice is as delicious as the next. I will say that Charlie Chaplin was, by far, the greatest comedian. Laurel and Hardy were second best. I do think Curly was very funny. He had a Chaplinesque technique, although the Stooges' pictures were rowdy. They were living caricatures and I don't think they ever realized it."

As we clicked a few photos of White, we asked if he'd pose for a gag shot with the flat palm of his hand parallel to his nose as if he were about to fend off a two-fingered Stooges eye-poke. "I won't do that," he snorted, "it sends a bad message to the youngsters. They could get hurt."

We were a bit baffled by White's protective concern. It hadn't occurred to us that such a staple Stooges sight-gag could end in someone losing their sight, but he was in the process of loading his 12 gauge, so we didn't debate the matter.

In the final tally, The Three Stooges accounted for almost half of White's total career film output. Other movies of his featured such classic comedians as Buster Keaton, Harry Langdon and Charley Chase.

All told, they served their purpose keeping Depression-era audiences guffawing before and in-between the featured pictures and, as we watched the octogenarian lovingly slide cartridges into his gun, we found they kept the "Great White Hunter" well supplied in birdshot, too.

In the Swim with Neptune's Daughter

Esther Williams

Talk about carving out a niche. While MGM was loaded to the gills with actors, singers and dancers, there was one—and only one—aquatic star on the Culver City lot, Esther Williams. And the 20-foot-deep swimming pool built on Stage 30, complete with hydraulic lifts, hidden air hoses and special camera cranes for overhead shots, was built especially for her.

In fact, Williams was such an "X factor" in Hollywood when she began her career that someone from MGM's art department was her "choreographer." And before her own pool was built, she remembered filming scenes for her "Water Ballet" in *Ziegfeld Follies* in Johnny Weissmuller's "Tarzan" saucer tank. "You know, the one that he swam in where he had all the rubber crocodiles chasing him," Williams said. "They weren't real, because in that small tank he would have been legless—fast," Williams said, "and he had great legs so that would've been a shame."

Williams packed into her persona an irresistible combination of youth, beauty and athleticism, often swimming with waterlogged leading men (Van Johnson, Red Skelton, Ricardo Montalban, and future husband, Fernando Lamas) like she was Michael Phelps on a day off from training and working solely from muscle memory. And unlike her co-stars with their coifs teased by MGM's chief hair stylist Sydney Guilaroff, Williams wasn't afraid to get her hair wet during extended water-borne musical sequences.

Like ice skater Sonja Henie who preceded her in films by a decade, Williams was one of only a few athletes to hit it big in movies, matriculating from champion swimmer to model to Hollywood star—the last vouchsafed by a singular talent she knew couldn't easily be replicated.

"I worked through three pregnancies in bathing suits," she said. "Thank God my kids kept their knees in! But even pregnant, it got to a point where the studio couldn't replace me. It was a whole world that was mine. It was my terrain. The only one I worked with that could really swim was Fernando. He was a swimming champion in Argentina."

Luminous at age 74 when we met her in 1996, Williams appeared ready to challenge Olympic swimming star Dara Torres in a leg of the 4 × 100-meter freestyle relay. It was fitting then that she met us—where else?—but poolside at her Beverly Hills home. On an adjacent table rested two books that seemed totally appropriate to the setting: *Pools* by Kelly Klein and a copy of the *The MGM Story*. Williams was dressed in a white smock with gold lettering that read: "Swim with Esther" stitched onto a front breast pocket. We quickly learned that her storytelling contained a disarming ribald streak that gobsmacked us and seemed oddly incongruent with the bathing beauty image she had fostered in her movie heyday but that, nonetheless, made her stories even funnier.

A standout swimmer at 16, the Los Angeles native (Inglewood), lost out on her opportunity to swim for the 1940 Olympic team because the games were canceled due to the war. Williams' "form," however, did catch the eye of show business impresario Billy Rose, who cast her opposite Weissmuller in *Aquacade*, a live musical extravaganza performed mostly submerged.

Williams barely had time to towel off, when MGM offered her a screen test. As Williams recounted, it was not just "any" screen test; she was making it opposite arguably the biggest movie star of them all—the "King" himself—Clark Gable. She called it a "crazy fluke." "Louis B. Mayer was mad at Lana Turner because she married Artie Shaw without asking him," Williams said. "He wanted you to tell him everything. He said to me, 'I want to be a father to you.' I said, 'Mr. Mayer, I have a father.' That line of his worked on a lot of girls."

As "punishment" for Turner's insubordination, Mayer threatened to replace her in an upcoming Gable film with an "unknown." Williams unexpectedly was that unknown quantity and Gable willingly played along.

Williams fully expected her screen test to lead nowhere, and in fact, she was swimming laps in the Beverly Hills Hotel pool when she was summoned to Mayer's office located in Culver City. Dressed in old clothes and wearing no make-up, Williams dutifully reported to the studio. When the time came to enter Mayer's office, much to her shock, there sat Gable.

"It's the knees that go," she said. "I loved him so much in *Gone with the Wind* when I was in high school. I thought this was the man of my dreams, if I could only find someone like him when I got married. And there he is! He put out those big paws. I'm touching him. He shakes my hand and I said, 'Oh Mr. Gable, I've heard so much about you.' He very sweetly smiled and said, 'I've heard a lot about you, too.'"

Director George Sidney was assigned to make the test, and no one, including Williams, actually thought Gable would report to the set to shoot it. Williams rehearsed the scene with actor Dan Dailey, who fully expected to film the scene with Williams, when Gable walked in, tapped Dailey on the shoulder and said, "O.K., kid, I'll take over now." Dailey stormed off the set leaving the neophyte Williams even more flustered. To make matters worse, Gable's wife, Carole Lombard, had accompanied her husband.

"Lombard is situated right under the camera and she's so blonde and she's wearing a black velvet suit with a beret with black fox everywhere and diamonds in her ears," recalled Williams. "I thought she's going to sit there and watch this barely out of the chlorine swimmer do a scene with her husband. So I said to myself, 'O.K., swimmer take your mark. I've been under pressure before and I've gotten to the end of the pool. So now I just got to get out of the pool first.'"

No sooner did Sidney yell "action," than Gable planted a big juicy kiss on an unsuspecting Williams.

"There's no kiss in the scene," she told us. "Not a single kiss. This screen test is to determine whether I'm going to get this role. Recovering from the kiss, I say my line, 'Do you really have to go?' And Gable says, 'No, I'm not going,' and he gives me another kiss. That's not the line and he's not supposed to kiss me again. After the fifth kiss, I look at Georgie (Sidney), and he said, 'cut.' Gable said, 'This is great. Good luck. Hope you get the part.' He gets up and leaves with Lombard on his arm and the two of them are laughing and having a wonderful time. As they walked off the stage, Gable says to his wife, 'I told you I was going to kiss me a mermaid today.' I'm sitting there not realizing that they often played jokes on each other. That was legend. I was the joke of the day. This is something you could cry over, but I didn't. I just didn't get to the end of the pool first."

At the time, Williams thought the test an exercise in futility and said, "At least I'll have something to tell my grandchildren." Much to her surprise, the test resulted in a long-term contract, and although she never made the picture with Gable, Williams made her film debut opposite Mickey Rooney in 1942's *Andy Hardy's Double Life*.

The popular "Andy Hardy" series helped launch the careers of such stars as Donna Reed, Lana Turner and Judy Garland. Audience response to Williams was positive, and in 1944 she was cast in *Mr. Coed* starring Red Skelton. Midway through production, studio brass, after viewing the rushes, renamed the movie, *Bathing Beauty* and awarded Williams top billing. It would become Hollywood's first swimming musical and launch a series of successful aquatic tuners starring MGM's very own diva of the deep.

According to Williams, the movie also spawned something else, an Olympic event—synchronized swimming—that outlasted even the studio itself. "After *Bathing Beauty*, I got a tremendous amount of mail from girls in swimming clubs that didn't want to swim fast; they wanted to swim 'pretty' like they saw me do in the movies," Williams said. "My mother was answering my fan mail at the time. She was a psychologist and took these requests very seriously, so she created a filing cabinet with mimeographed sheets where she would describe how I would do a 'back dolphin.' I told my mother how all the moves were done move by move and breath by breath and how to keep your body positioned where you wanted it to be."

Williams said that the short, choppy strokes in *Bathing Beauty* that have become a hallmark of many synchronized swimming routines were due to the big band music in the film. "If you're going to swim to Harry James, you don't swim long, smooth strokes to 'Sleepy Lagoon,'" Williams said. "You swim to 'One O'Clock Jump,' and that's when they began to do things in the water to jazz and that's how an Olympic sport was born."

From birthing an Olympic event, Williams, in 1953, inaugurated another first for MGM; she took the studio's signature animated characters, "Tom and Jerry," for a dip. "Bill Hanna and Joe Barbera (the creators of the cartoon) were so cute," Williams remembered. "They asked if I would have lunch with them and I thought, 'Why would I want to have lunch with a couple of guys who do cartoons?' Then they asked me if I had seen the movie *Anchors Aweigh*. Then I remembered Jerry the Mouse on Gene Kelly's arm doing all kinds of wonderful things and Gene and Jerry tap dancing together. I told them how brilliant they were with Jerry in that picture and they said, we want them to go underwater."

Williams brought up the possibly inconsequential point that cats (even cartoon felines) don't really swim to which she said Bill Hanna replied: "This cat will or he's fired!"

The movie in which Williams swam with the animated duo is *Dangerous When Wet* and she claimed it was the first time she ever had to "act" underwater. "It was a hoot to do, because, obviously, Tom and Jerry weren't there (they would be superimposed later), so I had to do double-takes and whatnot as if they were there. We had index cards and a whole storyboard laid out so I would know what my 'costars' were doing at all times so I could react to them."

At about this time during our visit, we heard what we thought was the echo of a doorbell. "That's the gate buzzer," Williams said. "It's probably a fan that would like to come and stay for dinner. They do that all the time. (*Williams coquettishly burlesqued a fan's voice*) 'Hello, I've loved you all my life, can I come in?' I say: 'What is it you want, sweetheart?' (*fan's voice*) 'Well, first of all I'd like to take a swim in your pool, and then, if I have time, I hear you're a wonderful cook.'"

"I guess some fans are all wet," Dave said.

"It's because they think they know you when they saw you 40-feet high on a screen and you smiled right at them in the theater," Williams said. "Every time you smiled at them, they thought, 'She loves me!'"

After about a minute, the buzzing stopped.

Williams estimated she swam more than 1,000 miles through such movies as *Neptune's Daughter*, *Pagan Love Song* and *Easy to Love*. Through them all, pregnancies notwithstanding, she managed to stay true to her size nine bathing suit. However, she said the pregnancies (Williams was married three times and had three children) did create havoc with the shooting schedule of her films and particularly with producer Joe Pasternak.

"They had to rearrange the entire shooting schedules so I could get into the size nine swimming suits and be photographable because we didn't finish those pictures until five or six months," she said. "I remember calling Joe and telling him, 'Joey, I'm sorry. I know we've had this conversation before, but I'm pregnant.' And he said, 'God damn it, why do you keep doing this to me?' And I said, 'It's not being done to you Joe, it's being done to me!' And he replied, 'I know, I know, but if you don't tell that husband of yours to knock it off, he'll be barred from the lot.' And I said, 'Joe, it doesn't happen on the lot!'"

In addition to being America's swimming sweetheart, Williams was one of the first stars to parlay her name recognition into successful business ventures. Sticking to what she knew best, Williams' name was attached to a line of swimming suits as well as above-ground pools. However, her first venture into swimwear was more of an educational experience than a profitable venture.

"I guess life imitated art," she said. "I played a swimsuit designer in *Neptune's Daughter*. Fred Cole from Cole's California called me and said I should have a tie-in with him. What he did was get me for peanuts. I was doing fashion shows from movies and after seven years, I finally smartened up." It was also during this time, in the early '60s, that Williams said director Federico Fellini approached her to star in *8½*.

Williams eventually left the swimwear business, but she dove headfirst back into it after the death of Lamas in 1982. "He really didn't want me to do anything, but wait for him to come home," she said. "It's just the way he was. My sister Maureen said to me one day, 'Why do you think you devoted 20 years to a man who really wanted you not to be famous anymore,' adding, 'what do people in show business call it when you take time off and then go back?' And I said, 'A hiatus; a 20-year hiatus.' And she said, 'From the time they said, swimmer take your mark and you became a swimming champion, you had a spotlight on you and maybe you needed a rest.'"

Ever since Lamas' death and until she died in 2013, Williams made up for lost time. She became a popular fixture at film festivals meeting old fans who had rediscovered her movies and new audiences that thrilled to the kitschy delight to be had the instant she started treading water. But as Williams told us, she really didn't have much choice in the matter either when her career began or when it reached its nadir. For her "keeping on" was always a straightforward proposition, crystalline: a case of sink or swim.

His Favorite Things

Robert Wise

More than 50 years ago the film version of the long-running Broadway musical by Rodgers and Hammerstein had its unheralded sneak preview at the Mann Theater in Minneapolis. The movie, *The Sound of Music*, generated favorable response from the audience, but director Robert Wise had no idea then that it would be the biggest blockbuster since *Gone with the Wind*.

Three decades later in 1995, sitting in his modest office tucked on a commercial street in the flatlands of Beverly Hills, Wise, then 81, was still quizzical about the root cause for the movie's monolithic success. "*The Sound of Music* had a universality about it that my other films don't have, not even *West Side Story*," he mused. "I think it's because it is a family picture from beginning to end. To this day, the film is like an international passport. People in every corner of the world recognize me through the movie."

Mementos collected from the era scattered about his nondescript office testified to that statement and included a Russian language poster of the film and the disembodied head of one of the marionette puppets featured in the "Lonely Goatherd" song. The head served as a comical bookend on an overstuffed shelf. Wise himself radiated a certain tidy contentment like a sagacious old owl (which he resembled), and an unrufflable one at that.

Wise told us to read the letter framed in Lucite that hung just below the Russian *Sound of Music* poster. It was from someone named Bella and had a kind of unintended, sing-song lyricism that innocently attaches to some foreign letters transcribed into English.

Because of your stay in our country so long ago yet almost yesterday, here's a little present for you. I kept it quite a few years. Back in 1973, I spent my summer in a tiny fisherman village in Latvia at the

Wised up

Baltic Sea and they were screening at that time Sounds of Music *every Saturday night in a different village. People followed the film from one village to another.*

*   This poster I got in my village from the projectionist who came in with the film and equipment. The
people enjoyed the film so much that even the elderly women, I overheard two of them whispering,
"We'll go next Saturday to the neighboring village to see it again." I thought this little token may please
you.*

Yours,
Bella.

"About three years ago Julie Andrews and I were awarded a state medal from Austria
because of the movie," Wise said, upping the token ante considerably. "I've even had people say to me in all earnestness that *The Sound of Music* has done more for Salzburg and
Austria than Mozart."

    Wise said that he had his heart set on casting Julie Andrews in the lead as Maria
Von Trapp from the very beginning. "The only problem was that there was this buzz
going around Hollywood at that time that Julie wasn't photogenic," he said. "I called the
producer of *Mary Poppins*, which hadn't been released yet, and asked if I could see a reel
or two of the film. Ernie Lehman, *Music's* screenwriter, Saul Chaplin, the musical director
and I went over to Disney and put those rumors to rest—Julie was our girl."

    The casting of the role of Captain Von Trapp, however, was more problematic. "I
remember that Yul Brenner desperately wanted to be the Captain," Wise said. "But I
thought he would be too 'on the nose' somehow. I had seen Christopher Plummer in
some plays in New York and thought he could bring a certain edginess to the role that I
felt was needed and was lacking in the stage version."

    Plummer turned the film down, so, at the urging of Plummer's agent, Wise flew to

London and over drinks at the Connaught Hotel convinced the actor to take the part. "My only reservation—and it was slight—was over Chris's age," Wise said. "He was only about 35 then and he refused to do a filmed makeup test. However, he did allow us to come up to his apartment one day with a makeup man and still photographer. We had to convince the studio that Chris could look old enough to be the father of a 17-year-old daughter. We pulled it off."

According to Wise, the search for actors to play the Von Trapp children spanned two continents and included tests of Rex Harrison's granddaughter and a young Mia Farrow. With the exception of Nicholas Hammond who played Friedrich, all the children ended up coming from Los Angeles.

Wise said he was initially approached to direct the film when William Wyler dropped out after a dispute with 20th Century–Fox over the treatment of several Nazi-related scenes in Lehman's script. "I think Willie wanted to bear down on those scenes," Wise said. "I, on the other hand, loved the script in total. The only problem was that the aerial shots that open the movie were too eerily like the opening aerial shot that began *West Side Story* for which Ernie was also the screenwriter. I told him, 'We can't open the picture that way, we'll be accused of stealing from ourselves!' He couldn't come up with anything better, so we bit the bullet and went with it. To this day, I get more comments on that aerial opening than on the *West Side Story* opening."

The son of a meat packer, Wise had hoped to become a journalist, but was unable to continue his studies during the Depression. Looking for work, he traveled to Hollywood where he found a job as a film porter in the shipping room at RKO Studios. "One of my main jobs was to carry prints of pictures up to the projection booth for screenings," he said. "After about six months, I was spotted by a man named T.K. Wood who gave me a start as sound effects editor, then music editor, then assistant editor. It was on-the-job training and I became a full-fledged editor five years after I began."

Among the films Wise "cut" in those early days, were two musicals starring Fred Astaire and Ginger Rogers: *Carefree* and *The Story of Vernon and Irene Castle*. "Years later, when Jerry Robbins and I shared the Oscar for best picture for *West Side Story*, Fred was the presenter. I have a picture of that at home which means a great deal to me." Wise said that early editing experience on the Astaire-Rogers movies effectively demystified musicals—a genre that has perplexed many other directors. In fact, Wise credits those films with giving him the boost of confidence to direct both *West Side Story* and later, *The Sound of Music*.

"When I was approached by the Mirisch Company to take on *West Side Story*, I was not nervous about it all," Wise said. "In fact, I knew all about the pre-scoring and working the playback and the rehearsals for all the dance numbers. I knew the whole *modus operandi*. I had been through it in the editing room. Had I not had that background I might've said, 'Well, gee, I don't know. How do you make a musical?'"

Wise's high-water mark as a film editor was reached when he worked on *Citizen Kane* with Orson Welles. "Pauline Kael, film critic of *The New Yorker*, stirred a tempest years ago about who really was responsible for the film's greatness: Orson or Herman Mankiewicz, Orson's co-scriptwriter," Wise said. "To me, Orson's stamp is on every frame of that film—as star, producer, director and writer. I never saw Herman on the set. It's Orson's film, no question about it."

By the time he came to work on *Citizen Kane*, Wise said he was well established as an editor having just finished editing *My Favorite Wife* starring Cary Grant and

Irene Dunne. "My boss, Jimmy Wilkinson, called me in and asked me if I knew this fellow Orson Welles," Wise said. "I told him yes and Jimmy said, 'Well, he's pulled a fast one on the studio.' He explained that Welles had gotten the green light to shoot three test scenes for his proposed movie but, in fact, had shot three real scenes. Anyway, the studio gave in and decided to let him film the rest of the movie but Welles said he wanted a new editor."

Wise went down to see Welles who came out after a break made up as Kane in old age. "The first time I ever saw Orson he was an old man," Wise said. "We chatted for a few minutes and I can't tell you what went on but I guess he liked the 'cut of my jib' and the fact that we were about the same age. When I got back to RKO, Jimmy got a call and said, 'You got it, it's a start.'"

After some second unit work on films like *The Fallen Sparrow* with John Garfield and Maureen O'Hara, Wise admitted that it might be "more fun" to sit in the director's chair instead of standing behind it and second-guessing whoever was in it. "Those were the days when studios were making a lot of B pictures; low-budget films on short schedules," he said. Wise got his wish on *The Curse of the Cat People* a film he had been editing, produced by Val Lewton.

"It was tremendously big," Wise said. "The studio was not unhappy with the work of the director on the film, Gunther von Fritsch. It was his first feature. But they were unhappy with the pace of his shooting. They couldn't seem to speed him up. He had used up all his schedule and only shot half the script. I took over on a Monday morning and they gave me 10 days to finish the movie. I did and that was the start."

In a directing career that spanned nearly half a century, totaled 39 films, and garnered four Academy Awards, Wise pointed to only about 12 personal favorites. "*The Day the Earth Stood Still*, is a favorite," he said. "Next to the two musicals, that is perhaps my best-known movie." Another is *The Sand Pebbles* with Steve McQueen.

"He was not the simplest guy to work with. He was moody and you never quite knew where the mood was going to come from one day to the next," Wise said. "He seemed to work from the end of his fingertips. I never knew a star that knew better what worked for him on the screen than Steve. He studied himself and knew exactly what he could do. He would say, 'Bob, I think I can do that bit of business with a look. I don't have to speak the line.'"

During his long directing career, Wise sampled almost every genre from musicals to horror pictures. He told us the only two "no's" he would never attempt again were spectacle films (he directed *Helen of Troy* in 1956 for Warner Bros. to tepid box office results) and Westerns (his *Tribute to a Bad Man* also in 1956, and starring James Cagney, was a box office bomb for MGM).

But sci-fi was definitely not off the table. In 1951 Wise had directed the classic *The Day the Earth Stood Still* starring Michael Rennie, Patricia Neal and "Gort." Twenty years later, Wise had followed that up with *The Andromeda Strain*. Based on that track record, in 1978, he was approached by Paramount Pictures to see if lightning couldn't be captured in a bottle a second time with the big-screen movie version of the classic 1960s TV show, *Star Trek*.

It couldn't.

"It was not a happy experience," Wise said about directing *Star Trek: The Motion Picture*. We had to start shooting when we only had the first act of the script in shape, so we were rewriting all the way through to the very last day. That's a lousy way to work."

Wise said that Michael Eisner (President and CEO of Paramount Pictures at the time) called him "out of the blue" to ask him to direct. "I said, 'Well, you know, I've done two science-fiction films and they were both earthbound.' I thought maybe it's time I did science fiction up in space."

One of the reasons the movie devolved into a gassy giant in most critics' minds (in addition to the lack of script problem) was that Wise was staggeringly unfamiliar with the *Trek* universe. "I told Eisner I wasn't a 'Trekkie.' I never got hooked on it when it came out originally so I would have to see some of it. Some fellows over there picked out what they thought were scripts of the 10 best episodes. I thought five or six of them were excellent, a couple were good, and two of them were pretty awful."

In the years following cancellation of the original TV series in 1969, Leonard Nimoy who played "Mr. Spock" had famously railed against being so closely associated with his iconic alien character from the planet Vulcan. He was so adamantly against being typecast, that the original script for the movie had excluded his character. "Of course I wasn't aware of the importance of the Spock character," Wise said. "I came home and my wife read the script and she and my daughter said, 'You can't have *Star Trek* without Spock. He's a vital part!' So I went back to the studio and said, 'Listen, what about this?' And they said, 'Yes, we kind of need Leonard.'"

At the time we met him, Wise said that offers to direct feature films had largely dried up. "The young studio heads want younger directors," he said with no regrets, telling us he kept busy by attending film festivals and doing committee work for the Directors Guild of America.

In his clear-eyed view of Hollywood's notorious short-term memory, Wise said he was inspired by Maria's remark as she leaves the convent to embark on her great adventure as governess of the Von Trapp children. "Every time God closes a door," he said, "somewhere he opens a window."

Amen to that!

Afterword:
A View from the Terrace

New York's Algonquin Roundtable during the "Roaring '20s" was the preferred lunching spot for such literary wits as Dorothy Parker, Robert Benchley, George S. Kaufman and Alexander Woollcott. *Bon mots* were in as generous supply as the bouillabaisse, and it was during these fraternal noontimes that the Roundtable became the birthplace of the wisecrack and catalyst for much of America's humor.

There was a roundtable at the budgetel were we stayed during our pivotal first interview trip to Los Angeles in 1978. It was called the Beverly Terrace Motor Hotel and it's still in business on the corner of Doheny Drive and Santa Monica Blvd. just inside the eastern border of Beverly Hills. But the trenchant comments and stinging barbs we witnessed there 40 years ago were of a decidedly lower caliber than the witticisms once bantered about at the Algonquin. The people who regularly gathered at the Beverly Terrace roundtable (a poolside metal table painted battleship grey with a large umbrella canopy over it), were all men of letters it is true—but these guys corresponded to collection agencies, bookies and offbeat religious sects. Most of them seemed to be human flotsam that had been drawn to the West Coast to remake their lives or bury troubled pasts. In that regard, to many, Los Angeles still represents the same kind of hopeful beacon.

It was customary at the Beverly Terrace after the workday was over, to gather in the Southern California twilight for poolside drinks at the roundtable.

A transplanted New Yorker named Ludwig Aarons was the ringleader of our group. He was a small man with a copper-toned beer belly and a bald head so splotched with freckles that when looming over him, it was like looking down on a bowl of bran flakes floating in almond milk. Ludwig had a curious habit of tape-recording everything that was said at the roundtable. His favorite amusement was to read vast stretches of the work of Henry Miller, and then replay the tape. As he listened in rapt concentration, Ludwig often chain-smoked a couple of packs of cigarettes. We noticed that the sound of Ludwig's own voice never failed to have a tranquilizing effect on him.

Ludwig also had thorough contempt for any kind of convention. Every morning prior to his first cup of coffee, he would forego showering and instead swan-dive into the motel pool from the second-story walkway in nothing but his Fruit of the Loom underwear. It was after one such brief interlude that he spotted Tom at the roundtable eating a bear claw pastry just purchased at the Hughes supermarket across the street from the hotel.

"You'll shorten your life with all that sugar content," he sneered, dripping wet and lighting a Pall Mall.

"Tell me, Ludwig," Tom chided, "have you ever tape-recorded the Surgeon General's warning on the side of your cigarette pack?"

Ludwig stalked off in a tirade sputtering about the "damned insolence" of the younger generation. He then called Tom some names that we both thought we recalled from his previous night's declamation of *Tropic of Capricorn*.

Ludwig's morning dip and continual yakkity yak drove another motel denizen, Frieda, a German woman, into fits. We had learned she was on the trail of her runaway son and had tracked him to L.A. She said she hated the city and that went double for most of the Americans she had met. But most of all, she couldn't abide loud noises or anything coming out of Ludwig's mouth.

Jim Patricola, Ludwig's constant companion, was a devout follower of the Rosicrucian religious order and had made a recent pilgrimage to its holy headquarters in Santa Barbara. One evening he came to the roundtable filled with pyramid power and looking for converts.

"We have a lot in common," he told Tom. "I'm infused with the A-polarity and so are you. We don't get along with B-polarity people. They're always buzzin' 'round us like a damn beehive." Patricola's profundity was lost on us. The last time we saw him, he was poolside, chatting up one of the hotel's resident "working girls" who was trying to sunbathe having undergone her own conversion long before.

There were two fringe members of the Beverly Terrace Roundable who sat in on our nightly discussions when the mood hit them. Fred Underhill was a cinematographer who had worked on *Woodstock*. He puffed Tiparillo cigars, blew perfect smoke rings and affected at all times a disinterested but benevolently superior posture. The other man, a college professor from Bemidji, Minnesota, was hooked on watching *Star Trek* TV episodes. "I just lucked upon an original cast script of 'The Squire of Gothos,'" he once said excitedly. "I found it in a memorabilia shop on Hollywood Blvd. I'll go get it and we can have a dramatic reading. Dave, you'll be Dr. McCoy. Ludwig can play Mr. Spock and I'll impersonate Capt. Kirk."

The Algonquin Roundtable in New York City enjoyed a vogue of about 10 years. Beverly Terrace's Roundtable disbanded after two weeks. The Algonquin Roundtable ended when the Great Depression condemned as frivolous the carefree frolic of a more innocent America. The Beverly Terrace Roundtable ceased activity when Frieda threatened the membership with a butcher knife. Her poolside cabana was just a few feet from our metal table, and she was averaging only three hours of sleep a night.

But to us, it hardly mattered. We had just interviewed Gene Kelly and our visit with Fred Astaire was scheduled for the next day. We were on our way.

Index

Aarons, Ludwig 285
Abbott, George 12
ABC 32, 92, 143, 251, 254
ABC News 27
Academy Awards 47, 59, 65, 78,
    100, 109, 120, 147, 202, 234, 272;
    Best Actor 26, 45, 57, 148–149,
    214; Best Director 282; Best Pic-
    ture 75, 87, 100, 108, 128, 196,
    202, 219, 281; Best Score 217,
    219; Best Short Film 176; Best
    Song 69, 74, 137, 155–156, 180,
    182, 244, 269; Best Supporting
    Actor 14, 162–163, 184, 219, 250;
    Best Supporting Actress 145;
    Ceremony 219, 140, 160; Dance
    Direction 210; Honorary 26, 142,
    237; Lifetime Achievement 106
The Academy of Motion Picture
    Arts and Sciences 224
Actors Studio 163, 235, 237, 247,
    259
Adam-12 231
Adams, Nick 122
Adamson, Harold 164
Addams, Charles 92
The Addams Family 10, 51, 90, 91,
    92
Adler, Stella 250
*The Adventures of Ozzie and Har-
    riet* 191
The Adventures of Tom Sawyer 91
The Agony and the Ecstasy 128
Ah Wilderness! (play) 271
Ahern, Gladys 8, 9
Ahern, Will 7–11
"Ain't That a Kick in the Head" 63
Air Force One 130
Airplane! 248, 251
Airport 39
Alaska 129
Albert, Eddie 11–14, 146
Albert, Edward, Jr. 14
Albert, Maria 14
Alda, Alan 31
Algonquin Roundtable 247, 285,
    286
"All the Way" 59, 212
Allen, Fred 34, 35
Allen, Gracie 51, 52, 54, 95; *see
    also* Burns, George

Allen, Steve 14–19, 97
Allen, Woody 177, 178, 206
Allyson, June 122, 146, 157, 198
Altman, Robert 41
Alton, Bob 264
Ameche, Don 45
American Academy of Dramatic
    Arts 226
American Film Institute 26, 46
An American in Paris 75, 76–77,
    78, 155, 200, 202, 218
Amos & Andy 186
Amsterdam, Morey 80
Anaheim Stadium 213
Anchors Aweigh 60, 116, 157, 242,
    244, 245, 278
Andrews, Bart 29
Andrews, Dana 195–196
Andrews, Julie 61, 114, 219, 280
The Andrews Sisters 15, 191
The Andromeda Strain 282
The Andy Griffith Show 110
Andy Hardy's Double Life 277
Andy Hardy's Private Secretary 116
Andy Hardy series 116, 228, 277
Animal Crackers 209
Animals 149
Ann-Margret 242
Annie Get Your Gun 242, 245
Aquacade 276
Arkin, Alan 111
Arlen, Harold 190, 271, 272
Armstrong, Louis 133, 240
Arnaz, Desi 30
Arness, James 32, 48
Arnold, Buddy 34
The Arts and Humanities Act of
    1965 213
Asner, Ed 19–24, 212
Astaire, Adele 25
Astaire, Ava 257
Astaire, Fred 1, 3, 24–27, 55, 61,
    62, 76, 82, 106, 120, 132, 157, 164,
    166, 198–199, 212, 240, 254–255,
    257, 272, 286; Astaire and Kelly
    4, 85, 79, 154, 158, 202–203; *see
    also* Astaire-Rogers musicals;
    *The Band Wagon; Easter Parade;
    Funny Face; Holiday Inn; Royal
    Wedding; Ziegfeld Follies*
Astaire, Peter 254

Astaire, Phyllis 257
Astaire, Robyn 198–199, 257
Astaire-Rogers musicals 27, 209,
    211, 247, 266, 271, 281
Astin, John 92
At the Circus 53, 247
Auberge La Lucarne aux Chouettes
    75

"The Babbitt and the Bromide"
    202
Babe 230
Babe: Pig in the City 230
Babes on Broadway 166
Baby Doll 259, 261
Bacall, Lauren 50, 74, 100
Bacharach, Burt 99
The Bachelor 17
BAFTA 120
Baker, Carroll 261
Baker, Jack 258
Baker, Josephine 94
Baker, Sheila 258
Balanchine, George 24
Ball, Lucille 1, 27–31, 38, 82, 88,
    161, 264, 274
Ballet 38, 39, 75, 84, 128, 199; in
    films 76, 77, 78, 85, 275
Ballet des Champs-Élysées 75
Ballet Russe de Monte Carlo 84
The Band Wagon 82, 85, 200
Banderas, Antonio 124
Barbera, Joe 278; *see also* Hanna-
    Barbera
The Barefoot Contessa 183
Barish, Seymour 49, 50
The Barkleys of Broadway 263,
    265, 266, 271
Barnet, Charlie 190, 192
Barrett, Rona 31–34
Barrymore, Ethel 8
Barrymore, John 216
Barter Theater 46
Barton, Jack 11
Barton, Ralph 132
Bathing Beauty 277
Batman 257, 261
"Be My Love" 60
Beach Party 120
Beat Generation 119
Beatles 171, 272

Beaton, Cecil 220
Beatty, Warren 119, 143
Bedtime for Bonzo 94
Beerbohm, Max 132
Beery, Wallace 216
"Begin the Beguine" 3, 262
Beiderbecke, Bix 72
The Bel Air Hotel 108
The Bel Canto Trio 116
The Belle of New York 267, 272
Ben-Hur 128, 129
Benchley, Robert 285
Benedict Canyon 41
Bennett, Tony 72
Benny, Jack 36, 43, 51, 62, 95, 136,
   203, 231, 232, 233, 247, 250
The Benny Goodman Story 15
Bergman, Ingrid 108
Berkeley, Busby 104, 194, 210, 228,
   270, 271
Bernstein, Leonard 213
Berle, Milton 34–38, 46, 80, 187,
   189, 232–233, 258
Berlin, Irving 15, 16, 72, 73, 77,
   164, 245, 269, 270, 272; songs
   198, 212; *see also Holiday Inn*
Berlin Airlift 137
Berlinger, Sarah 35, 36
Berman, Pandro 120, 247
The Best Years of Our Lives 74,
   194, 195–196, 215
Beta Sigma Rho Fraternity 180
The Beverly Hills Cab Company
   49
The Beverly Hills Hotel 119
The Beverly Hills Unlisted Jazz
   Band 58
Beverly Terrace Motor Hotel 24,
   285–286
The Beverly Wilshire 248
BF Goodrich Tires 238
Big Band 190, 191, 238, 243, 277
   see also Swing music
The Big Broadcast of 1938 137
The Big Country 130
The Big Slide 147
Big Street 27
"Bill" 218
The Birds 123, 125, 126
Bishop, Joey 82
Bisset, Jacqueline 38–41
Blair, Linda 124
Blake, Robert 189
Blanc, Mel 41–44
Blanc Communications 42
Blane, Ralph 265
Bloch-Bauer, Adele 135
Bloom, Claire 179
Bloomington, Minnesota 136
Blondell, Joan 256
"Blues in Hoss Flat" 177
BMI 137
The Bob Newhart Show 205, 206
"Body and Soul" 16, 20
Bogart, Humphrey 14, 50, 74, 100,
   108, 149, 150, 158, 216, 230;
   Casablanca
Bojangles see Robinson, Bill
"Bojangles of Harlem" 210

Bolger, Ray 175
Bonanza 183, 184
Bongart, Sergei 57, 59
Boone, Richard 48
Borgnine, Ernest 44–49
Borne, Hal 211
The Borscht Belt 146
Borzage, Danny 256
Borzage, Frank 256
The Boston Strangler 171
"Bouncin' the Blues" 271
Bowling for Columbine 126
Boy on a Dolphin 40
Boyle, Johnny 57
The Boys from Brazil 215
Bradley, General Omar 184
The Brady Bunch Movie 148
The Brain That Wouldn't Die 3
Branagh, Kenneth 129
Brando, Marlon 35, 119, 147, 148,
   149, 186, 235
Brazzi, Rossano 121, 183
Brecher, Irving 247
Brice, Fanny 94
The Bride Wore Boots 257
Brigadoon 158
"Broadway Ballet" 85
The Broadway Melody of 1940 187
Broadway Rhythm 83
Broccoli, Albert R. 257
Broccoli, Cubby 258
Brokaw, Tom 111
Brooks, Mel 114
Brooks, Richard 147, 178
Brother Rat 12, 13
Brown, Jim 125
Brown, Nacio Herb 225
Bruce, Lenny 81
Bruce, Nigel 80
Bryan, Arthur Q. 43
Buble, Michael 72
Bugs Bunny *see* Looney Toons
Bullitt 38
Burbank, California 95, 100, 190,
   221
Burnett, Carol 82
The Burning Bed 104
Burns, George 49–55, 60, 82, 86,
   95, 125, 142, 247; and Gracie
   Allen 51, 53, 233
Burns, Lillian 170, 245
Burns & Allen in Lamb Chops 52
Burton, Richard 170, 237
Burton, Tim 163
Butterflies Are Free 14
*The Button-Down Mind of Bob
   Newhart* 204
Buttons, Red 81
"Buttons and Bows" 180, 182
Buzzell, Edward 52–53, 54
Bye Bye Birdie 242

Cabaret 202
Caesar, Sid 81
Cagney, Bill 58
Cagney, James 1, 46, 55–59, 70,
   146, 175, 216, 230, 256, 282; *see
   also* White Heat; *Yankee Doodle
   Dandy*

Cahn, Sammy 59–63, 212
"Call Me Irresponsible" 59, 62, 212
Calloway, Cab 206
Cameron, Jim 130
Camino Real (play) 261
Camus, Albert 141
Cancel My Reservation 236
Cantor, Eddie 27, 35, 141, 143, 247
Canyon Passage 74
Capital Records 182
The Capitol Theater 137
Capone, Al 251
Capra, Frank 63–72, 111–112, 213
Captain Binghamton 45
Captain Newman, M.D. 101
Cardinale, Claudia 255
Carefree 26, 211, 281
"The Carioca" 27
The Carlton Celebrity Room 136,
   176
Carmichael, Hoagy 17, 72–75
Carney, Art 44, 257
Caron, Leslie 75–79, 220, 224
Carousel 145, 146
Carson, Johnny 17, 19, 82, 93, 94,
   95, 97, 98; *see also The Tonight
   Show*
Carter, Jack 79–82
Carter, Roxanne 79
Caruso, Enrico 35, 114
Casablanca 108, 179
Cash, Johnny 183
Cassatt, Mary 195
Cassidy, David 147, 148
Cassidy, Jack 147
Castle, Nick 208
Castle Keep 113
Castro, Fidel 120
The Cat and the Canary 182
The Catered Affair 46
Cathedral of St. Paul 65
Cavalcade of Stars 81
CBS 20, 21, 22, 23, 88, 89, 159, 205
Champion, Gower 211, 268
Champion, Marge 211
Chan, Jackie 166
Channing, Carol 11, 61, 132
Chaplin, Charlie 35, 65, 133, 177,
   179, 209, 275; *see also The Kid*
Chaplin, Saul 60–61, 86, 280
Charisse, Cyd 82–86, 157, 158, 197,
   198, 199
Charisse, Nico 199
Charles, Ray 72
Charlie's Angels 104
Chase, Charley 274, 275
Chase, Chevy 91
Chasen's Restaurant 97
"Chattanooga Choo-Choo" 269,
   272
Cheever, John 99
Cheret, Jules 155
Cheshire Cheese Restaurant 67
Chesterfield Cigarettes 191
Chez Panisse 12
"(Chicago Is) My Kind of Town"
   59
The Chicago Playwrights Theatre
   20

China Corsair 46
Citron, Herman 247
Chodorov, Edward 133
choreography 25, 85, 116, 156, 157–158, 166, 263, 264
Churchill, Winston 148
Cinderella 177
Citizen Kane 108, 281
City Across the River 171
City Lights 179, 218
Civil Rights Movement 131
Clark, Sam 210
Clinton, Hilary 104
Clooney, Rosemary 27
Club TCM 225
Cohan, George M. 57
Cohen, Mickey 89
Cohn, Harry 68, 274
Col. Sanders 117
Cole, Fred 278
Cole, Natalie 72
Colette 78
The Colgate Comedy Hour 100
Colman, Ronald 68
Columbia Studios 53, 60, 273, 274; Actors 104, 170; *see also* Cohn, Harry
Columbia University 139
Columbo 110–111, 113, 261
Comden, Betty 218, 219
Come Dance with Me! (album) 191
Come Fly with Me (album) 191, 192
"Come Fly with Me" (song) 59
Come Swing with Me! (album) 191, 193
The Commodore Hotel 67
Communist Party 133
Como, Perry 269
Conan Doyle, Arthur 111
Conklin, Chester 60
Connaught Hotel 281
Connecticut Budget Bureau 112
Conners, Marylou 89
Conners, Mike 86–90
Consolidated Foods 121
Conte, Richard 99
Conway, Tim 89
Coogan, Jack 10, 91
Coogan, Jackie 10, 90–93
Coogan and Parks 9, 10
Coogan Law 91–92
Cooper, Gary 120, 150, 216
Costner, Kevin 251
The Cotton Club 206
Count Basie 177
Count Basie Band 18
The Countess of Hong Kong 35
The Court Jester 62
The Court Martial of Billy Mitchell 150
Covarrubias, Miguel 132
Cover Girl 104
Coyne, Jeanne 77
Crawford, Joan 89, 164
"Crazy Veil" 85
Crichton, Michael 114
Crime and Punishment, USA 119
Crime Magazine 249

Crimes and Misdemeanors 162
Crosby, Bing 15, 34, 182, 191, 272; and Bob Hope 137–138; and Frank Capra 68, 69
Cross, Jimmy 92
Cry Terror! 100
Crystal, Billy 140
Cukor, George 39
Cul-de-Sac 39
Culver City, California 120
Cummings, Bob 100
Cummings, Jack 106, 107
Cummings, Nate 121
Current Biography 28, 29
The Curse of the Cat People 282
Curtis, Jamie Lee 168
Curtis, Tony 15, 147, 166–173
Curtiz, Michael 94, 108, 109
"Cute" 177

D-Day 133
Daddy Long Legs 76
Dailey, Dan 122, 219, 276
Dainty Marie 52
Daley, Bill 205, 206
Damn Yankees 104
"Dancing" 9
The Dancing Co-ed 239
"Dancing in the Dark" 85
Dancing Lady 164
Dancing on the Ceiling: Stanley Donen and his Movies 106
Dancing on the Edge 38
Dandridge, Dorothy 219
Danese, Shera 111
Dangerous Beauty 39
Daniel Boone 257
Darwin, Charles 108
Daves, Delmer 186
David, Jacques-Louis 198
Davis, Bette 257
Davis, Geena 185
Davis, Mac 138
Davis, Sammy, Jr. 81, 231
Day, Doris 183
A Day at the Races 41
Day for Night 39
The Day the Earth Stood Still 282
Dayton's 124
Dean, James 46, 119, 150, 161
Dean Martin Roasts 81
The Dean Martin Show 88
Debbie Reynolds Hotel, Casino, and Hollywood Movie Museum 223
De Carlo, Yvonne 94
de Cordova, Fred 93–98
de Cordova, Janet 93
The Deep 39, 40
de Havilland, Olivia 121, 122
Del Mar Racetrack 137
Dell, Gabe 92
DeMarco, Renee 266
Demarest, William 182
DeMille, Agnes 213
DeMille, Cecil B. 126, 128, 129–130
Democratic Party 131
Deneuve, Catherine 255
DePalma, Brian 101

DePaul, Gene 269
Derek, John 119, 170
Desilu 28, 88, 89
Desperate Housewives 81
Devine, Andy 195
Diaghilev's Ballets Russes 84
Diamond Horseshoe 195
DiCaprio, Leonardo 230
The Dick Van Dyke Show 80
Dickens, Charles 114
Dickinson, Angie 98–102
"Dig-Dig-Dig for Your Dinner" 263
Diller, Phyllis 81, 227
Dinner at Eight 216
Directors Guild of America 283
The Dirty Dozen 46
Disney 261, 280
Disney, Walt 144
The Dixie Four 9
Dixon, Harland 57
Dmytryk, Edward 254
"Do I Love You?" 268
Doctor Doolittle 189
Donaldson's Department Store 124
Donen, Stanley 39, 102–107, 258; and Gene Kelly 157, 218–219
"Don't Fence Me In" 192
Dostoyevsky, Fyodor 119
Douglas, Jack 138
Douglas, Kirk 170, 202, 216
Down Argentine Way 207
Dragnet 189
Dressed to Kill 101
Dressler, Marie 35
Du Barry Was a Lady 27, 262, 264
Dubin, Al 268, 270
Duchin, Eddy 16
Duets (album) 194
DuMont Television Network 81
Dunne, Irene 282
Durante, Jimmy 34, 81, 100
Durbin, Deanna 63, 94, 115, 250

Eagleton, Thomas 195
Easter Parade 25, 197, 198, 263, 265, 266
Eastwood, Clint 247, 259
Easy to Love 278
Ebsen, Buddy 122
The Ed Sullivan Show 81, 150
Ed Wood 161, 163
The Eddy Duchin Story 242, 246
Edens, Roger 86
Edwards, Gus 141
Eisenhower, Dwight D. 261
Eisner, Michael 283
Elizabeth II 142
Elizabethan England 128
Ellington, Duke 206
Elmer Gantry 147
Emmy Award 26, 111
The Empath 152
England 41
Entenmann's 133
Entratter, Corinne 158
Entratter, Jack 158
Enya 39

Epstein, Julius 107–110
Epstein, Phillip 107, 109
Erie, Pennsylvania 187, 188
The Errand Boy 177
Escape from New York 46
Esculente Brothers Circus 13
Ethel Barrymore Theater 186
Evans, Bill 17
Evans, Ray 180–184
Evans, Robert 119
Exodus 234, 236
The Exorcist 31
Eyman, Scott 254

Fairbanks, Douglas 35
Falk, Peter 110–113, 261
The Fallen Sparrow 282
Fallon, Jimmy 89
Family Guy 81
The Family Jewels 178
The Fatal Weakness 236
Fawcett, Farrah 104
Faye, Alice 269
Feather, Leonard 15
Feldman, Marty 9
Felix, Seymour 264
Fellini, Federico 176. 278
Ferdinand Strauss Toy Company
  187
Ferrer, Mel 78
Fields, Dorothy 72
Fields, W.C. 41, 94, 137
Films on Wheels 4
Fine, Larry 273, 274
Finian's Rainbow 164, 166
Fink's Mules 52
Finney, Albert 103, 258
First Love 250
Fisher, Carrie 221, 224
Fisher, Eddie 32, 170, 222
Fisher, Gail 88
Fisher, Todd 225
Fitzgerald, Ella 3, 72, 190, 193
Fitzgerald, F. Scott 62, 67, 168
Fleming, Erin 56
The Flintstones 44, 73, 171
Flying Down to Rio 27, 209, 210
Flynn, Errol 14, 122
Flynn, Joe 45
Folsey, George 114
Foote, Horton 236
For Me and My Gal 155
Ford, Glenn 112, 122, 147
Ford, John 255
Ford Coppola, Francis 162
Fordin, Hugh 158
42nd Street 268, 269
Fosse, Bob 24, 211
The Four Garbage Cans 17
Foxx, Redd 64, 81
Frampton, Peter 3
Frank, Mel 138
Franklin, Joe 36
Frasier 38
Frawley, William 30
Free and Easy 244
Freed, Arthur 3, 84, 99, 100, 106,
  122, 175, 202, 218, 225, 264, 265,
  270; *see also An American in*

Paris; *Babes on Broadway*; *The
  Barkleys of Broadway*; *Freed
  Unit*; *Gigi*; *Light in the Piazza*;
  The Pirate; *Singin' in the Rain*
Freed Unit 3, 105, 157, 217–218,
  219, 262, 264
Freedland, Michael 26
Freedman, Izzy 247
Freleg, Friz 43
Friars Club 34, 35, 37, 141, 258
Friday the 13th 168
From Here to Eternity 45, 46, 120,
  146, 219, 261
The Front Page 104
Frueh, Al 132
The Fugitive 248
Funny Face 78

Gable, Clark 117, 164, 216, 230,
  250, 261, 276, 277
Gabor, Eva 11, 14, 265
Gainsborough, Thomas 174
The Gallant Hours 57
GAP 158
Garbo, Greta 71
Gardner, Ava 115, 120, 183, 239
Garfield, John 282
Garland, Judy 3, 154, 155, 166, 203,
  218, 239, 245, 263, 266–267, 272;
  and Vincente Minnelli 77, 157,
  200, 202; *see also Andy Hardy*
  series; *Easter Parade*; *The Har-
  vey Girls*; *Meet Me in St. Louis*;
  The Wizard of Oz
Garner, Errol 16–17
Gates, Bill 88
Gaultier, Jean-Paul 260
Gavin, John 169
Geller, Bruce 88
Gene Kelly: The Legacy 158
Gentleman's Agreement 213
George Washington Bridge 260
"Georgia on My Mind" 72
Gershwin, George 15, 16, 36, 99,
  219, 264, 270, 271
Gershwin, Ira 27, 99, 270, 271
Gershwin, Lee 99
"Get Happy" 3, 266, 271
Get Smart 51
The Getty Center 171
Giant 120
Gielgud, John 129
Gigi 75, 76, 77, 78, 100, 200, 265–
  266; and the Academy Awards
  100, 120, 202, 219
Gilligan's Island 59
The Gingerman 58
Girl Crazy 263
Gish, Lillian 235, 236
Gleason, Jackie 61, 81, 91, 206, 232
Glover, Savion 208
Go Set a Watchman 215
Go West 53, 247
The Godfather 108
Goldberg, Rube 134
Goldberg, Whoopi 261
Golden Boy (play) 185
Golden Earrings 184
Golden Globe Awards 87

Goldwyn, Samuel 27, 195, 242
Gomer Pyle, U.S.M.C. 174
Gone with the Wind 276, 279
Good News 263, 265
*The Good, the Bad, and Me: In My
  Anecdotage* 261
The Good, the Bad and the Ugly
  260
Goodman, Benny 15, 238
Gorme, Eyde 17
Gould, Dave 210
Grable, Betty 31, 262, 274
Graham, Martha 260
Grahame, Gloria 146
Grain Belt Premium 136
Grand Hotel 216
Grand Prix 235
Grant, Cary 100, 120, 125, 253,
  258; and Tony Curtis 172–173;
  see also My Favorite Wife; *North
  by Northwest*
Grauman's Chinese Theater 225,
  274
"Gravy Waltz" 15
Gray, Steven 63
Grayson, Kathryn 84, 113–117, 218,
  245
Great American Songbook 269
Great Depression 180, 270, 286;
  audiences 275
The Great Dictator 179
Great Expectations 114
"The Greatest Inventor of Them
  All" 183
The Greatest Show on Earth 128
The Greek Tycoon 14
Green, Adolph 218, 219
Green, Guy 121
Green, Johnny 20, 218
Green Acres 11, 13
Greene, Shecky 81, 82
Griffin, Merv 82
Griffith, Melanie 124, 125
Group Theater 185
Guarding Tess 14
Guilaroff, Sydney 275
The Gulf War 135
Gunga Din 178
Gunsmoke 189, 231
Gus Edwards' Kid Kabaret 141
Guys and Dolls 111
Gypsy 174

Haans, Cole 113
Haas, Dolly 132, 133
Hackett, Buddy 81
Hahnemann Medical College 245
Haley, Jack 122
Half a Sixpence 244
Half Wit's Holiday 274
Hall, Monty 247
Halloween 168
Halloween H20: 20 Years Later 168
Hamilton, George 117–123
Hamlet 128, 129, 130
Hammerstein, Oscar 146, 147
Hammond, Nicholas 281
Hampton, Lionel 15
Haney, Carol 85, 179

The Hanging Tree 186
Hanna, Bill 278; *see also* Hanna-Barbera
Hanna-Barbera 43, 44
The Happy Hooker 142
Harburg, E.Y. (Yip) 164, 165
The Harder They Fall 150
Harlem 206
Harley-Davidson 115
Harmetz, Aljean 174
Harold Teen 174
Harper 252
Harper, Valerie 21, 22
Harris, Barbara 20
Harris, Sam 264
Harrison, Rex 220, 281
Harry & Tonto 257
Harry Potter 201
Hart, Lorenz 270
Hart, Moss 69, 214, 264
Hart to Hart 1, 257
Hartman, Don 138
Harvey (play) 46
The Harvey Girls 242, 244–245
"A Hatful of Ralph" 97
Have Gun Will Travel 48
Hawkins, Coleman 16
Hawks, Howard 74, 100, 101
Hayden, Darrell 235
Hayden, Jeffrey 234
Hayes, Kathryn 152
Hayworth, Rita 104, 197, 211
"Heart and Soul" 72
The Heart of New York 174–176
The Heartbreak Kid 14
Heatherton, Joey 32
Heche, Anne 169
Hecht, Ben 104
Hedren, Tippi 123–126
"Heigh-Ho, the Gang's All Here" 164
Held, John, Jr. 133
Held, Maggie 133
Helen of Troy 282
Hello, Dolly! 9, 155
Hello, Frisco, Hello 269
Hemingway, Ernest 67
Henie, Sonja 94, 276
Henreid, Paul 108
Henry V 21, 130
Hepburn, Audrey 38, 78, 20, 219, 220, 215, 222, 261
Hepburn, Katharine 5, 104, 132
Herbie Goes to Monte Carlo 144
Here Comes the Groom 68, 69, 74
"Here's to the Ladies" 84
Heston, Charlton 47, 122, 126–131
Heston, Fraser 129
Heston, Lydia 131
"High Hopes" 59
High Noon 146
High Society 263
"The Highway Polka" 182
Hilfiger, Tommy 185
Hill Street Blues 33
Hiller, Arthur 111
Hinckley, John 139
Hirschfeld, Al 131–135, 164

The Hirschfeld Century: The Art of Al Hirschfeld 132
Hitchcock, Alfred 123, 125, 126, 162, 163; *see also The Man Who Knew Too Much*; *North by Northwest*; *Psycho*; *To Catch a Thief*
Hitler, Adolf 84, 172
Holden, William 30, 46
Holiday in Mexico 170
Holiday Inn 69
Holland America Cruises 180
Hollander, Xavier 142
Holliman, Earl 101
Hollywood Center Studios 51
Hollywood Gold Cup 26
Hollywood Military Academy 254
Hollywood Palm Cafe 224
The Hollywood Walk of Fame 79, 233
Home from the Hill 120
The Honeymooners 44
Honolulu 53
Hope, Bob 11, 27, 36, 94, 135–141, 182, 237
Hope, Dolores 136, 137
Hopper, Dennis 41
Hopper, DeWolfe 35
Hopper, Hedda 33
Horne, Lena 157, 266
The House I Live In 176
House of Destiny 168
The House on Greenapple Road 21
"How Could You Believe Me When I Said I Loved You When You Know I've Been a Liar All My Life!" 165
"How Little We Know" 74
How the West Was Won 222
Howard, Curly 92, 273, 274
Howard, Moe 273, 274
Howdy Doody 269
H.S.H. Grace de Monaco *see* Kelly, Grace
Hudson, Rock 32
The Huffington Post 21
Hughes, Howard 81
The Human Comedy 87
The Hunter 189
Hutton, Betty 182, 221, 245
Hutton, Lauren 44
Huston, Anjelica 161
Huston, John 39, 261
Hyatt Hotel 228

I Am a Fugitive from a Chain Gang 174
I Am Curious (Yellow) 138
"I Can't Get Started (with You)" 137
"I Cover the Waterfront" 20
I Love Lucy 27, 30, 31, 51
I Loved Her in the Movies: Memories of Hollywood's Legendary Actresses 254
"I Only Have Eyes for You" 269
"I Wanna Be a Dancin' Man" 271
I Was a Teenage Werewolf 3
iCarly 81

Ice Capades 124
The Iceman Cometh 112
"I'm Just a Square in a Social Circle" 182
"Impossible" 15
Incognito 149
In God We Tru$T 9
The In-Laws 111
"In the Cool Cool Cool of the Evening" 69, 74
In the Heat of the Night 148
In the Wee Small Hours of the Morning 192
The Incredible Hulk 30
Indiana University 72
Indianapolis, Indiana 139
Inside Daisy Clover 103
The Invisible Man 151
Invitation to the Dance 218
Irving G. Thalberg Memorial Award 176
"It Only Happens When I Dance with You" 197
It Takes a Thief 1, 253, 254
It's a Wonderful Life 65, 68
It's Always Fair Weather 85, 102, 218
Iturbi, Jose 170
Ivanov 21
"I've Grown Accustomed to Her Face" 61
"I've Heard That Song Before" 59, 61, 69

"Jack and the Beanstock" 219
The Jack Carter Show 81
Jack Daniels 122
Jack London 195
Jackson, Anne 260, 262
Jackson, "Baby Laurence" 208
Jackson, Dorothy 203
Jackson, Michael 189, 203
James, Harry 15, 191, 192, 277
Janis, Conrad 58
Janssen, David 248
Jazz 16, 72, 76, 133, 181, 190, 193, 217, 240
Jazz & Jokes 224
Jazz Dance: The Story of American Vernacular Dance 208
The Jazz Singer 143
The Jean Hersholt Humanitarian Award 180
"Jeepers Creepers" 269
Jessel, George 34, 51, 141–144, 171, 232, 233, 247
Johnson, Edward 115
Johnson, Van 158, 275
Johnston, Jaye 24
Jolson, Al 143, 179, 271
Jones, Dean 144
Jones, Quincy 254
Jones, Shirley 144–151
Jordan, Michael 206
Jourdan, Louis 265
Jubilee 262, 264
Judge Magazine 133
Jumbo 263, 267
Just for You 272

Kael, Pauline 281
Kansas City, Missouri 20
Karatz, Abe 162
Kardashian, Kim 31
Kaufman, George S. 69, 214, 285
Kaye, Danny 60
Kazan, Elia 185, 235, 237, 261
Keaton, Buster 65, 274, 275
Keel, Howard 245
Keeler, Ruby 271
Keller, Helen 174
Kelley, DeForest 151–154
Kelly, Bridget 155
Kelly, Gene 1, 3, 5, 24, 26. 55, 60, 75, 78, 79, 102, 103, 104, 107, 154–158, 166, 194, 197, 221, 269, 271, 272, 286; Astaire and Kelly 4, 85, 79, 154, 158, 202–203; and Stanley Donen 258; *see also* *Anchors Aweigh*; *Du Barry Was a Lady*; *It's Always Fair Weather*; *The Pirate*; *Summer Stock*; *Ziegfeld Follies*
Kelly, George 236
Kelly, Grace 38, 203, 253
Kelly, Patricia 158
Kelly, Tim 155
Kennedy, John F. 98, 99, 131
Kenny Barron Live at Maybeck Recital Hall 17
Kerkorian, Kirk 223
Kern, Jerome 270, 272
Kerouac, Jack 260
Keyes, Evelyn 239
KFC 117
The Kid 10, 91
Kid Kabaret 142
Kidd, Michael 219
The Killers 101
Kimmel, Jimmy 100
King Cole, Nat 183
Kirby, Pat 17
Kismet 218
KISS 3
Kiss Me Kate 116, 196, 198, 242, 245
Kita Banzai Jap Acrobatic Family 8
Klimt, Gustav 135
KNBC 32
Knievel, Evel 122
Knight, Ted 21, 158–161
Knott, Ella 124
Knotts, Don 110
Koch, Howard 108
Koehler, Ted 271
Krupa, Gene 15

Lady for a Day 70
Lake Minnetonka 136
Lamas, Fernando 275, 276, 279
Lamour, Dorothy 139
Lancaster, Burt 113, 147, 170, 216
Land of the Giants 160
Landau, Martin 161–163
Lane, Burton 26, 164–166
Langdon, Harry 65, 275
Langdon, Jack 51
Lantz, Walter 43, 99

Lanza, Mario 60, 114, 116
LAPD 230
The Last Film Festival 41
The Last Great Ride 45
Latin Lovers 89
Laurel and Hardy 133, 134, 135, 222, 275
Lauren, Ralph 156
Laurie, Piper 147
Laverne and Shirley 31
Lawrence, Steve 17, 89
Lawry's The Prime Rib 49
Leachman, Cloris 21
Lee, Gypsy Rose 36
Lee, Harper 215
Lee, Ruta 225
Le Gallienne, Eva 112
Légion d'honneur 176
Lego 189
Lehman, Ernie 162, 280, 281
Leigh, Janet 147, 166–173, 198
Leigh, Vivien 186
Lemmon, Jack 47, 172, 173
The Lemon Drop Kid 182
Leno, Jay 17
Leonard, Burt 21
Leopold, David 132, 135
Lerner, Alan Jay 26, 78, 86, 164, 165, 219
LeRoy, Hal 174
LeRoy, Mervyn 173–176
"Let It Snow! Let It Snow! Let It Snow!" 59
Let's Dance 211
Levant, Oscar 15, 99
Lewis, Danny 179
Lewis, Jerry 91, 176–180, 272
Lewis, Sinclair 147
Lewton, Val 282
Liberty Films 70
Lt. Cmdr. Quinton McHale 46
The Life and Times of Judge Roy Bean 39
Life Magazine 133
Light in the Piazza (book) 121
Light in the Piazza (film) 103, 120, 121
Lili 75, 78, 263
Lillie, Beatrice 202
Limelight 179
Lincoln, Abraham 67
Lincoln, Evelyn 99
Lindbergh, Charles 246
Little Caesar 174
Living It Up 178
Livingston, Jay 180–184
Lobel, Carl 188
Lockheed Aircraft 100
Loewe, Frederick 78, 219
Loews, Inc. 242
Lombard, Carole 216, 276–277
The London Palladium 257
"Lonely Goatherd" 279
"Long Ago and Far Away" 158
The Long Kiss Goodnight 185
The Longest Day 252
"Look to the Rainbow" 166
Looney Toons 43, 174
Lord Fletcher's 136

Loren, Sophia 35
Loring, Eugene 85
Lorre, Peter 139
The Los Angeles Orpheum Theater 91
The Los Angeles Philharmonic Hall 84
The Los Angeles Public Library 201
The Los Angeles Times 50, 141
The Los Angeles Tribune 19
Los Angeles Water Department 126
Lost Horizon 68
Lost in Space 257
"Love and Marriage" 59
The Love Boat 196
The Love Bug 144
Loy, Myrna 195
Lucasfilm 189
Lucia di Lammermoor 114, 115
"Luck Be a Lady" 111
Lucky Me 100
The Lucky Strike Hit Parade 192
Lucy and Ricky and Fred and Ethel 29
Lugosi, Bela 161, 163
"Lullaby of Broadway" 268, 269, 272
Lumet, Sidney 39
Lund, Deanna 160
Lupino, Ida 133
Lust for Life 202
The Lyric Theater 7

MacArthur, Charles 104
Macbeth 128, 130
MacDonald, Jeanette 115
MacLaine, Shirley 77, 179, 211
MacLeod, Gavin 22
MacRae, Gordon 146
Madame Burkhardt and her Cockatoos 52
Madame Curie 174
Madison Square Garden 166
The Magnificent Seven 247, 259
Major Bowes' Amateur Hour 80
The Making of the Wizard of Oz 174
Malden, Carla 185
Malden, Karl 184–187, 255
The Man Next Door 196
The Man Who Knew Too Much 183
Manilow, Barry 166
Mankiewicz, Tom 257, 258
Mannix 88
Marc Antony 130
March, Fredric 195
Margo 14
Marie Antoinette 254, 255
Marnie 123, 126
Marsalis, Branford 17
Marshall, Gen. George C. 68
Marshall, Marion 255, 258
Marshall, Noel 123
Martin, Dean 30, 31, 63, 87, 98, 227, 269
Martin, Dick 205

Martin, Hugh 265
Martin, Steve 18
Martin, Tony 83
Marty 45, 46, 47
Marvin, Lee 46
Marx, Chico 41, 209
Marx, David 187
Marx, Groucho 18, 50, 56, 81, 92, 180, 209, 227
Marx, Harpo 29, 209
Marx, Louis 187–190
Marx, Minnie 36
Marx, Zeppo 209
Marx Brothers 12, 27, 29, 36, 53, 133, 155, 209, 247
Mary Poppins 280
The Mary Tyler Moore Show 21–22, 158, 160, 204
*M*A*S*H* 31, 257
Mason, James 100, 162
The Masonic Lodge 100
Max Rose 178, 179
May, Billy 190–194
Mayer, Louis B. 26, 114, 121, 157, 202, 222, 214; affair 258; and George Sidney 242, 244; and Kathryn Grayson 116–117; and Lillian Burns 245; and Lana Turner 276; *see also* MGM
Maynard, Don 213
Mayo, Virginia 194–196, 255
MCA 170
McCarthy, Charlie 187
McClay, Howard 27, 31
McClelland, Lois 154
McCoo, Marilyn 254
McCormack, Catherine 39
McGovern, George 195
McHale's Navy 45, 48
McMahon, Ed 93–98
McQueen, Steve 122, 123, 144, 186, 189, 282
Me and Juliet 146
Meet John Doe 64
Meet Me in St. Louis 200, 202, 63, 265
Meir, Golda 142
Mel Jass Matinee Movie 3
Melville, Herman 157
Memphis, Tennessee 117, 209
Mencken, H.L. 152
Mercer, Johnny 62, 74, 182, 269
Merman, Ethel 46
Merrick, David 268
Merry Melodies 43
The Merv Griffin Show 81
Metro-Goldwyn-Mayer *see* MGM
Metropolitan Museum of Art 132
Metropolitan Opera 115
Metropolitan Stadium 4
MGM 3, 43, 53, 57, 82, 84, 99, 103, 105, 114, 115, 116, 117, 120, 121, 164, 166, 167, 197, 198, 216; assembly line 243; auction 223; contract 262, 270; films 69–70, 76–78, 155, 239, 264, 266, 270, 277–278, 282; head of production 255; studios 242; *see also*

An American in Paris; Caron, Leslie; Charisse, Cyd; Donen, Stanley; Garland, Judy; Green, Johnny; Kelly, Gene; Mayer, Louis B.; Minnelli, Vincente; *Singin' in the Rain; Summer Stock; That's Entertainment!*
Michelangelo 129
Midler, Bette 189
That Midnight Kiss 116
Midway 14, 252
Milian, Tomas 121
Miller, Ann 5, 158, 196–200
Miller, Arthur 158, 261
Miller, Bill 192
Miller, Glenn 190, 191, 272
Miller, Henry 285
Mimieux, Yvette 103, 121, 122, 258
Minneapolis, Minnesota 3, 12, 19, 25, 55, 63–68, 71, 124, 177, 243, 279
Minnelli, Lee 200
Minnelli, Liza 77, 200, 202
Minnelli, Vincente 26, 77–78, 121, 157, 200–203, 262, 263; *Gigi* 202, 265–266; *Meet Me in St. Louis* 265
The Minnesota Daily 4, 159
Miranda, Carmen 271
Mirisch Company 281
The Misfits 259, 261
Mississippi River 65, 67, 71, 245
Mr. Bubble 84
Mr. Coed 277
Mr. Deeds Goes to Town 65
Mr. Ed 183, 184
Mister Roberts 174
Mr. Smith Goes to Washington 65, 250
Mr. Wonderful 81
Mitchum, Robert 120
Mix, Tom 243
Moby Dick 158
Mojave Desert 123
"Mona Lisa" 180, 183
"Monday Mourning on Saturday Night" 181
Monet, Claude 200
Monroe, Marilyn 133, 158, 162, 172, 222, 259, 261
Monsieur Beaucaire 138
Montalban, Ricardo 89, 153, 275
Montgomery, Elizabeth 150
Montgomery Ward 186
Mooney Sisters 242
The Moon's a Balloon 261
Moore, Dudley 33
Moore, Grace 115
Moore, Michael 126
Moore, Roger 257
Moreau, Jeanne 261
Mork and Mindy 58
Morton, Gary 27, 31, 88
Mosconi, Willie 257
"Moses Supposes" 155
Mostel, Zero 132
Motion Picture Country Home and Hospital 93

Movie Moguls 195, 230, 231
Mozart 218, 280
MTV 158
Murder on the Orient Express 39
Murder She Wrote 196
Murphy, George 212, 262
Murray, Jan 81, 82
Muscular Dystrophy Association (MDA) 176
Museum of Modern Art 132
The Music Man 145, 146
Musician's Guild of America 20
My Fair Lady 58, 61, 78, 217, 219
My Favorite Brunette 139
My Favorite Wife 281–282
My Lost City 62
My Name Is Aram 87

Nabors, Jim 174
Naked City 21
Namath, Joe 213
The Name Above the Title 68, 112
The Name of the Game 249
Nashville, Tennessee 209
National Endowment for the Arts (NEA) 213
The National Enquirer 177
National Retail Federation 189
National Rifle Association 126
Nazi Germany 217
NBC 31, 33, 38, 47, 153
NBC Radio Orchestra 43
NCIS 1, 252
Neal, Patricia 282
"The Nearness of You" 72
Nelson, Gene 122
Nelson, Ricky 101
Nelson, Willie 72, 74
Neptune's Daughter 278
Ness, Eliot 247
Neue Galerie 135
Nevada Smith 185
"Never Let Me Go" 183
New Girl 81
New Orleans, Louisiana 117
New York Film Critics Award 138
New-York Historical Society 132, 135
New York Police Department 36
The New York Times 131, 143
The New Yorker 281
Newhart, Bob 89, 203–206, 228
Nicholas Brothers 206–209, 212
Nicholas Collegiates 207
Nichols, Mike 20
Nicholson, Jack 161
Nielsen, Leslie 250
A Night at the Opera 133
"The Night They Invented Champagne" 265
Nimoy, Leonard 152, 153, 283
Ninotchka 82
Niven, David 119, 147, 261
Nixon, Marni 220
Nobel Peace Prize 176

Nolte, Nick 40
Normand, Mabel 35
Normandy 133
North by Northwest 162, 235–236
North Dallas Forty 138
Northwestern University 94, 131
Notorious 125
Novak, Kim 246
Nureyev, Rudolf 211
The Nutty Professor 178

Oakley, Annie 7
Oates, Warren 161
O'Brien, Margaret 198
Ocean's 11 99
O'Connor, Carroll 59
O'Connor, Donald 155
Odets, Clifford 260
O'Hara, Maureen 282
Oklahoma! 145, 146, 150
"Old Devil Moon" 164
The Old Man and the Sea 67
"An Old Piano Plays the Blues" 17
"Ole Buttermilk Sky" 74
Oliver Twist 91
Olsen and Johnson 181
Olympics 276
The Omen 215
"On a Clear Day You Can See Forever" 166
"On the Atchison, Topeka and the Santa Fe" 244, 269
On the Road 260
On the Town 78, 102, 155, 157, 196, 219
On the Waterfront 148, 234
Once in a Lifetime 214
"One O'Clock Jump" 277
One, Two, Three 55
O'Neill, Eugene 271
Orchestra Wives 191
Orpheum Circuit 7–10, 25, 43, 51, 52, 91, 142, 231–232
Orpheum Theater 51, 52
Oscars *see* Academy Award
O'Shea, Michael 195
O'Toole, Peter 258
Our Gang 243
Outcault, Richard F. 185
The Owl and the Pussycat 58

Paar, Jack 17
The Pacific Coast Highway 151
Pacino, Al 99
The Paddlewheel Hotel & Casino 223, 259
Pagan Love Song 278
Page, Geraldine 236
The Pajama Game 179
Pal Joey (film) 242
Pal Joey (play) 104
Palace Theater 7, 36, 141, 266, 267
Palance, Jack 89
The Paleface 182
Paley, William 205
Palm Springs, California 64, 65, 74, 137, 272
Palomar Hale Telescope 273

Pan, Hermes 209–212
Panama, Norman 138
Pansy the Horse 195
Papa's Delicate Condition 61
Papp, Joseph 21
Paramount Studios 62, 68, 69, 78, 129, 137, 139, 153, 178, 214, 253, 270; films 211, 251, 282–283
Paramount Television 89
Paramount Theater 166
Park Central Hotel 190
Parker, Charlie 17
Parker, Dorothy 285
Parker, Col. Tom 122
Parks, Eddie 7–11
Parsons, Louella 33
The Partridge Family 147
Pasternak, Joe 106, 120, 271, 278
Patric, Jason 149
Patricola, Jim 286
The Patsy 178
Patterson, Russell 133
Patton 184
Pavlova, Anna 84
The Pawnbroker 148
Pearl Harbor 181
Peck, Gregory 1, 38, 212–216, 234, 257
Peck, Tony 213
Peck, Veronique 257
Peckinpah, Sam 46
Peck's Bad Boy 91
The Peking College 138
People Magazine 27
Peppard, George 120
The Pepsodent Show 137
Perito, Nick 269
Perkins, Anthony 168
Perry Mason 100, 231
Pete Smith Specialty 274
Peter Pan 61
Petit, Roland 75
Pfeiffer, Michelle 99
"The Piano Dance" 211
Picasso Summer 258
Pickford, Mary 7, 35
Pickup on South Street 56
"Picnic" 15
Pinocchio 163
The Pirate 194, 195, 208, 218
Planet Hollywood 207
Playhouse 90 147
The Plaza 266
Pleshette, Suzanne 206
Plummer, Christopher 280–281
A Pocketful of Miracles 111–112
Point Blank 99
Poitier, Sidney 219
Polanski, Roman 39
Police Story 101
Police Woman 100, 101
Pollack, Sidney 161
Popeye 187, 188
Porgy and Bess 219
Porter, Cole 3, 86, 245, 262, 264, 270
"The Portland Fancy" 155
Portland Orpheum Vaudeville Theater 43

The Poseidon Adventure 46
Powell, Dick 271
Powell, Eleanor 3, 197, 199, 208
Powell, Jane 168
Powers, Stefanie 257–258
Power's Elephants 52
Preminger, Otto 219, 236
Presley, Elvis 122, 179, 242, 272
Preston, Robert 147
Previn, André 216–221
Princess Astrid of Norway 203
Princess Margaret 204
Princess Margaretha of Sweden 203
Prinz, LeRoy 210
Producers Releasing Corporation 182
Prom Night 168
Pryor, Richard 81
Psycho 147, 168, 169

"Que Sera, Sera (Whatever Will Be, Will Be)" 180, 183
The Queen of England *see* Elizabeth II
Quo Vadis 234

Radio City Music Hall 69, 202
Ragtime 55
Raiders of the Lost Ark 138
Rainbow Rehearsal Studio 7
Rainger, Ralph 182
Rains, Claude 108, 109
"Rancho Grande" 7
Randall School of Dramatic Arts 46
Randall School of Fine Arts 159
The Rat Pack 99, 113, 246
Rathbone, Basil 80
Reagan Ronald 13, 94, 101, 109, 117, 212; as president 128, 138, 139, 143, 161, 226
Real People 30
Rebecca 125
"Red Blues" 85
Redford, Robert 100
Reds 143
Reed, Donna 68, 116, 234, 277
Reese, Herb 190
Reiner, Carl 82
Reiner, Rob 141
Remington Steele 196
Rennie, Michael 282
Revenant 149
Reynolds, Burt 119
Reynolds, Debbie 157, 170, 221–225, 258–259
Rich and Famous 39
Rickles, Don 46, 79, 81, 89, 225–228
Riddle, Nelson 192, 193
Riding High 68, 69
Rigoletto 114
Rio Bravo 100, 101
"Riverboat Shuffle" 72
Rizzoli & Isles 38
RKO Studios 209, 210, 212, 281, 282
Road House 133

The Road to Happy Days: A Memoir of Life on the Road as an Antique Toy Dealer 188
Road to Singapore 137
Road to Zanzibar 138
Robbins, Jerry 133, 281
Robin, Lee 272
Robin and the Seven Hoods 113
Robin Hood 94
Robinson, Bill 57, 199, 233
Robinson, Edward G. 174, 245
The Rockford Files 51
"Rockin' Chair" 72
Roddenberry, Gene 151, 152
Rodgers, Richard 146
Rodgers and Hammerstein 147, 279
Rodgers and Hart (Lorenz) 270
Rodgers and Hart (Moss) 104, 182
Rogers, Ginger 24, 27, 197, 198, 211; and Fred Astaire 209, 266, 271, 281; *see also* Astaire-Rogers musicals
Rogers, Will 7
Rogers & Cowan 252
Roman Holiday 14, 215
Roman Scandals 27
The Romance of Rosy Ridge 168
Rona Barrett's Hollywood 32
Ronald McDonald House 4
La Ronde 20
Ronstadt, Linda 72
Room Service 12, 29
Rooney, Charlene 231
Rooney, Mark 230
Rooney, Mickey 116, 157, 228–231, 255–256; Andy Hardy 228, 230, 277
Roosevelt, Eleanor 142
Rose, Billy 195
Rose, Jack 138
"Rose of the Rio Grande" 270
The Rose Tattoo 259
Roseville IV 138
Royal Wedding 26, 106, 107, 165
Rubin, Benny 231–234
Ruiz, Pepe 57
Ruman, Sig 133
Runyon, Damon 27
Russell, Harold 195
Russell, Rosalind 216
Rutherford, Ann 198
Rydell, Mark 161

Sadagursky, Stephanie 188
Saint, Eva Marie 162, 234–238
Saint-Exupéry, Antoine de 148
St. John, Jill 257, 258
St. Louis Municipal Opera Amphitheater 114
The St. Louis Municipal Opera Company 195
St. Paul, Minnesota 3, 9, 11, 25, 51, 52, 65, 67; audiences 143, 232

San Fernando Valley 15, 48, 55, 86, 141, 239, 255
San Remo 104
The Sand Pebbles 282
Sanders Brothers 119
The Sandpiper 237
Sands Hotel 203
Saroyan, Aram 87
Saroyan, William 87
Sarris, Andrew 262
Saturday Night Fever 26
Saturday Night Revue 81
Saturn 3 104
Schary, Dore 77
Schell, Ronnie 174
Schlesinger Productions 43
Schnitzler, Arthur 20
School of Dramatic Expression 195
Schubert, J.J. 94
Schubert, Johnny 94
Schulberg, Budd 234
Schwarzenegger, Arnold 129, 130, 261
Schweigert Hot Dogs 4
Scott, George C. 173
Screen Actors Guild 128, 212, 256
Sears, Roebuck, & Co. 186
Seaton, George 39
Second Chorus 240
"The Second Time Around" 61
Segal, George 58
Sego Milk 124
Seldes, Marian 119
Self, Bill 257
Selznick, David O. 195
Selznick Pictures 132
"September in the Rain" 269
"Serenade in Blue" 269
Sgt. Pepper's Lonely Hearts Club Band 171
Seven Brides for Seven Brothers 106
The Seven Little Foys 140
Severinsen, Doc 17
Shakespeare, William 128, 130
Shakespeare in the Park 21
"Shakin' the Blues Away" 198
Shambala Preserve 123–124
Shameless 81
Shatner, William 151, 152
Shaw, Artie 168, 238–242, 255, 276
Shaw, Robert 40
Shearer, Norma 254, 255
Shelton, John 114
Sheraton-Ritz Hotel 64
Sherlock Holmes 80, 111
Shields, Brooke 135
Shore, Dinah 248
Shoup, Gen. David M. 13
Show Boat 218, 242
Showstoppers 166
"Shuffle Off to Buffalo" 268
Sidney, George 158, 242–247, 276, 277; *Tom and Jerry* 277–278
Silk Stockings 61, 82, 85–86
"Silver Bells" 182
Silvera, Frank 119
Silverman, Stephen 106
The Simpsons 44
Sinatra, Frank 16, 46, 80, 87, 98,

100, 113, 116, 120, 133, 191, 197; and Eli Wallach 261–262; Recording 192, 193; *see also* *Anchors Aweigh*; *Carousel*; *From Here to Eternity*; *Pal Joey*; *The Rat Pack*
Singin' in the Rain 85, 102, 103, 155, 157, 218, 221, 225
Silverman, Fred 31
Silvers, Phil 263
Simon and Schuster 185
Singer Sargent, John 198
The Single Guy 47
60 Minutes 30
Skelton, Red 91, 147, 216, 275, 277
"Skip to My Lou" 268
"Skylark" 72
"Sleepy Lagoon" 277
Small Town Girl 196
Smart Set Magazine 133
Smith, C. Aubrey 80
Smith & Dale 174
Soledad Canyon 123
Some Like It Hot 171, 172
Something's Got to Give 261
Sondheim, Stephen 5
Song and Dance Cinema Society 4
Sony 116
Sorell, Helena 253
Sotheby's 189
Sothern, Ann 31
The Sound of Music 153, 279–280, 283
South Pacific (play) 146
"South Rampart Street Parade" 15
The Specialist 149
Spencer, Elizabeth 121
Spiegel, Sam 235
Spielberg, Steven 111
Spock 152, 153, 283, 286
SpongeBob SquarePants 23
Sputnik 34
Stack, Robert 247–252
Stack, Rosemarie 251
Stage Door 198
Stagecoach 88
Stalking Moon 234
Stallone, Sylvester 149
Stanley, Kim 162
Stanwyck, Barbara 257
Stapleton, Maureen 162
Star Trek 151, 153, 282, 286
Star Trek: The Motion Picture 282
Star Trek II: The Wrath of Kahn 153
Star Wars 138, 189
"Stardust" 72
State of the Union 70
Stearns, Marshall 208
Steiger, Rod 100, 144–151, 235
Steinbeck, John 213
Steps in Time 26, 211
Stern, Isaac 213
Steve Allen Plays Jazz Tonight 17
Stevens, Connie 135
Stewart, Jimmy 27, 28, 68, 175–176, 250
Stewart, Rod 72

Stone, Irving 202
Stop Death in Our Lifetime 141
Stordahl, Axel 61, 192
Stork Club 32
The Stork Club (film) 182
Stormy Weather 207, 208
The Story of Vernon and Irene Castle 209, 281
Strasberg, Lee 161, 162, 237
Stravinsky, Igor 76
A Streetcar Named Desire 184, 185, 186
Streets of San Francisco 185
Streisand, Barbra 9, 58, 155, 166, 262
Strickling, Howard 167
Strike Force 249
Sudden Fear 89
Studio City, California 19
Summer Holiday 218, 271
Summer Stock 263, 266, 271
Sun Valley Serenade 191, 211
Sunset Boulevard 141
"Sunshine Boys" 174
Superman II 138
Styne, Jule 59, 60, 61
Swing Easy! (album) 192
Swing Hostess 182
Swing music 239, 243
"Swing Sonata" 181
Swing Time 210
A Swingin' Affair! (album) 192
Swit, Loretta 124
Switch 252

Tandy, Jessica 186
Tarzan 275
Tashlin, Frank 43
Taylor, Elizabeth 170, 222, 237, 239
Taylor, Rip 224
Taylor, Rod 125
TCM *see* Turner Classic Movies
TCM Classic Film Festival 224–225
The Tempest 21
The Ten Commandments 128, 129
The Tender Trap (film) 63
"The Tender Trap" (song) 62, 63
The Terminator 130
Terpsichore 199
Terror Train 168
Texaco Star Theater 36
Thalberg, Irving 255
Thalberg, Irving, Jr. 254
The Thalberg Building 121
"Thank Heaven" 76
"Thanks for the Memory" 137, 182
That Certain Feeling 237
"That's Amore" 269
That's Entertainment! 3, 26, 197
Thau, Benny 121, 122
There Really Was a Hollywood 168
"There's Beauty Everywhere" 84, 87
"They Can't Take That Away from Me" 271
"This Could Be the Start of Something" 15, 17

This Side of Paradise (book) 67
The Thomas Crown Affair 88
Thompson, Marshall 170
Thoroughly Modern Millie 61
"Three Coins in the Fountain" 59, 212
The Three Musketeers 242
"The Three Penny Opera" 21
Three Stooges 27, 92, 273, 274–275
Tidelands Motor Inn and Nightclub 204
Tightrope 88
Tillie's Punctured Romance 35
Tilton, Martha 182
Time Limit 186
The Time Machine 103
TIME Magazine 187
Tin Pan Alley 72, 267
Tinker, Grant 21
"Tinkle Bell" 182
Titanic (1953) 130, 257
Titanic (1997) 230
TMZ 32, 255
To Be or Not to Be 250
To Catch a Thief 125, 253
To Each His Own 184
To Have and Have Not 74, 100, 101
To Kill a Mockingbird 214, 215
The Toast of New Orleans 61, 116
The Today Show 124, 125
The Tomorrow Show 33
The Tonight Show 15, 18, 93, 95, 96, 97, 228, 241
Tony Award 259
Too Close for Comfort 159
Top Hat 210
Top Speed (play) 210
Tormé, Mel 16, 270
Torres, Dara 276
Tower, Senator John 139
Toys in the Attic 103
Tracy, Spencer 46, 67, 70, 95, 230
Travanti, Daniel J. 33
Travolta, John 26
Tribute to a Bad Man 282
Trilogy (album) 193
The Trip to Bountiful 236
Tropic of Capricorn 286
The Trouble with Harry 77
True Lies 129, 130
Truffaut, François 39
Truman, Harry 142
Trump, Donald 104, 213
Tucker: The Man and His Dream 162
Turner, Lana 89, 116, 173, 277; and Artie Shaw 239, 247, 276
Turner Classic Movies 172, 177, 178, 224–225, 258
Twain, Mark 65, 67, 71
Twentieth Century–Fox 253, 269, 281
20/20 30
Twitty, Conway 183
Two for the Road 39, 103

UCLA 87, 234
Undercurrent 133

Underhill, Fred 286
"Unforgettable" 183
U.S. State Department 85
Universal Studios 101, 111, 170, 181, 254
University of Chicago Theatre 20
University of Minnesota 4, 24, 133
University of Pennsylvania 180
University of Pittsburgh 155
University of Southern California 263
The Unsinkable Molly Brown 222, 263
Unsolved Mysteries 247, 249
The Untouchables 189, 248, 251
Up 18, 23
"(Up a) Lazy River" 73
Updike, John 158
USO 137

Valentino, Rudolph 117
Vance, Vivian 30
Van Gogh, Vincent 202
Van Heusen, Jimmy 59, 60, 62
Vanity Fair 94, 133
Vaudeville 18, 25, 43, 80, 141, 143, 165, 177, 179, 204, 232; Acts 9, 51–52, 57, 91, 92, 174, 233; *see also* Ahern, Will; Burns, George; Orpheum Circuit; Parks, Eddie
Vaughn, Sarah 190
Vaughn, Vince 169
Vera-Ellen 83, 211, 267
Verney Farm 256
Versailles Peace Conference 7
Vertical Whorehouse 142
Vertigo 184
Vietnam War 14, 135
Violent Saturday 46
Viva Las Vegas 242
von Fritsch, Gunther 282

Wagner, Lindsay 257
Wagner, Natasha 257
Wagner, Robert 1, 117, 170, 252-259
The Waldorf Astoria 69
Wall Street 260
Wallace, Marsha 205
Wallach, Eli 259–262
Wallis, Hal 179
Walsh, Raoul 196
Walters, Barbara 32
Walters, Charles 262–267
Wambaugh, Joseph 101
Warner, Jack 94
Warner Archive Collection 274
Warner Brothers 13, 43, 94, 101, 109, 143, 146; films 28, 39, 43, 44, 108, 196, 219; studio 31, 101, 221, 270
Warren, Harry 15, 155, 267–273, 268
"Washboard Blues" 72
The Washington Post 143
Wasserman, Lew 111, 254
"Water Ballet" 275
Waters, Alice 12
Wayne, John 30, 100, 101, 131

Webb, Chick 190, 206
Weissmuller, Johnny 275, 276
Welk, Lawrence 34, 241
Welles, Orson 45, 176, 281–282
Wellman, William 87
"We're in the Money" 268
West Side Story 279, 281
Weston, Paul 61
What Price Glory 256
Wheeler and Woolsey 232
When Do I Start? 185
White, Betty 22, 124
White, Jules 273–275
White Heat 194, 196, 255
Whiteman, Paul 247
Who Do You Trust? 97
Who's Afraid of Virginia Woolf? 103
Widmark, Richard 56, 133
The Wild Bunch 46
Wilder, Billy 172, 200, 220
Wilkinson, Jimmy 282
Williams, Andy 17, 74, 254
Williams, Esther 116, 198, 275–279
Williams, Audrey 17, 122
Williams, Hank 122
Williams, Tennessee 185, 259

Willson, Meredith 147
Wilson, Teddy 15
Wilson, Woodrow 7
Winant, Ethel 21
Winchell, Walter 32, 34, 140, 141
Wings 87
Winter Garden Theater 242, 268
Winters, Jonathan 189
Winters, Shelley 94
Wise, Robert 153, 279–283
Withers, Jane 189
The Wiz 203
The Wizard of Oz 4, 5, 122, 173, 175, 176, 222
Wood, Natalie 257, 258
Wooden, John 57
Woollcott, Alexander 285
Woolley, Monty 264
Woolworths 187
World of Entertainment 157
Wyatt, Jane 152
Wyler, William 64, 129–130, 195, 196, 215–216, 281
Wyman, Jane 69
Wynn, Steve 223, 259

Yaged, Saul 15
Yankee Doodle Dandy 57, 94, 109, 225
Yates, Peter 39
Yatsko, Bill 188, 189
Yellen, Linda 41
You Can't Take It with You (film) 69
You Can't Take It with You (play) 214
"You'll Never Know" 269, 273
Young, Lester 17
Your Cheatin' Heart 122
Your Hit Parade 269
Your Show of Shows 81
"You're All the World to Me" 26

Zanuck, Darryl 143, 214, 215
Ziegfeld, Florenz 73
Ziegfeld Follies 84, 137, 202, 264, 265, 275
Zimmerman, Marge 56, 58, 59, 256
Zinnemann, Fred 146, 150, 151
Zucker Brothers 251